The Shape of the Roman Order

STUDIES IN THE HISTORY OF GREECE AND ROME

Robin Osborne, James Rives, and Richard J. A. Talbert, editors

Books in this series examine the history and society of Greece and Rome from approximately 1000 B.C. to A.D. 600. The series includes interdisciplinary studies, works that introduce new areas for investigation, and original syntheses and reinterpretations.

THE SHAPE OF THE ROMAN ORDER

THE REPUBLIC AND ITS SPACES

Daniel J. Gargola

THE UNIVERSITY OF NORTH CAROLINA PRESS
Chapel Hill

© 2017 The University of North Carolina Press

All rights reserved

The University of North Carolina Press has been a member of the Green Press Initiative since 2003.

Cover illustration: marble bust, mid-first century A.D., courtesy of the Metropolitan Museum of Art.

Library of Congress Cataloging-in-Publication Data
Names: Gargola, Daniel J., author.
Title: The shape of the Roman order : the republic and its spaces / Daniel J. Gargola.
Other titles: Studies in the history of Greece and Rome.
Description: Chapel Hill : The University of North Carolina Press, [2017] | Series: Studies in the history of Greece and Rome | Includes bibliographical references and index.
Identifiers: LCCN 2016036907 | ISBN 9781469631820 (cloth : alk. paper) | ISBN 9781469668703 (pbk : alk. paper) | ISBN 9781469631837 (ebook)
Subjects: LCSH: Rome—Politics and government. | Space perception—Rome—History. | Public spaces—Rome—History.
Classification: LCC JC83 .G37 2017 | DDC 320.937—dc23
LC record available at https://lccn.loc.gov/2016036907

FOR

AMY

Contents

Acknowledgments xi
Abbreviations xiii

INTRODUCTION 1
Rome and Its "Constitution" 3
The Republic as a Territorial Order 7
The Plan of the Work 11

1 REPRESENTING THE *RES PUBLICA* 12
Rome and Its History 12
Rome as a Spatial and Temporal Order 21
Rome and Its Gods 25
Antiquarianism, Priestly Knowledge, and Jurisprudence 33
Laws and Legislation 38

2 ROME, ITS MAGISTRATES, AND ITS EMPIRE 44
Rome and the Cycle of Public Life 44
Rome and Its Roads 51
Conceptions of Empire 55
The Magistracy and the *Provincia* 59
The Spatial Implications of Extra-Urban *Provinciae* 69
Provinciae and Their Limits 78

3 ROME AND ITS ITALY *83*
Italy and the "Land of Italy" *83*
Citizens, Latins, and Allies *88*
Rome and Its Officials *95*
Prodigies and Their Expiation *99*
Census and *Dilectus* *105*

4 THE AUGURS AND THEIR SPACES *119*
Rome, Its Spaces, and Its Gods *119*
The Augurs and Their Discipline *122*
The Augurs and Their *Templa* *124*
The Augurs and Rome's Boundaries *130*
Imperium and the *Pomerium* *132*
The Augurs and Rome's Hinterland *140*
Inside and Outside *149*

5 SCIENCES OF THE CENTER *154*
Templa, Their Orientations, and Their Divisions *154*
Rome and Its Colonies *167*
Polybius, the Roman Army, and Its Encampments *178*
Spaces and Their Centers *181*

6 LAWS, DECREES, EDICTS, AND THEIR SPACES *187*
Magistrates, Laws, Edicts, and Spaces *187*
The City and Its Limits *190*
Rome and Italy *201*
Some Examples *206*
At the End of the Republic *220*

CONCLUSION *224*

Notes 231
Bibliography 267
Index 287

Maps

1 Rome and its major roads in Italy 53
2 The *via Latina*, the *via Appia*, and the colonies along them 54
3 The *via Aemilia* and the colonies along it 55
4 The distribution of the Roman tribes after circa 244 95
5 Towns with multiple prodigies, 218–167 103
6 Rome and its environs 120

Acknowledgments

In the course of writing this book, I have incurred many obligations. The University of Kentucky provided the sabbatical during which much of it was written, while its interlibrary loan librarians secured with great efficiency many obscure works. Over the years, I have presented parts of various chapters to audiences in Quebec, Odense, Leiden, Dresden, and Sydney, and I have found their comments informative and useful. Among individuals, I am especially grateful for the encouragement of R. J. A. Talbert during the book's long gestation and for the observations of the readers for The University of North Carolina Press, M. Jehne and J. Rich. Dr. Amy C. Clark was helpful in all stages of the project. The remaining errors, of course, are my own.

Abbreviations

In the text and notes, the works of Greek and Latin authors are cited according to the abbreviations of the *Oxford Latin Dictionary* (Oxford, 1968) and Liddell and Scott's *A Greek-English Lexicon* (Oxford, 1940), with the exception of texts within the *Corpus Agrimensorum Romanorum*, where the texts and translations in B. Campbell, ed., *The Writings of the Roman Land Surveyors: Introduction, Text, Translation and Commentary* (London, 2000) are used. Modern works are cited by the author's last name and publication date. Complete citations of books and articles are listed in the Bibliography, where the title of the journals in which articles appear are abbreviated according to the system in *L'Année philologique*. Certain modern works, however, are regularly cited in the following forms:

    AE   *L'Année épigraphique* (cited by year and number of the inscription).

    ANRW   H. Temporini et al., eds., *Aufstieg und Niedergang der römischen Welt. Geschichte und Kultur Roms im Spiegel der neueren Forschung* (Berlin, 1972–).

    CIL   T. Mommsen et al., *Corpus Inscriptionum Latinarum* (Berlin, 1863–).

    FGH   F. Jacoby, ed., *Die Fragmente der griechischen Historiker* (Berlin, 1923–55).

    FRHist   T. J. Cornell et al., *The Fragments of the Roman Historians* (Oxford, 2013).

IG	*Inscriptiones Graecae* (Berlin, 1873–).
ILLRP	A. Degrassi, ed., *Inscriptiones Latinae Liberae Rei Publicae* (Florence, 1957–63).
ILS	H. Dessau, ed., *Inscriptiones Latinae Selectae* (Berlin, 1892–1916).
Inscr. Ital.	A. Degrassi, ed., *Inscriptiones Italiae*, XIII (Rome, 1937–63).
ORF[3]	E. Malcovati, ed., *Oratorum Romanorum fragmenta liberae rei publicae*, 3rd ed. (Turin, 1967).
SIG[3]	W. Dittenberger et al., eds., *Sylloge Inscriptionum Graecarum*, 3rd ed. (Leipzig, 1915–24).

Introduction

From as far in the past as we can see, Romans often made a simple and sharp distinction between the city and everything under its sway or within the reach of its armies and embassies. At different times and in different contexts, this dichotomy might be expressed in terms of a contrast between "at home" (*domi*) and "on campaign" (*militiae*), between the city (*urbs*) and the surrounding fields (*ager*), between the city and the "towns and villages" (*fora et conciliabula*), between the *urbs* and "all of Italy" (*tota Italia*), between the city and the provinces (*provinciae*), or, more grandly, between the *urbs* and the "inhabited world" (*orbis terrarum*). When the Augustan historian Livy proclaims in the general preface (*praef.* 9) to his history of Rome that he intends to examine "through what men and by what policies, at home and on campaign [*domi militiaeque*], the *imperium* was established and enlarged," he announces his intention to survey those crucial acts at Rome and in war that contributed to the acquisition of Rome's empire.

This emphasis on Rome certainly had deep roots. After all, the city provided the core around which the Roman state developed and from which its power expanded, and it long served as the primary locus of the most important decision-making groups; as S. E. Finer notes, the ways in which states were built is one of the most important factors in determining how they came to be governed.[1] But the dichotomy between the city and its hinterlands is also a representation of the broader polity as a spatial order, and here controversy has arisen. Because our sources focus on events in Rome and with its magistrates, embassies, and armies in the field, developments and arrangements away from the center or the regions of active campaigning often remain obscure, resulting in different reconstructions of the realities of Roman power. Some regard the depiction of Rome in terms suitable to a city-state as largely accurate and suggest that Roman government away from the city and its armies remained relatively simple into the first century.[2] For others, the emphasis on Rome masked a different reality in which Rome had ceased to be a city-state and had become a "territorial state" instead.[3]

All polities organize their activities spatially and temporally. They occupy territories, more or less clearly defined; they distribute crucial functions over time and space; they represent and rank places and spaces and the activities and groups that are associated with them. In these matters, they are influenced by their histories, by local topography, by relations with their neighbors, by the forms of their political, religious, military, and economic activities, and by a range of other factors that set the context for their actions. At the same time, people make space through their movements, their experience, their memories, and their traditions. In this way, the "space" and the "time" that any group occupies are, to a large degree, social constructs.[4]

The present study investigates the Roman republic and its empire, especially in the third, second, and first centuries B.C., as a spatial order. The aim is not to produce a historical geography examining how Roman officials imposed their city's power on specific towns, peoples, or regions. Instead, its emphasis lies on the ruling elite's views of their polity and its power, their personal experience while performing public functions, the kind of activities that they undertook at Rome and abroad and how they sought to regulate and describe them, and the ways that they conceptualized spatial relationships over the broad range of Rome's activities. After all, the Roman elite's worldview undoubtedly was related to the ways that they sought to organize their political order and to the form and purpose of their activities within it. The anthropologist M. E. Bloch stresses the importance of natives' conceptions of their societies to any attempts to describe them, while the political scientists M. Bevir and R. A. W. Rhodes maintain that one should think of a political order not in terms of formal structures but against the background of the actions of individuals shaped by specific cultural practices and the meanings associated with them, which arise out of a community's history and situation.[5]

Thus, literary accounts will bulk large in the following chapters, as will magistrates and their actions; normative statements by public officials (edicts), by the senate (decrees), by legislative assemblies (laws); and the opinions of priests and jurists (*responsa*). As we shall see throughout the following chapters, enactments of all kinds were with some regularity to apply to particular spaces, either directly by specifying a place or its limits or indirectly by linking a rule or rules to occasions, institutions, or statuses that only functioned in particular places or had spatial implications, more or less closely defined. Spatial considerations, in other words, permeate histories and public and sacred law, and they serve quite well as points of entry into the ways that members of the ruling elite viewed their polity and its empire.

ROME AND ITS "CONSTITUTION"

When we begin to see Roman public life more clearly in the last decades of the third century, we encounter a wide range of public offices and collectivities. The two consuls and a variable number of praetors were Rome's most prominent public actors in the city and abroad.[6] During their year in office, they had, or could take up, the command of armies, presidency of the senate and of citizen assemblies, and a range of other roles. When the number of praetors was increased from one to two around 244, then to four circa 227, and next to six for 197, the position of praetor may have been more clearly and firmly distinguished from the consulship.[7] From the last decades of the fourth century, moreover, popular assemblies and eventually the senate as well might extend the terms of a serving magistrate, enabling him to continue "as if" a consul or praetor (*pro consule* or *pro praetore*), functionaries whom modern scholars call promagistrates.

The occupants of other offices had more restricted areas of activity, functionally and spatially. The two curule and the two plebeian aediles can be found supervising roads and markets in and near the city, prosecuting perpetrators of a range of public offenses in trials that could take place only at Rome, arranging for the performances of certain religious festivals in the city, and maintaining temples.[8] The ten tribunes of the plebs operated only in and very near the city, where they presided over citizen assemblies and, at some uncertain point, meetings of the senate; proposed laws; and protected the rights of citizens through their powers of obstruction.[9] The quaestors, at least eight in number from the middle of the third century, can be found supervising the treasury in Rome and assisting consuls and praetors on campaign. Some offices were filled at irregular intervals for very specific tasks: *duumviri aedi locandae* or *duumviri aedi dedicandae* to construct or dedicate new temples at Rome; *triumviri coloniae deducendae* to found colonies; *decemviri agris dandis* to make viritane assignments.

Although they were not part of the annual cycle of magistracies, in the late third and second centuries these colleges were formed with some frequency and were associated with their own sets of procedures.

Tenure in these offices rested upon assemblies of citizens. Officials who possessed the right to summon the citizenry—consuls, praetors, and tribunes of the plebs—might call them together either to hear speeches or receive commands in gatherings known as *contiones* or to vote in elections or on laws in assemblies known as *comitia* or *concilia*. Voting assemblies came in two basic forms, distinguished primarily by the ways in which their members were ordered and the functionaries who could preside over them. In the census, the two censors, elected in and after the third century once every five years, assigned male Romans to centuries (*centuriae*) according to their wealth and to tribes based on their place of residence. Assemblies of centuries (*comitia centuriata*) met under the presidency of a consul to elect consuls, praetors, and censors. Tribal assemblies met under a praetor or a tribune of the plebs to elect the other magistrates. In our period, tribal assemblies under a tribune usually approved legislation.

Over the course of the third and second centuries, the senate took on a leading role in public life.[10] Ostensibly only an advisory body, certain magistrates—consuls, praetors, and, at some point, tribunes of the plebs as well—could summon the senate to give advice on specific matters. In practice, the senate can be found acting as the locus for debates on foreign policy; receiving ambassadors from other states and in turn sending out embassies, usually composed of senators; determining military commands; managing Rome's relations with its gods; resolving disputes among allies; and granting honors to the deserving. Rome's own historians generally held the senate to be as old as the city, but the enactment of a law, the *lex Ovinia*, late in the fourth century put its composition into the hands of the censors, rather than the consuls who had supervised the task earlier, thus beginning a process by which the senate was steadily freed from the overarching power of the chief magistrates.[11] By the end of the third century, the censors regularly enrolled all former consuls, praetors, and aediles, but the principles that they used to fill out the remainder of the membership, perhaps three hundred in all, are unknown; tribunes of the plebs would gain admittance because of their office late in the second century, and quaestors only in the first. As a gathering of former officeholders, the senate came to be seen as a store of virtues, prestige, and experience, and, despite its advisory role, it came to set policy in a range of matters, perhaps taking on, or attempting to take on, a coordinating function that the actual magistracies lacked.

The senate's growing centrality may have focused the lives of politically active members of the elite more firmly on Rome, where it conducted its deliberations, and it may have given to its senior members a permanent institutionalized position in Rome's public life.[12]

Rome also possessed a great variety of priesthoods, priestly colleges, and sodalities, some of which advised magistrates and the senate on points of religion, while others possessed ritual programs of their own.[13] The Salii or the Luperci performed very specific rites during the year. Certain priests, such as the *flamen Dialis* or the *flamen Martialis*, were closely connected to the cult of a single god. The best-known priestly colleges acted more broadly and in ways that closely affected the conduct of public life: pontiffs, augurs, and the college known at various times as the "two men," "ten men," or "fifteen men for the performance of sacrifices" (*duumviri, decemviri,* or *quindecemviri sacris faciundis*). Unlike magistrates, who served for terms of one year and were selected by citizen assemblies, priests served for life (or until some fault or physical imperfection led to their dismissal), and they usually were selected by other priests.

How should one view this collection of offices and collectivities? In his monumental *Römisches Staatsrecht*, the most influential single work on Rome's political order, Theodor Mommsen saw republican government as a formal and autonomous system of institutions regulated and defined by laws that rested in turn on the sovereignty of popular assemblies, a view that owes much to nineteenth-century German ideas about constitutions and a properly ordered state.[14] He saw change as taking place according to the internal logic of the system rather than through shifts in external circumstances, a view that was widely shared among nineteenth-century students of public and private law. His Rome was very much a *Rechtstaat*.

While still influential, Mommsen's views about the foundations of the Roman political order have received justifiable criticism. Christian Meier has noted that the concept of the state as an autonomous object is a modern one and that systematic and formal constitutions as well as elaborate and integrated legal codes were the result either of some clear and distinct founding act or of some thorough reform.[15] A. Magdelain and J. Bleicken stress that magistracies possessed no clearly defined core, an observation that is especially true of the consuls, who were involved, or came to involve themselves, in many areas of public life.[16] Their fundamental existence, in other words, rested on custom, *mos maiorum*, and was largely unquestioned.

Still, reports of laws, senatorial decrees, and priestly or juristic opinions attempting to regulate various matters are quite common, although the measures themselves are generally specific and particular. Enactments fall into two broad groups, one addressing specific situations that would soon pass and the other without temporal restrictions.[17] Jochen Bleicken has described a process though which customary procedures were transformed slowly, sporadically, and partially into law beginning in the fourth century and continuing throughout the remainder of republican history.[18] In matters of cult, Jörg Rüpke suggests that the Roman elite, from circa 300, began a slow process of ordering and clarifying ritual activities.[19] Claudia Moatti detects a broad movement toward regularizing traditional practices from early in the second century.[20] As Martin Jehne notes, setting limits to customary actions was an important element of the republican order.[21] The development of a more formal jurisprudence began to appear at the end of the third century, while, from the last decades of the second, Roman legal practice became more ambitious, laws more complex, and legal concepts more abstract, although the codification of law would lie far in the future.[22]

In this way, then, offices and collectivities ought to be viewed in terms of the tasks that they took up or were given, some of which were "customary," while others were the results of deliberate and overt attempts to address conflicts and special circumstances. At the same time, the procedures regulating the interactions of officials, senate, and assemblies and the processes by which magistrates acted upon those who were subject to their authority are probably best seen as not established in any fixed and formal fashion but rather the result of "habit" or "custom." In such an order, explicit rules, enshrined in laws, senatorial decrees, magisterial edicts, or priestly and juristic opinions, may be seen less as attempts to regulate broadly offices or social groups than as efforts to address specific situations or to reduce or resolve disputes and uncertainties. They may be understood, then, as attempts to "rationalize" offices and practices, if such a process is understood not in terms of some supposedly universal standard of reason but rather as an effort to render customary practices more explicit and free of conflict.

Mommsen also viewed Rome's constitutional order as autonomous and rather firmly separated from other areas of Roman life. This too has come to seem less likely. The republic's governmental apparatus, to the extent that it possessed one, was not functionally distinct from other elements of social and political life. The republic was markedly hierarchical, and despite the prominence of citizen assemblies, public life focused rather sharply on a small elite. In such a polity, one might expect the boundaries between the public and private lives of members of the ruling elite to be poorly defined.

Thus, Rome's public order might be viewed also in terms of its ruling elite, their way of life, and their values. This elite—the so-called nobility, a segment of the broader landholding class—began to take shape in the closing decades of the fourth century.[23] Membership in it and status within it rested on the ability to win positions and honors. In this competitive and hierarchical environment, members liked to think that the elite, both individually and collectively, possessed manly courage (*virtus*) and good faith (*fides*) and displayed respect for the gods (*pietas*) and that their lives were characterized by the pursuit of praise or fame (*laus*) and glory (*gloria*). Offices and honors—and those attributes such as *dignitas* and *auctoritas* that were dependent on them—were in the gift of others, whether the senate, popular assemblies, or the soldiers in one's army.

One can also turn to the modes of interaction that characterized public life. Roman political culture has been justly described as a culture of spectacle and Rome itself as a theater of power.[24] During the course of the year, games, festivals, and processions were often conducted with considerable grandeur, as were more occasional performances, such as the triumphant return of victorious generals or the funerals of prominent members of the elite. The city itself was dotted with temples, altars, and shrines, each of which served as the locus of recurring cult acts, many of which involved Rome's most prominent public actors. Official action in the city, moreover, was accompanied by sacrifices, rites of divination, and processions. Magistracies and priesthoods possessed their own costumes, attendants, and emblems of rank. Public acts were often accompanied by ritual gestures as well as formal language. Magistracies, priesthoods, and the senate, then, may have been constructed in large part not by formal rules but by what their occupants were seen to have done, how they went about doing it, and the many symbols that surrounded and accompanied their actions. Any examination of the office of consul, for example, may be more a matter of historical anthropology than of any settled constitutional law.[25]

THE REPUBLIC AS A TERRITORIAL ORDER

From the earliest days of the city, Rome controlled or dominated lands away from the center, and from the beginning of the fourth century its reach steadily expanded. Models and debates about the ways that the Roman elite organized their power away from the city parallel controversies over the degree of formalism and systematization in Roman public life. Modern nation-states preside over populations that possess, or are thought to possess, some cultural unity, while their administrations enclose territories under their control within clear boundaries and some overarching administrative and legal system.[26] With their bureaucratic organizations, the making of decisions is highly concentrated in a capital, while the responsibility for implementing them is dispersed among officials who supervise defined territories, often at some distance from the center.

Modern scholars have long detected, with varying degrees of justification, similar features in republican Rome, but more recently, some have come to view Rome's empire of the late third and second centuries rather differently. In their view, the ruling elite did not regard their city's power in terms of territories to be governed in some more or less direct fashion but rather as subordinated communities that owed Rome deference and obedience.[27] Indeed, the republican elite may often have possessed little detailed knowledge about many of the lands and peoples that had fallen under Rome's sway or were within the sphere of operation of its magistrates and armies. Archaeological excavations in China have revealed the use of maps for military and economic purposes as early as the third century B.C.[28] Even in later periods, however, the Roman elite did not use maps for administrative services, except for schematic drawings (*formae*) of distinct tracts that had received the attention of some magistrate, usually by preparing for its assignment to colonists or its sale or lease.[29] When added to poor communications, primitive transport, and uneven control over subordinated territories, the elite's worldview, which encompassed their restricted knowledge, the traditions of their polity, and the limited nature of public institutions, may have long impeded the formation of any overarching system or firm controls.

Italy is a different matter, for from the third century the Romans imposed upon it an organization that served to raise their great armies. The creation of some greater functional unity in Italy, in cultural terms or in organizational ones, is and has been one of the central problems in the historiography of republican Rome. Much of the debate has emphasized integration outside the formal apparatus of government. One approach focuses on the ties that linked elite families at Rome with the elites of the towns of Italy. From as far in the past as we can see, prominent persons had moved to Rome in order to participate in its public life, while maintaining ties with family members who remained at home, creating in the process links that could persist for generations. At the same time, some members of the ruling elite formed patron-client relations with members of local elites.[30] Unfortunately, the lack of evidence makes it difficult to assess just how pervasive these connections actually were and how thoroughly they penetrated all parts of the peninsula. In any case, links such as these would have grown over time, leaving earlier conditions uncertain.

For others, the creation of an "Italian" culture appears central, an approach whose roots may lie, at least in part, in the nationalist assumptions of the late nineteenth century, when scholarly discussion of these matters largely began.[31] At one extreme, some place the appearance of a common culture or community of interest in the late third century, following closely upon the establishment of Roman hegemony over the peninsula.[32] Others doubt that Roman Italy was very united in the last decades of the third century, pointing to polities that maintained imperial ambitions of their own, and occasions when Roman leadership increased tensions as communities and factions sought Roman favor as a weapon against rivals.[33] But when, then, did a more unified order appear? Some place such a development in the aftermath of the Social War, when Roman citizenship was extended to the free population of the peninsula.[34] Others see the gradual creation of a common political culture in the second century, when greater integration emerged as a consequence of more frequent contacts among elites, especially in the context of military service; broad economic changes resulting from the influx of wealth and slaves gained in foreign wars; the development of extensive markets in the peninsula's larger cities; and greater mobility among the population at large.

Still others emphasize the formal institutions of the Roman state, which required some actions on the part of its subordinates, if only service in Rome's armies and acquiescence or compliance to those laws, edicts, and decrees that concerned them and were made known to them. From the late third century, the Roman order in Italy was largely identified with Rome's citizens, Latins, and other allies, who gained the status because of their membership in some subordinate polity. Through the lens of these statuses, some scholars view Italy of the middle republic as a formally regulated order in which subordinated polities occupied clearly defined positions with respect to Rome. Thus, Latin colonies possessed the charters that their founders had given them, along with the general rights and privileges pertaining to all such polities, while allies had their treaties (*foedera*), which performed the same broad function. Roman citizenship, we are told, came in two basic forms, one with full rights and the other, *civitas sine suffragio*, without the right to vote or hold office at Rome. Citizens, moreover, occupied colonies (*coloniae*) and *municipia*, which, as fully developed communities, possessed their own civic organizations to which the Romans delegated certain essential functions, most notably involving the *census* and conscription. The result, then, was an ordered countryside in which the inhabitants lived in settlements that possessed clearly defined rights and duties with respect to Rome and sometimes performed very specific functions for Roman officials. The depiction of Roman Italy as a formal legal order, so necessary for viewing the republic as a *Rechtstaat* rather than a *Machtstaat*, is one of the most enduring representations of the republican system.

At one level, one might raise the same objections that have already been examined in the context of Rome's constitution, primarily its concern with system and with well-developed legal forms and its failure to set out any course of historical development. Relatively few allied communities may have possessed treaties that defined their relations with Rome, for many, if not most, would have been absorbed into the Roman order, from the ruling elite's point of view, through a *deditio in fidem* in which the entire community and its possessions passed into Rome's power.[35] In the third and second centuries, numerous examples of the ruling elite overriding the supposed privileges of Latin or allied towns can be found. Citizens and the polities in which they resided present a further range of problems. Recent studies, for example, emphasize that crucial terms such as *municipium* had tangled and complex histories, while others such as citizenship without the vote (*civitas sine suffragio*) appear to have been retrospective attempts to clarify or fix earlier arrangements.[36]

Furthermore, in its pervasive legalism, the model envisions the relationship between Rome and subordinated communities as constructed through a series of legal forms, rather than through the sometimes irregular actions of individuals and groups, and in this way it parallels attempts to describe Rome's own political order as somehow different from the culture and society in which it was embedded and from the contingent circumstances in which its officials acted. It also assumes or can be taken to assume stability in the relations between Rome and individual settlements, which is perhaps unlikely in a region that witnessed wars, the spread of large estates with servile workforces, and substantial population movements. Furthermore, the status, if any, of many of the settlements that can be detected through literary works, inscriptions, or archaeological surveys is unknown. Were smaller settlements dependent on some larger neighbor? Did they all possess formal political structures and some formalized relationship with Rome from an early date?

Studies of Rome's political order, its hegemony in Italy, and the organization of its transmarine empire, then, have frequently been conducted in terms of formal institutions and overarching structures and against the background provided by the modern state. One can find, however, firmer traces of other ways of conceptualizing and organizing space. The next step, which will be carried out in the remaining chapters, is to clarify the ways that the republic functioned spatially, by identifying the relevant elements of the worldview of the Roman elite; the republic's modes of operation; the ways that official tasks away from the city were conceptualized, defined, and represented; and the manner in which groups who were to be the targets of official activity were characterized.

THE PLAN OF THE WORK

The remainder of this work is divided into six broad chapters. The first examines Roman modes of representing the polity and its institutions along with the literary forms in which we encounter them. The second focuses on the ruling elite's conceptions of their empire, the ways that they deployed their polity's most prominent official actors over it, and the adjustments needed to accommodate an ever-growing sphere of operations. The third chapter investigates the organization of Roman Italy, especially in the distribution of roles and statuses, and the ways in which subordinate polities were integrated into the republican order. The fourth focuses on the perceived connection between the site of Rome and the republic's relationship with its gods. Here, the priestly college of the augurs occupied a prominent position, not only by defining places suitable for a range of actions in the city but also by establishing procedures for legitimate activities away from it. The fifth chapter examines the orientations and subdivisions of certain spaces, including camps and colonies, places and spaces that Roman magistrates created while operating away from Rome. The sixth chapter turns from the actions of magistrates, senate, and the institutions that they commanded to the concepts and practices of jurists and the authors of laws, edicts, and decrees. As will soon become clear, any examination of Roman practices in the third and second centuries rests to a large degree on texts produced in the first century or even later. A persistent problem, then, is to escape from this filter, which one might achieve, if only in part, by following multiple lines of evidence and argument.

ONE

Representing the
Res Publica

Ascertaining the ways that the Roman elite broadly conceptualized and represented their polity is an essential first step. After all, reconstructions written only from the perspective of a modern observer may miss many of the concerns and constraints that limited and directed members of the elite as they went about their tasks. Surviving texts provide valuable insights into the ways that some members of the Roman elite viewed their republic, and some permit glimpses that reach back to the beginnings of Latin literature in the late third century and beyond. This chapter examines these ways of depicting and regulating republican institutions in order to clarify their methods and their conventions.

ROME AND ITS HISTORY

Two explicit attempts to describe the republican political order survive, if only in part. In the middle of the second century, Polybius, a Greek resident at Rome, wrote a long account setting out how Rome had come to dominate the known world between the First Punic War, which began in 265, and the destruction of Carthage in 146, and, in the sixth book, he provided a long description of the constitution that had made this feat possible. A century later, Marcus Tullius Cicero, former consul, priest, orator, and philosopher, composed two long dialogues, *On the Republic* (*De republica*) and *On the Laws* (*De legibus*), in conscious imitation of Plato's *Republic* and *Laws*. In the second book of *On the Republic*, his chief interlocutor set out a brief description of the Roman political order, while in the second and third books of *On the Laws* a character bearing Cicero's name put forward the laws that he thought would best govern Rome. Since Polybius's version is more fragmentary, the discussion focuses first on Cicero's.

For his examination of Rome and the ideal polity, Cicero produced a dialogue set during the Latin Festival early in 129. His main speaker is Scipio Aemilianus, twice consul, censor, and victor over Carthage and Numantia, who, at the dramatic date of the dialogue, within a few days of his death, may have been the most influential senator. His fictional interlocutors are also prominent men: three had been consuls before 129 (C. Laelius in 140, M.' Manilius in 149, and L. Furius Philus in 136) and three more would hold that position later (C. Fannius in 122, Q. Mucius Scaevola the augur in 117, and P. Rutilius Rufus in 105). In the first book, Cicero's Aemilianus argues for the value of the political life and for the rational examination of it and, after defining the constitutional forms of monarchy, aristocracy, and democracy, sets out why a mixed constitution, one combining elements of all three, is best. Then, in the second book, he applies this theory to Rome, the best example of a mixed constitution.

When Cicero sought to link the peculiarities of his city to broader philosophical concerns in the second book, he provided a brief description of Rome's constitution that was based on historical works rather than philosophical ones. Cicero's history is strongly focused on the city's first centuries. His Scipio sets out a connected narrative, interrupted only by comments of the interlocutors, that begins with Rome's foundation and ends with the Decemvirs and the Twelve Tables long before the dialogue's dramatic date. In this history, he emphasizes the beginnings of institutions and practices. He associates Romulus with the foundation of the city, the creation of the senate, the patriciate, the college of augurs, and the division of the people into three tribes and thirty *curiae*. His successor, Numa Pompilius, promulgated the "laws of Numa" that regulated religious observances, established the priests of the major gods, and instituted markets and games. Tullus Hostilius began the rituals of the *fetiales*, necessary for the proper declaration of war and the ratification of treaties; established the *comitium* and *curia*, meeting places of the people and the senate; and secured the permission of the people to have twelve lictors bearing *fasces* precede him, prominent emblems of legitimate power. Tarquinius Priscus added new families to the patriciate, reorganized the equestrian centuries in the manner "that is still retained," performed the first Roman Games, and vowed the Temple of Jupiter Best and Greatest on the Capitol. His successor, Servius Tullius, created the census and the *centuriae* as well as the voting assembly based on them, while Tarquinius Superbus, the last king, dedicated Jupiter's temple. The account of the first half-century of the republic is shorter and contains fewer innovations. The origins of the consulate are lost in a lacuna, but notices survive of the first dictatorship, the first tribunes of the plebs, and the beginnings of the conflict between patricians and plebeians. The Decemvirs set out the Twelve Tables, long the fundamental text in Roman law.

In his sixth book, Polybius too introduced his account of the Roman order with a brief survey of the origins of states and the value of a mixed constitution, and he ended by comparing Rome with other exemplary constitutions. He began with an account of Rome's early history, the Archaeology, which survives only in fragments. Like Cicero's history, Polybius's also ends around the time of the Decemvirs, and it may have included an account of their deeds.[1] Polybius, however, followed this historical introduction with a description of Rome's public order at the time when he deemed it to have been at its height, the years of the Second Punic War. First, he describes in an abstract and schematic manner the powers of the consuls (the royal element), the senate (the aristocratic element), and the people, and the ways that each kept the others in check (6.11–8). In the process, he mentions only a few other offices—the tribunes of the plebs, the quaestors, and the censors—to show their dependence on (or, in the case of the tribunes, their independence from) the consuls or the senate. After setting out the balancing act between consuls, senate, and people, he then takes up Rome's military order, first describing how magistrates conscripted soldiers for their armies and then the layout of Roman camps and the manner in which officials maintained discipline within them (6.19–42). Next, he describes in some detail aristocratic funerals, which, he holds, exalted civic virtue and encouraged others to emulate it. Finally, he praises Roman religious beliefs for encouraging obedience and discipline among the masses and honesty among the elite.[2]

In their historical sections, Polybius and Cicero both wrote in a tradition, although the works of their predecessors and most of their successors are known only through fragments, which give an imperfect sense of the texts from which they were drawn.[3] Roman historical writing began in the last decade of the third century, when Q. Fabius Pictor, a senator, wrote, in Greek, the first Roman history, which covered the wanderings of heroes in Italy, Rome's foundation and early centuries, and the wars with Carthage that dominated his own day.[4] Several decades later, the poet Ennius wrote a long history in Latin verse, while the Elder Cato produced the first such work in Latin prose. A long series of writers, sometimes called "annalists," continued the practice throughout the second and first centuries. Histories in this fashion had clear Greek precedents. From the fourth century, Greek writers produced accounts of individual cities that stretched from their origins to the authors' own times and included mythical figures, the origins of institutions, and events of the more recent past.[5]

Now, Polybius based his account, at least in part, on the Elder Cato's *Origins*, the first Roman history in Latin prose, and on the history of Fabius Pictor.[6] In *On the Republic*, Cicero mentions Ennius's *Annals*, Cato's *Origins*, and Polybius's history, all available at the work's dramatic date.[7] In *On the Laws*, set in his own day, Cicero cites Q. Fabius Pictor and a long list of writers of the second and first centuries: Cato, L. Calpurnius Piso, C. Fannius, Vennonius, Coelius Antipater, Cn. Gellius, and C. Licinius Macer, which may reflect more accurately the range of his reading.[8] He also mentions as sources the Twelve Tables (*Rep.* 2.54), the pontifical annals (*Rep.* 1.25), other priestly books (*Rep.* 2.26 and 2.54), antiquarian works (*Rep.* 2.34), and tradition (*Rep.* 2.4 and 2.28).

A generation after Cicero, the historian Livy produced a much more fully developed account of Rome's rise and the spread of its power. Livy too began before Rome existed as a city and ended in his own day, producing in the process a work of 142 books. Today, only 35 books survive largely or completely intact—1 through 10, which cover Rome's foundation and its history to the end of the Samnite Wars, and 21 through 45, which set out the years from 218 to 167, when Rome became the dominant Mediterranean power—but epitomes of all but two books, the *periochae*, preserve in some limited way the contents of the lost books or the lost portions of the fragmentary books (41, 43, 44, and 45). For this reason, subsequent chapters often emphasize the period between the outbreak of the Second Punic War in 218 and the end of the Third Macedonian War in 167.

Cicero and Livy wrote in much the same historiographical tradition, but one that had evolved considerably from the works that Cicero claims as his sources. Earlier historians had set out the origins of Rome and its institutions in the distant past, along with a fuller and more detailed account of events in their own day or in the recent past, but it is far from clear how fully they treated the intervening period. In the last decades of the second century, some writers began to produce continuous year-by-year accounts of republican history, while still maintaining extensive sections on the distant past. L. Calpurnius Piso Frugi, consul in 133, was the first historian who certainly composed his history in such a fashion.[9] At the same time, works began to increase notably in scale. Piso wrote seven or eight books, while his near-contemporary Cassius Hemina, wrote five. By way of contrast, Cn. Gellius, who wrote later in the second century, reached the Gallic sack in book 15 and the early years of the Hannibalic war in a book numbered in the thirties.[10] In the first century, historians such as Licinius Macer, Valerius Antias, and Claudius Quadrigarius continued to produce annalistic histories, although Claudius began his account with the Gallic sack, not the foundation of the city; Valerius Antias's annals contained at least seventy-five books.[11]

This expansion need not have resulted in any broad challenges to the framework of Roman history. Later writers, as far as can be told, largely worked within the conventional structure of events, accepting the broad stages of Roman history, its major actors, and its most significant events. Within these limits, historians expanded on the work of their predecessors by adding new elements or lesser characters or by elaborating some episodes and figures into more fully literary accounts. Sempronius Asellio (*FRHist* 20 F 2), who wrote only about contemporary history, complains that annals did not inspire their readers to virtue, which may mean that they did not contain fully developed *exempla* in the way that an orator might do. Livy would later remedy this failure. Another means of expansion would have been the steady assimilation of more accounts of the origins of cults, rites, and offices: the history of Livy's contemporary Dionysius of Halicarnassus clearly achieved much of its great bulk in this fashion.

Livy's Roman order developed much as Cicero's. He includes, in either brief notices or fully developed episodes, the addition of new magistracies, priesthoods, and practices and the modification of old arrangements in a long sequence that stretched from Romulus through the republican centuries. At another level, and much more vividly, Livy presents Rome's history as a series of exemplary figures and their deeds.[12] While setting out these figures, Livy, like Cicero, often places his actors in the main settings of Roman public life—addressing the senate, the people, or soldiers; sacrificing; proclaiming vows and prayers—and he often imitates the formal language of prayers that so permeated Roman public life.[13] He also took care to place his events carefully within the city of Rome, its temples, monuments, and public spaces.

At yet another level, Livy shows that the power and reach of Roman institutions had continually expanded over the course of its history. In a sense, Livy, and perhaps his predecessors too, took a form of local history that in the Greek world set out the history of a single city and used it to encompass eventually the known world, while still retaining its focus on the central city, its institutions, its public life, and its political history.

When recounting events away from Rome, Livy often described the routes of armies and embassies and steadily noted the creation of new tribes, the foundation of colonies, the granting of citizenship to defeated communities, and arrivals in Rome of embassies from distant states. This vision of Rome's steady expansion provides the bulk of our evidence for Roman imperialism before the first century.

As an activity, the writing of Roman histories was a highly conventional one. To state the obvious, historians built on what went before. At one level, they possessed some "evidence" upon which they would construct their narratives. On another level, they had some form of relationship, often polemical, with their predecessors. The manner in which Roman historians went about assembling their material only reinforced the conventional nature of their activities. Most did not do "research" in a modern sense, although some clearly had done so. Instead, historians largely appropriated portions of their predecessors' narratives, to which they added contrasting tales from other authors, constructed variants of their own, or inserted new "events" or "facts." In the process, they turned this material to their own purposes, creating speeches to delineate character and making moral or political statements through the use of exemplary characters and events. In a very real way, the histories of Livy and of Dionysius of Halicarnassus represent the culmination of this historiographical tradition. J. Marincola considers this pattern of appropriation followed by an attempt to exceed one's model as yet another aspect of the concern over exemplary figures that permeates the histories themselves.[14]

Although much about earlier histories is obscure, and undoubtedly will remain so, Cicero's and Livy's predecessors did sometimes locate the origins of key institutions in the distant past and link them with clearly identified persons or occasions. Thus, Fabius Pictor, Cato, and Vennonius all make Servius Tullius the creator of the tribes; Cato associates the foundation of Rome with the formation of its *pomerium*, the essential divide between the city and the surrounding countryside; Cassius Hemina attributes certain cultic practices to Numa and the establishment of market days (*nundinae*) to Servius Tullius; and Cn. Gellius has Numa establish the college of fetials.[15] Historians did not limit their innovations to the monarchy and the very beginning of the republic. Piso sets forth the first *lectisternium* or sacred banquet in 399, while Livy places such developments in almost every part of his history that survives.[16] To some unknown but probably substantial degree, such histories recorded the gradual development of the Rome of the historians' own times.

How might one view this mass of anecdotes and descriptions that seek to assign to Roman institutions and practice some definite origin, often quite remote in time? Some modern historians are primarily concerned with their value as evidence for Rome's early history, providing a source of controversy that shows no signs of resolution. It does seem reasonably clear, however, that our sources contain a mixture of fact, fiction, idealization, and anachronism, and the boundary between them will never be identified with certainty. One possible approach shifts the emphasis from Rome's more distant past to the age in which the histories were composed. History, after all, has its own history, which varies from time to time and place to place, revealing different interests, purposes, conceptions of what is important, and ideas about how the world works. As David Schaberg has noted with respect to early Chinese historiography, "habits of representation and plot construction are highly durable, both because they belong to lasting communities that have a stake in them and because ... they tend to create invisible standards of interpretation and judgment."[17] Roman historical writing developed within the ranks of the ruling elite, and in subsequent periods its members and their associates continued to play a prominent role. While the number of authors was rather small and their audiences not necessarily a great deal larger, the images of Rome that they presented were widely shared, at least among the elite. Thus, these Roman histories may be seen less as versions of a "real" history of Rome and more as elements, perhaps even central elements, in Roman political culture, where they serve quite well as a point of entry into Roman conceptions of their polity.

Here, the concern over exemplary figures provides a starting point. The Roman nobility stressed personal and familial merit as revealed in the competition for magistracies, priesthoods, and other honors. One could represent a person's life and social position as a series of offices and awards, and one could identify a family with the collective accomplishments of its members, past and present.[18] From the fourth century, leading Romans sought to enshrine the memory of their deeds in votive temples and altars, statues and other dedications in temples or other prominent places, and displays of spoils.[19] The deliberate erasure of someone's name from monuments, a *damnatio memoriae*, which was sometimes imposed on those condemned of certain crimes under the empire, should be viewed in this context.[20] As we shall see in later chapters, this tendency to view the republic in terms of exemplary figures finds a parallel in the way that the republican elite sometimes saw their city's empire through the deeds of successful commanders and sought to regulate that empire by setting out the movements of their magistrates over it.

This concern with offices and memorable acts shaped the elite's cultural ideals and their representations of the civic order. Romans, much more than Greeks, stressed the desirability of patterning one's behavior on exemplary figures and on having as a goal the creation of exemplary actions of one's own that would be imitated in turn, a concern that lies at the heart of much of Roman literature.[21] The creation of *exempla*, in effect, made the republic a moral order. From the middle of the third century, moreover, some figures featured prominently in public performances, revealing the past to be not merely a matter for scholars. Officials who staged festivals or *ludi* sometimes included dramatic performances on historical subjects, *fabulae praetextae*, that "presented a Roman aristocrat, wearing the garb denoting his office and rank, and fulfilling his official duties for the good of the state."[22] The protagonists were often figures from the distant past—Naevius wrote a *Romulus*, while Ennius produced a *Sabinae*—but some were contemporary: Naevius's *Clastidium* honored M. Claudius Marcellus, Ennius's *Ambracia* focused on M. Fulvius Nobilior, Pacuvius's *Paullus* depicted L. Aemilius Paulus. Plays about contemporary figures and events may also have been staged in the first century, although this is less certain. At the same time, inscriptions and funeral orations, like histories, reveal a desire to claim that some ancestor had been the first to initiate some practice or perform some exemplary deed.[23]

Linking institutions to individuals in such a fashion is certainly older than Roman literature. Romulus, at least in his role as founder of the city, can be detected as early as the late fourth century.[24] Early in the third century, the Greek historian Timaeus, who probably relied on some Roman source, identified Lavinium, already under Rome's power, with the arrival of Aeneas in Italy and claimed that Servius Tullius had first marked minted bronze with a specific design, although the objects in question were produced only in the late fourth and early third centuries.[25] By the end of the century, Fabius Pictor would report that one of the consuls of 294 had vowed in battle a temple to Jupiter Stator, just as Romulus had done long before, viewing a remote figure as a proper model for later imitation.[26]

In this way, accounts of Rome's past may be seen as a kind of "collective memory," the shared knowledge held by members of a society about its essential nature and its roots in time and place.[27] Accounts of past figures and events, in other words, explain the social and political order and enable individuals and groups to function within it. Viewed in this fashion, Rome's "history" is more than a collection of exemplary figures and their deeds, for it clearly envisioned such figures as acting in meaningful places and on significant occasions, such as festivals, anniversaries, and rituals, that might also symbolize, in some fashion, the collectivity and its order.

In the city, Rome's idealized history was always present, creating in effect a "landscape of memory." Livy, along with other Roman writers, often took care to locate the events that they were describing in the city and at important nearby locations, most notably Lavinium and the Alban Mount, places thought to be ancestral to Rome and in later periods closely associated with the ceremonies surrounding Roman magistrates' entry into office.[28] At one level, one might view this link between these sites and the development of the Roman political order as appropriate for the time the historians supposedly were describing, for Rome's sphere of activity then was certainly limited, but these locations remained of great significance for most of republican history.

This connection between persons, deeds, and places was not merely a matter for writers. The association of Romulus with the Palatine is at least as early as the first decade of the third century. The curule aediles of 293 erected a statue near the *ficus Ruminalis* of the twins "below the she-wolf's teats," an image that would also appear on one of the earliest issues of Roman silver coins, minted probably in 269 or 268, demonstrating that the legend provided a suitable emblem for the city.[29] By the end of the century, Q. Fabius Pictor knew of the hut of Romulus, the *casa Romuli*, which a later author assures us, was rebuilt when necessary according to the original plan and with the original materials.[30] Elsewhere, the Romans linked at some point the dedication of Jupiter's Capitoline temple with the foundation of the republic, and probably around 300 they erected statues of Rome's kings on the hill.[31] In the *comitium*, statues of the legendary augur Attus Navius and of the hero Horatius Cocles were installed, probably in the aftermath of the *comitium*'s reconstruction in the late fourth or early third century.[32]

From the last decades of the fourth century, these areas had come to provide prime sites for monuments—votive temples, dedications, and freestanding statues or displays of spoils in public spaces—that honored the gods for granting benefits while preserving the memory of some accomplishment and the name of the political figure who had achieved it. Thus, monuments honoring living members of the ruling elite, their ancestors, and even figures from the remote past clustered around the spaces where their successors acted out their own roles. This concentration of memorials was itself sometimes the focus of public activity. One of the censors of 179 removed statues and spoils that he deemed inappropriate from the Temple of Jupiter Best and Greatest on the Capitol.[33] According to the late second-century annalist, L. Calpurnius Piso, the censors in 158 removed from the forum statues of all those who had held office, except for those that had been authorized by the senate or a popular assembly; one of the statues was said to have been of Sp. Cassius, who supposedly had aimed at tyranny in the fifth century.[34]

Thus, Roman conceptions of their polity were closely connected to accounts of its history, real or imagined, which in turn were linked to prominent persons, their offices, and the public spaces in which holders of these posts customarily acted, a practice that was already in place, if only in some basic form, by the last decades of the fourth century. Roman citizens, however, often lived far from the city, and its armies and allies were spread even farther—an aspect of depictions of the polity to which we will now turn.

ROME AS A SPATIAL AND TEMPORAL ORDER

Livy's account of republican history broadly follows a format that scholars call "annalistic," which had a clear connection to the way that Rome functioned as a polity. The basic compositional unit—the consular year, which began when two consuls entered office and ended when their successors did—reflects its annual cycle of elections, a basic element in Rome's temporal organization. Rome's consuls, along with its praetors, were its highest annual magistrates. As possessors of *imperium* and thus of the ability to command armies or punish without restraint beyond the city's boundaries, they were also its chief official actors away from Rome. Roman writers did not view the consular year as separate from the consuls themselves. Thus, in Livy's history, and probably in annalistic histories in general, the role of the consular year was not purely calendrical.[35]

The consular year was not always in accord with the sequence of the seasons or, until the middle of the second century, with the city's civic calendar. From the outbreak of the Second Punic War, Rome's consuls and praetors entered office on March 15 until 153, when the date shifted to January 1, bringing the consular year and the civic calendar into alignment for the first time. Between the beginning of the war against Pyrrhus and the end of the First Punic War, the consular year may have begun on May 1, shifting to the ides of March at some point between 233 and 217.[36] Earlier, the entry date may have been quite variable.[37] Rome's civic calendar, moreover, was not always in alignment with the solar year. In 190, it was almost four months in advance of the seasons, while it was almost two and a half months ahead in 168.[38] In the first years of the Second Punic War, the calendar may also have been a month or two ahead, although this is less certain.[39] The conventions of the civic calendar, rather than the cycle of seasons, set the basic temporal framework for official activity.

Livy's consular year was linked to the political order in other, subtler ways. Throughout the surviving portions of his history, he narrated the course of major military campaigns and domestic conflicts, but he also inserted passages that have been called "annalistic"—simple declarative sentences, straightforward grammatically and often formulaic in nature, that record events without giving much, if any, context or purpose. These passages, which contain a wealth of information, have often been deemed "archival," but the underlying sources, especially for the earliest periods, are controversial. In general, the amount of detail increases as the history progresses, possibly because of the greater amount of information that was available for later periods. In any case, it is only with book 10, which covered events in the first decade of the third century, that we begin to encounter details on the scale of the later books.

Although his practice in the first ten books was more irregular, Livy followed a fairly consistent pattern in books 21 through 45, which covered the years between 218 and 167, and for an uncertain interval before and after, where his text does not survive. Here, annalistic passages, now fuller and more formulaic, give structure to the narrative of the year's major events.[40] A year usually begins with the consuls' entry into office and ends with the return to the city of a consul to conduct the election of his successors. Livy's narration of events lies between these two points, although, in some years, Livy has the consul resume campaigning after the election. Although the loss of the remaining books makes certainty impossible, Livy may have followed this pattern until the outbreak of the Social War, when the disruption of republican institutions would have made it untenable.

Additional annalistic passages expand upon this structure in one of two basic ways. In the first, Livy often recounts a series of events that set the stage for the consuls' departure to their assignments, usually military in nature and away from the city, that were clustered around the beginning of the consular year. In the second, usually placed at the very end of the year, he reports, in various combinations and only vaguely dated within the year, triumphs, temple dedications, the foundation of colonies, the performance of rites of thanksgiving, the staging of festivals, and the imposition of fines. Here, the basic vocabulary often varies little from entry to entry. History on this pattern, then, emphasizes events that are formally similar or even identical year after year, and this yearly pattern, in turn, represents the republican constitution as a continuing operation that transcends men and events.[41] Livy probably adopted this structure and the vast amount of detail contained within it from an earlier author, who may have been Valerius Antias, probably active two generations earlier, who clearly did research on some scale; the results, where they can be checked, are largely accurate.[42]

Except for armies, neither Cicero nor Polybius regarded the organization of Roman power away from the city as relevant to his purpose. When Polybius wrote his history, Rome not only dominated Italy, which provided the core of its military forces, but also dispatched magistrates, ambassadors, and armies far outside the peninsula, and, in the century that separated Polybius from Cicero, Rome's reach only grew. As we have seen, Polybius and Cicero imposed on their Romes concepts derived from a Greek philosophical discourse on the ideal city. Rome did share some features with Greek city-states or *poleis*—elected officials, an advisory council, and popular assemblies—and ancient authors had no great difficulty in finding Greek terms for their supposed Roman analogs, although much was undoubtedly lost in the process.[43] But the Rome of Polybius's or Cicero's age, or of any period after the middle of the fourth century, was vastly larger in its civic territory and in the number of its citizens than any Greek city, so that the convention of treating Rome as a kind of *polis* obscures important elements in its political organization that may also have contributed to its success.

In setting out this spatial distribution of functions, Polybius (6.12) describes the consuls in terms of a simple dichotomy between their duties first in Rome and then on campaign, just the distinction that Livy would later make between "at home" (*domi*) and "on campaign" (*militiae*). The senate and popular assemblies, of course, met only in the city, where the senate appeared to be in charge when the consuls were away. From Rome, the senate also conducted investigations into suspicious occurrences within Italy, and received embassies from outside the peninsula while dispatching its own embassies to resolve disputes, issue ultimata, and settle wars, thus dividing its activities into distinct zones—the city, Italy, and beyond—in which the senate performed different functions, although Rome remained the essential core.

Some find this brief description of Rome's spatial order problematic. Arnaldo Momigliano, for example, has suggested that Polybius's insistence on viewing Rome in Greek terms has obscured its alien features along with its actual modes of operation, most notably by excluding any mention of the towns in which many Roman citizens actually lived, Rome's colonies, and the allies who provided the bulk of its military power.[44] Fergus Millar, however, notes that Polybius compared Rome's order with the exemplary constitutions of Sparta, Mantinea, the cities of Crete, and Carthage, all city-states, and that he praised the Achaean League for having the same magistrates, councilors, and jurors, so that it operated as if it were a single city.⁴⁵ Rome clearly did not meet this exacting standard.

When Cicero set out in *On the Laws* the rules that he thought would best govern Rome, he had his chief speaker, who bore his own name, proclaim two codes, one dealing with cult and the other with magistracies. In the second of these codes, Cicero makes the same basic distinction that Polybius had made and that Livy would make. After proclaiming that citizens have the right to appeal from magisterial decisions and that trials should be conducted before popular assemblies, he adds that "there shall be no appeal from orders given by a commander in the field; while a magistrate is waging war, his commands shall be valid and binding." He divides minor magistrates into those who served "on campaign" and those who operated "at home" under the supervision of the senate. "There shall be aediles who shall be curators of the city [*urbs*], of the markets, and of the customary games." The censors "shall have charge of the temples, streets, and aqueducts within the city." In the field, the consuls "shall hold the supreme power; they shall be subject to no one." Finally, "magistrates and ambassadors shall leave the city when the senate decrees or the people command; they shall wage wars justly; they shall spare the allies; they shall hold themselves and their subordinates in check; they shall increase the glory of the people; they shall return home with honor."

Indeed, Cicero may have used the image of the "two fatherlands" in *On the Laws* (2.3–6) to address the great extent of the Roman polity. There, he announces that he, like many Romans, had two *patriae*, one by nature, that is, the city of his birth, and the other, Rome itself, by common citizenship, and he proclaims his intention to focus on the latter. The Elder Cato, he claims, had held much the same position a century earlier. While Cato and Cicero were prominent members of Rome's elite, they were also citizens of Tusculum and Arpinum, communities whose inhabitants had received Roman citizenship in the past, and thus they were able to function in Rome as Romans, while participating at home in the civic life of towns that had retained their own magistrates, cults, and customs. For Cicero, these two *patriae* were clearly separate: one could discuss Rome's institutions without any reference to other settlements occupied by citizens.

Rome's continuing centrality in the management of empire and the dichotomy between the spheres "at home" and "on campaign" form a clear contrast with the situation in other contemporary empires, headed by kings and without the marked annual structure of public life that characterized Rome and other city-states, in which the ultimate source of legitimate authority often moved and was not as clearly tied to a specific place.[46] From such a perspective, polities might appear differently. In his letter to the people of Larisa in Thessaly in 215, Philip V of Macedon noted that the Roman practice of admitting noncitizens to citizenship had made it possible for them to send out many colonies.[47]

ROME AND ITS GODS

Public cult bulks large in Livy's history. Especially for the years after circa 300, he often records the deaths of pontiffs, augurs, *decemviri sacris faciundis*, and other priests and identifies their replacements. But his notices, both in scale and in regularity of occurrence, primarily concern the performance of cultic acts by magistrates, priests, and senate: the expiation of prodigies, the making of vows, the performance of major festivals (*ludi*), and ceremonies of thanksgiving, *supplicationes*, their repetition if the first performance was deemed to have been flawed (*instaurationes*), and the dedication of temples. Livy did not invent this material, although he did expand it, shorten it, change the order of events, and alter its position within the year.[48]

The result was to represent Rome's gods as deeply involved in the polity, to link Roman piety with Roman success, and to explain failures by acts of impiety, which would prove temporary when magistrates, senate, and priests had regained the gods' goodwill through the performance of rites.[49] Livy did not establish these connections through explicit statements. Instead, they often arise from the juxtaposition of religious events with their apparent consequences. F. Hickson-Hahn notes that Livy's use of the language of prayer, when combined with passages recording the performances of rites, "reminded Livy's contemporary audience that the Roman state, with its political and religious machinery, had been and continued to be a stable and enduring entity."[50]

Livy was not the only Roman author to give to the city's public cult a prominent role. Toward the end of his life, Cicero produced three works addressing the gods and their role in human life: *On the Nature of the Gods* (*De natura deorum*), *On Divination* (*De divinatione*), and the fragmentary *On Fate* (*De fato*). The central points at issue in *On the Nature of the Gods* and *On Divination*—the nature of the gods (not their existence) and the validity of divination—had a long history in Greek philosophy. In the first century, some of Rome's elite had begun to measure their city's practices against philosophical arguments.[51] The Epicureans held the gods to be remote and uninterested in human affairs; worshiping them was useless. Other schools sought out universal standards, which devalued local peculiarities. Few Romans, as far as can be told, rejected entirely their city's practices. Instead, those who were attracted to philosophical arguments sought to purge Roman practice of "superstition" and then to find acceptable reasons to preserve the rest.[52]

For Cicero, the validity of public cult was closely linked to the political order. Both dialogues center on long established debates about the gods and the validity of divination, and both contain many Greek examples. Still, Roman institutions and figures are prominent in both, while speakers frequently stress the importance of the matters at issue to the republic. Cicero set *On the Nature of the Gods* in the house of C. Aurelius Cotta, a pontiff and later a consul, during the Latin festival of 77 or 76. In it, Cotta represents the New Academy, C. Velleius is an Epicurean, and Q. Lucilius Balbus, a Stoic, while Cicero, then a young man, listens. Early in the first book (1.14), Cicero proclaims in his own voice his central concern: that rituals, piety, oaths, temples, shrines, sacrifices, and the auspices might all be deemed valueless unless it could be shown that gods were involved in human affairs and that they could be influenced by cult. In the dialogue, Velleius and Balbus both assert that they expect Cotta, a pontiff, to defend Rome's religion.[53] At the very end (*ND* 3.94), Balbus, disliking Cotta's arguments, proclaims that he had to fight against Cotta "on behalf of our altars and hearths, of the temples and shrines of the gods, and of the city's walls, which you as pontiffs declare to be sacred and are more careful to hedge the city around with religious ceremonies than even with fortifications."

Cicero organized the dialogue around three contrasting presentations: Velleius and Balbus take an Epicurian and a Stoic stance, respectively, while Cotta puts forward arguments against both. At the beginning of his presentation (*ND* 2.3), Balbus announces this intention to prove that the gods exist, to explain their nature, to demonstrate that they govern the world, and to show that they are concerned about humanity (not just the Romans) and its fortunes. He attempts to demonstrate the existence of the gods through epiphanies and accurate prophecies.[54] He seeks to show the gods' benevolence by noting the practice of erecting temples to admirable qualities, such as Honor (*Fides*), Harmony (*Concordia*), Hope (*Spes*), and Reason (*Mens*), and by constructing etymologies linking the names of gods to useful elements in the natural world. In his response, Cicero's Cotta never questions the gods' existence or the validity of most Roman cultic activity. Balbus has quite definite views about the gods, whereas Cotta merely wishes to demolish his opponents' doctrines, while not putting forward any of his own. In his reply to Velleius, Cotta announces that "in natural philosophy, I am more ready to say what is not true than what is."[55]

Cicero's Cotta, then, may be seen as a defender of Roman practices, divorced from any particular theory of the nature of the gods, as long as they are purged of what he considers to be absurdities.[56] In his response to Velleius, Cotta criticizes his opponent for ignoring Ti. Coruncanius and P. Mucius Scaevola, famous chief pontiffs of the third and second centuries, and relying instead on Epicurus, "who destroyed the very foundations of religion and overthrew, not by force like Xerxes, but by argument, the temples of the immortal gods."[57] Later, he proclaims that he was guided on questions of religion by the chief pontiffs Ti. Coruncanius, P. Scipio, and P. Scaevola and by the augur C. Laelius and not by any Greek philosopher, and he pronounces that: "All the religion of the Roman people is made from rites and auspices, to which a third is added consisting of all prophetic warnings as the interpreters of the Sibyl or the *haruspices* have derived from portents and prodigies. I have always held that none of these departments of religion were to be despised, and I have held the conviction that Romulus by his auspices and Numa by his establishment of our ritual laid the foundation of our city, which assuredly could never have been as great as it is had not the fullest measure of divine favor been obtained for it."[58] Indeed, Cotta (*ND* 3.9–10) explicitly criticizes Balbus for relying on argument when tradition would have sufficed.

Cotta, it is important to note, reduces Roman public cult, with its wide variety of rites, priesthoods, priestly colleges, and sodalities, to three categories, which he connects to different sets of practitioners. Rites formed the sphere of the pontiffs, whose many functions included a general expertise in rituals and prayers. The augurs were guardians of the auspices, which accompanied all significant public acts. The third category included two sets of experts. The *quindecemviri sacris faciundis* interpreted the Sibylline Books, the Books of Fate, which had an important role in the expiation of prodigies. The *haruspices*—in this case, experts summoned from Etruria and not the sacrificial attendants of magistrates—also interpreted and helped expiate portents, especially those concerned with lightning and monstrous births. The first three of these groups formed the most important and prestigious of the priestly colleges.

In the following year, Cicero produced *On Divination*, in which Cicero's brother Quintus is the spokesman for the Stoic position, while Cicero himself represents the New Academy. Since a character bearing Cicero's own name makes the arguments against divination, scholars have often seen the dialogue as having a clear conclusion that condemns the practice in all its forms.[59] Some have suggested that the apparent change in Cicero's position from the more positive valuation of divination in *On the Laws* represents the collapse of Cicero's political hopes during the civil wars. Others, however, have pointed out that Cicero sometimes signaled in his dialogues written in a skeptical manner that one should not seek to find his own beliefs in the work.[60] In any case, the dialogue's form implies that positive arguments could be made for both sides, although he may have thought that arguments against the practice had more force.[61]

The dialogue's structure is simple. In the first book, Quintus makes his arguments in favor of the validity of divination, while in the second, Marcus seeks to counter his brother's arguments. Cicero begins by proclaiming the centrality of divination to Rome's order, for Romulus had founded the city through the auspices, his successors had employed augurs, and, after the expulsion of the kings, no business at home or abroad (*nec domi nec militiae*) was begun without taking the auspices. The Romans, moreover, had also sought out Etruscan *haruspices* to aid in interpretation and to give advice, and they had established the *quindecemviri sacris faciundis* to interpret the Sibylline verses. In Rome, divination involved the central institutions of the polity.

Quintus divides divinatory practices into two broad categories: divination by art, which included the rites of the augurs and the interpreters of entrails, portents, and prodigies, and divination by nature, which included dreams and prophetic frenzy, a distinction that was old in Greek thought.[62] He stresses, and would stress again and again, that divination by art was a systematic form of knowledge, based on long observation, that made valid predictions by revealing the signs that precede certain events.[63] Erroneous interpretations did not undermine its status as an art, since no system of knowledge, no *ars*, was without error, especially since the augurs of his own day had lost much earlier knowledge.[64]

Throughout his presentation, Quintus stresses that divination was primarily concerned with associations between signs and the events that they portended and not with events and their causes; for him, the practice was based on experience, not theory. Indeed, Cicero (*Div.* 1.5; 1.29), in his own voice, earlier claims that "the ancients" had been guided more by what had actually taken place than by reasoned argument, while his Quintus emphasizes that omens were not causes but rather signs that foretold what would happen unless precautions were taken. Toward the end of his presentation, he asserts: "The truth is that no other argument of any sort is advanced to show the futility of the various kinds of divination ... except that it is difficult to set out the cause or reason of every kind of divination. You ask: 'Why is it that the *haruspex*, when he finds a cleft in the lung of the victim, even though the other vitals are sound, stops the execution of an undertaking and defers it to another day?' 'Why does an augur think it a favorable omen when a raven flies to the right or a crow to the left?'"[65] Wishing to know why divination worked, he claims, was not really important: one could know that a magnet was drawn to iron without knowing why. John North has emphasized that Roman ideas about divination did not include any overt theorizing about causes, and he has warned against attempting to determine the ideas of causation that "must" have underpinned Roman actions, for theorizing in such a fashion was alien to Roman practice.[66] More than a century before Cicero wrote the dialogue, Plautus too considered ravens and crows on the right or left as clear signs.[67]

The bulk of Quintus's argument rests on successful predictions. His Roman examples of divination by nature run from the beginning of the city to his own day and are usually derived from literary works. Thus, he claims that Q. Fabius Pictor had held that all of Aeneas's adventures had been foretold in a dream, that the second-century poet Accius had claimed that Tarquinius Superbus's dream had predicted Rome's greatness, that one could find the dream of P. Decius Mus "in the annals" (*in annalibus*), and that a number of historians, including Fabius Pictor and the second-century writers Cn. Gellius, and Coelius Antipater, had reported a dream that revealed a flaw in the votive games at the end of the Latin War in 338.[68]

Next, Quintus turns to divination by art, which he (1.95) connects to well-run polities. Here, we find (1.98–99) that the *haruspices* and the *quindecemviri sacris faciundis* were in agreement on the interpretation of signs such as the appearance of two suns, meteors, earthquakes, statues of gods that sweat, showers of stones, of blood, and of earth, births of hermaphrodites, and lightning that strikes temples and the gates of the city and that their predictions had come to pass. Then, he sets out his examples: Ennius's account of the augural contest between Romulus and Remus; predictions of victory over Veii as found "in the annals"; and the disaster at Lake Trasimene in 216.

Marcus's critique is less overtly positive toward Roman practice than was Cotta's in *On the Nature of the Gods*. The arguments in the first book are largely from historical experience: Quintus acknowledges that he does not know why divination works but only that it does, while Marcus later claims that such a position is not acceptable philosophically.[69] In the second book, Marcus adopts two basic lines of argument. In one, he uses the great variety of divinatory practices and their arbitrary and seemingly ridiculous nature against them. Thus, he (*Div.* 2.27.59) notes that the *haruspices* had once pronounced that the mice who had gnawed at the sacred shields at Lanuvium portended disaster, and he suggests that it matters little what mice gnawed, for gnawing was what they do. At another level, he also accumulates counterexamples in which divination had spectacularly failed, leaving untouched the equally impressive successes that formed Quintus's strongest arguments.[70] Throughout his presentation, moreover, Cicero does present an argument for the efficacy of the auspices and the practices of the *haruspices*: although invalid as methods of divination, they are, and have been, of great use in preserving the *res publica*.[71] Viewing rites in this fashion permitted augurs to continue to perform them, for philosophical arguments affected only the rationale behind them.[72]

But Cicero had his Quintus argue not only for the validity of divination but also for divination of a very specific kind. At the beginning of the dialogue (1.1), Cicero proclaims it to have been the ancient belief, in Rome and elsewhere, that divination is the "presentiment and knowledge of future events," a position that would be central in his fragmentary dialogue *On Fate* (*De fato*), written shortly after *On Divination*. Later (*Div.* 2.70), he held that, while Romulus "believed that augury was an art useful for seeing things to come," the augurs of Cicero's day did not foretell the future, preserving the discipline instead "out of great respect for the opinion of the masses and because of its great utility for the republic."

Roman divination, however, was not quite this simple. The augurs did not view their signs as predictive. Officials sought through the auspices to ascertain whether there was some divine impediment to performing a specific act on the day on which the rite was performed. Cicero's Quintus (*Div.* 1.29) asserts that such signs warn of what might happen if precautions are not taken. If the signs were negative, they might repeat the rite on other days until a positive result was achieved. When interpreting prodigies, moreover, pontiffs, decemvirs, and *haruspices* were concerned primarily with signs that the *pax deorum* had been disrupted and with proposing expiatory rites that would restore Rome's good relations with its gods. There are indications, however, that the decemvirs and *haruspices* also made predictions about future developments, a practice that may have been an innovation of the late third century.[73]

Works of this kind, which sought to judge Roman practice against the standards of Greek philosophy, mark a clear departure in the ways that the elite wrote about their city's cults. Scattered traces in a range of texts mention books and other documents, sometimes thought to be old, in the possession of various priestly colleges. The Salii and the *fratres Arvales* preserved cult hymns, the *carmen saliare* and the *carmen arvale*, that were probably composed before the end of the fourth century; the pontiffs maintained a rather complicated calendar that may have reached its developed form at about the same time; the *decemviri sacris faciundis* consulted the Sibylline Books, whose date is uncertain.

Priestly collections, however, apparently did not contain doctrinal works or even detailed instructions for the performance of rites. Instead, they were limited to prayers, calendars, opinions on specific ritual matters, and records of the performances of rites and must have been surrounded by oral commentary and exegesis;[74] Cicero was able to consult such records for events as far back as the third century.[75] Although rites and signs could be discussed with some sophistication, cult, even at an elite level, did not involve any systematic theology. John Scheid has noted that the Romans' ideas about the gods, from as far in the past as we can see and persisting well into the Empire, were much less developed than their views about the rites used in conciliating them.[76] Religion itself, in other words, had not been the object of self-conscious reflection.

Despite Quintus's assertion that Roman divination rested on long observation, there are few signs that Roman priests kept written records matching signs and outcomes over long periods, as did diviners in the Near East, the ultimate source of many of the divinatory practices of the ancient Mediterranean world. Here, the chronicle that chief pontiffs had maintained from some uncertain time in the past to the late second century is the most likely possibility.[77] The Elder Cato reports that the chief pontiffs posted a tablet (*tabula*) that recorded grain prices and eclipses of the sun and moon, while later authors also held that it recorded all the significant events of the year.[78] Grain prices certainly were objects of divinatory speculation in the Near East, as were eclipses at Rome and elsewhere, but the few passages that mention the pontifical annals do not link it explicitly to divination. Certain phenomena, however, were viewed as signs over substantial periods, so that some sign-lore did exist, if only orally. In his dialogue *On Friendship* (*De amicitia* 7), set in 129, one of Cicero's speakers asserts that the augurs met monthly to discuss augural matters (*commentandi causa*), which may indicate that their knowledge was transmitted in such a context. One of

Cicero's signs in *On Divination* may have first been deemed significant in Mesopotamia.[79] Against this background, it is important to note that our knowledge of these matters does not derive directly from these priestly archives or from accounts of consultations. Instead, as we shall see in the following section, we largely hear of them through the intermediary form of "antiquarian" texts, some of which were compiled by writers who were also priests.

How should one view this collection of offices and practices? Cicero found Roman divination to be philosophically acceptable, if only in part, because it was politically useful. In the second century, Polybius (6.56.6–8) viewed Roman religiosity as a chief factor in Rome's success, for it instilled self-discipline in the elite and a willingness to follow orders in the populace. In his *Human and Divine Antiquities*, written around the middle of the first century, M. Terentius Varro outlines a "tripartite theology," which, he claims, the chief pontiff and jurist Q. Mucius Scaevola, consul in 95, had earlier set out.[80] Varro holds there to be three basic views of the gods: one, found in the poets, was both false and useless; the second, the creation of the philosophers, might be true but provided little help in governing a city, for most citizens would be confused by it; the third, the actual religion of a city, which had developed over time and not according to the theories of any philosopher, might be false, but was also useful and necessary for governing it. Jörg Rüpke has suggested that arguments for the utilitarian value of Roman practice are best seen as attempts by members of the ruling elite to preserve traditional practices against universalizing and rationalizing criticisms.[81]

Now, members of the Roman elite clearly saw the worship of the gods as useful, but not necessarily because—or only because—their position in public cult separated them sharply from their supposed inferiors. Roman gods were powers that affected the world and people in it for good or ill. Through cult, public officials sought to secure divine favor through vows and prayers; to determine through the auspices or the examination of the entrails of sacrificial animals whether or not such favor had, in fact, been gained; to interpret signs or portents that might indicate that the *pax deorum*, the peace between Rome and its gods, had been ruptured; and to identify the expiatory rites that would led to its restoration. Linderski has noted that the Roman attitude toward supernatural powers was that "one should do whatever one can to appease them, but also whenever it was possible one should try to gain control over them."[82] These acts, which directly involved magistrates, the senate, and priestly colleges, bulk large in our sources.

From a different perspective, Roman cult formed a central element in a system of signs and symbols that help to interpret and explain reality, provide orientation within it, and even control or shape events in the phenomenal world.[83] Indeed, Roman practices might be seen as a system of communication and negotiation, through signs that are ultimately arbitrary as all such signs must be, by which magistrates sought warning of divine anger and approval of their own actions. Links between effects and their supposed causes are not always obvious, and their identification often rests on fundamental assumptions about the way that the world works. For a long time, the Roman elite was highly successful in achieving the goals that they had set for their polity, and when they begin to express skepticism in the first century, their order was experiencing sharp strains.

The cultic activities of Rome's elite, then, ought not to be regarded as distinct from their "political" or "administrative" functions. In the performance of their tasks, magistrates, priests, and senate assessed the state of Rome's relations not only with its allies and competitors but also with its gods, they sought to ascertain whether circumstances were favorable or unfavorable for a range of possible activities, and they attempted to influence outcomes by the performance of cult tasks or by giving magistrates more "useful" assignments. Indeed, no clear divide existed between the human and divine worlds, for defeats, conspiracies and crimes might be seen as signs of divine disfavor. Roman cult, in other words, was central to the elite's worldview.

ANTIQUARIANISM, PRIESTLY KNOWLEDGE, AND JURISPRUDENCE

Cicero and Livy reveal a written tradition of depicting the Roman polity historically through exemplary figures and successive innovations in magistracies, priesthoods, and practices. In some of his dialogues, moreover, Cicero provided glimpses of the more arcane knowledge of priests, which rested in turn on oral tradition and on collections of documents that set out calendars, prayers, changes in the membership of priestly colleges, notices of the performances of rites, and opinions of colleges or individual priests about disputed points of ritual and of law. When we come to have a clearer view of these written forms, however, it comes through the intermediary of antiquarianism, which shared many features and practitioners with jurisprudence. Antiquarians, as we shall see, shared with historians a concern for the supposed origins of institutions, but they also were concerned with the meanings of terms and the establishment of norms for contemporary practices.

Antiquarianism is a broad category that may include, or disguise, a variety of practices with a number of ends. It has often been defined by the kinds of text that its practitioners were thought to have produced: learned treatises without literary pretensions, usually descriptive rather than chronological in structure, that could quote documents, argue about interpretations, set out alternate views, and use questions and answers as an organizing device.[84] Antiquarians often set out the origins of a city, an institution, or a rite through foundation myths or *aetiae* or by constructing etymologies that supposedly revealed the fundamental meaning of associated terms and phrases, a practice that brought them close to grammarians. They sometimes exhibited an interest in monuments and old documents, which could bring them close to historians and jurists. In many ways, antiquarianism was central to Roman intellectual life.[85]

Antiquarian elements began to appear in Roman works around the end of the third century, for Rome's first historians included passages that might be deemed antiquarian. The origins of the form lie in fifth-century Greece, when some writers began to produce works on genealogies, foundation stories, and lists of eponymous magistrates, from which more fully developed chronologies could be produced.[86] From the end of the fourth century, others began to encompass in their works the monuments of a city and its religious customs and political institutions. Greek antiquarianism, then, was often closely connected to the production of local histories.

In historical works, antiquarian elements would have been assembled into a larger whole through the encompassing narrative, but the second century also witnessed the appearance of treatises that were devoted to, and probably organized around, a particular institution or practice or even a single text. Early in the century, M. Fulvius Nobilior, consul in 189, produced a work on the calendar, *De fastis*, which he deposited in the temple of Hercules Musarum, although it remains unclear whether this work was a text or a painted calendar with commentary. Later in the century, L. Aelius Stilo composed works on the hymn of the Salii, the *carmen Saliare*, and the Twelve Tables. In the middle of the first century, M. Terentius Varro, the greatest antiquarian of them all, is said to have produced more than seventy works distributed over more than six hundred books. His most ambitious works, possibly the only ones that attempted to set out the entire Roman order, survive only in scattered citations: the twenty-five books of his *Human Antiquities* (*Antiquitates rerum humanarum*) and the sixteen books of his *Divine Antiquities* (*Antiquitates rerum diuinarum*), both organized around Roman institutions.

From the beginning of the second century, or even earlier if one credits reports of Ap. Claudius Caecus's *De usurpationibus*, some writers also began to produce formal commentaries and works of exposition on law. The fundamental text guiding Roman legal practice was the Twelve Tables, perhaps the reason why the Decemvirs occupied such a prominent place in Roman histories. The basic *legis actiones*—legal actions preparatory to litigation that were encompassed in fixed sequences of words and deeds—were at least as old as the end of the fourth century, and they may have been still older. In matters of law, eminent men thought to be especially knowledgeable, the *iuris periti* or the *iuris consulti*, were often consulted about points at issue in sacred or public matters or in disputes between citizens. In such cases, they either constructed the verbal *formulae* so essential to legislation or litigation or issued an opinion, a *responsum*, about a specific matter. When the sources permit us to view such *responsa*, they are very much concerned with setting out lawful actions, with identifying who could properly perform them, or with identifying the contexts, times, and places where their performance was valid. Ti. Coruncanius, the first plebeian chief pontiff and apparently the most active jurist in the second quarter of the third century, held to be valid certain sacrifices made on an unlucky day, a *dies ater*; denied to be pure certain sacrificial animals; and thought that the person who inherited the largest portion of an estate ought to be responsible for continuing the family's rites.[87] More than a century later, Q. Fabius Maximus Servilianus, a pontiff and consul in 142, deemed it improper to perform rites for one's ancestors on a *dies ater*, since it was necessary to invoke the names of Jupiter and Janus, whose names could not be spoken on such a day, while P. Mucius Scaevola, consul in 133 and *pontifex maximus*, again linked responsibility for continuing family rites with the inheritance of the largest portion of the estate.[88]

The earliest formal work of jurisprudence may have been the *Tripertita* of Sex. Aelius Paetus Catus (cos. 198), which linked clauses in the Twelve Tables with the associated *legis actio* and some commentary. Others jurists would continue to write on the Twelve Tables throughout the century. Pomponius (*Dig.* 1.2.2.39–41), who probably wrote in the second century of the empire, reports that P. Mucius Scaevola (cos. 133), M. Iunius Brutus (who held the office of praetor in an unknown year during the same period), and M.' Manilius (cos. 149) were in some fashion founders of the civil law. Scaevola's, Brutus's, and Manilius's works appear to have been collections of *responsa* addressing related matters.[89] Jurists, moreover, made little effort to generalize. Cicero (*De or.* 2.142) claims that Brutus, along with the Elder Cato, had recorded in his opinions particular names and circumstances, which, he maintains, discouraged students, who had to learn a large number of cases. Early in the first century, Q. Mucius Scaevola, consul and *pontifex maximus*, produced eighteen books on the civil law (*de iure ciuile*), which, we are told, set out the civil law *generatim*, that is, by categories. Scaevola, in other words, attempted to create a unified whole by arranging the individual elements into larger categories and subcategories much like Varro would later do with Roman antiquities. He also had a crucial role in the development of processes of abstraction that would turn jurisprudence slowly away from immersion in particulars.[90]

Jurisprudence and antiquarianism shared practitioners, concerns, and some conventions. Early in the second century, M. Fulvius Nobilior addressed in some fashion the calendar, *De fastis*, a topic beloved of antiquarians but also essential to the operation of much of Rome's public life, including litigation. Cicero (*Brut.* 81) claimed that a Fabius Pictor, probably Numerius Fabius Pictor who was active late in the second century, was skilled in law, literature, and antiquities; he is known to have written on pontifical law (*de iure pontificio*). C. Sempronius Tuditanus (cos. 129) wrote on magistracies, while Iunius Gracchanus (who probably was sometimes called Iunius Congus) wrote a treatise *de potestatibus* on magisterial powers. In the following century, authors continued to mix concerns over the law with more "antiquarian" pursuits. The shadowy L. Cincius, probably active around the time of Sulla, produced a *Mystogogica*, virtually a guidebook to the city's monuments, and also wrote on old words (*de uerbis priscis*), voting assemblies (*de comitiis*), the powers of consuls (*de consulum potestate*), military matters (*de re militari*), the calendar (*de fastis*), and on the duties of jurists (*de officio iurisconsulti*).[91] In the 50s and 40s, four prominent augurs, all Cicero's colleagues in the college, wrote on the auspices, *de auspiciis*: M. Valerius Messala; Ser. Sulpicius Rufus, who was also active in the civil law; Ap. Claudius Pulcher; and C. Claudius Marcellus. Still later, the Augustan jurist M. Antistius Labeo wrote on priesthoods, rituals, and the edict of the peregrine praetor, while his contemporary, C. Ateius Capito, wrote on pontifical and augural law as well as on private law.

When we turn to discussions of specific institutions and practices, we find that antiquarians, and occasionally jurists too, were often concerned with the origins of the offices or practices that they were describing. Here, there was a clear tendency to link them with prominent Romans or important events, often of the distant past, just as historians did. M. Fulvius Nobilior attributed the names of some months to Romulus or Numa Pompilius. L. Cincius thought that a method for identifying the commanders of joint Roman and Latin armies had begun with the destruction of Alba Longa by Tullus Hostilius, Rome's third king.[92] M. Valerius Messala, Cicero's contemporary, his colleague on the augural college, and a noted authority on the law, explained why the Aventine Hill was not included within the *pomerium*, the augural boundary of the city, by noting that Remus had taken the auspices from this hill, so that it had become ill-omened.[93] Some claimed that certain rules formed part of the "laws of Numa," or the *leges regiae*, a collection that can first be detected in the annals of Cassius Hemina, or the *ius Papirianum*, attributed to a Papirius who was *pontifex maximus* under Tarquinius Superbus.[94] Historians, antiquarians, and jurists shared some of the same anecdotes and occupied similar conceptual worlds.

Since antiquarian works are known only through fragments, little about their overall organization can be determined with any confidence. The scattered extracts, which may well not be very representative of the original works, display an interest in the origins of institutions and practices, often revealed through etymologies and aetiological tales, in the meaning of terms associated with them, and in a large amount of detail about some aspect of public or sacred practices. As a good illustration, one might turn to Aulus Gellius's discussion (*NA* 10.15.1–32) of the rules covering the priest of Jupiter, the *flamen Dialis*, which he claims to have found in certain unnamed books on public priests (*de sacerdotibus publicis*) and in the first book of a work, probably in pontifical law, by a Fabius Pictor. These priests, we are told, may not ride on a horse, see the citizens arrayed as if an army outside the city's boundary, take an oath, wear a ring or a knot, pass under an arbor of vines, sleep three nights in succession away from their bed, go outdoors without their cap or *apex*, or touch a corpse or bread made with yeast. Norms such as these float vaguely in time and are without context.

Roman antiquarianism has not enjoyed a good reputation among modern scholars. Arnaldo Momigliano saw it, and the production of local histories with which it was closely allied, as politically and intellectually marginal activities.[95] Some students link it to reactionary opinions, nostalgia for a distant and vanished past, or the elevation of this past over the concerns of the present.[96] Elizabeth Rawson connects the appearance of antiquarian practices in Rome with the turbulence of the age of the Gracchi and their later development with the disorders at the end of the republic.[97] Antiquarians, then, sought escape from the turmoil of their own times either by immersing themselves in an idealized, and often mythical, past or by seeking to revive it in some fashion. Andrew Wallace-Hadrill suggests that Augustan antiquarianism served to legitimate reforms, while delegitimizing the very recent past, the source of so much turmoil.[98] Assessments such as these clearly cannot account for the practice in its entirety: after all, the works of Nobilior and Cato—and of Polybius too, for he used "antiquarian" elements in his "Archaeology"—all appeared before the age of the Gracchi, when the traditional order is usually seen to have been at its height.

Now, republican antiquarians, like jurists and historians, certainly thought the past to be exemplary. Concern for the past, then, did not require an abandonment of the concerns of the present. Indeed, many Roman antiquarians may not have exhibited much interest in bygone days for their own sake, except perhaps for the occasional curiosity. None of the institutions and practices set out in Cicero's account of the history of early Rome, with the exception of the monarchy itself, can be shown to have been abandoned in his own time. Jörg Rüpke has suggested that assigning origins to contemporary cult practices was one of the ways that members of Rome's elite in the second and first centuries ordered and made sense of the cultic practices of their city.[99] The same observation can be made about their city's magistracies, assemblies, priestly colleges, and many of the practices associated with them. Antiquarian information helped order public life by explaining institutions, procedures, and customs, although its controversies and polemics are now largely invisible.[100]

LAWS AND LEGISLATION

Drafting laws was an old practice in Rome. Later literary works report the existence of laws and treaties from the sixth and fifth centuries, some of which may be genuine.[101] A few damaged inscriptions preserve traces of laws of the sixth and fifth centuries, which reveal the presence of verbal forms resembling those that were central to later legislation, an illustration of some continuity in scribal practice. From the second half of the fourth century, historians and antiquarians record the passage of measures that sought to regulate elements of public life: opening the highest offices to plebeians, preventing or eliminating iteration of the consulship, expanding the pontifical and augural colleges and opening them to plebeians, and banning debt bondage or *nexum*.

Laws, *leges*, were authoritative statements intended to bind groups of people, certain places, or individuals who had entered into some contractual relationship with the larger polity, usually to buy or rent public property or to collect certain revenues or provide specific services. A *lex* was closely associated with the official who had proclaimed it, either to the assembled citizens who would then accept or reject it, or to some group to be bound by it, or at some place whose use was to be governed by its provisions; they usually bore the name of the official who had successfully placed them before an assembly. Intended to be read aloud, *leges* possessed their own linguistic forms, some of which were certainly quite old.[102]

Once again, one of Cicero's dialogues, *On the Laws*, the companion to *On the Republic*, provides a useful introduction. In it, he set out the laws to govern his exemplary Rome, providing a synchronic view of Rome's institutions, in contrast with the diachronic one in *On the Republic*. Cicero clearly envisioned a close connection between the two.[103] In *On the Laws*, where a character bearing his name is the main speaker, Cicero is regularly identified as the author of *On the Republic*, while the dialogue's focus is explicitly said to be on the laws of the city of *On the Republic*. His attempt to link ideas of natural law, primarily Stoic in inspiration, with the laws of an idealized Rome is not entirely successful. After all, Stoics rejected the authority of the law of real communities and sought to substitute reason instead, a practice that made it difficult to apply their theories to existing polities.[104] Although Cicero did appropriate the techniques of Roman jurists, much as he had used Roman historiography in *On the Republic*, he was also out of sympathy with them: he (*Leg.* 1.14–5) criticizes jurists on the grounds that they wrote only on minor matters, while in his *In Defense of Murena* (21–9) and in *On Duties* (3.69), he describes jurisprudence as trivial, overly concerned with the meaning of words, and far from true justice.

For present purposes, our focus will rest on Cicero's rules for his Rome, which he set forth in two codes, each surrounded by a debate conducted according to philosophical norms. In book 2, Marcus sets out his laws concerning cult in a long series of clauses (*Leg.* 2.18–22), which, his brother Quintus notes, did not differ much from the laws of Numa or from customary practice; the remainder of the book is essentially a commentary on these rules. Book 3 follows the same pattern. Marcus (*Leg.* 3.6–11) proclaims rules that were to govern the senate; Rome's most prominent public officials, including consuls, censors, aediles, and tribunes of the plebs; and the holders of several lesser magistracies. In the ensuing commentary, he places his regulations within the requirements of a mixed constitution and, in the process, identifies the sources for his laws in modified Roman practice, in the opinions of famous jurists, and in the Twelve Tables.

In the two sets of laws, Cicero set out idealized versions of offices and practices that were deeply embedded in Roman public life, which he then justified by linking them to central issues in Greek political thought. His clauses—often obscure, highly detailed, and narrowly focused—mix concerns over the proper organization of the republic with instructions to perform arcane rites and are expressed in a language that often appears fussy and deliberately old-fashioned. It is just these features that connect the dialogue most directly to juristic practices.

The relationship between Cicero's laws and Roman legislative practice can be seen at several levels. First, he sought to regulate cult and magistracies in separate codes rather than as intertwined in action as they actually were practiced. Inscriptions of the late third or early second century show public and sacred already presented as distinct categories.[105] Second, each code is largely a collection of separate and narrowly focused provisions. In general, laws were groups of separate clauses, which either ordered magistrates or private citizens to perform specific tasks, or declared some action to be lawful, or prohibited magistrates or citizens from doing certain things by setting a fine for violators and identifying potential prosecutors. Abstractions were rare and crucial terms never defined. Drafters of laws, moreover, sometimes described the powers and functions of magistracies or priesthoods by noting only that they were like those of some other office, thus eliminating the need for closer definitions.[106] Laws rarely set out reasons for their provisions.[107]

Finally, there is Cicero's language. A *lex* was closely associated with a distinctive language and syntax. Through the use of assonance and alliteration, compositions possessed a rhythmic quality suitable for oral recitation. Repetition was common, while sentences usually involved either a substantive clause of purpose ("I beg you that . . ."), or a subjunctive following an indirect command ("it is decreed that . . ."), or a conditional clause followed by a command in the third-person future imperative—for example, from the Twelve Tables, "if he is summoned to court, let him go" (*si in ius uocat, ito*). Often, the subjects were left unclear or changed without notice. Laws, moreover, were collections of clauses that were, in turn, constructed by segments that set out the matter at hand. The construction of laws in this fashion was a long-lived practice but not a static one. Earlier laws tended to deploy a narrower range of forms. Conditional clauses followed by third-person future imperatives dominated. From the late second century, some measures began to become more ambitious and to exhibit a fuller and more flexible style. The simpler forms of earlier rules, however, were still present in later laws, where they often expressed the most vigorous commands and prohibitions.[108]

This linguistic practice was not merely a matter for legislators. Romans deployed many of the same forms in magisterial edicts, in senatorial decrees, in legal agreements between private citizens, and in prayers, vows, dedications, and treaties. Although each possessed its own peculiarities, together they formed a fairly unified style that has been called archaic, archaizing, or the *carmen* style.[109] Statements in this manner formed elements of highly formalized performances in which the speaker sought to impose rules on the citizenry, or to confirm the arrangements in private contracts or sales, or to secure benefits from a god, or to ascertain a divinity's will. The *carmen* tradition, along with its relation to oral performances and its connection to normative statements in public, sacred, or private actions, was a distinctive and pervasive cultural phenomenon.[110]

The clauses in Cicero's codes clearly are related to this practice, although they are not fully of it. His clauses contain commands and prohibitions, almost always expressed in third-person future imperatives, although the penalties that usually formed part of a *lex* are frequently absent. Some of Cicero's clauses, moreover, are too abstract or all-encompassing to provide enforceable rules: "Let them approach the gods in purity, let them display piety, let them move away from luxury. He who acts otherwise, the god himself will punish him";[111] "Let the powers be just and let citizens obey them without refusal. Let the magistrate check the disobedient and harmful citizen by fine, chains, or whipping if no great or equal authority prohibits it. Let there be the right of appeal to the people";[112] "Let commanders, lesser magistrates, and ambassadors leave the city whom the senate has chosen and the people commanded, let them wage just wars justly, let them spare the allies ... let them return home with praise."[113]

The relationship between Cicero's clauses, especially the ones in his second code, and the legislative practice of his day may be clarified by comparing them with a law, enacted only a few years later, that was to govern Caesar's colony at Urso in Spain, the so-called *lex coloniae Iuliae Genetivae*, and thus was also intended to provide the basic laws of a community. Perhaps as much as a third of the original, inscribed on bronze tablets under the Flavians, survives in three large blocks.[114] Most of the chapters couple a rule with some punishment for noncompliance, although a few do not establish any penalty. The surviving sections are primarily concerned with magistrates, their tasks, and their jurisdiction; priests figure only in their public attributes or when their responsibilities intersect with those of magistrates.

Both codes exhibit a concern for magistracies, their powers and duties, and the relationship between magistrates, the senate or colonial *curia*, and priests. Thus, Cicero proclaims, "Let the aediles be curators of the city, the market and of the games, and let this magistracy be the first step to higher honors," whereas the framers of Urso's law establish the colony's aediles partly by describing their emblems of rank and attendants (a scribe, a *praeco* or herald, a *haruspex*, a flute player, and four slaves "with girded aprons") and partly by setting out specific tasks for them: "Let whoever shall be aedile put on, during his magistracy, a show or dramatic spectacle for Jupiter, Juno, and Minerva, during three days . . . and during one day [games] in the circus or [gladiators] in the forum for Venus."[115] Even when Urso's measure does set out provisions that were more general than Cicero's, they often are accompanied by provisions that were much narrower. For example, Cicero instructs those who presided over meetings of the senate and people: "Let those who conduct public business observe the auspices; let them heed the public augur."[116] In Urso's law, we read: "Concerning auspices and whatever things shall pertain to those matters, jurisdiction and right of judgment are to belong to the augurs."[117] This rather general statement is immediately followed by another permitting augurs to wear the *toga praetexta*, like magistrates, at public games, where they too were to have privileged seating.

Cicero's laws clearly fit into Roman tradition. His laws and Urso's both exhibit a concern for the proper relationship between magistrates, priests, and senate, both set out in some fashion the operation of the courts, and both provided for sacrifices, festivals, and other cultic practices. The civic order in its entirety emerges—to the extent that it can be said to have emerged—only out of the accumulation of details. Comparison with other laws reveals that Roman legislation began to have an overt formal structure after the foundation of the colony at Urso, and the law's authors may have given to the measure its overall shape primarily by grouping similar matters together.[118] Nevertheless, Cicero did push the limits of the form. Some clauses are broader than would have been the case in true *leges*, are often overtly moralizing, and occasionally contain brief statements about the rationale behind them. Cicero's laws, moreover, were embedded in a larger dialogue that made the philosophical concerns behind the rules even more explicit. Cicero, in other words, turned juristic practice, prestigious but not well suited to describing a functioning order, to a broader end through the use of explicit exegetic statements.[119]

Today, we see how Romans conceptualized their polity and its institutions through literary and scholarly forms that derive from the Greek world—first, local histories and works of antiquarian scholarship and, later, dialogues on the ideal city, the nature of the gods, and natural law—which Roman writers used to give structure to their examinations of Roman practice. In the process, they turned these literary forms to their own uses and embedded within them traces of more-localized practices that were deeply rooted in elite political culture and the learning of priests and jurists. Roman historians, antiquarians, and jurists represented the republican order historically through exemplary figures and the origins of institutions, often in the distant past. They connected their city's success to its public cult and the rites that composed it. They emphasized the city itself over the territory that it dominated, even those regions and settlements that were inhabited by Roman citizens. They show a reluctance to construct overarching schemes and structures or to define crucial concepts and terms. Discussions of particular institutions and attempts to regulate them, both perhaps occasionally very elaborate, seemingly contained collections of detailed provisions. Although our knowledge of these matters is largely derived from texts of the first century, their authors, no doubt correctly, viewed them as characteristic too of Rome's past. Some of these practices can be traced through the second century and occasionally even into the third or fourth, although their contexts and significance may have shifted over time.

TWO

Rome, Its Magistrates, and Its Empire

In the years between 218 and 167, when our evidence is most complete, Roman commanders and their armies operated over an immense range, campaigning as far east as the Taurus Mountains, approximately twelve hundred kilometers from Rome, as far west as the mouth of the Baetis in Spain, one thousand kilometers from the city, and as far south as the environs of Carthage, five hundred kilometers from Rome's walls. In the following decades, this range would only increase. At the same time, while its commanders and their armies were operating so far afield, Rome remained the clear center of public life, the seat both of the citizen assemblies that filled the magistracies that would constitute Rome's public actors in the coming year, accepted or rejected laws that had been placed before them, or received magisterial edicts or reports about significant events and of the senate that assigned tasks and recommended courses of action. In this chapter, the primary focus is on the place of Rome in its empire, the Roman elite's views about their city's power, the manner in which they defined the assignments of the chief magistrates, and the development of spatial limits to their exercise of power.

ROME AND THE CYCLE OF PUBLIC LIFE

Rome's political order was closely linked to the annual cycle of magistracies, and the entry of the consuls into their office began with a period of decision making. Here, Livy provides the bulk of the evidence in annalistic passages interspersed in his narrative, so that the resulting reconstruction best fits the years between 218 and 167 and an uncertain period before and after. In Rome, the consuls were closely connected with the Temple of Jupiter Best and Greatest on the Capitol, the dedication of which, at the end of the sixth century, Roman writers later would synchronize with the beginning of the republic. As they entered office, each year's consuls first tested their acceptability by taking the so-called auspices of investiture, by sacrificing in front of the temple and then examining the entrails of the sacrificial animals, another divinatory rite, followed in turn by vows for the safety of the republic.[1] Next, they met with the senate, which was waiting within the building. In this meeting, or in another close to it in time, consuls and senators made the year's most important decisions, determining the two assignments or *provinciae*, usually military in nature, that the consuls would divide among themselves, either by lot (*sortitio*) or by agreement (*comparatio*), along with the larger number to be divided by lot among the year's praetors, four in number from circa 227 and six from 197.[2] Then, they identified which of the previous year's magistrates would continue to serve beyond their terms in office "as if consuls" (*pro consule*) or "as if praetors" (*pro praetore*), functionaries that modern scholars generally call promagistrates. This process of linking persons to their assignments also involved decisions about the size of armies, the conscription of new soldiers and the discharge of old, the contingents that Rome's allies were expected to contribute, and the number of citizens to be enrolled in the legions. J. S. Richardson notes that the annual definition of assignments provided a flexible mechanism that matched Rome's available resources, expressed in terms of holders of *imperium*—the power to command armies—with the demands of the situation.[3]

Between their entry into office and their departure for their commands, an interval that might take several months, higher magistrates completed a number of essential tasks. Here, the conscription of soldiers may have taken the most time. Consuls—and sometimes praetors as well—notified representatives of Latin and allied polities within Italy of the number of soldiers that they were to provide and the place where their contingents were to assemble, and they announced through edicts first read aloud in Rome and then dispersed by messengers the day on which eligible citizens were to assemble for conscription, the *dilectus*. In these activities, and sometimes others as well, consuls and the senate were guided by certain lists. The *formula togatorum*, which can be detected as early as 225, provided a means to calculate the military contributions of Latin and allied polities within peninsular Italy, while the census produced a number of lists, some of which guided the conscription of citizens.[4]

At the same time, the consuls also secured the goodwill of the gods by proclaiming the days for the performance of the Latin Festival (*feriae Latinae*) on the Alban Mount (*mons Albanus*), twenty-seven kilometers southeast of Rome and the seat of Jupiter Latiaris, and then leading a procession of magistrates, priests, senators, and citizens there for sacrifices and communal meals.[5] Finally, the consuls, in consultation with the senate and the members of the priestly colleges of the pontiffs and the *decemviri sacris faciundis*, along with Etruscan *haruspices*, performed or arranged for the performance of the rites needed to expiate prodigies, signs that the *pax deorum*, the peace between Rome and its gods, had been ruptured and a crucial means of assessing the situation on the eve of the consuls' departure from the city.[6]

On the day of their departure, magistrates left Rome to take up their commands first by taking the auspices, the so-called auspices of departure, and then by making vows on the Capitol and processing through the city to one of the gates.[7] As part of this formal departure, they and their lictors put on their military cloaks or *paludamenta*, thus indicating symbolically that they were entering a sphere suitable for war, and their lictors put axes within their *fasces*, showing that the commander now possessed the power to punish without restraint. According to A. Feldherr, "The spectacle of the consul's *profectio* provides a representation of the Republic in microcosm; the consul's progress takes him from the physical and religious center of the city, the Capitolium, where he has just attempted through his prayers to engage the power of the gods on the state's behalf, to its periphery and the distant battlefield, where, if he has been successful, that power will manifest itself in Roman victory.... The citizens' glimpse of the consul provides their link to the totality of the state, the *summa res publica*, that he is entrusted to defend."[8] Livy (44.22.17) claims that an especially large crowd accompanied L. Aemilius Paullus in 168 in anticipation of his victory over King Perseus of Macedon. Most of Rome's higher magistrates served much of their terms abroad, and the regular movement of magistrates out from Rome permeated Roman conceptions of their empire and shaped important cultic practices.[9]

Successful commanders reversed this ceremonial departure, when on their return and after securing the senate's approval they entered the city in triumph and marched in procession to the Capitol from which they had departed long before.[10] The phrase *auspicio imperio felicitate ductuque* ("by his *auspicium, imperium*, the good fortune that comes through divine favor, and personal leadership"), or some close equivalent, served to designate qualities that merited triumphs.[11] According to Livy, L. Aemilius

Regillus (pr. 190) had placed a tablet on a votive temple proclaiming that "under his *imperium* and *auspicium* and with his good fortune and leadership" he had defeated the fleet of King Antiochus, while Ti. Sempronius Gracchus (cos. 177) proclaimed on his dedication: "Under the *imperium* and *auspicium* of Ti. Sempronius Gracchus, the legion and army of the Roman people conquered Sardinia. In his *provincia* more than eighty thousand of the enemy were slain or captured.... He brought back home the army safe and secure and enriched with plunder. For the second time, he entered Rome in triumph."[12] In a surviving dedicatory inscription (*CIL* I, 2, 626), L. Mummius, consul in 146, claimed that "under his leadership, his auspices, and his *imperium*, Achaia had been captured and Corinth destroyed, and he had returned to Rome in triumph." Note the persistent link between possession of the auspices and *imperium*, achieving victory, and returning to the city in triumph. From the perspective of Rome and its inhabitants, the departure and subsequent return of higher magistrates would have been the most visible aspects of command and thus the ones most easily subject to definition and regulation. As we shall see in later chapters, they occupy prominent places in cult and law.

When we see the ceremony closely, a returning magistrate assembled with his army on the *campus Martius* and sought permission from the senate to enter the city in triumph, the only occasion when an army was permitted to cross the city's boundary. If granted, the commander and his troops entered the city through a special gate, the *porta triumphalis*, and marched to Jupiter's temple on the Capitoline Hill. In the procession, commanders displayed the spoils that they had taken in war, along with prominent captives that they had seized. From the third century, victors also displayed artistic representations of their victories, an important element in the development of Roman representational art.[13] Although fleeting as ceremonies, triumphs were permanently enshrined within the city. Triumphant commanders frequently constructed votive temples that contained proclamations of their accomplishments, displays of spoils, and pictorial depictions of their successes.

Matching magistrates to their commands and preparing for departure required an assessment of the broader circumstances and the crafting of an appropriate response. In Italy and beyond, the Romans encountered polities that were often expansionist, aggressive, and opportunistic along with others that were politically unstable, facts of international life that would sometimes have fed a sense of insecurity in Rome, just as Rome itself would have made its neighbors insecure.[14] In all periods, the ruling elite undoubtedly possessed some knowledge, more or less accurate, of famous and distant polities or rulers, but these need not often have figured greatly in Roman calculations. Powerful states closer to Rome's horizons of operations would have been a different matter. Here, the ruling elite possessed few institutionalized means of gathering information about their competitors.[15] Polybius (10.8) praises Scipio Africanus for seeking to learn upon his arrival in Spain about the disposition of Carthaginian forces, the relationships between the Carthaginian generals, and the state of their alliances in a manner that makes his behavior seem exceptional; Livy (32.28) claims that the first commander in the Second Macedonian War spent much of his term looking for the Macedonian king and his army.

Instead, our sources give a prominent role in decision making to the complaints and reports of others, which Roman magistrates, ambassadors, and the senate may sometimes have solicited. Decisions about assignments often were reached following the representations of embassies, which had come to Rome to influence the senate either by assuaging or diverting anger from their own polity or by laying charges against others. As we shall see later in this chapter, consular and praetorian *provinciae* away from Rome were often set out in terms that required little detailed knowledge beyond the identification of a foe. In this way, then, the senate and magistrates at Rome may have been better informed about the few polities that were the focus of their attention at any one time than they were about many others, including some that they viewed, if only vaguely, as within their city's power.

Still, much of the senate's information about affairs on the margins of Rome's power would have come from its commanders and often involved claims to status and honors. Magistrates and promagistrates made representations about developments in their areas of operation in order to secure the continuation of their commands or to request new troops, supplies, or money. Commanders who had returned to Rome set out their successes when away, often in support of a claim for a triumph. In this way, Roman perceptions of their city's empire were shaped by the claims of allies and their own commanders—and by earlier commanders, whose accomplishments were enshrined in Rome's many monuments. Andrew Feldherr suggests that the observation of the ceremonial departures of magistrates from the city would have brought to mind similar departures and triumphant returns in the past.[16] Some claims were contested by rivals.

Although many crucial decisions concentrated around the consuls' entry into office, the process of formal decision making did not cease with the determination of assignments. During the year, the senate sometimes made adjustments to existing *provinciae* or instructed magistrates to raise new armies to meet developing situations; it decided whether returning commanders should receive triumphs or ovations, retrospective judgments about the way in which they had conducted themselves while on campaign. Magistrates often issued edicts, the senate made its decrees, and popular assemblies authorized laws, some of which sought to regulate life in the city while others ordered or prohibited official actions or sought to regulate private activity away from Rome, a process that required publication at home through heralds (*praecones*) or abroad through messengers (*viatores*).

Some subsequent decisions also led to the departure of functionaries from the center. From time to time, the senate dispatched ambassadors, *legati*, to present demands to foreign states or declare war upon them, to mobilize support in crucial areas of Roman activity, to resolve disputes between subordinate polities, to engage in investigations, or to assist in groups of ten successful commanders in imposing settlements upon the defeat of a major foe. Legations were a central element in Rome's exercise of power. In 225 legates dispatched to Hasdrubal, the Carthaginian commander in Spain, secured an agreement that Punic armies would not cross the Ebro River.[17] During Rome's wars in the Greek world, groups of legates mustered support for Rome's armies, sometimes through the threat or use of force. On several occasions after the end of the Second Punic War, Rome dispatched ambassadors to mediate between Carthage and the king of Numidia, maintaining Rome's influence in the region.[18] As Roman predominance became ever greater, some ambassadors proved highly assertive. In 168 C Popillius Laenas pressed the Seleucid Antiochus IV to leave Egypt, which he had just successfully invaded, by threatening war.[19]

After the supervision of military operations, the foundation of colonies was probably the most common form of official activity away from Rome. From the late third century, and probably in some form at least as early as the late fourth, a senatorial decree or a popular law provided for the election of a college of magistrates, *triumviri coloniae deducendae*, to found one or more colonies in localities sometimes defined broadly as the land (*ager*) of a named polity or polities or on other occasions a particular town or encampment.[20] Less frequently, the senate and popular assemblies also ordered the selection of *decemviri* to make viritane assignments in some polity's land as well. When given the task of founding multiple colonies, the proposed settlements were sufficiently close to enable their triumvirs to establish them in a single journey from the city.[21]

In this, Roman practice resembles other occasions when senate and popular assemblies matched a magistracy, a task, and a place or even movable objects. In 212 a senatorial decree and plebiscite instructed the urban praetor to see to the election of *quinqueviri* to repair Rome's walls and towers, one group of *triumviri* to recover sacred vessels and record temple gifts, and another college of triumvirs to rebuild the temples of Fortuna and of Mater Matuta inside the *porta Carmentalis* and of Spes outside the gate, all of which had been destroyed by fire.[22] On other occasions, *duumviri aedibus locandis* or *duumviri aedibus dedicandis* were chosen to supervise the construction or the dedication of a temple or temples on designated plots in or near the city.[23] Much of the management of Rome's empire consisted of the definition of specific and limited tasks rather than general administrative ones.

Within Italy, local initiative too remained important. Towns might petition the senate to resolve some local dispute, address some persistent problem, or avoid official anger.[24] Upon receipt of their petitions, the senate in 210 permitted the people of Acerrae to rebuild their town and allowed the people of Nuceria to settle in Atella, while in 180 it granted the Cumaeans' request that they be permitted to use Latin in certain circumstances.[25] In response to local requests, the senate sought to resolve boundary disputes between the allied city of Pisa and the citizen colony of Luna in 168, between Ateste and Vicetia in 134, and between Genoa and the Veturii in 117, usually by dispatching senatorial delegations to investigate the matter.[26] During the first third of the second century, the senate appears to have largely decided to send additional settlers to existing Latin colonies in response to requests from them.[27] In the East, Greek cities too dispatched embassies to Rome seeking to resolve disputes with Roman commanders or conflicts with their neighbors or seeking confirmation of some privilege. Successful cities put up inscriptions recording the senate's decisions.[28]

Away from the city, the senate sometimes learned of conspiracies, rebellions, and the march of hostile armies through the reports of communities or individuals closer to the scene.[29] Without such reports, magistrates and the senate may largely have been ignorant of events, even rather close to the city. In the aftermath of the disaster at Cannae in 216, as rumors flooded Rome, the senate proposed sending cavalry from the city along the *via Appia* and the *via Latina* in order to find out, by interrogating fugitives, what had happened to the consuls and their armies, and where these armies might be, if they still existed.[30] In the same year, Hannibal's ambassador came fairly close to Rome before magistrates and the senate became aware of his approach.[31] In 186 a consul reported that in his investigation of the Bacchanalian conspiracy, which had taken him along the coasts of Italy, he had found abandoned the colonies of Sipontum and Buxentum.[32] More dramatically, while one of the praetors of 171 was being attacked in public assemblies in Rome, his defenders justified his absence by maintaining that he was away on public service, although he was then on his estate less than sixty kilometers from the city, an incident that led Livy (43.4.5–6) to comment that even Rome's immediate vicinity was unknown at the time.

To some uncertain but probably significant degree, members of the ruling elite would have known about their city's empire and the developments that affected, or might affect, it through the filter provided by Rome's public life: its meetings of the senate and popular assemblies, its great public ceremonies, its conflicts over precedence and honors, and its rumors and reports of distant events, whether human or divine. Rome's centrality had certain consequences. The city had long drawn elites of some subordinate communities into its own political life. The consolidation of the senate as a collectivity and its subsequent accumulation of functions, which began in the late fourth century, undoubtedly strengthened this tendency, for its members could be summoned at any time so that prolonged absence, if not on public service, would only have weakened the influence of those who failed to attend regularly.[33] As we saw in chapter 1, the Elder Cato and Cicero, who both operated as members of the Roman elite in Rome while maintaining a presence in their ancestral communities, used the image of the "two fatherlands" to describe their continued presence in two political and social worlds.

ROME AND ITS ROADS

Rome was central to the political order because members of its ruling elite had their primary residences there and because many of its most important institutions were based in its public and sacred structures and spaces, but its centrality was more than merely metaphorical. At one level, the Roman polity and the communities that it had subordinated spread, and would continue to spread, in various directions from the city, but at another level the regular movement of magistrates and citizens to and from Rome was a prominent structural feature of its public life. Because of their military service, members of Rome's elite would have seen much more of their world than other members of their society, and they would have experienced it largely in the form of journeys to and from the center.

From the last decades of the fourth century, this movement was facilitated by the construction of great radial roads, which had as their points of origins the gates in Rome's walls. At some uncertain time, perhaps after the formation of closer ties with Capua, the most powerful city in Campania, the *via Latina*, which linked Rome with Capua down the Liris Valley, was either established or improved. Later in the fourth century, Ap. Claudius Caecus began construction of the *via Appia*, the first road to bear the name of its builder, to connect the two cities by a more secure coastal route, a matter of some importance at this stage in Rome's wars with the Samnites. A few years later, the first segment of the *via Valeria* was laid out through Tibur to the Fucine Lake during Rome's wars with the Aequi. From at least as early as the middle of the third century, inscribed milestones marked distances along these great routes. The earliest surviving example (*ILLRP* 1277) was erected along a road linking Agrigentum and Panormus on Sicily during the First Punic War. Two others (*ILLRP* 448 and 449), bearing the names of aediles of the late third or early second century who had undertaken repairs, marked points along the *via Ostiensis* and the *via Appia*.

Although these routes and those that would follow had profound effects on the life and landscape of Italy by channeling and facilitating commerce, travel, and migration, Roman magistrates constructed these roads, while others continued to maintain them, to ease the movement of officials, embassies, messengers, and armies to and from the center.[34] For this reason, the construction of others in subsequent years reflects Rome's growing sphere of operation. The *via Appia* was first extended, probably in the context of the Samnite or Pyrrhic wars, to Venusia and then, later in the century, to Brundisium on the Adriatic. In the late 220s, C. Flaminius established the *via Flaminia*, which ran through Umbria to Fanum Fortunae and then north along the Adriatic coast to Ariminum, providing the chief route for armies and officials into the Po Valley. In the late third or early second centuries, the *via Cassia* was laid out through Sutrium, Volsinii, and Clusium to Arretium, and the *via Aurelia* to Pisae and Luna, while from 187 the *via Flaminia minor* crossed the Apennines from Arretium to Bononia, then an important center in an area of intense campaigning. In the early second century the *via Aemilia* linked Arminum with Placentia and Cremona, while later in the century the *via Egnatia* connected Dyrrhacium, where Roman officials and armies often landed after crossing the Adriatic, with Thessalonike, at a time when Roman commanders were regularly campaigning in Macedonia.

Founding colonies and making viritane assignments rendered more secure lines of movement. Latin settlements and the larger citizen colonies

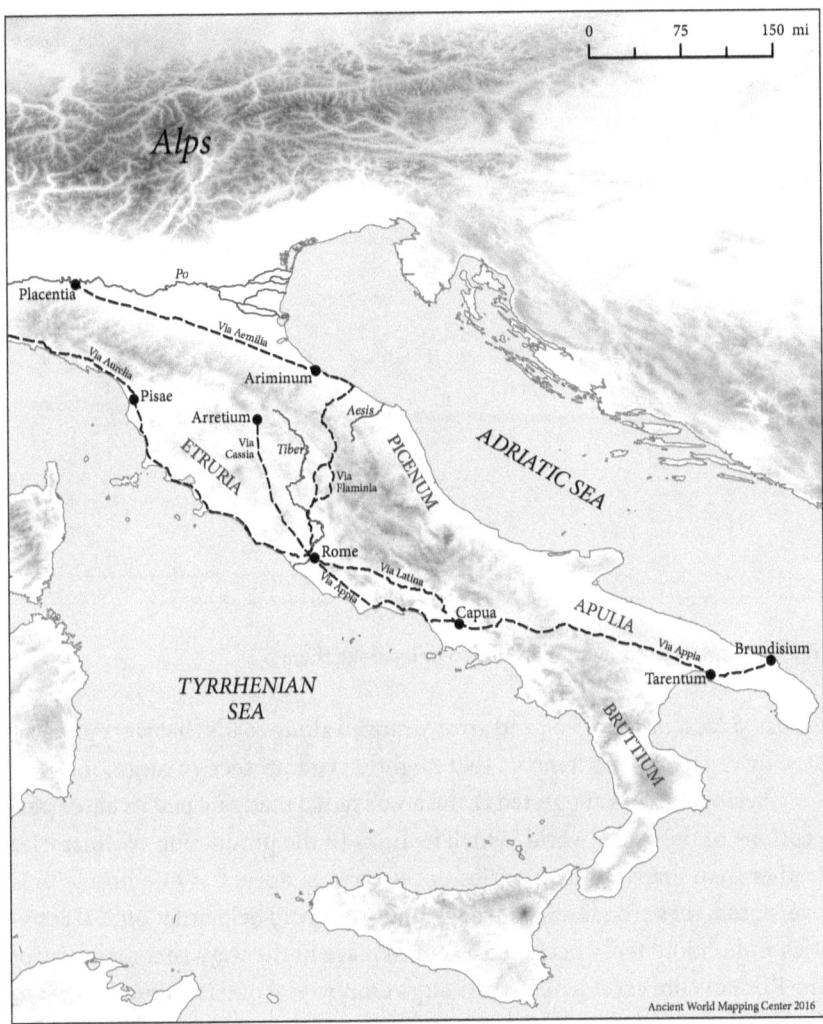

Rome and its major roads in Italy

that seem to have replaced them early in the second century were often closely associated with roads.[35] Thus, Cales (334) and Fregellae (328) guarded the *via Latina*, while Carseoli (298) and Alba Fucens (303) stood watch over the *via Valeria*. In the third century, extensions of the *via Appia* went first to Venusia (291) and then to Brundisium (244). The *via Aemilia*, laid out early in the second century, passed through Bononia (189), Mutina (183), and Parma (183) and ended at Placentia (218), while viritane assignments filled the interstices between them. As a result, officials,

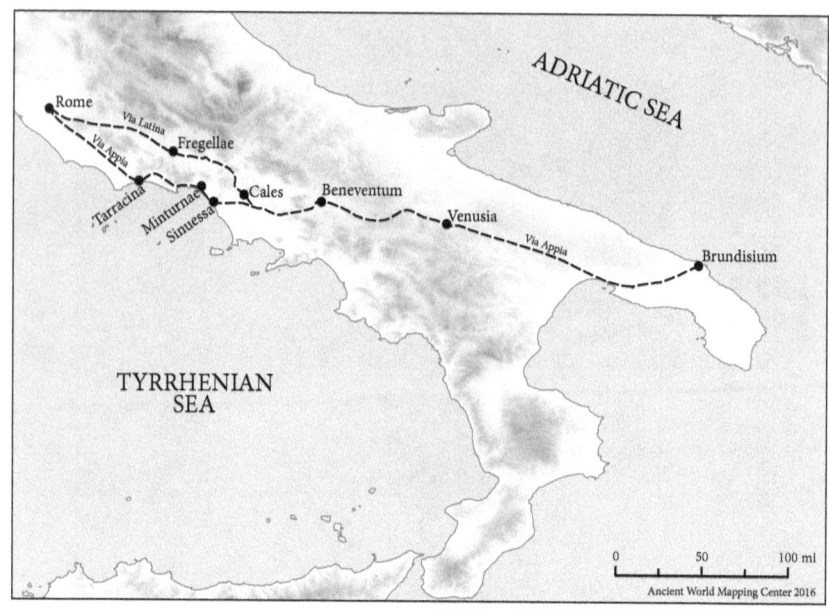

The *via Latina*, the *via Appia*, and the colonies along them

ambassadors, messengers, and armies moved along roads that were punctuated by organized settlements that might serve a protective function.

Pietro Janni has suggested that Rome's radial roads shaped its elite's perceptions of the larger world, which he links to the production of itineraries (rather than maps) in later periods of Roman history.[36] While his claim is overstated, these roads and journeys along them did help order official activities and undoubtedly occupied a central place in the ways that members of the Roman elite experienced their city's empire and official action within it. In addition to setting channels for the movement of magistrates and armies, from the third quarter of the third century, Rome's radial roads may also have served to order the conscription of Roman citizens in the *dilectus*, and from at least as early as the last decades of the century, certain official tasks or subsets of the citizenry were defined in terms of distances along them.[37] The triumvirs who implemented the *lex Sempronia agraria*, most active between 133 and 129, arranged their operations each year by successive forays down different routes.[38] Although there is little evidence for the process, magistrates and the senate almost certainly used these roads to organize the movement of orders and messages to and from the center: Livy (40.2.1–4) reports that notice of a prodigy at Caieta in 182 came through Formiae (*a Formiis*) on the *via Appia*; some polities communicated with the center through intermediaries.

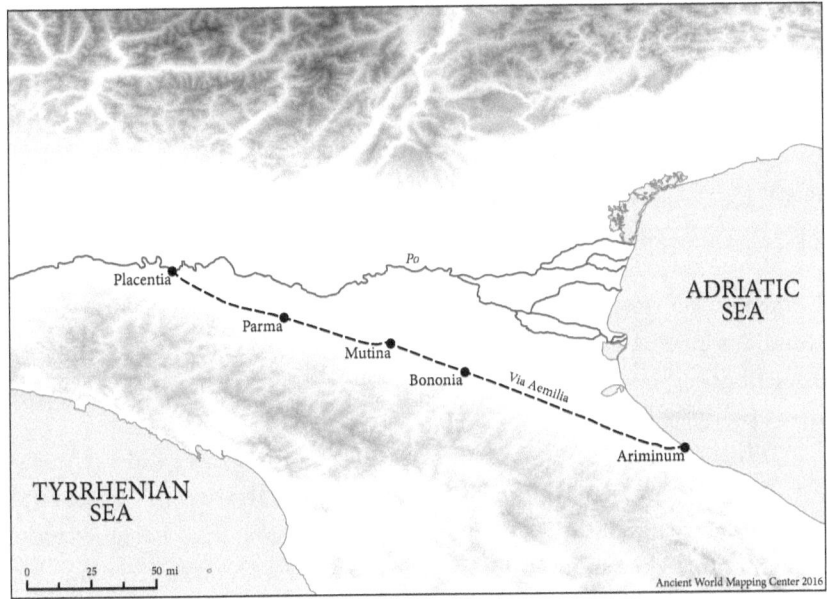

The *via Aemilia* and the colonies along it

CONCEPTIONS OF EMPIRE

Roman representations of their empire were linked to the elite's conceptions of it and their attempts to act in it. Rome's elite in the late third and second centuries—and undoubtedly earlier as well—largely saw their city's empire in terms of its power over peoples or polities, not over territories, and until the first century they did not connect the sphere over which their city's armies operated with any perceived need to govern it. Polybius's claim (1.1) that Rome had subdued practically the entire inhabited world, the *oikoumenē*, within a period of fifty-three years—from, that is, 220 to 167—does not mean that Rome dominated, much less ruled the known world, but rather that it might exercise power in each region if it chose and that it had no serious rivals.[39] Polybius clearly associated Rome's empire, its *archē*, with its ability to defeat competitors and compel obedience.[40]

The concept of *imperium*, which had deep cultic associations, was central to Roman views of the city's power. *Imperium* possessed a wide range of meanings.[41] In scattered passages in the works of writers of the second century—the comic poets, fragments of the works of other poets, orators, and historians, and in its last decades laws preserved in inscriptions—the most common use of *imperium* is to denote a magistrate's ability to issue orders and, by extension, the power lying behind these orders. Here, it was associated with consuls, praetors, dictators, and *magistri equitum*, all of whom could command armies, rather than with lesser officials, who could not, and in this sense it was linked with *auspicium*, the right to take the auspices in matters of public concern.[42] On other occasions, *imperium* might also designate instructions that a superior gave to an inferior or even a magistracy itself. At times, it could also signify the power of the Roman people—or of other polities as well. The Elder Cato (*ORF*[3] frag. 164) called Rome's power over others "our *imperium*" in his speech in defense of the Rhodians in 167. With respect to Rome, then, *imperium* primarily served as an attribute of the most important magistrates and secondarily as the power of the polity itself.

While Romans of the late third and second centuries did not imagine their city's power in terms of territories under the control of a central government, they did give to it spatial associations that warrant closer examination. After an intensive examination of the literary and epigraphic evidence, John Richardson asserts that the Roman elite had no word for—and thus no concept of—the empire as a space until the age of Augustus.[43] For him, the empire would have been territorial only if firm boundaries encompassed it. The Latin word *finis* denoted limits of various kinds, but while some were temporal, most were spatial, although some might be notional and others quite specific. Polities, for example, had their own *fines*, although they might be contested by their neighbors. Others might be attributed to offices and functions—thus, the *pomerium*, the city of Rome's augural boundary, was the *fines* of the urban auspices—or to settlements or subgroups of larger populations.[44]

From the late third century, and probably earlier as well, Roman magistrates and legates occasionally determined the boundaries of subordinate or competing polities that had gained their attention: in 225, Roman ambassadors pressed the Carthaginian commander in Spain to agree not to cross the Ebro River; during the war with Antiochus III, a Roman magistrate established an old royal road as the Macedonian kingdom's boundary in Thrace;[45] when Cn. Manlius Vulso (cos. 189) and the senatorial legates who assisted him imposed a treaty on Antiochus III, they required that the king withdraw from cities, lands, villages, and strongholds on "this side" of the Taurus Mountains and prohibited his ships from sailing beyond the promontories of Calycadnus and Sarpedon;[46] in 168, a senatorial commission, in response to an appeal from the citizens of Pisae, sought to resolve a boundary conflict with the recently founded citizen colony of Luna; and in the first half of the second century, legates set the limits separating the Carthaginians and the Numidians on several occasions. In none of these instances did magistrates or the senate seek to establish the limits of Rome's own power.

At present, however, our concern lies with still grander limits. In the opening decade of the first century, the author of the *Rhetorica ad Herennium* claims that Rome's *imperium* covered the inhabited world, the *orbis terrae*, and all the peoples, nations, and kings within it.[47] When writing of the achievements of Pompey, Cicero holds that his *imperium* was not bounded by the earth, but by the regions of the heavens, that he had made the boundaries (*terminis*) of the *imperium* of the Roman people the *orbis terrarum*, and that he had won victories over all peoples by land and by sea.[48] The Augustan historian Dionysius of Halicarnassus (*Ant.Rom.* 4.13.4–5) remarks that the seemingly endless extent of the tombs that spread along the roads leading from Rome's gates reflects the boundless nature of the Roman world. As we saw in chapter 1, the Greek historian Polybius set out in the middle of the second century to describe how Rome had come to dominate the inhabited world between 220 and 167, and some members of the ruling elite of his day may have also viewed their city's power in the same way: Plutarch (*TG* 9) puts in a speech that he attributes to Ti. Gracchus the claim that the Roman people were masters (*kurioi*) of the *oikoumenē*, although it remains uncertain whether the assertion is the biographer's or his subject's.

For Richardson, these instances that involved no firm boundaries form a clear contrast with passages in imperial authors in which Rome's frontiers were sometimes associated with specific places.[49] The author of the *Rhetorica ad Herennium* (4.44), however, uses a grandiose claim about the limitless nature of Rome's empire—one measures the greatness of Rome's *imperium* by the rising and the setting of the sun—as an example of a rhetorical device in which the truth is exaggerated to make a point. Statements extending Rome's power over the inhabited world are clear examples of such exaggeration, but they rest on the assumption that Rome had, might have had, or ought to have had *fines*, although members of the ruling elite may have been unable or unwilling to say with any conviction where they were at any time.

That said, while Romans of the republic did not seek to give their polity definition by seeking to draw boundaries around it, they undoubtedly did view it, to some extent, in spatial terms. Members of the ruling elite almost certainly could have located, if only broadly and approximately, major subordinates and competitors by their directions from Rome and perhaps by the time it would take delegations and armies to make the journey. Recall that in Italy, the Romans constructed roads radiating from the city to areas of frequent operations, which they would have connected to particular allies and opponents. In the first third of the second century, when the evidence is reasonably clear, Roman magistrates and legates often departed from Italy for the East at Brundisium, the terminal point of the *via Appia*, those campaigning in the North used Ariminum on the *via Flaminia*, Arretium on the *via Cassia* or Pisae or Luna on the *via Aurelia*, while officials and soldiers bound for Spain embarked at ports on the west coast of Italy near Rome or north of it or took the long, and probably ill-defined, land route through what is now southern France.[50] In this way, then, the elite would have associated to some degree their city's empire with the routes needed to reach distant places that they deemed to be under their power or that were the focus of their attention. The imperial practice of depicting the empire in graphic form as an assemblage of roads radiating from Rome may have had deep roots.[51]

For long, of course, such roads were limited to Italy, leaving routes to theaters outside the peninsula unfixed and less secure. In 188 the proconsul Cn. Manlius Vulso, while returning from Asia with his army, fought his way through an ambush that Thracians had set to block him in order to seize the vast amount of plunder that his army was conveying.[52] Journeys by land to and from Spain were especially dangerous and arduous. When the former praetor M. Helvius left Farther Spain in 195, he and his escort encountered and defeated a large force that attempted to block his return to Rome.[53] In 189 ambassadors from Massilia reported that Ligures had ambushed another praetor as he attempted to make his way by land to Spain, killing him and most of his retinue.[54] Only in the 120s—almost a century after the first Roman armies had landed in Spain—would campaigns in Transalpine Gaul begin to make this route more secure.

It is in the sense of distance from the center that one should probably regard certain claims about the *fines* of the Roman people.[55] In *On the Republic* (3.15.24), with the dramatic date of 129, Cicero has a speaker proclaim it to be the custom to inscribe the words "he expanded the boundary of empire" (*finis imperii propagauit*) on the tombs of great commanders. One of Pompey's dedications provides the earliest clear example of such a practice, and over the following decades others would make similar claims.[56] A few scattered annalistic passages in Livy's history indicate that similar associations were made by the end of the third century.[57] In 200, for example, the *haruspices* reported that an examination of the entrails of sacrificial animals foretold victory in the war against Philip V of Macedon, a triumph, and the extension of boundaries, while in 191 they claimed that the entrails from a sacrifice made before the division of the consular provinces again predicted victory, a triumph, and the extension of the boundaries of the Roman people.[58] Boundaries such as these, connected to the most distant places that Roman armies would reach against major powers to Rome's east, would have had no administrative significance. In practice, moreover, Rome's sphere of operations would sometimes have overlapped with those of other polities, producing contested sovereignties, while some communities within such bounds would have viewed themselves as independent. That said, while the Roman elite did not set clear limits at the outer edges of their sphere of activity, as we shall see in the following chapters, they did proclaim clear internal boundaries to magistracies, functions, and groups of people, generally with greater density and specificity near the city than at a distance.

THE MAGISTRACY AND THE *PROVINCIA*

In the annual distribution of *provinciae*, the consuls and the senate sought to link the management of Rome's empire to the cycle of its civic life. In the process, they also revealed a marked tendency to match as closely as possible consular and praetorian *provinciae* with the actual occupants of some magistracy, although the steady expansion in the number of theaters of operation and the marked increase in the distance to assignments would place great stress on their arrangements. Indeed, no solution would prove entirely satisfactory until the direct link between actual tenure in an elective office and the possession of some extra-urban *provincia* was severed in the middle of the first century.

Polybius (2.23–27), who probably followed Fabius Pictor, reveals the way that the two consuls and four praetors of 225 were matched to armies and tasks. One consul was sent to Sardinia with his army, while the other was dispatched to Ariminum in preparation for a war against the Gauls. He does not name the four praetors or give their commands, but he does report the locations of four armies: one in Rome, another on Sicily, a third at Tarentum, and a fourth in northern Etruria, where it apparently was dispatched in the form of an emergency levy directed against Gallic invaders. Events soon disrupted this arrangement, for upon the defeat of the army in Etruria, the consul on Sardinia returned to the mainland with his army. The simplest solution would be to suggest that each of these four armies was under one of the year's four praetors and that two were sent to Sicily and Tarentum, while the remaining pair were in Rome, from which one would depart when Gauls threatened Etruria.[59] In this year, then, the senate managed Rome's empire by dispersing six occupants of two annual offices over it.

The Second Punic War was fought in many theaters, and the number of commanders greatly exceeded the number of annual magistrates, with the result that Rome made extensive use of promagistrates. Indeed, the war in Spain, the most distant area of operations and the least amenable to central control, was directed first by long serving promagistrates and then by private citizens given commands. Within a few years of the war's end, however, the ruling elite returned to an expanded version of the earlier practice. When the number of praetors was increased to six for 197, the new officials were almost certainly intended to serve in Spain. The consuls and the senate decided to divide among the praetors two positions at Rome—the urban and peregrine *provinciae*—along with Sicily, Sardinia, and Nearer and Farther Spain, and to divide among the consuls Italy and the ongoing war with Philip V of Macedon. According to Livy (32.28), the tribunes of the plebs objected on the grounds that the time needed to reach the scene of operations had served as an obstacle to victory, for it resulted in the replacement of a commander in the field in the middle of the campaigning season. As a result, Ti. Quinctius Flamininus (cos. 198) continued to command as proconsul against Macedon, while the consuls shared Italy. The only other promagistrates were two proconsuls returning from Spain.[60] The senate clearly wished that all assignments be held by serving magistrates, which presumably was the reason for the increase in the number of praetors.

Over the following decades, the original arrangements for 197 provided the fundamental pattern. The consuls and the senate used consular *provinciae* to address the most serious challenges with the result that they varied markedly from time to time. Consuls were the most common commanders in wars to the east of the Adriatic, and they frequently campaigned against Gauls or Ligures in the north of Italy; in 195 one even was assigned Nearer Spain. Praetorian assignments, on the other hand, exhibit more regularity. Entering praetors generally divided the urban and peregrine *provinciae* at Rome as well as Sicily, Sardinia and Nearer and Farther Spain.[61] Indeed, from 197 through 193, the senate matched the six praetors to these six assignments with only a single exception: in 195 the praetor who had received Sardinia in the previous year was prorogued so that the new praetor might command at Pisae in a war against the Ligures. With the exception of

Flamininus (cos. 198), who commanded in Macedonia from 198 to 194, the only promagistrates were former praetors either returning to Rome from their *provinciae* or waiting there for the arrival of their successors.

The senate originally distributed the assignments in 192 in the same fashion, but the impending war with Antiochus III led them to shift the praetors who would go to Spain to other assignments and continue the old commanders in their commands. Except for the war's last year, the senate dispatched new consular commanders yearly, but the annual distribution of praetorian *provinciae* became markedly more flexible. The six core praetorian assignments were regularly filled, but occasionally the urban and peregrine *provinciae* were combined, and praetors of the previous year were continued with some frequency in their extra-urban assignments, permitting more magistrates to serve in the east, in Gaul, or in some region in peninsular Italy, where their commands too were sometimes extended.

Perhaps the most notable feature of praetorian assignments in the 180s is the regular presence of *provinciae* in peninsular Italy. Thus, a praetor received Bruttium and Apulia in 190, where he was prorogued in 189 and 188; in 187 praetors were assigned Tarentum and Gaul; in 185 one received Tarentum where he was prorogued in the following year; in 183 and 181 Gaul and Apulia again were praetorian *provinciae* and the latter pair were prorogued for 180. At the same time, extensions for one year of magistrates sent to the Spanish *provinciae* became common, perhaps because of the time needed to travel there. For much of the decade, the two praetors freed every other year in this fashion served in Gaul and Apulia, where they too were continued in their commands, creating in effect a situation in which annual elections of six praetors produced eight praetorian *provinciae*.[62] Because of lacunae in Livy's text many of the assignments of the 170s are unknown. Still, one can often detect the continuing assignment of the urban and peregrine *provinciae* along with others in Sicily, Sardinia, and Nearer and Farther Spain. In 174 and 173 serving commanders on Sardinia were prorogued so that their would-be successors could campaign on Corsica. In 171, 169, and 168—and possibly 170 as well—the two Spanish *provinciae* were combined so that a praetor could serve in the east in the Third Macedonian War.

Beginning in the 180s, the senate began to assign to some magistrates a task in Italy to perform before going abroad. In 184 the praetor who received Sardinia was to investigate poisonings in Italy, which delayed his departure for four months; in 179 another praetor destined for Sardinia was to search out poisoners beyond the tenth milestone from the city, an operation that proved so protracted that he never took up his chief assignment; in 173 a consul who shared the Ligures with his colleague was given the task of going to Campania to separate public land from private, an assignment that took most of the year; in 167 a praetor who had received Sardinia was unable to go to the island because he had been kept back to investigate capital crimes.[63] Recall that Polybius (6.13) claims that the senate had charge of public investigations of crimes such as treason, conspiracy, poisoning, and assassination, an assertion that may indicate that these assignments continued in the years after 167, when the loss of Livy's text renders much obscure. Praetors assigned Sardinia received supplementary assignments in Italy with greater frequency than their peers, perhaps because the island's presence among assignments was not as pressing.[64]

The nature of the six regular praetorian assignments warrants closer examination. When Livy or his epitomator reported the addition of two praetors circa 227 and two more for 197, they did not link these additions with any explicit decision to send them to particular places:[65] for the first expansion, the epitomator merely notes that the number of praetors was increased to four, while Livy maintains that the second was intended to meet the increasing number of *provinciae* and the expansion of *imperium*, leaving open the possibility that the senate considered assignments to be flexible. That said, the senate clearly decided to dispatch, if only for the foreseeable future, the first group to Sicily and Sardinia and the second to Spain. T. C. Brennan and J.-L. Ferrary, however, suggest that the additional praetors of circa 227 and 197 were specifically linked by law from the beginning with these assignments, which thus differed fundamentally from the ephemeral *provinciae* given to commanders for specific wars that would soon pass.[66] Deviations, and there would be many, would require other laws to permit them. For others, their seeming permanence may have been the result of the failure of successive tenants to resolve the problems, primarily military in nature, that had led to their assignments, so that the perception would have grown that they were necessary for the foreseeable future. In the first reconstruction, the senate would have envisioned establishing a permanent presence in certain regions outside of Italy, while in the second, it would have remained flexible and only sought to increase the number of theaters in which it might act at any one time.

The evidence for the fixity of certain assignments is limited at best. Brennan and Ferrary point to Livy's reports of the distribution of *provinciae* in two specific years as evidence that exempting Sardinia and Nearer and Farther Spain from the annual sortition required a popular law to permit it. In 208 Livy notes that the senate chose to keep the praetor assigned to Gaul in his command and then decided to do the same for his colleague in Sardinia, so that a law was carried proroguing the latter's *imperium*.[67] For 192 Livy reports the distribution of assignments and then notes that in preparation for the impending war against Antiochus III the senate wished to shift the praetor given Nearer Spain to Bruttium and his colleague who had been granted Farther Spain to Macedonia and the fleet, so that a plebiscite was passed.[68]

At core, this interpretation rests on the assumption that the laws of 208 and 192 were, in fact, typical and that Livy normally excluded them from his history, perhaps for considerations of space and style. Livy certainly did compress his annalistic notices. As we shall see in chapter 3, his accounts of prodigies and their expiation often leaves uncertain whether an expiatory rite was performed for one or all of the prodigies that he had just listed. But other matters may have had a place in the decision to put forward these two laws. Livy reports that the law of 208 prorogued the commanders' *imperium* without mentioning the assignment in which he was to exercise it.[69] In the second passage, he notes the changes in assignments and then, after mentioning the law, reports that the previous commanders in Spain were prorogued. In this way, then, Livy's notices may be connected to another matter, which his regular silences also leave obscure. Popular authorization for the prorogation of *imperium* appears to have been deemed necessary, if only occasionally, down to the end of the Second Punic War, but some scholars suggest it may have long persisted, if only as an occasional formality.[70]

It is in the context of supposedly fixed assignments that Brennan wished to see the *lex Baebia*, which may have been enacted in 181 but affected only the praetors of 179 and 177.[71] This measure instructed that only four praetors be chosen in alternate years, and its framers may have intended that praetors be dispatched to Spain only in the years in which six were chosen and that they serve two years there. T. C. Brennan suggests that the law ended the supposed fixity of certain assignments, which might now be held for longer periods, but it should also be noted that the law was enacted when assignments of *provinciae* in peninsular Italy were ending, for the last was given in 181 and extended in 180. Thus, those who supported the *lex Baebia* may have intended to reduce the number of praetors because the number of necessary assignments also appeared to be decreasing. The *lex Baebia* quickly fell into abeyance, perhaps because the two praetors lost every other year were needed elsewhere. It is the last known attempt before the first century to link directly the number of assignments and the number of magistrates, although it required the formation of a biennial cycle to do so. The ruling elite abandoned or modified only slowly its desire to make the management of their city's empire conform to its annual cycle of offices.

We are best informed about *provinciae* between 225 and 167, but Roman practice in these matters did not begin or end there. Because of the loss of Livy's second decade and of his narrative for the years after 167, our knowledge of arrangements before 225 and after 167 is limited. From the middle of the fourth to the middle of the third century, Rome had three annual holders of *imperium*—two consuls and one praetor—although in exceptional circumstances, a consul might appoint a dictator, who, in turn, would nominate a *magister equitum*. The sole praetor's responsibilities probably would have been set by custom, and if, as seems likely, they largely remained in or near Rome unless an emergency drew them away, only the two consuls would usually have acted away from the city. As we shall see in chapter 4, the power to command soldiers rested on a fundamental distinction between the city of Rome, where it could not be exercised in normal circumstances, and an essentially unlimited zone beyond the city's boundary, where it had full force. This way of conceptualizing magisterial power fits well a situation in which Rome's sphere of operations was limited and commanders might face several enemies during the course of a year. Indeed, in the wars of the late fourth and early third centuries, magistrates and armies are occasionally depicted as shifting their theaters of operation and even their opponents during the course of a year.[72]

In the last decades of the fourth and the opening decade of the third centuries, these arrangements proved to be inadequate with the result that the *imperium* involved in the command of soldiers was distinguished in some fashion from tenure in one of the magistracies that usually exercised it. The earliest known prorogation enabled the consul Q. Publilius Philo to continue the siege of Neapolis in 327.[73] On other occasions, terms were extended to enable officials to retain command of their armies for their triumphs. During the Third Samnite War, the use of promagistracies broadened. In this war, Rome faced the largest group of enemies that it had ever encountered at once—Samnites, Lucanians, Etruscans, Umbrians, and Gauls—and thus the necessity of fighting simultaneously in more theaters than it ever had in the past. In 296 both consuls of the previous year were prorogued for six months to command in Samnium, and in 295 five men, some given *imperium* while private citizens, held commands as promagistrates in order to command in minor theaters of operation or to make attempts to draw enemy forces away from Rome's main armies.[74] During the same war, consuls also delegated *imperium* to *privati* to command their armies in their absence, the earliest trace of the practice. Two years later, Livy's text ends and Roman practice becomes largely invisible. The earliest known prorogations for an entire year are to be found during the Second Punic War.[75]

During the Third Samnite War, one also encounters clear signs that some commanders were matched formally to particular enemies or areas of operation. Livy (10.37.1–12) reports that a consul of 294 was denied a triumph because he had left his *provincia* against the Samnites to campaign in Etruria, while Dionysius of Halicarnassus (*Ant.Rom.* 17/18.4.4–5.4) claims that a consul of 291 was prosecuted for interfering with another's command since he had intruded into a proconsul's *provincia* while not acknowledging his authority. But there are problems. Livy (10.17) notes that his sources assigned the same deeds in 296 to different commanders, and after reporting the denial of a triumph to the consul of 294, he (10.37.13–4) complains that his sources differed over the theater in which each consul had operated or left the division of consular responsibilities unstated. For the latter year, moreover, the *Fasti Triumphales* reverse the areas in which Livy places the consuls.[76] Similarly, Livy (10.12.3–8) reports that L. Cornelius Scipio Barbatus (cos. 298) campaigned in Etruria, but Scipio's own *elogium*, inscribed around the end of the third century, credits him with victories in Samnium and Lucania.[77] Indeed, Livy (8.40) complains about the falsehoods in his sources, especially regarding magistracies and commands.

In a practice that may reach back to the fourth century, consuls were also matched by lot to two of the four legions that they would raise together but command separately, with one receiving the first and third and the other the second and fourth. And, as we shall soon see, some later *provinciae* were defined in terms of command of a specific army. Could a consul's *provincia* once have been only the legions that he would command without any formal decision about whom he would lead it against or where he would operate? Here, the early practice of using popular laws to authorize promagistracies may provide a suitable context for the beginning of the formal link between a command and an opponent or an operation. If so, the practice of assigning areas of operation may have been an innovation of this period, when the temporary proliferation of promagistracies increased the number of commanders and thus the need to deploy them properly in pursuit of some overall strategy.

Then, at some point between 246 and 242, the closing years of the First Punic War, Roman assemblies began to elect a second praetor, the beginning of the distinction between the urban and peregrine *provinciae*.[78] In later periods, as military operations moved ever farther from the city, these functionaries were associated primarily with the city and its courts, but their original duties are obscure, lost with Livy's second decade. T. C. Brennan has plausibly suggested that the second praetor was added to perform a defensive function in Italy during the last years of the First Punic War, when Carthaginian commanders attempted to shift the theater of operations from Sicily to the Italian mainland while the consuls were occupied on the island.[79] In the same period, Rome founded the citizen colonies of Alsium and Fregenae along the coast of Etruria to the north of the Tiber and the Latin colony of Brundisium on the Adriatic, most probably to guard against such threats.[80]

For long, the consuls had been Rome's chief actors away from the city, where the sole praetor apparently remained, probably in command of the urban legions, which he would lead away from Rome on the seemingly few occasions when thought necessary.[81] As the official with *imperium* most regularly present in the city, they—and the urban praetors who would be their successors—undoubtedly performed, or came to perform, a range of functions in Rome. The addition of a second praetor would not have changed this basic arrangement. The consuls continued as the chief commanders. Like urban praetors, the peregrine praetors combined some, presumably less onerous or pressing, duties in Rome with the ability to operate away from Rome against hostile intrusions or subversive activities.

Against this background, the increase in the number of praetors from two to four at some point between 227 and 225 marks a clear break. This change took place in the context of frequent warfare in the Po Valley and occasional wars in Illyria and on Corsica that regularly drew one or both consuls far from Rome. At the same time, the expansion of Carthaginian power in Spain may have led to worries about a Carthaginian resurgence and concern for Rome's position in Sicily, Sardinia, and perhaps southern Italy, all far removed from areas of operation to the north. When military operations were confined to peninsular Italy, commanders might change their area of operation as circumstances dictated, but when armies began to operate at greater distances from the center, protecting areas far from the scene of operations may have seemed necessary and appropriate. In any case, for the first time praetors were specifically chosen so that they might be dispatched to command garrisons at threatened places. Polybius's account (2.23–27) of arrangements in 225 reveals the consequences of the shift.

After 167, when Livy's text again fails, matters became equally obscure. All, or virtually all, of the consuls are known, although their *provinciae* often are not. We can occasionally detect consuls performing certain functions in Rome or elsewhere in Italy, while others fought in Transalpine Gaul, against Carthage in the Third Punic War, in Asia after the dissolution of the Attalid kingdom, or in Africa against Jugurtha. On still other occasions, consuls held *provinciae* that were usually praetorian. From the second half of the 150s to the late 130s, a consul often held one of the Spanish assignments, while consuls also fought on Sicily in the later stages of the First Slave War. About half of the praetors can be identified, often only because they later served as consuls, but only a very few are associated with *provinciae*. Promagistracies are largely invisible.

As a result, one can say little about the ways that the senate distributed holders of *imperium* across Rome's sphere of operations. Certain assignments undoubtedly persisted. We can assemble a series of names of the men who held Sicily and Nearer and Farther Spain and some from the 140s and circa 130 in Macedonia and Asia as well.[82] For only one year, 139, can we be certain that both the urban and peregrine praetorships were assigned, while there is no evidence that any praetors were dispatched to Sardinia between 165 and 122.[83] Little can be said about more ephemeral *provinciae* or about the assignments of praetors who might be displaced when consuls held commands in Spain or Sicily. In the 140s and 120s, the senate also dispatched praetors with some regularity first to Macedonia and then to Asia, but without increasing the number of praetors, so that the regular use of promagistrates almost certainly expanded.

In the aftermath of the Social War and the civil wars of the 80s, when so many institutions were in flux, the dictator Sulla increased the number of praetors to eight and shifted the relationship between tenure in a magistracy and occupancy of a *provincia*.[84] First, consuls and praetors remained in Rome for much if not most of their terms, departing to their assignments only toward their terms' ends, so that each year's ten magistrates with *imperium* might easily accommodate the ten extra-urban *provinciae* of the time. While perhaps originally intended to be only of a year's duration, so that election would have been followed by two years of service, these assignments permitted the easy possibility of expansion. Indeed, over the following decades, the number of *provinciae* would steadily increase, partly as a result of Rome's growing sphere of operations, but partly because more *provinciae* were formed closer to the center, a development that may be linked to an increasing tendency to grant *provinciae* greater territorial specificity. At the same time, since C. Gracchus's law on consular provinces, which required the setting of consular assignments before the elections, remained in force, the senate would have had to decide what the new consuls were to do perhaps as much as eighteen months before they would begin to do it—yet another example of the continuing power that Rome's public life exercised over the management of its empire.

Sulla's adjustments marked the culmination of a process.[85] Standing courts, which had begun to appear in 149, were usually under the presidency of some praetor, who had it as his *provincia*, thus increasing the number of urban assignments. At the same time, urban praetors, and perhaps their colleagues who spent their terms in the city as well, began to receive *provinciae* away from Rome and Italy on the expiration of their magistracies. The separation of *provinciae* outside of Italy from tenure in an office became more marked in 52, when C. Pompeius carried a law requiring that at least five years must elapse between the end of a magistracy and the assignment of a command.

From one perspective, the slow shift from magistrates to promagistrates in the management of empire reflects views about the proper relationship between the city of Rome and its dependencies. By the middle of the first century, magistracies were becoming, or had become, largely phenomena of the city, while operations at a greater distance were in the hands of persons who once had held such an office, but did not do so when carrying out most or all of their assigned tasks. Consuls, it should be noted, took precedence over proconsuls, although both possessed the same *imperium*, so that this change may represent an attempt to elevate the city over its hinterland, a goal that may also be detected in other areas of official activity, including laws and the auspices.[86] Revealing his own desires in the midst of civil war, Cicero (*Att.* 8.15.3; *Phil.* 4.4.9) proclaims that consuls had the right to pick the command that they wanted and that they had power over every *provincia*, even those not assigned to them.

If Sulla's reforms were intended to reinforce the primacy of the city and the senate, they did not achieve this goal. In the aftermath of his dictatorship, a few powerful political figures—L. Licinius Lucullus, Pompey, and Caesar—came to have especially broad and lengthy commands, creating what were in effect other loci of decision making, if only for a time. In 67 Aulus Gabinius proposed that Pompey be given a command against the pirates for three years throughout the Mediterranean, the power to appoint fifteen legates with praetorian *imperium* without senatorial approval, and an *imperium* greater than other commanders who would have to give way before him. In the law as passed, however, this last prerogative was modified to give him *imperium* equal to that of proconsuls within fifty miles of the sea. Ten years later, another measure gave him complete control of the grain supply throughout the *orbis terrarum* for five years. And, in 55, yet another measure gave him the Spanish *provinciae*, which he was to manage from Rome through *legati pro praetore*.[87]

In the middle decades of the first century, then, one can detect a clear tendency to divorce extra-urban *provinciae* from actual tenure in a magistracy, although holding such a position in the past served as a necessary qualification. In this way, the governing of Rome's empire began to be separated from the annual cycle of the city's public life. In these measures and others enacted during the civil wars and under Augustus, a single person, usually not the occupant of a regular magistracy, was given the power to supervise certain operations over broad spaces and the ability to appoint direct subordinates, a clear sign of Rome's coming "bureaucratization." In much the same period, other laws permitted one man to serve as the founder of many colonies simultaneously through delegates who actually installed the settlers, instead of the small number that earlier founders established through their direct actions.[88] In the last decades of the republic, the importance of the occupants of magistracies, so central to Rome's public and ceremonial life, clearly had declined, while the management of much of Rome's empire shifted to others.

THE SPATIAL IMPLICATIONS OF EXTRA-URBAN *PROVINCIAE*

The relationship between *provinciae* and places or spaces warrants a more detailed examination. In the first century and into the empire, some *provinciae* were clearly viewed as territories or groups of peoples and polities under the supervision of a Roman magistrate.[89] Caesar occasionally used the phrase *in provinciam redacta* (to force into a province) to indicate the forceful imposition of Roman taxes and laws.[90] Under Augustus, we first hear of provinces as characterized, and perhaps even defined, by lists, *formae* or *formulae provinciarum*, of the communities within them and their tributary burdens; at the same time, the *imperium* of the Roman people could be depicted as a collection of provinces.[91] The Latin word *provincia*, however, at first and for long did not denote a territory or its inhabitants but rather the task that the senate or, less frequently, a popular assembly assigned to some magistrate, either in Rome itself, in Italy, or outside the peninsula entirely.[92]

The spatial implications of various *provinciae* were complex. As we have seen, the Roman elite of the third and second centuries viewed their city's power not in terms of places or regions that were to be governed in some direct fashion but rather as a poorly defined set of subordinate communities that were thought to owe Rome deference and obedience. For J.-L. Ferrary, Romans of the third and second centuries viewed their empire largely in terms of their ability to compel obedience when they chose to do so, but they also established within the broader sphere of their city's subordinates some *provinciae* in which magistrates regularly were to keep watch, maintain order, and administer justice.[93] Here, he suggests that the Adriatic largely divided Rome's empire into two zones. In this way, he sees considerable continuity between republican and imperial practices.

But for others, and with greater probability, extra-urban *provinciae* into the first century were primarily military in nature. Many were clearly linked to the conduct of an ongoing or impending war, but in the absence of such a conflict, the place of some assignment in the sortition indicated an intent to go to war, a desire to exert pressure, or an announcement that certain interests would be asserted forcefully. Thus, praetors might be dispatched to regions that were too unstable to allow the preservation of Rome's position without the regular threat, and occasional use, of force or were vulnerable to intrusion from the outside.[94] Spain provides a good example of the former, while Sicily and Sardinia may be examples of the latter, given Roman suspicions about Carthage that persisted until its destruction at the end of the Third Punic War. Fred Drogula sees the more regular assignments as attempts to intimidate neighboring polities and as forward bases that served to project Roman power as much as defend it.[95] The ruling elite, then, long viewed the management of empire in military terms, as the contrast between "at home" (*domi*) and "on campaign" (*militiae*) illustrates.

The military nature of second century extra-urban *provinciae* finds some confirmation in the second half of the century when magistrates came to be assigned with some regularity to a *provincia Macedonia* and a *provincia Asia*. At the end of the Third Macedonian War in 167, L. Aemilius Paulus, the victorious commander, with the assistance of ten senatorial legates, imposed a complicated settlement on the region. The Macedonian monarchy was dissolved, its territory was divided into four republics, and some of its subordinates were declared "free." Paulus and his associates also proclaimed some polities to be liable for the payment of tribute, although they did not impose it, while certain lands were to be public property. The senate next dispatched a magistrate to the region in 149 in order to prevent Andriscus, a pretender to the Macedonian throne, from reestablishing the monarchy. When this praetor died in battle, they sent a successor, Q. Caecilius Metellus (pr. 149), who first defeated Andriscus and then other pretenders as well and returned to Rome in triumph in 146. As Robert Kallet-Marx notes, magistrates were then sent with some regularity in the following decades because of persistent military problems along its northern frontier.[96] Asia presents a similar picture. The last Attalid king, who died in 133, willed his kingdom to Rome, but the senate assigned a magistrate to the region only in 130 when Aristonicus sought to revive the monarchy, and it continued to do so until the settlement that ended the war in 126, which declared some polities to be free, granted lands and communities to Rome's allies, and declared others tributary. The senate probably continued to dispatch praetors there in subsequent years because of the proximity of ambitious and predatory dynasts.[97]

The nature of late third- and second-century *provinciae* may be clarified by examining the ways that tasks were defined. Livy provides the bulk of our evidence, but his nomenclature may reproduce only imperfectly the language of his sources, for there are occasional anachronisms, and he varied his presentations for stylistic reasons. By the end of the second century, and perhaps earlier as well, the senate's instructions could be quite complex, adding additional tasks to the primary one or spelling out the main assignment in some detail. Here, Livy's practice may make earlier instructions appear simpler than they were: on one occasion, he (37.50.4) reports that a consul of 189 was not only to make war against the Aetolians but also to cross to Cephallenia, although he does not reveal what the consul was to do there; on yet another occasion (36.1.8) he notes that the senate instructed a consul holding *provincia Graecia* in 191 to add to his army troops from allies outside Italy as long as he kept within certain bounds. Still, a closer examination does reveal certain consistent patterns, some of which can be paralleled elsewhere. Note the persistent connection between consular or praetorian *provincia* away from Rome and the use of military force or judicial coercion against those suspected of specific infractions.

First, Livy regularly links such *provinciae* with armies and with enemies whom he often identifies closely. Occasionally, he even designates a *provincia* in terms of a specific army, identified by the town where it had wintered, the name of its previous commander, or its place of assembly. Flaminius (cos. 217), for example, received the legions wintering at Placentia, while the consuls of 215 divided armies at Teanum and Rome.[98] The close connection between tenure in some provincial assignment and command of an army would long continue. Indeed, after the Second Punic War, when armies in Spain and in the great wars in the East served for extended periods, new commanders must have arranged the journeys from Rome to culminate in their new army's chief encampment.

At other times, and with greater frequency, Livy's *provinciae* are the intended targets of military activity, identified either by commander (i.e., "the war against Hannibal"), by ethnicity (i.e., the Ligures), or by the enemy's homeland: Africa, Macedonia, or Aetolia.[99] (In his account of the Jugurthine War at the end of the second century, Sallust too characterizes the consular commanders' *provinciae* as "Numidia" or the "war against Jugurtha.")[100] In wars with many theaters, Livy's *provinciae* sometimes are both the enemy and the broad region in which the recipient was to conduct operations. When the senate defined Hispania as a province in 218, for example, it identified where the consul was to fight the Carthaginians; when it assigned a praetor of 192 "Macedonia and the fleet," it indicated where he was to prepare for war against Antiochus III and the force he was to command during the conflict; when it assigned to consuls of 190 and 189 first Greece and then Asia, it specified, if only broadly, where it expected them to wage war against the Seleucid king.[101]

Livy's depiction (35.20.10–14) of the assignments of 192 illustrates the close connection between the designation of a *provincia* and the identification of a target. In the midst of his account of preparations for war against Antiochus III, two praetors received as their tasks "the Bruttii" and "the fleet and Macedonia." He goes on to claim that these two praetors were said to be preparing for war against Nabis, king of Sparta, who was attacking Rome's allies, but in reality they were aimed against the Seleucid king, waiting only for the return of ambassadors to begin their operations. At the end of the second century, the Law of Praetorian Provinces of 100, which addressed Roman commands in Macedonia, Asia, and Cilicia, contains clauses intended to reassure neighboring rulers and polities that pirates were Rome's only intended opponents. To a large degree, when it placed a *provincia* in the sortition, the senate was identifying a perceived threat to their order and directing a magistrate to act against it.

In some cases, these objects of attention were more diffuse or perhaps not even closely identifiable. The senate probably designated *provinciae* such as Sicily, Sardinia, or Nearer and Farther Spain to guard against potential enemies, to prevent challenges to Rome's position, or to preserve in unstable circumstances an order favorable to Rome, and it occasionally assigned commands in Italy for the same ends. While Hannibal was in Italy, the senate instructed a promagistrate in 215 to conduct a levy in "the land of Picenum" (*in agro Piceno*) in order to garrison it; in 212 it sent a praetor to Apulia along with "the legions that had been at Luceria"; in 210 it dispatched a consul and his legions "into Etruria" (*in Etruriam*); in 208 it ordered a promagistrate to Etruria to guard against subversion there.[102]

At times, Livy's senate instructed recipients of a *provincia* to search out and punish malefactors identified by crime as well as by polity or region. Late in 207 a promagistrate was sent to Etruria to conduct investigations into which communities had considered defecting from Rome or had helped Hasdrubal in any way.[103] In the aftermath of the Hannibalic War, a praetor of 200 was dispatched to "the Bruttii" and continued in the following year to complete his investigations of conspiracies among them.[104] In 186 both consuls were to seek out participants in the Bacchanalian conspiracy who had fled Rome or failed to respond to summons.[105] In the following years, magistrates and promagistrates received assignments to continue the search for conspirators, to seek out poisoners, or to defend against pirates.[106] Livy (45.16) reports that a praetor of 167 was to investigate certain unspecified capital crimes.

Many of Livy's provincial designations within Italy are as much ethnic groups as regions. Thus, a praetor of 212 received "the Etruscans" (*Tuscos*) along with the urban legions of the previous year, which were thus intended for service "among the Etruscans."[107] Other commands are "among the Bruttii," or "the Bruttii," or "the Brutti and Lucani."[108] The limits of such assignments may have been rather vague. Livy often refers to Apulia as a *provincia*, but Michael Fronda notes that the frontiers of Apulia were essentially undefinable.[109] Indeed, Aulus Cornelius Mammula (pr. 191), who had received "the Bruttii" in the sortition, was also instructed to defend "the entire coast around Tarentum and Brundisium," neither of which was in Bruttium, although he probably was the nearest higher magistrate.[110] And, finally, during the first decades of the second century, the senate regularly defined Gaul or the Ligures as *provinciae*, even though the necessary operations might encompass some of the same places.

Yet another way of designating *provinciae* illustrates a similar indeterminacy. For five years—213, 209, 205, 203, and 199—Livy calls the assignment in the Po Valley Ariminum and once adds "thus they called *Gallia*."[111] Founded as a Latin colony in 268, Ariminum served as Rome's first major base of operations in the plains south of the Po, and in subsequent years it was used as a mustering point for armies intended to fight in the north and provided winter quarters for existing armies. Livy (32.1.6) reports that the praetor who received Ariminum in 199 also obtained the army necessary to hold the lands around it. Pisae and Tarentum sometimes played a similar role. In the late third and early second centuries, Pisae, an allied city, occasionally served as an embarkation point for voyages to and from Sardinia and Spain, and it was frequently a consular or praetorian assignment during the Lugurian Wars. Livy claims that the senate assigned Pisae to a praetor in 195 so that he might be in the rear of the Ligures, that they made Pisae and the Ligures a consular *provincia* in 188, and that when the senate made the Ligures the *provincia* of both consuls of 185, one began his march from Pisae.[112] In the aftermath of its rebellion during the Second Punic War, Tarentum was a common assignment, especially as Hannibal was increasingly confined to the southwestern portion of the Italian peninsula. In 208 a praetor received Tarentum and the Sallentini as his command.[113] Tarentum was sometimes linked to Apulia. In 185 a praetor assigned to the Greek city put down a slave revolt in Apulia, while in the following year, another praetor who had received it sought out and punished fugitives from the Bacchanalian conspiracy who were hiding in that part of Italy.[114]

Still, Livy does give a few *provinciae* boundaries. In 215 as events in Syracuse began to turn against Rome, the commander in western Sicily placed his army in garrisons along the boundary between his *provincia* and the kingdom, while two years later the senate assigned two *provinciae*, one within the limits of the kingdom of Syracuse and the other the "old *provincia*."[115] Then, in 197, when the senate first assigned as *provinciae* Nearer and Farther Spain, it instructed the praetors who received them to mark the boundaries of their *provinciae*. The resulting limits ran from south of New Carthage to the headwaters of the Baetis River, but they probably did not go further inland, for Roman power had not penetrated these regions, and they certainly did not encircle the two assignments.[116] J. S. Richardson notes that the Spanish *fines* "made little or no difference to the activities of the commanders in Spain, who over the next few years were frequently to be found fighting in what was properly the territory assigned to their colleagues."[117] Cicero (*Pis.* 38) claims that *provincia Macedonia* had once been bounded by the swords and spears of its commanders.

Just what did these boundaries signify? The frontier in Sicily may best be seen as the boundary of the kingdom of Syracuse—the Romans did set limits to their dependents and the defeated—so that its role as provincial frontier may have been only secondary. As we shall see many times during the course of this investigation, the Roman elite of the late third and early second centuries frequently set boundaries, some more precise than others, to the activities of various magistrates, most frequently in or near Rome, but occasionally at greater distances as well. The practice may well have been most urgent when functionaries possessing the same powers operated in close proximity. In Spain the limits served to separate the exercise of *imperium* by praetors operating in a region that was not well known to the Roman authorities.

Other, more abstract, boundaries illustrate the principle more clearly. Livy (25.5.5–7) reports that in 212, in the midst of recruitment problems, the senate ordered the establishment of two triumvirates to search the countryside for recruits, one on "this side" and the other "beyond the fiftieth milestone" from the city (*alteros qui citra, alteros qui ultra quinquagensiumum lapidum*). In 180, in order to investigate poisonings in the midst of a panic set off by the death of a consul, the senate ordered the peregrine praetor to conduct investigations in Rome and within ten miles of it (*quod in urbe propriusue urbem decem milibus passuum esset commissum*) and another praetor the task of conducting investigations beyond the tenth milestone (*ultra decimum lapidem per fora conciliabulaque C. Maenio*).[118] These limits clearly concern magistrates of equal status and function, whom they separate, without taking any note of local conditions.

The Law on Praetorian Provinces of 100 provides a glimpse of how detailed the senate's instructions for the holders of various *provinciae* for a single year were or would become.[119] Portions of the measure survive in very fragmentary condition on damaged stone blocks found at Cnidos and Delphi. These versions represent separate translations, probably by Latin speakers, of the original Latin into a Greek that is occasionally awkward. The law's scope is uncertain. Lacunose passages mention the assignment of magistrates to Macedonia and Cilicia, and probably Asia as well. The law is much more concerned with the actions of magistrates and promagistrates than it is with polities or individuals that might be encompassed within their spheres of action.

The law's framers set out a series of very specific instructions and qualifications. A consul was to send letters to various rulers and polities, including the kings in Cyprus, in Alexandria, and in Cyrene, proclaiming that the Roman people would take care that Roman citizens, Latins, allies, and residents of foreign states that were friends of the Roman people might sail the seas in safety, the reason that they had made Cilicia a praetorian *provincia*.[120] The praetor who holds *provincia Asia* should send letters proclaiming the statute to a range of polities and take care that these cities display it in inscriptions posted in prominent locations.[121] This element of the law was apparently intended to justify the formation of a command in Cilicia, which, like other *provinciae* in the past, was defined against a particular opponent.

Other clauses set out very specific instructions for commanders. The magistrate who would hold *provincia Macedonia* should not receive certain troops that an earlier measure had granted him.[122] While in his command, he was to travel to the Caenic Chersonese—or perhaps to the Chersonese and Caenice—which Titus Didius had just taken, where he should collect public revenues, establish the boundaries of the tribute, and remain for at least sixty days.[123] Magistrates who had received *provincia Macedonia* or *provincia Asia* were to swear an oath to follow the statute within ten days of hearing of it, while other magistrates in Rome were to do so within five days.

Some scholars find in the law signs that *provincia* had taken on, or was beginning to take on, a territorial significance. The crucial passage occurs among the clauses that concern the holder of *provincia Asia*: "Nothing is enacted in this law to the effect that the praetor or proconsul holding the *provincia Asia* should not hold Lycaonia or that the *provincia Lycaonia* should not be his, just as it was before the passing of this law."[124] For J. S. Richardson and A. Lintott, the clause represents the earliest surviving appearance of *provincia* in the sense of a "geographical entity," Lycaonia, in which a magistrate was to carry out his designated task or tasks.[125] The passage will not bear this weight. As we have seen, *provinciae* were long associated with tasks, but these were to be performed in certain places or regions or against certain opponents, although they might be rather indeterminate. After all, *provincia Sicilia* or *provincia Sardinia* or the *provinciae* of Nearer and Farther Spain carried with them clear references to the regions, if only broadly defined, in which their recipients were to undertake their assigned operations.

The spatial implications in the definition of a *provincia*, however, go beyond the mere matching of a magistrate, a task, and an opponent, polity, or some broad, if often ill-defined region. First, the relationship between the nomenclature of an assignment and its object or focus might vary. In some instances, such as Africa in the opening year of the Second Punic War or Macedonia at the same point in the Second Macedonian War, the name of the *provincia* identifies the ultimate goal of the intended operations. The Hispania of the first year of the Hannibalic war indicates the broad region to which the consul was to go and begin operations against the Carthaginians, while the assignment "among the Bruttii" of 192 denoted the area in which the praetor assigned it was to prepare for war farther to the east. Still other assignments—Nearer and Farther Spain, "among the Etruscans," or "among the Brutti—identify regions or ethnic groups to which the assigned official was to go and assert Roman interests.

Two structural features of the republican order may have increased the spatial and temporal indeterminacy of many *provincia*. As we shall see in chapter 4, from as far in the past as can be seen with any clarity the powers of higher magistrates were defined spatially in terms of a fundamental contrast between the city, where they did not possess military functions, and lands away from it, in which they might deploy military powers provided that they had left Rome properly. In this way, the formal definition of *provinciae* which appears to have become more prominent in the last quarter of the third century, would represent an attempt to focus the attentions of a magistrate more specifically against a particular enemy or problem. Since taking up most assignments required that a magistrate travel from Rome to the scene of operations, while laying one down involved a return to the city, this movement, in some fashion, was also part of the *provincia*. An inscription (*ILS* 4041 = *ILLRP* 401) reveals that Ap. Claudius Pulcher (cos. 54) vowed as consul the reconstruction of a gate at Eleusis on his way to his *provincia Cilicia*.

In addition, magistrates sometimes constructed, apparently on their own authority, roads leading to their *provinciae*, a practice that indicates that the task was not easily encompassed within an easily definable space. When he was consul in 223, C. Flaminius campaigned in northern Italy against the Insubres, and in either his consulship or his term as censor in 220 he also laid out the *via Flaminia* from Rome to Fanum Fortunae on the Adriatic and then north along the coast to the Latin colony of Ariminum. The praetor Cn. Egnatius, who held office in the 130s, arranged for the construction of the *via Egnatia*, which ran from Apollonia and Epidamnus on the Adriatic to Cypsela on the Hebrus River in Thrace.[126] The *elogium* from Polla (*ILLRP* 454), if it is properly attributed to P. Popilius Laenas, who commanded in Sicily in 132 in the midst of the First Slave War, has the honorand build a road from Capua to Rhegium, neither of which were on the island.

The connection between an assignment and movement sometimes continued within the area in which an official was to perform his assigned tasks. Livy (37.50.4) reports that a consul of 189 was not only to make war against the Aetolians but also to cross to Cephallenia, while the Law on Praetorian Provinces instructs the holder of *provincia Macedonia* to travel to the Caenic Chersonese, which his predecessor had taken, where he should collect public revenues, establish the boundaries of the tribute, and remain for at least sixty days.[127] A decade earlier, the Agrarian Law of 111 set out a complicated schedule of movements and actions for the duumvirs that it would create (see chapter 6). In 111, it should be noted, a consul was active in Africa for the war against Jugurtha, but his presence was irrelevant.

To this, one should add the difficulty in determining when a magistrate's powers and his tenure in his *provincia* began and ended, temporally and spatially. The Elder Cato delivered an address (*ne imperium sit ueteri ubi nouus uenerit*) in which he recommended that a commander's *imperium* should end when his replacement arrived in the *provincia*, but the Law on Praetorian Provinces asserts that a magistrate's powers of jurisdiction end only with the return to Rome.[128] Some returning officials kept their *imperium*—and occasionally command over their returning soldiers—for lengthy periods while waiting just outside Rome's urban boundary for the senate to grant them triumphs. From the late second century laws were enacted to keep officials in their *provinciae*, while early in the first century Sulla required that previous governors leave their *provinciae* within thirty days of the arrival of their successors, perhaps a sign that some were not departing promptly. Indeed, when Cicero arrived in Cilicia in 51, his replacement neither met with him nor surrendered his assignment but continued for a time to hold judicial hearings. Rome provided a clearer reference point—and one more amenable to supervision—than distant camps and commands, a situation that persisted in a more limited fashion into the much different administrative climate of the empire: the *Digest* (48.4.2–3; 1.16.1) sets penalties for failing to hand over one's *provincia* on the arrival of one's successor, and it also announces that proconsuls possess the insignia of their rank as soon as they leave the city, although they can exercise power (*potestas*) only in their *provinciae*. Although *imperium* encompassed the power to command armies and to punish without restraint when away from Rome, these two functions of higher magistracies would steadily be distinguished, much as *imperium* itself was separated from actual tenure in a magistracy.[129]

PROVINCIAE AND THEIR LIMITS

The senate and popular assemblies at Rome occasionally took care to keep magistrates focused on their assigned tasks. After Hannibal had returned to Carthage leaving his army in Bruttium behind, Cn. Servilius Caepio (cos. 203), who had received "Bruttium and the war against Hannibal," crossed into Sicily with the intention of going to Africa in pursuit of the Carthaginian commander;[130] the senate secured the appointment of a dictator to order him back to Italy. The tribunes of the plebs questioned one of the consuls of 178, who had returned from his province in northern Italy, about his war against the Istrians when the senate had not decreed one.[131] When envoys from Aquileia informed the senate that C. Cassius Longinus (cos. 171) had abandoned his *provincia* of Gaul and was seeking to invade Macedonia through Illyria, the senate sent three senatorial legates to find him and remind him that he should not begin new wars without the senate's approval.[132]

Occasionally the relationship between a commander's supposed accomplishments and his *provincia* was an issue when weighing his request for a triumph. In general, of course, any discussion in the senate about such matters involved some assessment about the quality of a commander's victory and his role in obtaining it. Here, we should not expect hard-and-fast rules, since the process was so caught up in elite rivalries, although contestants sometimes proclaimed that certain norms should govern the decision.[133] Perhaps the most important criterion was that the successful commander ought to have been in supreme command of his army and that he ought to have been present at the decisive battle. In the give-and-take of debates, other matters sometimes come to the fore. Did the commander fight the crucial battle as a magistrate or as a promagistrate? How many of the enemy were slain? Did the commander bring his army back to Rome, a strong sign that his victory was complete, or did he leave it behind for his successor, which may indicate that his success was incomplete?

Senators discussing possible triumphs sometimes took note of whether the magistrate had gained his victory while pursuing the task that he had been given. Livy (10.37.1–12) reports that a consul of 294 was denied a triumph because he had left his *provincia* against the Samnites to campaign in Etruria. Almost a century later, in 197, M. Helvius received Farther Spain. Illness kept him in Spain after his relief. To escort him on the first stages of his journey back to Rome, Ap. Claudius Nero, the praetor in charge in 195 and his successor's successor, gave Helvius soldiers as an escort, and with them he defeated a large force of Celtiberi who sought to block his passage.[134] When he reached Rome and sought a triumph, the senate rejected his request on the grounds that he had fought "under another's auspices and in another's province."[135] Indeed, M. Porcius Cato (cos. 195), who held Nearer Spain at the time, may have had a crucial role in blocking Helvius's triumph, for the former praetor's success may have overshadowed his own. Cato did assert in some unknown context that a magistrate's *imperium* ended when his successor arrived (*ne imperium sit ueteri ubi nouus uenerit*).[136] The senate, however, did grant Helvius an *ovatio* or lesser triumph, which may indicate that they found some justice in his claim and some ambiguity in the situation, while the *Fasti triumphales* identify Helvius as proconsul and thus in possession of *imperium*.[137] Despite various questions raised about actions at remote locations, the fact that Helvius had not formally surrendered his powers by entering Rome may have been a factor.

The most dramatic conflict concerned Cn. Manlius Vulso, who, as consul in 189, received Asia as his *provincia* with the understanding that he would continue operations against Antiochus III.[138] Because peace negotiations were well advanced, Vulso began a war against the Galatians in the interior of Asia Minor, apparently on his own initiative and without a declaration of war. When he returned to Rome in 187, controversy erupted when he successfully sought a triumph, with supporters and opponents giving different representations of his actions. The ten legates who had assisted Vulso and his predecessor in negotiations with the king proved his most vigorous opponents, and they apparently focused on Vulso fighting a war that had not been formally approved—that was not, in other words, his *provincia*. Indeed, they even claimed that he had attempted to sabotage peace negotiations and cross the Taurus Mountains into Syria and was restrained only with difficulty.[139]

Around the beginning of the final quarter of the second century, we can begin to detect the enactment of legislation designed to keep magistrates in their *provinciae*. At some point, probably in the late 120s, the praetor M. Porcius Cato proposed and carried a law, a *lex Porcia*, which established limits for certain forms of behavior by magistrates who were abroad.[140] This same broad period, it should be noted, also saw the passage of C. Gracchus's law on consular provinces that required the senate to name the following year's *provinciae* before the consular elections, thus impeding any attempt to tailor assignments to favored individuals, as well as the enactment of the Extortion Law of 123, aimed against magisterial depredations. The *lex Porcia* is known only through passages in later laws, usually recorded on fragmentary inscriptions, that cite the measure.[141] It prohibited magistrates or promagistrates "with wrongful deceit" from assembling an army or marching or traveling outside their *provinciae*, except when instructed by the senate or for purposes of transit or for reasons of state, and it also limited what a magistrate or promagistrate might demand of a free city. Rules such as this may have been or become fairly common, perhaps an indication of persistent problems. Sulla carried a law that forbade magistrates or promagistrates from leaving their *provinciae* with their army or starting a war without the permission of the senate or people, required commanders who had been replaced to leave the province within thirty days of the arrival of their successors, and permitted replaced commanders to retain their *imperium* until their return to Rome.[142] Cicero (*Pis.* 50) states that the *lex Antonia de Termessibus* of 72 also forbade magistrates from leaving their *provincia* or leading their army outside it (*exire de prouincia, educere exercitum*).

Finally, we should return to the Law of Praetorian Provinces of 100. As we have seen, one of its clauses proclaims that the praetor or proconsul holding *provincia Asia* should also hold Lycaonia and *provincia Lycaonia*. Another instructs the consul, praetor, or proconsul who holds *provincia Macedonia* to go the Caenic Chersonese—or the Chersonese and the Caenice—and mark certain boundaries and collect certain revenues and then proclaims that "he who has the Chersonese and the Caenice as his *provincia* is to hold this *provincia* along with Macedonia."[143] Just before this passage, the framers of the law included a reference to the *lex Porcia*. Could these clauses have been intended to make clear that the Chersonese and Lycaonia were within the proper sphere of operations of the commanders in Macedonia and Asia? Did the passage of measures such as the *lex Porcia* lead to efforts to define more firmly the limits of *provinciae*?

As the center of public life, Rome was the primary locus for decision making in its empire, a role that the ruling elite regularly sought to strengthen. From it, they regarded their city's empire in terms of powers over peoples and polities and not over administered territories, they associated it with the accomplishments of magisterial commanders, and they sought to manage it on a large scale by directing generals and their armies against their opponents or to guard against uprisings, rebellions, or other significant threats to their order. As we have seen and shall see, Romans had clearer ideas about boundaries near their city than they did about the farthest reaches of their empire. Indeed, they may have been better informed about events in Rome and in areas of active campaigning than they were about developments in many intermediate regions.

The spatial indeterminacy of Rome's empire was mirrored in its extra-urban *provinciae*, which the senate defined in the late third and second centuries primarily to address some specific threat or opportunity. Regular journeys of magistrates from Rome to the sites of their proposed activities and their eventual return formed a prominent structural element in the polity, one made manifest in Rome's great radial roads, a feature that did not favor viewing *provinciae* as defined spaces. The beginning and ending of commands, moreover, were conceptualized in terms of an exit from the city and an eventual return to it, while magisterial powers, in some fashion, were in force during travel to and from distant assignments. These tasks, while they possessed clear spatial implications, were not always clearly defined, except in relationship to the city, although over time some would harden into administrative districts, at least in part as a result of efforts to limit the ability of magistrates and promagistrates to operate freely.

THREE

Rome and Its Italy

The ruling elite of the late third and second centuries did not view their city's empire as a space with clear boundaries, and the assignments, *provinciae*, that they gave to senior magistrates were often poorly defined and tailored to address specific situations. At the same time, much of the government of Rome's empire consisted of official journeys to and from increasingly distant areas of concern. Italy was an exception, however, for Romans from the third century gave to it formal frontiers, imposed upon it a level of organization not found elsewhere in Rome's empire, and raised from it the armies with which they would assert power more widely in the Mediterranean world. This chapter, which focuses on Italy, primarily in the third and second centuries, examines the organization that the Roman elite imposed on the peninsula and surveys the spatial distribution of roles, statuses, and functions.

ITALY AND THE "LAND OF ITALY"

By the last quarter of the third century, Romans had come to draw at least one major boundary far from the city itself, beyond their direct observation and almost certainly not clearly defined throughout its length. The word *Italia*, which probably came into Latin from Greek, has a long and complicated history, for it once designated only a region in southern Italy, but through obscure stages it eventually came to denote first peninsular Italy and then the mainland to the Alps, extensions that are almost certainly linked to the expansion of Roman power.[1] Polybius (1.6.6; 6.50.6) claims that around the time of the Pyrrhic War, the Romans began to make war on the rest of Italy as if it belonged to them, and he asserts that Rome had only intended to rule Italy but had come to dominate the *oikoumenē* by chance. When he wrote the *Origins*, Polybius's contemporary the Elder Cato devoted several books to the beginnings of Rome and of other Italian polities, an attempt to bring all of Italy into a common framework.² A century earlier, P. Sempronius Sophus (cos. 268) enshrined the memory of his triumph over the Picentes by placing on the wall of the Temple of Tellus a painted representation of *Italia*, the earliest known attempt to depict peninsular Italy as a geographic and political unit and an apparent sign that he, at least, viewed Rome's domination of the peninsula as complete.³

At the beginning of the last quarter of the third century, when arrangements first become clearer, any broad cultural or political unity would have been illusory. Many polities remained mutually hostile, some maintained imperial ambitions of their own, and communities and factions sought Roman favor as a weapon against their rivals.⁴ In his description of preparations to meet a Gallic invasion in 225, Polybius (2.23.11–13) holds that the inhabitants of Italy for the first time felt that they had a common cause, but he did not see this cause as the defense of Italy but rather as each defending his own city.⁵ The responses of various polities to Hannibal's invasion during the Second Punic War and to the outbreak of the Social War early in the first century indicate that some local identities long maintained considerable force and that Rome's hegemony was not always welcomed.

At first and perhaps for a long time, Romans may have had clearer ideas about *Italia*'s boundaries than of the realities of the polities encompassed within them. For Polybius (2.14.7–11), Italy extended to the Alps, and for the Elder Cato (*FRHist* 5 F 150 = Serv. *ad Aen.* 10.12–13), the Alps protected it as if a wall. Polybius, however, divides Italy into two unequal portions, separating the peninsula from the Po Valley by a boundary south of the citizen colony of Sena Gallica, founded in the 280s. Much later, the geographer Strabo (5.1.11), who sometimes used Polybius as a source, holds that the boundary between Cisalpine Gaul and the rest of Italy was once at the Apennines and the Aesis, just to the south of Sena Gallica, but later it was shifted to the Rubicon, just to the north of the Latin colony of Ariminum, founded in 268. Slightly later (5.2.10), he again makes the Aesis the boundary between Italy and Gaul and notes that it was later changed to the Rubicon. Sulla was almost certainly responsible for the shift.

These differing limits represent more than the expansion of Roman activity into the valley of the Po. The Aesis and Arnus Rivers and the surrounding seas defined the boundaries of the augural and juristic "land of Italy" (*terra Italia*).⁶ For the augurs, an *ager* denoted the territory of a specific community, while a land, a *terra*, consisted of the *agri* of many communities that were thought to share some identity. Thus, we hear of a *terra Etruriae*, while C. Gracchus took note of kings in *terra Graecia* and an annalist, probably Valerius Antias, assigned a speech to Scipio Africanus in which the great commander referred to his victory *in terra Africa*.⁷

Terra Italia was not the only large space that the Romans defined by rivers and seas, for water boundaries occupied a prominent place in augural thought. The Elder Pliny (*HN* 3.56–59) claims that ancient Latium was bounded on the north and south by the Tiber and the city of Circeii on the coast and that it was later extended to the Liris River. If these boundaries are genuinely old, they probably point to the middle of the fourth century, when Rome first incorporated the surrounding Latins in its polity, which Rome then extended to the margins of Campania. Pierangelo Catalano suggests that the sea, the Tiber, and the Anio once constituted Latium's western, northern, and eastern limits, while the southern limit was not clearly defined until Roman expansion made possible lines drawn first at the Liris River and then at the Volturnus.⁸ The Twelve Tables uses the words "across the Tiber" (*trans Tiberim*) to mean "outside of Latium," although Roman citizens almost certainly occupied lands across the river when the code was promulgated.

What was the significance of the concept of *terra Italia* and in what contexts was it important? As noted in the following chapter, the augurs regularly emphasized inner spaces over outer ones, and they often associated the largest with a magistrate's ability to auspicate and not with the polities and persons encompassed within them. In this regard, it is significant that *terra Italia* appears in reports of the formulas of some laws, edicts, and decrees of the late third and early second centuries, where it serves to denote a kind of privileged space (see chapter 4). In 225, moreover, it served to separate noncitizen polities that had a regular and prominent place in Rome's armies from others that did not play such an essential role. The Agrarian Law of 111 mentions allies and Latins in "the land of Italy" who provided soldiers according to the *formula togatorum*, but the first detectable appearance of the list is over a century earlier.⁹ In the face of an impending invasion of Italy by Gauls in 225, Polybius (2.23–24), probably following Fabius Pictor, reports that the senate ordered allies and Latins to provide a summary of their manpower that was available for military service.¹⁰ Although he did not specifically limit the returns to the "land of Italy," Polybius took note only of polities outside it—the Veneti and the

Cenomani—in the context of additions to forces raised within the peninsula during an emergency levy.

The list's name, the *formula togatorum*, is particularly striking. The word *togatus* designates the wearer of the *toga*, a civic costume associated with Romans and Latins. The *formula togatorum*, however, included other allies as well as Latins, thus proclaiming them to be in some especially close relationship with Rome.[11] From the late third century, we hear of lists of "friends" (*formula amicorum*), of "allies" (*formula sociorum*), or of "friends and allies" (*formula sociorum et amicorum*), which may be the same list or two or even three different lists.[12] This list, or these lists, identified individuals and polities outside of Italy that had the right for their representatives in Rome to be introduced into the senate and to receive public lodging. The differing treatment of allies inside and outside peninsular Italy is clearly reflective of a perceived qualitative difference (a matter pursued in greater depth in chapter 6).

Although the term *terra Italia* is first detectable in the last quarter of the third century, its origins are almost certainly earlier. Pierangelo Catalano holds that the augurs probably formed the category during the age of the Pyrrhic Wars, while W. V. Harris suggests that the Aesis and Arnus Rivers must have been set as boundaries before the foundation of the Latin colony at Ariminum in 268, since any later limit probably would have included the settlement, a short distance to the north.[13] Like other Roman limits, the boundaries of the early *terra Italia* would not have marked, or long have marked, the outer reaches of Rome's power, and they may have been set before they matched realities on the ground. The Roman victory over a grand coalition in 295 was won at Sentinum near the headwaters of the Aesis, while Roman officials had founded the citizen colony of Sena Gallica to its north before the outbreak of the Pyrrhic War. In 268, the year of Sophus's triumph, other magistrates founded the Latin colony of Ariminum north of the river, which moved Roman power to the fringes of the greatly different environment of the Po Valley. In 232 a Roman commission, acting under the authority of a law put forward by C. Flaminius when tribune of the plebs, settled Roman citizens in Picenum and the *ager Gallicus*, that is, to the north and south of the Aesis. The boundaries of *terra Italia* may once have served, if only notionally, to separate a Roman from a non-Roman world, thus marking the limits of Rome's ambitions, but in the age of the Punic Wars, Roman power would spread beyond peninsular Italy. In these circumstances, *terra Italia* would take on the role of a privileged core within the larger sphere of Roman activity.

The perceived or desired unity of Italy is a clear theme in the third century, although the evidence is often difficult to evaluate. Here, the Secular Games (*ludi saeculares*) of 249 provide one indication. Roman writers gave to these games, a periodic festival that was celebrated every century or *saeculum*, a history reaching back to the beginning of the republic, but the third-century celebrations are the earliest certain performance.[14] The imperial antiquarian Verrius Flaccus reports that in 249 the *decemviri sacris faciundis* interpreted a prodigy—lightning striking Rome's walls—as predicting that the war with Carthage would go well if Dis and Prosperina were conciliated with a hymn—that is, a *carmen saeculare*—and a sacrifice.[15] According to Phlegon of Tralles, an author of the second century of the empire, and Zosimus, a late antique historian, a hymn that accompanied these games mentioned a Sibylline oracle predicting that, if the proper rites were performed, "your laws would be observed not in Latium alone but would extend to all of Italy."[16] F. Russo suggests that the reference to Latium must derive from a fourth-century performance, when Rome had just achieved or was on the verge of achieving domination of Latium, while the extension to all of Italy would have been an innovation of the third-century rites.[17] Lily Ross Taylor has suggested that another prayer preserved in the epigraphic records of the Augustan performance requesting that Rome's power grow at war and at home (*duelli domique*), and that the Latins always remain loyal, derived from the same period.[18]

A shift in vocabulary, broadly datable to the middle or late third century, confirms an elite concern for some form of unity across polities in Italy. In the Twelve Tables, *hostis* appears in a context that indicates that such a person might enter into some binding agreements with citizens, and here "foreigner" is a better translation than "enemy."[19] In Plautus's comedies, written early in the second century, *hostis* can mean either "foreigner" or "enemy," while, slightly later, fragments from the works of the elder Cato reveal only the meaning "enemy." The earliest attested use of *peregrinus* is also to be found in Plautus's works, which invites the suspicion that the meaning of *hostis* shifted, or began to shift, only when *peregrinus* came to be used for some intermediate category between citizens and hostile or potentially hostile foreigners. When categorizing a person, *peregrinus* usually appears in contrast to *civis*, citizen, but when denoting a thing or a practice, it can designate something brought more fully into the Roman civic order.[20] According to Festus (p. 268 L), "peregrine rites" (*peregrina sacra*) were those that the Romans adopted either to weaken the enemy or to expiate some prodigy. Although our earliest sources for the word *peregrinus* come from the early second century, the appearance of the *praetor peregrinus* points to an origin in the middle decades of the third century. As we shall see in chapter 6, laws of the second and first centuries would continue to draw the polities of Italy into an ever greater formal unity.

CITIZENS, LATINS, AND ALLIES

By the last decades of the third century, Romans divided the free inhabitants of the peninsula into three broad status groups—citizens, Latins, and allies—largely on the basis of the polities to which they belonged. In these years, after almost two centuries of expansion, Rome's citizens had come to occupy two broad bands of territory, one along the west coast of Italy from southern Etruria to Campania and the other stretching to the northeast of the city in Sabinum and Picenum. Allied states and Latin colonies that had been established during the wars of expansion in the late fourth and third centuries filled peninsular Italy to the north and south of this strip, although a few might be found closer to the center, relicts of earlier phases of expansion. Before the outbreak of the war with Hannibal, Rome had founded three Latin colonies in the Po Valley, had made at least one viritane assignment there, and had established new alliances and subordinates in the region. After the Second Punic War, Roman magistrates installed citizens in citizen colonies and viritane assignments first in the south of Italy on lands seized from rebellious allies and then in the Po Valley to the north. In this way, citizen settlements came to be more widely dispersed, although western central Italy long remained the core.

"Citizenship without the vote" (*civitas sine suffragio*), one of the most obscure of republican institutions, adds to the complexity. The inhabitants of some citizen settlements possessed full rights even though they may have been too far from Rome to exercise many of them with any frequency. Others possessed citizenship without the vote, granted to entire communities from the middle of the fourth century through the subordination of Picenum in 268. Although it has long been seen as a fully formed legal category and a transitional one, intended to ease the movement of communities into full citizenship, Henrik Mouritsen has plausibly asserted that citizenship without the vote is a retrospective category, intended to make sense of a variety of arrangements, not quite citizenship but closer than the alliances that would replace it.[21]

A similar obscurity surrounds the history of the *municipium*. In later periods, *coloniae* and *municipia* ranked at the top of the hierarchy of settlements, for both possessed the institutions appropriate to a fully developed polity. Colonies were viewed as created communities, owing their governing institutions to their Roman founders, while *municipia* were preexisting communities, absorbed into the Roman order, that preserved their magistracies and cults. In the aftermath of the Social War, when Roman citizenship was extended to the free population of Italy and many institutions were adjusted to accommodate the new situation, the Roman authorities clearly delegated important public functions to municipal officials, and some scholars have suggested that they had already done so as early as the late fourth century. The institution of the *municipium*, however, almost certainly took on greater specificity against the background of the expansion of the citizenry in the first century.[22]

Municipia, moreover, may have once been associated primarily with citizens without the vote.[23] Indeed, the term *municeps*—someone who takes up some burden—is linguistically, and probably historically, prior to *municipium*, which would merely denote an aggregation of *municipes*.[24] The Roman elite may first have identified a status that they associated with persons and only later connected it to communities.[25] One clause in the Agrarian Law of 111, the earliest epigraphic evidence, sets out rules that apply not only in *coloniae* and *municipia* but also in towns that it likened to colonies and *municipia*: "as if *municipia* and colonies" (*pro moinicipieies colonieisue*).[26] The law's authors conceptualized certain polities only by likening them to others. The sparse evidence, then, may indicate some process of development, in which the Roman elite gradually took more overt and formal notice of the settlements in which many citizens lived.[27]

Such a conclusion finds some confirmation in the difficulties that late republican and imperial jurists and antiquarians encountered in defining crucial terms. They largely agreed that *municipes* shared some burden with Roman citizens and that they derived from a *municipium*, a self-governing polity under its own laws and practices, except for the performance of their duties (*munera*) that linked them to the larger Roman order.[28] A late republican author, who may have been the jurist Ser. Sulpicius Rufus (cos. 51), defines *municipes* as those "who had become Roman citizens in this condition, that they always kept their *res publica* separate from the Roman people, the Cumani, Acerrani, and Atellani, who <were both Roman citizens, and used to serve in the legions, but did not take up offices>."[29] Here, the link with citizenship *sine suffragio* is clear, but the examples are limited geographically and perhaps chronologically, for while all three came into Roman hands in the fourth century, their relationship with Rome was redefined in the aftermath of the Campanian rebellion during the Second Punic War, which affected even the loyal Cumani.

Festus's epitomator (p. 155 L), on the other hand, provides three different definitions. In the first, he claims that a *municipium* was a class of men (*genus hominum*) who were not Roman citizens but, when they came to Rome, shared certain duties with Roman citizens but could not vote or hold office, and he gives as examples the Fundani, Formiani, Cumani, Acerrani, Lanuvini, and Tusculani. His second includes men whose entire community had come into Roman citizenship, such as the Aricini, Caerites, and Anagnani. His final group consists of men who came into Roman citizenship in such a way that they would be *municipes* of their own community, such as the Tiburtes, Praenestini, Pisani, Urbinates, Nolani, Bononiensis, Placentini, Nepesini, Sutrini, and Lucrenses. The last category includes Latin and allied communities that achieved citizen status only after the Social War.[30] All the epitomator's examples, moreover, mix groups with full citizenship with others that possessed partial citizenship; he, or his source, may have known little about these polities or their legal circumstances.[31] H. Galsterer has suggested that the concept of a *municipium* was retrospective in nature, linking communities that were incorporated in broadly similar ways, while obscuring differences among them.[32] If this is correct, Rome and its full citizens would for long have been surrounded by polities with some varying and probably not fully defined relationship with the center.

The process of expansion created an uneven distribution of Rome's full citizens. Early in the fourth century, the capture of Veii, seventeen kilometers away, had increased by half Rome's civic territory, creating a zone around the city that after centuries of expansion would remain the region most thoroughly integrated into its political, cultural, social and economic life.[33] In the settlement that ended the Latin War in 338, most polities near Rome were fully incorporated into its citizenry: Aricia about thirty kilometers southeast of Rome and Lanuvium less than ten kilometers farther are good examples. The two largest Latin communities—Tibur, thirty kilometers northeast of Rome, and Praeneste, thirty-five kilometers east of the city—became allies. Beyond them were the hostile or potentially hostile Aequi and Hernici. Others retained the status of Latins and formed the core of the later Latin Name (*nomen Latinum*): Ardea about thirty-five kilometers south of Rome; Sutrium, fifty kilometers to its north; Nepete, slightly closer to the city. Sutrium and Nepete probably marked in some fashion the northern limits of Roman power when they were established after the fall of Veii. (Caere, slightly more than fifty kilometers to the northwest of the city, would have completed the ring around Rome, but its status is uncertain.)

The ring of Latin and allied settlements, however, did not fully delimit Rome's power or its citizenry, which extended beyond the slopes of the *mons Albanus* into an area with citizen polities possessing full or partial rights, allies, and Latins, reaching in some fashion as far as Campania, where Rome was in the process of forming a close relationship with the Campani. Two decades earlier, Roman officials had established two clusters of citizens, cores of the tribes Pomptina and Poblilia, well beyond the rest of its citizenry and separated from the rest by Aricia, Lanuvium, and Praeneste, and some polities whose inhabitants counted, or would come to count, among those possessing *civitas sine suffragio*. With the settlement of 338, this gap would be reduced, while neighboring settlements, such as Signia, Norba, and Setia, would form part of the Latin Name.

The central space bounded by polities in Latium that preserved some formal independence deserves a closer look. At the most basic level, the full absorption of polities within this zone into Rome's citizenry may well be a function, if only in part, of their proximity to the center—that is, that Rome's public, cultic, and economic life may already have dominated theirs. But, still, the preservation of the formal independence of polities, such as Ardea, Tibur, Praeneste, while absorbing more fully others at a greater distance, would appear to indicate that Rome's leadership saw some purpose in the continuation of their full self-government. Here, it should be noted that they constituted a kind of protective ring around Rome and its hinterland, for all preserved their own military organizations. At the same time, no communities possessing citizenship without the vote were within its bounds—Velitrae, on the farther slopes of the *mons Albanus* and thirty kilometers from Rome, may have been the nearest—and, as we shall soon see, no polity to which Roman magistrates dispatched agents, *praefecti iure dicundo*, was any closer.

The Roman elite's sense of security within this inner space soon became manifest. Beginning around 300, prominent families began to construct monumental tombs outside Rome's wall and along the roads that radiated from its gates. Around that time, Roman officials began to build aqueducts to supply the city's growing population, and these structures stretched well beyond Rome's walls. Ap. Claudius Caecus, as censor in 312, supervised the construction of the *aqua Appia*, which brought water to the city from an unknown spring located near the seventh and eighth milestones of the *via Praenestina*. Using spoils from the war with Pyrrhus, the censors of

272 constructed the *aqua Ania vetus* which drew water from a source above Praeneste. Much later, the senate instructed an urban praetor to repair the two aqueducts, and in the process he also arranged the construction between 144 and 140 of the *aqua Marcia*, which took its water from a source to the east of Rome at the thirty-eighth milestone of a minor road.

The importance of this central space emerges with still greater clarity if one examines the tribes that organized the duties of citizens, which may have assumed greater prominence during the fourth century.[34] Roman authors attributed their origin to Servius Tullius, but their number increased with Roman expansion until it reached thirty-five in circa 244—four within the city of Rome and thirty-one outside it. Later, new citizen settlements as well as polities raised from partial to full citizenship would be added, often as outliers, to existing tribes. In scattered notices in annalistic passages throughout the first decade of his history, Livy set out the steady expansion of the number of rural tribes. While opinion varies on the reliability of his claims about the earliest one, scholars largely have accepted his notices about the new tribes of the fourth and early third centuries, if only because they track reasonably well the course of Roman expansion.[35] Although the locations of some are uncertain, twenty-one of the twenty-three rural tribes reportedly in existence in 338 were located within this central zone.

Before proceeding, however, one matter should be clarified. For Theodor Mommsen, tribes possessed territories formed from the aggregate properties of their members.[36] Plinio Fraccaro, however, has demonstrated that the Romans viewed tribes as groups or clusters of citizens.[37] In the words of Lily Ross Taylor: "It is for *cives*, not land, that new tribes were organized, and it is to peoples, not places, that a tribe was assigned."[38] Livy, after all, claims that the Tusculani (not the city of Tusculum) were enrolled in a tribe in 381 and that the Formiani, Fundani, and Arpinates (not the towns of Formiae, Fundi, and Arpinum) were enrolled in tribes when made full citizens in 188.[39] That said, the first seventeen rural tribes, supposedly in place early in the fifth century and forming two, or in some directions three, concentric rings around Rome, may have been compact and their "territories" clearly identifiable. Livy (26.9) once describes Hannibal as leading his army "into Pupinia" where he encamped eight miles from Rome.

In the century following the end of the Latin War, the Romans established eight new tribes still farther afield, although it is often unclear whether they were to accommodate old citizens newly settled in some place or members of recently absorbed polities given citizenship or some combination of the two. In any case, they did not change the basic pattern of a homogeneous core surrounded by a broader zone in which polities of different statuses intermingled. The formation of the Maecia and the Scaptia in 332 partially filled the space between the Pomptina and the Poblilia and the core area of citizen settlement; the former appears to have received its name from a Volscian camp near Lanuvium, while the latter was named after a derelict *urbs Scaptia*.⁴⁰ The Oufentina and Falerna in 318 and the Terentina in 299 expanded the area in which scattered citizen polities might be found to the Volturnus River, the northern boundary of Campania, while the Aniensis, also formed in 299, was in the upper reaches of the valley of the Anio, beyond allied Tibur and perhaps near the Latin colonies of Alba Fucens and Carseoli founded just a few years before. The last two tribes, established circa 244, did not change this picture to a significant degree. The Quirina included citizens installed around Reate and the *lacus Velinus*, approximately eighty kilometers from Rome, but the core of the Velina is less certain: it probably encompassed individuals residing considerably farther to the east in territory taken from the Praetutti, possibly near the Latin colony of Hadria, thus creating another outlier.

In the third century, then, Roman citizens possessing full rights occupied a broad region stretching from north to south from southern Etruria to the northern limits of Campania and from west to east from the sea into the foothills of the Apennines. Within this space, citizen settlement was densest in a zone of about thirty to fifty kilometers around the city, and as the distance from the center grew, these settlements became more widely scattered and interspersed with polities that possessed a different legal status. If the settlement of 338 produced a kind of core around Rome, later expansion created an outer zone in western central Italy from southern Etruria to Campania, which would also long persist. Within the limits of our knowledge—the number of polities that made the transition from partial to full citizenship before the first century is unknown—the only communities known with any certainty to have been raised to full citizenship—Cures Sabini, forty-two kilometers from Rome, along with Arpinum, Fundi, and Formiae at greater distances—lie on its margins.⁴¹ Down to the outbreak of the war with Hannibal, almost all the citizen colonies—Sena Gallica is the sole exception—guarded vulnerable positions along its coast, while the first colonies founded after the war extended farther south, cutting off the Campani from the sea. In the aftermath of the Second Punic War, the first time the matter becomes visible to any degree, the bulk of known senatorial estates lies between southernmost Etruria and Campania, with a few outliers at a greater distance.⁴² After Rome and its environs, this broad space would have been the part of Rome's empire with which the ruling elite was most familiar—and most concerned.

In the third quarter of the third century, the ruling elite imposed on Rome's tribes an overarching organization, which may have been based on the city's radial roads. The thirty-five tribes in existence from circa 244 possessed a clear official order, distinct from the sequence in which they actually voted or came forward for conscription, which was determined by lot.[43] The four urban tribes came first, followed by the rural. Lily Ross Taylor has shown that the Romilia, immediately south of Rome and adjacent to the Tiber, was the first of the rural tribes, while the Arnensis to its northwest, was the last, an arrangement that suggests a counterclockwise enumeration from the perspective of an observer in the city of Rome who was facing to the south.[44] Although the numbers and approximate locations of some tribes remain unknown, scattered passages reveal the relative positions of other tribes in the tribal order, which again appear to have been set out in a counterclockwise fashion. Michael Crawford recently examined *tesserae* identifying some of the tribes along with their numbers that confirm the picture.[45] At the same time, nearer tribes in the same direction from Rome came before farther ones: thus, the Clustimina, the Quirina, and the Velina, all at increasing distances to Rome's northeast, were successively numbered the twenty-eighth, the twenty-ninth, and the thirtieth. As we shall see in later chapters, representing spaces or groups of people in terms of sequences out from a center was a common Roman practice.

Crawford also suggests, with considerable plausibility, that the rural tribes were grouped by road and numbered successively along each route. Thus, the *Romilia*, *Voltinia*, and *Voturia* were along the *via Ostiensis*, the *Aemilia*, *Horatia*, *Maecia*, *Scaptia*, *Pomptina*, and *Falerna* along the *via Appia*, and so forth following in succession the *via Latina*, the *via Praenestina*, the *via Valeria*, the *via Salaria*, and the *via Flaminia* until one reaches the *Galeria*, *Sabatina*, and *Arnensis* along the *via Clodia*, running to Rome's northwest. This tribal order, it must be stressed, encompassed all the tribes in existence from the 240s and thus must follow the creation of the last two tribes. Michael Crawford proposes that these arrangements, clearly part of a deliberate scheme, should be placed in 225, the year in which Rome, in the face of an impending Gallic invasion, required Latins and allies to report on their manpower available for military service, a suggestion that is possible but uncertain.

Still, the practice of using directions from the city, probably expressed in terms of Rome's radial roads, to orient tribes and outlying or additional clusters is older than circa 225 and persisted afterward. As old citizens were settled in new areas and as existing polities, or some of their inhabitants,

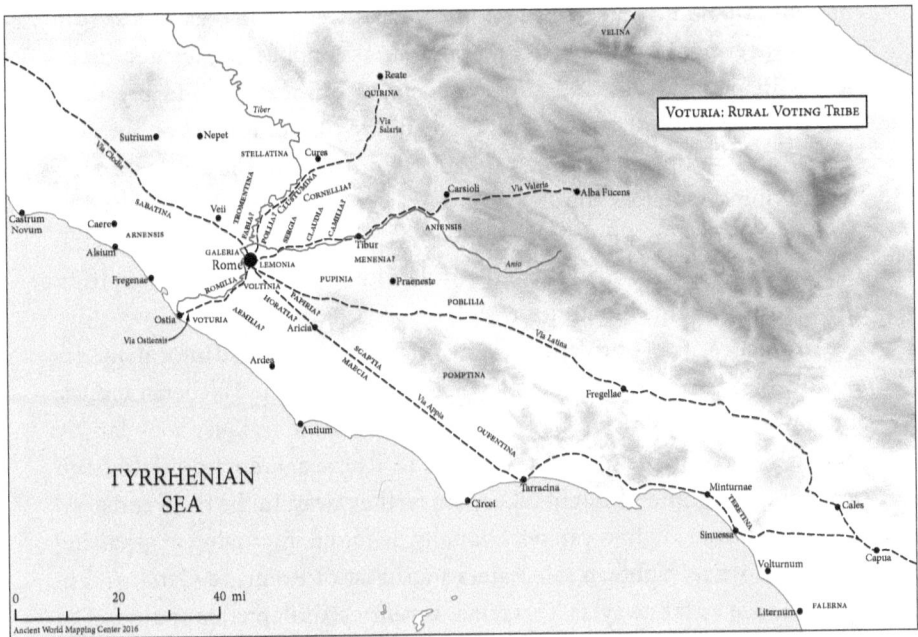

The distribution of the Roman tribes after circa 244

were granted full citizenship, new clusters were added to existing tribes. The inhabitants of Cures Sabini, who were raised to full citizenship in 268, were placed in the Sergia, the core of which was much closer to Rome and, like Cures, along or in close proximity to the *via Salaria*.[46] The settlers in the viritane assignments of 232 in Picenum and the *ager Gallicus*, after the addition of new tribes in circa 244 but before Crawford's proposed date for the arrangement, were placed in the Velina and the Pollia; all lay along or could be reached by the same route.[47] When the inhabitants of Arpinum, Fundi, and Formiae were granted full citizenship in 188, the Arpinates were assigned to the Cornelia and the others to the Aemilia, but the locations of these tribes are unknown. Crawford suggests that Arpinum may have been placed in the Cornelia because it marked in some fashion the beginning of the *via Valeria*, which led up the Anio Valley, and that Fundi and Formiae may have been granted to the Aemilia because it marked the start of the *via Appia*.[48]

ROME AND ITS OFFICIALS

The presence of Roman officials did not weigh equally on all parts of Italy. Rome's public life was most intense in or near the center. Here, magistrates

Rome and Its Italy

entered office (and sometimes laid it down) in formal ceremonies, conducted meetings of the senate and popular assemblies, prosecuted malefactors in public trials and supervised private litigation, and presided, with the assistance of priests, over many of the rites of Rome's public cult. Magistrates and priests also made annual journeys to the Alban Mount, twenty-one kilometers southeast of Rome, for the Latin Festival and to shrines at Lavinium, fifty-three kilometers south of Rome as well. Officials and priests also performed the bulk of the rites intended to expiate prodigies within the same broad space.

In practice, if not by rule, offices and functions established informal zones in and around the city. Tribunes of the plebs, the curule and plebeian aediles, and those quaestors given the task of supervising the treasury were largely limited as a consequence of their duties to Rome and environs, although occasional assignments might take them farther away. In the third and early second centuries, aediles can occasionally be found improving or repairing roads to Bovilae, eighteen kilometers southeast of Rome, to Ostia, and in one instance as far away as Tarracina, seventy-six kilometers southeast of the city.[49] Occasionally minor officials were dispatched farther from Rome. In 168 and 167, the senate dispatched quaestors to Capua or Brundisium to escort a favored ruler to Rome or to prevent one in disfavor from landing.[50]

The higher magistracies present a more complex picture. In the years between 218 and 167, when we can see their activities most clearly, consuls and praetors might receive *provinciae* that kept them in or near Rome, or they might be granted assignments that linked them to operations in some part of Italy or in the broader Mediterranean world, travelling to and from the focus of their activities. Most consular tasks that did not involve the command of armies took place in or very near Rome.[51] Here, one might encounter them supervising the expiation of prodigies; dedicating temples, altars, or shrines; presiding over meetings of the senate and public assemblies; granting audiences to foreign ambassadors and envoys of subordinate polities and corresponding with their governments; and issuing edicts what would be disseminated in the city and away.[52]

Urban praetors were supreme in Rome during the consuls' absences. They had a prominent role in public cult, supervised the courts that resolved disputes between private citizens, presided over assemblies and meetings of the senate, received foreign embassies and introduced them to the senate, transmitted to Italian towns or foreign states relevant decrees of the senate, and served as an intermediary between messengers dispatched by Roman commanders and the senate. As Roman power spread far beyond Italy, the activities of urban praetors came to be more restricted, formally or informally, to Rome and its environs.[53] The last known task that an urban praetor managed at any great distance from Rome involved the praetor of 165 going to Campania to buy private land that projected into public property.[54] The duties of peregrine praetors, who also possessed functions in Rome, are more obscure.

Consuls and praetors were widely dispersed away from Rome. In the first decades of the second century, some praetors received *provinciae* in peninsular Italy, a practice that appears to have ended early in the 170s. Occasionally, consuls departed from the city to carry out certain tasks in peninsular Italy that were not directly linked to the command of armies. In the third and second centuries, one finds widely scattered occasions in which they conducted a judicial inquiry aimed at suppressing the Bacchanalian conspiracy in 186, separated public and private land in Campania in 173, and on three occasions over a century and a half drained marshes to prepare the land for cultivation. At any great distance from the city, then, the presence of higher magistrates was intermittent. In the same period, colonial triumvirs and agrarian decemvirs installed settlers in peninsular Italy and the Po Valley, places that were distant from Rome but not as distant as some of the regions in which consuls or praetors acted. The triumvirate that founded the Gracchan colony at Carthage in 122 was the first to operate outside of Italy. In these colonial commissions, former consuls and praetors predominated, perhaps a sign that operations at any distance from Rome were best left in the hands of senior figures.[55] Beyond Italy, only consuls, praetors, and those acting as if consuls or praetors operated with any frequency.

The institution of the *praefecti iure dicundo* complicates the matter. These prefects came in two broad forms, each dispatched to towns, not polities. At some uncertain point, probably in the aftermath of the rebellion of the Campani in the Second Punic War, Roman assemblies began to elect four junior magistrates, the *praefecti Capuam Cumas*, who left Rome to exercise jurisdiction in ten towns: Capua, Cumae, Casilinum, Volturnum, Liternum, Puteoli, Acerrae, Suessula, Atella, and Calatia.[56] As a consequence of their rebellion, at least three and possibly as many as six—Capua, Casilinum, Acerrae, Suessula, Atella, and Calatia—lost their magistracies, senates, and assemblies. Before the outbreak of the war, three more—Volturnum, Liternum, and Puteoli—were small coastal communities dependent in some fashion on Capua. Cumae, the tenth town, remained loyal throughout the war. These four prefects may have been the only annual magistrates formally tied to specific places in Italy at a significant distance from the center.

The second form is probably older and still more obscure.[57] Festus (p. 262 L), the chief source, claims that the urban praetors had sent agents, *praefecti*, to twelve named towns along with "many more." Eight—Fundi, Formiae, Venafrum. Allifae, Privernum, Anagnia, Frusino, and Arpinum—lie to the southeast of Rome in regions that had come under its control by the end of the fourth century. None lie south of the Volturnus River, which marked the northern limits of the Campani. Two—Caere and Saturnia—are in southern Etruria and probably came into Rome's power in the early third century. Reate probably received citizenship without the vote early in the third century, and Nursia may well have done so at about the same time. Scattered inscriptions and literary references allow the identification of other *praefecturae* elsewhere in Sabinum and in Picenum, the last region to be granted *civitas sine suffragio*.[58]

The late fourth and early third centuries, then, serve as a terminus post quem for the formation of these prefectures, like grants of *civitas sine suffragio*, which almost certainly overlapped in space and in time, although the connection between the two remains unclear. As far as can be told, the seats of prefects were also the urban centers of communities of citizens without the vote, but some were near places occupied by citizens with full rights. The *ager Caletranus*, where Saturnia was located, may have come into Roman hands early in the third century, but until the establishment of a citizen colony there in 183, little can be said about its inhabitants. As a result, scholars differ about whether the prefects exercised their jurisdiction over full citizens, partial citizens, or both. The concentration of known prefectures in central Italy and the use of a different practice in Campania may indicate that urban praetors no longer sent *praefecti* to new places by the last decades of the third century, although this is controversial.[59]

What were prefects for? Scholars often assume that *praefecti iure dicundo* resolved in some fashion private disputes among citizens who lived in and around the towns in which they operated, largely because the urban praetors who appointed them performed, or came to perform, a similar function in Rome. Citizen polities, however, long continued to use their own laws, and the inhabitants of some did not speak Latin, making difficult the imposition of Roman legal practices: Cumae, for example, did not use Latin, and thus Roman legal *formulae*, in contracts and auctions until the senate gave it permission to do so in 180, while Arpinum did not follow Roman norms for inheritances in the second century.[60] In the late fourth and early third centuries, the seats of prefects and communities of *cives sine suffragio* marked the more distant parts of the Roman order at a time when Roman leadership over these regions was recent, untested, and still contested. Livy (9.20.5) reports that a Roman praetor sent prefects to Capua in 318 because of civil strife. Against this background, their spatial distribution warrants more attention. Over time, the seats of prefects came to cover with a "set of supervisory centers" the territory inhabited by Roman citizens, except for the regions closest to the city, for no known prefecture is less than fifty kilometers from Rome.[61]

In this way, then, one can detect certain informal and poorly defined zones around the city, constructed at least in part by the functions associated with various posts and distorted by the need for officials and their subordinates to travel to and from distant assignments: the city and its immediate vicinity, where Roman functionaries were present most intensively; a broader space in which Roman prefects were dispatched to towns; another in which major magistrates along with colonial and agrarian commissioners were occasionally present; and the most distant, the site of active campaigning. Away from Rome and its immediate vicinity, moreover, Italy was the most intensely governed part of Rome's expanding sphere of operations. In addition to the occasional presence of high officials, magistrates in Rome dispersed edicts and decrees and summoned citizens, Latins, and allies to the *dilectus*. The censors placed contracts to build or repair structures in Rome, but one of the censors of 179 also arranged for a project at the citizen colony of Tarracina, while the censors of 174 built bridges in "many places" (*multis locis*), contracted for the building of walls at Calatia and Auximum, and leased land around each town, using the proceeds to build a *forum* in each, temples at Pisaurum and Fundi, an aqueduct at Potentia, paved streets at Pisaurum, and suburbs at Sinuessa.[62] In the middle of the century, Polybius (6.12–3; 17) would claim that the censors placed their contracts throughout Italy, although they probably did not do so in Latin or allied polities.

PRODIGIES AND THEIR EXPIATION

Prodigies bulk large among reports of significant events that helped the ruling elite assess Rome's situation; they often took place at some distance from Rome, and they required some response in rituals of expiation.[63] Historians and antiquarians report prodigies from every period of republican history, although the historicity of some may be doubted. Our evidence is fullest for the years between 218 and 167 when reports of prodigies and their expiation formed a prominent part of the annalistic structure of Livy's history. Much later, Julius Obsequens, who may have lived in the fourth century A.D., assembled a collection of prodigies, the *liber de prodigiis*, primarily from Livy's history, giving us some idea of the contents of the lost books.[64]

From the late third century, one can detect a regular process for identifying prodigies, ascertaining their significance, and determining the means of averting the consequences of divine anger. First, the sign was reported to a magistrate, usually a consul or praetor, who then notified the senate, which either accepted or rejected the report as of public significance. If senators accepted the sign, they then decided which experts to consult: pontiffs, *decemviri sacris faciundis*, or Etruscan *haruspices*. Magistrates in command of armies, however, sometimes accepted prodigies and went on to expiate them, although other commanders did report prodigies to Rome.[65] We are much more poorly informed about expiations in the camps, either because they were less frequent than those in the city or because they were not as consistently reported at Rome or perhaps even known there.

Prodigies were highly varied. The persistent failure to secure favorable auspices or to find clear signs in the entrails of sacrificial animals that the god had accepted the sacrifice might indicate some underlying rupture in the relationship between Rome and its gods. Other signs were more dramatic: earthquakes, monstrous births, unusual behavior of animals, eclipses, meteors, comets, or odd meteorological events; they might include human actions, such as the discovery of otherwise unknown books of prophecy, theft from temples, defeats of Roman armies, the detection of conspiracies, or crimes. Some signs are especially prominent, perhaps because their links with specific deities seemed more certain or because the rites of expiation were viewed as more efficacious. Here, one can detect a persistent concern over signs that involved Roman magistrates and the walls, gates, temples, and major public spaces of Rome, other cities, and even army encampments. In the second half of the second century, the annalist L. Calpurnius Piso (*FRHist* 9 F 40 = Plin. *HN* 17.244) records incidents in which trees growing in shrines or on statues were seen as prodigies in his own day.

The acceptance of a prodigy necessarily led to decisions about the rite needed to expiate it. Most performances were at Rome without apparent regard for where they had been observed. In other words, the senate, magistrates, and priests in some fashion mapped the broad world of signs, detected in reports of widely dispersed phenomena, onto the spaces of their city. Our sources report expiations in the form of offerings at temples, shrines, or public places; banquets (*lectisternia*) shared with one or more gods at their couches; public prayers or *supplicationes*, often for several days and at the temples of several gods; the ritual purification of Rome itself; and a performance known as a "nine-day rite" (*novemdiale sacrum*). Some marked permanent changes to the fabric of the city and its public life by promising new temples or festivals.

On occasion, magistrates and priests performed rites of expiation a short distance away from Rome. In the late third and early second centuries, one can find prayers to Fortuna on Mount Algidus, about twenty kilometers to the southeast of Rome, as well as sacrifices to Juno at Lanuvium, in the forum of Ardea, a Latin city not a Roman one, and in the grove of Feronia in the *ager Capenas*;[66] none of the prodigies that led to these rites took place at Mount Algidus, Lanuvium, Ardea, or the *lucus Feroniae*. One time, the senate instructed that a sign at Crustuminum, not far from Rome, be expiated at the exact spot.[67] Later, seemingly atypical performances represent some specific circumstance. In 143, after a defeat by the Salassi, the decemvirs determined by reading the Sibylline Books that they were to sacrifice within enemy territory whenever the Romans were about to begin a war with Gauls.[68] In the aftermath of the death of Ti. Gracchus in 133, the *decemviri sacris faciundis* performed rites at a temple of Ceres in Henna on Sicily, probably to avoid turmoil in Rome.[69]

In these actions, magistrates and priests performed the necessary rites, but on some occasions they also broadcast through edicts instructions for others to participate. Some intended participants in or near Rome were to join rites in the city.[70] On other occasions, magistrates and priests dispersed edicts ordering people away from the city to conduct their own rites as well. In 188 the decemvirs ordered prayers at all rural crossroads (*in omnibus compitis*); seven years later, a senatorial decree followed by a consular edict instructed that there should be supplications and festivals for three days "through all of Italy" (*per totam Italiam*).[71] In 180 the decemvirs proclaimed two days of prayer to Salus not only in the city but also in all the *fora* and *conciliabula*, with all above the age of twelve instructed to wear garlands.[72] Because of the uncertainty in Livy's terminology, it is often unclear just how widely dispersed these performances were intended to be (see chapter 6).

Roman practice was not static. In the aftermath of the battle of Cannae in 216, the senate rarely turned to the *decemviri* for almost a quarter of a century, perhaps because of the failure of their recommendations to secure victory.[73] The senate first accepted a human hermaphrodite as a dire prodigy in 209, but when another was detected two years later at Frusino, a town about seventy-five kilometers from Rome on the *via Latina*, the response was more elaborate.[74] The *haruspices* recommended that the child be thrown into the sea, while the pontiffs proposed a complicated ceremony, involving three choruses, each of nine young girls, who were to process through the city while singing a hymn that the poet Livius Andronicus would compose for the occasion. While the choruses were practicing, lightning struck the temple of Juno Regina on the Aventine, and the rites expiating the two prodigies became intertwined. On the day of the performance, a procession that included the decemvirs, the choruses, and two wooden statues of Juno Regina entered Rome and proceeded to the forum, where the girls sang and danced. Next, they went to the *Forum Boarium* and finally to the temple of Juno Regina. This sign would be acknowledged as prodigious for over a century and expiated with much the same rite.[75] Much later, Pliny (*HN* 7.34) would note that such births were once see as prodigies but later were viewed as amusements.

As we shall soon see, magistrates and the senate accepted prodigies from a large number of places, some of which were occupied by Latins or allies. In this way, then, they centralized at Rome a crucial aspect of decision making about the state of the larger polity's relationship with the gods. Decemvirs, pontiffs, and *haruspices*, moreover, used the public spaces and cult places of the city, and occasionally others in its environs as well, to serve as the setting for rites intended to assuage divine anger, even when that anger had been made manifest in signs that were detected at some distance from Rome. In the same period and later, the ruling elite also explicitly and formally concentrated judgment in the city—and even in certain places within it—about a range of matters that had taken place at some distance (see chapter 6). In any case, the rites used to expiate prodigies are yet another indication of the close connection between the polity and the city of Rome and its structures and spaces.

In the late third and early second centuries, the senate is known to have accepted signs from over one hundred towns and their hinterlands, some occupied by citizens, with or without the vote, and others by Latins or allies. Scholars have sometimes argued that the senate accepted prodigies only from towns and territories occupied by citizens or from tracts of Roman public land.[76] The senate certainly accepted more signs from towns or territories occupied by citizens—more than 80 percent of the reports come from them—but it did not limit itself to reports that only pertained to such places for one-sixth of all prodigies came from places that were not settlements of citizens and did not clearly occur on tracts of Roman public land.[77] The senate may well have used a number of criteria in judging whether a portent was of public significance.

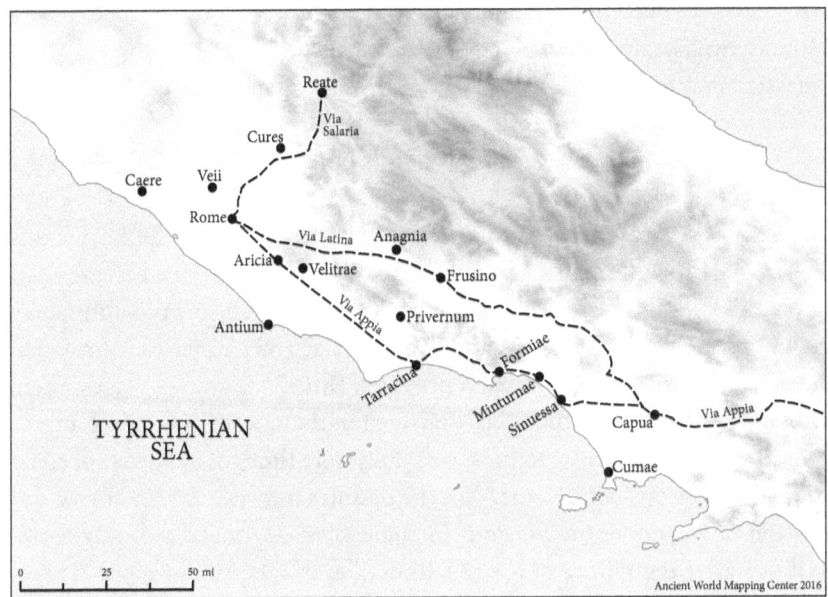

Towns with multiple prodigies, 218–167

Prodigies were not distributed evenly over Rome's sphere of operations or even over the territory occupied by its citizens. In the late third and early second centuries, almost 85 percent of all reported prodigies took place in Rome, Latium, southern Etruria, northern Campania, and the land of the Sabines, especially in a region about fifty kilometers wide that stretched from Caere and Tarquinii in the north to Capua in the south, just the region that contained the bulk of its citizens. For Veit Rosenberger, Roman practice constituted a space formed by the geographic barriers of the sea to the west and the Apennines to the east that included all the towns that had come into Rome's possession by the opening of the third century and represented the portion of Italy that was most firmly tied to it.[78] This space, moreover, was articulated by the great public roads that the Romans had begun to build from the last decades of the fourth century, for most prodigies away from Rome took place in or around towns on or very near to them.

On closer examination, however, additional distinctions can be made, for the senate did not acknowledge prodigies evenly over this space. Slightly less than a quarter of all the known events occurred in Rome or just outside its walls, and another fifth within one or two days' travel of the city, a zone that encompassed locations such as Lanuvium and its temple of Juno Sospita, the *mons Albanus* and the *lacus Albanus*, all sites with multiple prodigies.

Rome and Its Italy

More than 40 percent of all reports, in other words, pertain to places where Roman magistrates and priests were frequently present, and the events in question may have been reported by or through them directly.[79] Places in or near the city were better represented than those at greater distances.

Certain towns in western central Italy bulk large in our lists, perhaps a sign that they were better integrated into the Roman order or were deemed more important. Capua produced nine reports, and it may have been responsible for the reports from "Campania."[80] Anagnia and Reate each provided six.[81] Caere, Frusino, Sinuessa, Tarracina, Veii, and possibly Cures Sabini each produced five.[82] Aricia, Amiternum, and Cumae each provided four, while five more towns each provided three.[83] Eighteen places, then, provided five-sixths of the total. Fourteen of them were colonies, Latin as well as citizen, and these polities, we know, were thought to have especially close connections with Rome.[84] In the decades between 218 and 167, six of the ten towns under the *praefecti Capuam Cumas* witnessed prodigies, all but one after the failure of the rebellion. Ten of the places to which praetors dispatched prefects also produced prodigies, sometimes in number: Anagnia and Reate each provided six, Caere and Frusino each produced five. Some scholars have suggested that local officials reported prodigies to magistrates and the senate, a sign of their integration into the larger order, but many reports concerning events away from Rome may have been forwarded by Roman functionaries instead.

For the most-distant locations, Livy is our chief source. He often identifies the locations of these prodigies more broadly than the nearer ones—Apulia, Bruttium, Gaul, Lucania, Picenum, Sabinum or "among the Sabines," Sardinia, Sicily, and "among the Marrucini"—which invites the suspicion that more-precise locations meant less here than they did for the nearer events. (Note, however, that Sabinum or "among the Sabines" may sometimes refer to Cures Sabini, less than forty kilometers from Rome.)[85] During the Second Punic War, the senate accepted signs from Apulia, Arpi (its chief city), Gaul, the Latin colony of Hadria, Mantua, Sardinia, and Sicily. In the third of a century following the end of the Second Punic War, one finds signs from Ariminum, Arretium, Auximum, Bruttium, Lucania, Macedonia, Syracuse, and the *ager Gallicus*.

A concern for commanders, armies, the contexts in which they operated, and the actions of enemies may lie behind the acceptance of reports from more-distant areas and explain how they came to be reported. Here, any conclusions are necessarily tentative, since Livy usually reported prodigies without placing them chronologically in relationship with other events of the year. The signs from Gaul, Sardinia, and Sicily during the Second Punic War directly affected camps and armies.[86] (Prodigies much closer to Rome occasionally involved camps as well.)[87] In 199, within a few years of the war's conclusion, a commander reported a prodigy from Bruttium, while a proconsul reported a sign from Macedonia that involved his fleet.[88]

For other places, the connections are more tentative. In 217 the senate accepted the only known prodigy from Arpi, the chief town of Apulia, in the same year that Hannibal attacked it.[89] (Closer to Rome, the only appearance of Eretum took place in the year in which Hannibal passed through the place during one of his marches on Rome.)[90] The signs at Mantua, Apulia, Hadria, and Sicily in 214 all occurred in the midst of intense military activity.[91] In the third of a century following the end of the Second Punic War, one finds signs from Ariminum, Arretium, Auximum, Bruttium, Lucania, Macedonia, Syracuse, and the *ager Gallicus*.[92] We have seen how the reports from Bruttium and Macedonia came through Roman commanders on the scene. Ariminum and Arretium were staging areas for the wars in the northern Italy, which were a regular feature of these years. Sicily, and thus Syracuse, saw the regular presence of Roman magistrates. In 173, when a prodigy was detected in the fields in the *ager Gallicus*, a college of Roman decemvirs was involved in making assignments of land there.

Magistrates and the senate, then, took decreasing note of prodigies as distance increased, which may reflect the limits of their knowledge or indicate that signs closer to the center were thought to be more significant. Away from the city, but still within western central Italy, they focused on only a few polities, while at still greater distances, their attention was directed toward problematic regions in which magistrates were acting, much as they did when defining military commands. The paucity of reports from outside Italy may indicate that prodigies there were usually expiated in the camps (see chapter 5). In any case, signs of divine anger that were observed outside of Italy were usually not matters of concern to the senate in Rome.

CENSUS AND *DILECTUS*

In the last decades of the third century, and long before and after as well, the census and the *dilectus* were the chief means by which Rome's far-flung citizenry was incorporated into the structures of the Roman political order. In the present context, choosing between two contrasting models is important. In one, citizens came to Rome to be counted in the census and conscripted in the *dilectus*; in the other, local officials counted citizens and conscripted soldiers, forwarding their counts to Rome and dispatching conscripts to places of assembly. Each produces a markedly different picture of the spatial organization of Roman power. In the first, the Roman elite's emphasis remained focused on Rome and on operations under their direct supervision; in the second, they integrated at least some local governments into operations crucial to their city's power, which implies the possession of some knowledge of them and concern for their administrative structures and modes of operation.

When we can view the census with some clarity, the two censors put together a list of the senate and distributed citizens over thirty-five tribes according to their domiciles and over almost two hundred centuries (*centuriae*) on the basis of wealth. At first, and for long, the censorship was held primarily by men who had not yet reached the office of consul, but from the late fourth century more prominent men began to serve.[93] The increasing prominence of the censors was probably connected to a shift that placed at its center the formation of the ruling elite. The *lex Ovinia* gave to the censors the task of constructing a list of senators, an essential stage in the emancipation of the senate from the consuls' power and the beginning of its rise to a central position in the Roman state. The censors also constituted the equestrian order (*ordo equester*). Ideally, military service on horseback formed its functional core, for those whom the censors enrolled were to possess the public horse (*equites equo publico*), which meant that they received at public expense the horses that they were to ride in battle.[94]

At the center of the censors' task, however, was the assignment of the male citizenry to a range of subunits, each encompassed within a series of lists. On the basis of wealth, the censors distributed them over *centuriae* arranged in six broad classes.[95] Here, the primary distinction was between the relatively few centuries of cavalry (*equites*) and the much larger number of centuries of infantry (*pedites*), in which some were identified as *iuniores*, who served in the legions, and *seniores*, who usually did not. The centuries coexisted with an organization by tribes that may have assumed greater prominence in the fourth century as Roman citizens became more dispersed.[96] By the end of the third century, and probably earlier as well, Roman magistrates chose citizens for military service in the legions by tribe, which also provided the framework for the collection of tribute, now necessary in an increasingly monetized political order.

The division of the same citizens into parallel organizations of tribes and centuries was fundamental to Roman views of their polity. The centuriate organization resembled an army, and armies occasionally resembled the larger polity. In it, citizens were distributed over centuries of *equites* and *pedites* and its essential units shared a name with the primary subunits of the legions. Indeed, in the laws that he proposed for his ideal Rome, Cicero (*Leg.* 3.7) instructed his censors to summon the infantry and the cavalry to the census. Voting assemblies organized by centuries were clearly distinguished from gatherings arranged by tribes. The *comitia centuriata* formed a body that might be likened to an urban army (*exercitus urbana*), and, like armies, it could not meet within Rome's augural boundary, the *pomerium*. Among its central functions was the election of consuls and praetors, magistrates who could, and usually did, command armies. The dual structure of centuries and tribes, then, represents a clear tendency to view the citizenry in certain circumstances as if an army in contrast to other occasions in which war was more distant, a dichotomy that was certainly old.[97]

This dual system of centuries and tribes was very much focused on Rome. While conducting a census, the censors supervised several grand ritual performances, which played a role in integrating Rome's citizenry into the life of the city.[98] In the *recognitio equitum*, the censors took up their position in the forum, where those who possessed the public horse appeared before them with their horses and the honors that they had won in battle in order to receive a judgment on their suitability to continue. (The selection of the senate, which involved a similar judgment about candidates' characters, took place in private, although the list recording the final result was read in public.) The second great ceremony marked the census's formal conclusion. The *lustrum* was a ritual of purification that censors employed while constituting the newly reformed citizenry of Rome, that commanders used while organizing or reorganizing their armies, and that colonial triumvirs deployed when ordering the prospective citizens of a new colony (see chapter 5).

The subgroups of the census had a continuing existence in the life of the city, the only place where they ever assembled as formal entities. The senate, of course, met only in Rome or just outside its walls, although individual senators might be widely dispersed on public or private business. For some uncertain period after the end of the fourth century, the *equites* processed on the ides of July from the temple of Mars at the first milestone of the *via Appia* to the temple of Castor in the forum, the *transvectio equitum*.[99] Over time, senators and *equites* took on other honors. From 194 senators had separate seating in theatrical performances, clearly differentiating them from the mass of citizens, and from 149 they began to serve on juries set up to try former magistrates for offenses while on public service.[100] At some point, senators and *equites* acquired the privilege to wear costumes and other emblems of rank that clearly displayed their status. Centuries and tribes, moreover, were regularly recalled to existence in the voting assemblies that elected officials, enacted laws, and issued verdicts in certain criminal cases, conferring legitimacy even though a minority of citizens may actually have attended.[101]

Viewed from another perspective, the central operation of the census was the construction of a series of lists, some now more obscure than others. The selection of senators and *equites*, of course, resulted in lists that set out the senate's membership and distributed the *equites* over their centuries. At some point, the censors began to establish lists of widows and orphans for the payment of tribute. The *tabulae Caeritum*, named after Caere, a town of citizens without the vote, contained the names of citizens whom the censors had deprived of the right to vote.[102] The centuries and tribes too took form in lists of their members. In the third and second centuries, and no doubt earlier as well, the censors concluded the census by reporting a global number of adult male citizens, sometimes qualified by the phrase "who were able to bear arms."

The actual formation of these lists of tribes and centuries was an involved process, in which the censors relied on declarations made by heads of families about their places of residence, their dependents, and their property in order to assign individuals to centuries on the basis of wealth and to tribes according to residence. From at least as early as the beginning of the second century, the censors were assisted by *iuratores* who administered oaths, and probably no later than the second century they were also attended by tribal *curatores*, whose duties are unknown.[103]

Identifying where citizens made their declarations has proved contentious. The census was long associated with the *campus Martius*, just outside Rome's walls. In its earliest years, citizens undoubtedly came to Rome to be counted. Much later, the process was less centralized. The *tabula Heracleensis*, compiled in the middle of the first century, instructs those who held the highest offices in colonies, *municipia*, and *praefecturae* while a census was underway in Rome to receive the declarations of resident citizens.[104] In a reference to the census of 86, conducted soon after a major expansion of the citizenry and in the midst of civil war in Italy, which would have made travel difficult, Cicero notes that the local senate of Larinum had not sent its lists to Rome because of fear of their corruption.[105] These instances provide the earliest clear evidence for records constructed and organized by town.

When and through what stages did this decentralization take place? Some suggest that the assignment of crucial functions to local magistrates developed against the background of the great expansion in the number of citizens after the Social War, which would have made earlier arrangements untenable.[106] Others view the practice as old, rooted in the age when Rome began its expansion in Italy, a position, it must be stressed, that rests on a certain view of Roman hegemony in Italy in which not only citizens but also the formal institutions of the communities in which they lived were integrated into the Roman state. Evidence for decentralization in the third and second centuries is scant at best. During the Second Punic War, Latin towns performed their own counts, and when the Roman senate sought to punish the ones that had failed to provide the required soldiers, it did so by requiring them to conduct their censuses according to Roman norms.[107] Allies too must have made their own counts, although all may not have done so or have been very thorough. The members of the many polities that would be included in the Roman citizenry after the Social War were indeed counted locally, if they were counted at all. In any case, they were long outside the competence of Rome's censors.

But what about Roman citizens? Our sources generally present the census as taking place at Rome, although in the form of anecdotes rather than any global description of the process. Only a few scattered passages, difficult to interpret, may present a different view. Thus, in 189 the Campani asked the senate where they should be counted, and the senate decreed that they should be listed at Rome.[108] The inquiry and the response probably indicate that the Campani had earlier been counted at Capua, but because of the abolition of local magistracies after the suppression of their revolt, they were now to be counted in Rome. Some scholars, however, take the incident to reveal a general principle: that the inhabitants of towns, or at least some towns, had always been counted locally. But the Campani were far from typical. Before their rebellion during the Second Punic War, they were citizens *sine suffragio* and probably not enrolled in tribes. At the same time, Campanian soldiers appear to have sometimes fought in their own formations, so it seems likely that they were conscripted and counted locally, if only occasionally. Livy's description of two events—an extraordinary levy during the Second Punic War and the dissemination of an edict of the censors of 169—are examined later, since the question of the local census is closely linked to the matter of a local levy.[109]

One mechanism may have come to reduce the need for many citizens to travel to Rome. Heads of families reported the numbers of their dependents, even adult sons. While censor in 142, Scipio Aemilianus complained that censors were instructed to include in the census some who had not actually attended, which may indicate that he thought it proper for all to be counted at Rome.[110] Instead, we are told, those who chose not to attend might have others present their names—a practice that was probably a recent innovation, clearly reduced the numbers of those who had to come to Rome, and implies that citizen were expected to make the journey before it was in place. Here, the declarations of persons residing away from the city may have been carried in groups to Rome by private arrangement. If their bearers carried the names of significant numbers of their fellow townsmen, there would be little need for a local census, thus bypassing, if only for a time, any formal requirement for actions by local officials, although they may have come to take up the task informally.

As significant as the census, the conscription of armies was central to Rome's projection of power and one of the most important responsibilities of Rome's chief magistrates. Enrolling these armies depended on the status of the soldiers who would make them up and, to a degree, of the communities from which they came. As we have seen, the *formula togatorum* aided in the calculation of the contributions of Rome's Latin and Italian allies. Scattered references indicate that allied contingents equaled and often exceeded the Roman contribution. The central act in the mustering of armies, however, was the conscription of citizens for service in the legions, an operation that, except in emergencies, also appears to have long centered on Rome.

Polybius (6.19–26) provides the only systematic overview of the process in those portions of his sixth book in which he describes Roman military arrangements—the organization of the legion, the process of its conscription, and the camps that armies would occupy—as part of his larger description of the Roman constitution. The form of legion that he describes, the so-called manipular legion, probably first appeared during the Samnite Wars of the late fourth century, although little can be said about it in detail until the Second Punic War.[111] In it, soldiers formed three separate battle lines—the *hastati, principes,* and *triarii*—the first two of which used the same equipment, while those in the third bore a variant. Each encompassed ten maniples, and each maniple had two centurions, so that a single legion had sixty centurions and their *centuriae*. Each legion, moreover, was accompanied by *velites* or skirmishers, who were not organized into maniples but instead were attached to the maniples of heavy infantry, along with three hundred cavalry. Polybius holds that a legion contained 4,200 men, although the total might be raised to 5,000.

To raise such a legion, Polybius has the consuls first proclaim the time and place where citizens of military age were to gather, an edict that must have been disseminated in some fashion to communities of citizens away from the center, much as other magistrates would have done with theirs. The twenty-four military tribunes, elected to serve with the four legions normally attached to each year's consuls, chose the soldiers. On the appointed day, while potential recruits gathered on the Capitol, the tribunes divided themselves into four groups, one for each legion, and cast lots to determine the order in which members of the thirty-five tribes would come forward. Then, they chose the soldiers, tribe following tribe, until they filled out each legion. Although Polybius is not clear on this point, each legion appears to have contained contingents from all the tribes, making it a microcosm of the city. Next, the tribunes set a time for each legion's soldiers to assemble again so that they might be assigned to the units in which they would actually serve. Finally, they dismissed the men, after ordering them to equip themselves properly and setting a time and a place for them to gather again. While this was going on, the consuls sent to allied cities in Italy informing them of the numbers of men they were to contribute and the day and place that they too were to assemble.

The few known mustering places are widely scattered over Italy. During the Second Punic War, when Hannibal and his army were operating within the peninsula, armies sometimes gathered at Rome, the nearby allied cities of Tibur and Praeneste, and Cales and Sinuessa, on the margins of Campania where they were to operate.[112] After the war, commanders set mustering points farther afield: armies intended to serve in the East sometimes gathered at Brundisium, the chief crossing point for the Balkans; soldiers who were to fight in the North assembled at Ariminum, Pisae, or Arretium; units that were to fight in Spain sometimes collected at the port of Luna for their departure from the peninsula.[113] Earlier practice is more obscure. Livy (10.33) holds that a consul of 294 instructed his army to assemble at the Latin colony of Sora in preparation for a campaign against the Samnites. When discussing the foundations of the colonies of Placentia and Cremona at the outbreak of the Hannibalic War, Polybius (3.40.3–10) claims that the founding commissioners ordered colonists to assemble "at the site," which may indicate that magistrates mustering armies too used more distant mustering places before the war had spread to Italy.

Polybius, it must be stressed, focused on a very specific set of circumstances. In his levy, the twenty-four military tribunes raised four legions, two of which would serve under each consul. Immediately after his description of the levy, he sets out the layout of the camps that consuls and their tribunes formed when first mustering their army and at the end of a day's march, in which he first describes camps that both consuls and their armies shared and then the adjustments that would be necessary if they campaigned separately. Such an arrangement of armies and commands was old, but when Polybius wrote, in the decade of the 150s, it was far from typical. From the middle of the fourth century, Rome possessed three annual magistrates—two consuls and a praetor—who could command armies, although the praetor and the urban legions usually remained in Rome except in emergencies. By the end of the century, each consul commanded an army of two legions, while the tribal assembly elected the twenty-four military tribunes who would be distributed over them. Armies, moreover, were usually annual, like their commanders—that is, new consuls raised them for the operations that they would conduct—and, while the consuls sometimes campaigned together, they often conducted operations separately.

By the last decades of the third century, arrangements had become more varied. The creation of an additional praetor in circa 244, of two more circa 227, and of another pair for 197 resulted in the formation of additional armies. In the atypical conditions of the Second Punic War, Rome maintained many legions and a large number of commands. After the war, military operations continued in widely scattered locations. In these circumstances, armies varied in size, and, while some armies and their legions were mobilized only for a year, others continued in existence for years, discharging veterans and receiving supplementary levies in their place. While new consuls sometimes raised four legions that they would command, levies of this kind became less frequent.

In these circumstances, Polybius's source of information becomes central. When he described Rome's military arrangements, he clearly relied on some text rather than on direct observation, for he notes at least one element that differed from practices that he had seen in his own day.[114] Some suggest that Polybius derived his account of the legions, the *dilectus* and of the layout of the camps from the *commentarii* of a military tribune or perhaps a handbook composed to assist just them.[115] *Commentarii*, it should be noted, were records of, or directions for, the performance of a single event.[116] If Polybius did, in fact, use such *commentarii*, he would have preserved a relatively unmediated account of an actual operation. The chief question would be when the event had taken place, necessarily in some year in which the two consuls had raised their four legions and then campaigned together, if only for a time. This year, moreover, must lie between 216, when military tribunes began administering the military oath, as Polybius claims that they did, and 180, the last year in which both consuls are known to have raised two armies, each of two legions, and then campaigned together.[117] If so, the *commentarii* that supposedly underlie Polybius's account would have recorded an event that was already atypical.

But there are good reasons to doubt whether Polybius did, in fact, follow a military tribune's *commentarii*. He regularly describes these tribunes in the plural, and he occasionally sets out arrangements with some abstraction.[118] A literary form that was usually employed to describe a single performance of a particular event would appear to be an unlikely source for an extended account that included the selection of soldiers, the formation of units, and the organization of camps. For these reasons, it is perhaps best to regard the underlying work as "antiquarian" or "technical," although there may have been no clear distinction between them.[119] At least one such work was available when Polybius wrote his sixth book, although little can be said about it or any possible competitors. The Elder Cato, we know, wrote a work on military affairs (*de re militari*). The very few extant fragments reveal that he treated in some fashion *velites, hastati, principes*, and *triarii*, the taking of the auspices, formations on the march and in battle, the guarding of camps, and methods for maintaining discipline, most of which Polybius examined as well.[120]

Viewing Polybius's source as antiquarian or technical has important consequences, since, while scholars may view the use of *commentarii* as sources more positively, Roman antiquarianism has a much different reputation. As we saw in chapter 1, scholars often view antiquarian practices as overly concerned with the distant past and subject to idealization and even to invention, but practitioners often were concerned with contemporary matters. In later periods, "technical" works sometimes mix together detailed instructions for utilitarian operations with accounts of origins and contrived etymologies and combine idealized depictions of a process with the acknowledgment of variations in practice, usually presented as deviations from the norm.[121]

Polybius's account of the raising of four legions by the new consuls, of the camps that they occupied while campaigning together, and of the means to secure camps and to discipline the soldiers within them may be seen as just such an ideal, one that had long been practiced more or less closely, although it had been recently obscured by variants. After all, it was firmly rooted in "constitutional" practice. As we have seen, from the late fourth century citizen assemblies had elected the twenty-four military tribunes who would serve with the four consular legions. Despite the great increase in the number and size of Rome's armies and despite the extended service of some legions for years, Roman assemblies continued to elect twenty-four military tribunes, but, to accommodate additional legions, commanders began to appoint the tribunes that would serve with them. In some fashion, then, the four consular legions and their twenty-four tribunes long persisted as a norm.

If Polybius's account is idealized, how closely did it fit the practice in his own day and in the relatively recent past? We occasionally encounter in narratives legions of six thousand infantry, although their historicity has been doubted.[122] At the same time, accounts of the wars in Spain sometimes reveal Roman soldiers arrayed in cohorts, which provided a firmer battle line and made easier the formation of detachments.[123] Cohorts and maniples, however, could coexist, for each cohort contained a maniple each of *hastati*, *principes*, and *triarii*;[124] Cato mentions both in the context of training his army in Spain in 195.[125] The cohort was a tactical unit, not an administrative one, and perhaps for this reason, was not in Polybius's account.[126] Polybius also ignored the increasing use of senatorial legates as the chief subordinates of army commanders (although military tribunes continued to serve), while other authors present in brief passages minor variations in nomenclature of the classes of infantry and in their equipment. Elizabeth Rawson suggests that Polybius's depiction of the *dilectus* did not differ too greatly from practices in his own day, deeming it unlikely that an author, resident in Rome and familiar with military affairs, would have used a description of the levy that differed markedly from contemporary practice.[127]

But what about the *dilectus*? In an influential discussion of the matter, Peter Brunt put forward reasons why he thought that the *dilectus* of the late third and second centuries could not have been conducted in such a fashion.[128] Some objections concern the ability of the Capitol to hold large crowds, but they can be met by placing the process in some other place at Rome, such as the *campus Martius*, where it sometimes is said to have taken place, or by suggesting that selection covered several days rather than just one. Others question the degree of centralization, for Brunt suggests that requiring so many men to come to Rome for just a few days was impractical, and he deems it "unnecessarily inconvenient" for prospective recruits first to come to Rome, then return home in order to equip themselves properly, only to be ordered to assemble again for their service. Except for outliers in Picenum and the *ager Gallicus*, where Romans were installed in 232, citizens would have had to travel no more than circa 170 kilometers to the city, and most would have faced considerably shorter journeys.

Brunt's proposed solution is not entirely satisfactory. He suggests that Polybius has described the actual formation of units rather than the selection of soldiers, and he proposes that conscription for those citizens who resided at some distance from Rome took place in their towns, except for those resident in less urbanized regions, without sophisticated structures of local government, who would still have been conscripted at the center. If so, those chosen would still have to journey to Rome in order to be assigned to their units, they still would have to return to gather their equipment, and they would have to travel yet again to their place of assembly. His reconstruction, in other words, reduces the burdens of crowds on Rome and of travel for those who would not be selected, but still would require prospective soldiers to make the repeated trips that he finds so improbable. Brunt also notes that our sources sometimes portray the consuls in charge of the levy as reading out the names from lists, so that those who were absent might be identified and subjected to penalties.[129] He takes Polybius's failure to mention this aspect of the process as a sign that he did not describe its first stage. Still, any local levy would have depended on local census lists, but, before the first century, these lists appear to have been organized by tribe, not place.

In narratives, Rome still remains central. Passages in Livy's history are broadly consistent with Polybius's account, although they allow more variation. Although he never provided a systematic treatment of the process, the raising of soldiers does provide a regular element in the annalistic structure of the books that cover the years from 218 to 167. Some notices record emergency levies, but in them Roman magistrates still raised Roman soldiers, although they may have done so away from Rome.[130] Livy clearly envisions more conventional levies as taking place in the city. Like Polybius, he usually assigns to the consuls responsibility for the levy, although, during the Hannibalic war, he occasionally has dictators do so, along with praetors afterward.[131] Some accounts clearly were preserved because they had been accompanied by disorders at Rome or had come to involve other magistrates, usually the tribunes of the plebs, and the senate, active only in the city.[132] Note that Livy (42.32–35) reports that in 171 former centurions had protested to the plebeian tribunes over the way in which new centurions were selected, and the tribunes in turn referred the matter to the senate.

Once, Polybius (9.6.6) took note of a *dilectus* that differs from his model. In 211 Hannibal, who was campaigning near Capua, made a quick march on Rome. The two consuls, however, had recently enrolled a legion and had bound the conscripts to assemble with their arms at Rome on a day that, by chance, turned out to be when Hannibal was approaching the city. At the same time, they also were enrolling a second legion. These arrangements resemble one of Brunt's proposed solutions for addressing the limited space on the Capitol and for mitigating the disruption of great crowds—the enlistment of legions successively rather than simultaneously—but Brunt instead suggests that the two legions represented the urban legions of two different years, one already formed and summoned quickly to service and the other in the process of formation, which contradicts Polybius's depiction of events.

A mechanism for summoning separately groups of tribes did exist, and it preserved the centrality of Rome upon which it was focused. As we have seen, the thirty-one rural tribes of the time were stacked by distance and direction and probably grouped along the routes the radiated from the city. Michael Crawford plausibly suggests that the practice was intended to facilitate the *dilectus* by allowing tribes along the same road to be summoned to Rome simultaneously, a practice that might easily accommodate the selection of multiple armies that accompanied the expansion in the number of praetors.[133] Was any attempt made to match groups of tribes and allies with places of assembly, which were widely dispersed over Italy?

In the first century, when the bulk of the free population of peninsular Italy possessed Roman citizenship, local magistrates did register citizens for the census, but they do not appear to have conscripted soldiers for Rome's armies. If one excludes times of civil war, when more irregular practices prevailed, one still finds occasions in which troops were conscripted in Rome. At other times, the senate assigned to magistrates districts in which they or their legates might recruit. Thus, Caesar enrolled soldiers in Cisalpine Gaul, where he was governor, while L. Licinius Murena recruited in Umbria before proceeding to Transalpine Gaul.[134]

Aulus Gellius (*NA* 16.4.4) preserves traces of a similar practice early in the second century. When recounting a few brief elements from the Sullan antiquarian L. Cincius's work on military matters (*de re militari*), he begins with a description of the ways that the fetials had declared war and ends with the number of centuries, maniples, and cohorts in a legion and the reason why formations of cavalry were called "wings" (*alae*). In the middle, he sets out part of the oath that military tribunes had imposed on recruits under the authority of the consuls of 190.[135] In it, the new soldiers swear to "come and give service to him who had held the levy in that district, village, or town" (*eo die uenturum aditurumque eum, qui eum pagum, uicum, oppidumue delegerit*). Recruits, it must be stressed, owed service or obedience only to the commanders to whom they had been assigned or to their delegates. Plautus and Cicero, writing over a century apart, use the word *conquisitor* to denote an agent dispatched to recruit soldiers.[136]

Certain arrangements made in 212 reveal a different set of functionaries. In the face of recruitment problems as a result of losses in the Second Punic War Livy (25.5.5–9) claims that the senate ordered the creation of two triumvirates to search "rural districts, *fora*, and *conciliabula*" (*in pagis forisque et conciliabulis*) for recruits and that these officials did, in fact, seek them out "through the fields" (*per agros*). For some, the absence of cities, *municipia*, indicates that their citizens were conscripted locally, so that the triumvirs might focus on more poorly organized settlements.[137] Henrik Mouritsen, however, argues that Livy uses some form of the phrase "in *fora* and *conciliabula*," or, on occasion "in the fields," "in Italy," or "in all of Italy" to represent one side of the complementary pair "in the city and away from it" that appears in other contexts as *urbs* and *ager* or "at home" (*domi*) or "on campaign" (*militia*).[138] Livy's depiction (40.37.3) of an order requiring the performance of supplications "in the city and through all the *fora* and *conciliabula*" (*in urbe et per omnia fora conciliabulaque*) is a good example. His account of the triumvirates of 212, then, may indicate only that they were to seek out recruits away from Rome without specifying in any way the kinds of settlements that were to receive their attention. The use of a special college of magistrates, rather than the agents of existing ones that we encounter slightly later, may indicate that the practice of sending recruiting agents into the countryside began only with the Second Punic War.

Much about the use of agents in the second century remains obscure: how frequently did magistrates resort to the use of *conquisitores*, and how broadly did they operate over Italy? The practice may have expanded as Rome's citizens became more dispersed with land assignments in southern Italy in the aftermath of the Second Punic War and especially after the great increase in the number of citizens after the Social War. Still, Livy and Polybius do present the *dilectus* as concentrated at Rome, so the use of *conquisitores* may for long have been supplementary. At the same time, Polybius portrays military tribunes at Rome forming units and naming centurions, while Livy (42.32–5) records a conflict over the appointment of centurions at Rome. The use of agents leaves little room for the operation of local magistrates, but it also leaves obscure where and by whom the new recruits were formed into centuries, maniples, and legions. In the census,

Roman officials may have turned to local magistrates as intermediaries only late in republican history, but in the *dilectus*, they appear to have kept the process under the control of Roman magistrates and their agents.

Although many aspects of Rome's empire were spatially indeterminate, Italy was a special case, representing a core within Rome's larger area of operations. The Romans gave to Italy clear boundaries and imposed on it a set of overarching statuses through which they organized conscription. Within Italy, one can detect other informal or implicit zones, some the result of Rome's expansion from a single core, and others signs of a conviction that certain activities ought to be either close to or at some distance from Rome. Some marked degrees of integration into Rome's central institutions; others were formed by the actions of lesser officials based in the city. In general, the nearer were more closely linked to the center than the farther. Indeed, until the first century, the ruling elite appears to have made little effort to integrate local governments more fully into Roman operations; rather, they sought to exert control when necessary by dispersing agents occasionally and unevenly away from the center. Rome's radial roads, which had an important place in the regular movement of magistrates to their assignments, also served to organize the citizenry and its military service. In any case, creating uniform administrative spaces, except perhaps for lands quite near to Rome, was not a consideration.

FOUR

The Augurs
and Their Spaces

Rome's centrality was made manifest in its role as a center of decision making and as the point of origin and termination for journeys for public purposes. At the same time, official activities constructed a number of de facto zones around the city, formed by its citizenry and its allies, by the functions of its magistrates and priests, and by the willingness of the senate to accept prodigies as of public significance. These same features find more formal and explicit expressions in Rome's public cult and in the disciplines of its priestly colleges. This chapter focuses on certain aspects of this cult, especially when associated with the augurs, whose area of expertise, the auspices, permeated much of public life. As we have seen, these priests, probably in the middle quarters of the third century, separated the "land of Italy" from external regions by explicit boundaries and attributed some unity to the polities enclosed within its limits, but they also created other dividing lines closer to the city.

ROME, ITS SPACES, AND ITS GODS

Considerations of place bulked large in Roman public life and cult. At the outbreak of the Second Punic War, Rome had been a center of power for centuries. The institutions of Roman public life had grown with the city, shaping the urban fabric and being shaped by it. Central events took place in the city's public squares, in temples and sacred spaces scattered around the city or just outside its walls, and along the routes linking them. In and around these places, magistrates entered office and performed many, if not all, of their functions, priests carried out their

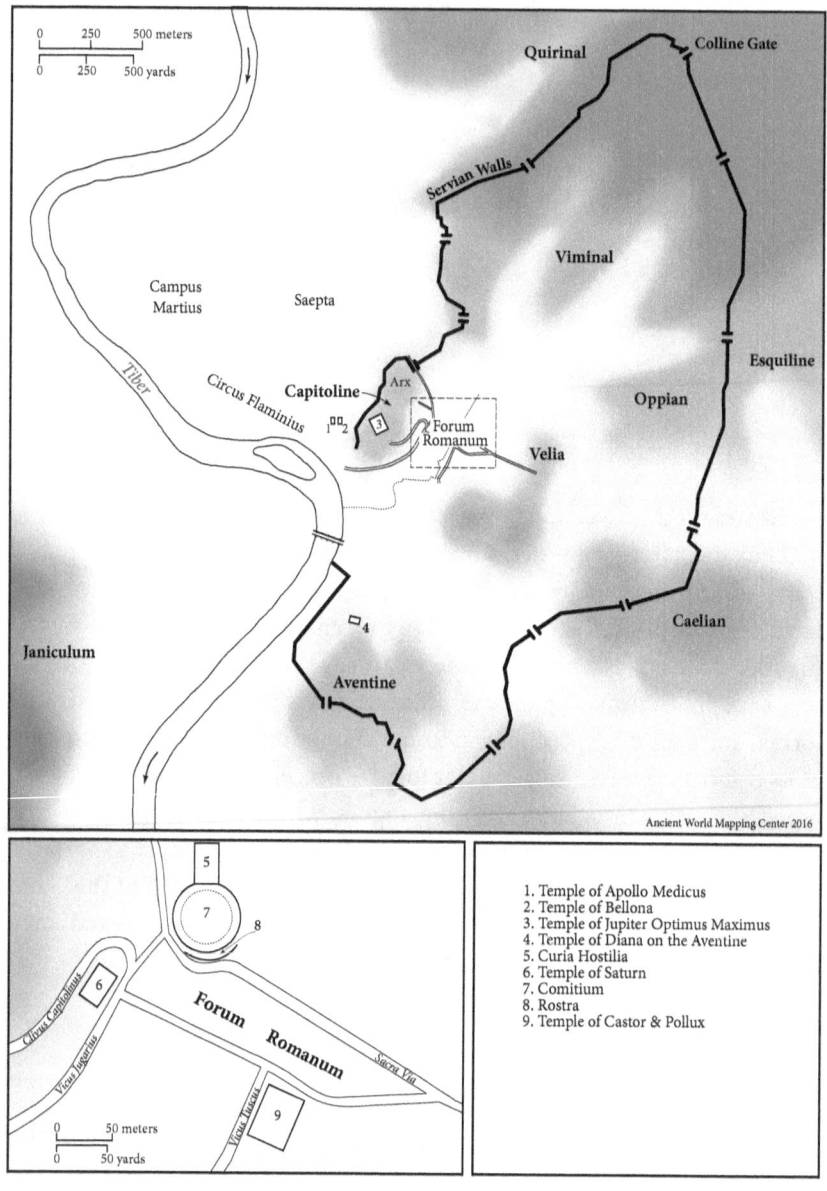

Rome and its environs

duties, the senate held its sessions and issued its decrees, and assemblies of citizens elected officials, enacted laws, and heard speeches and public announcements. Many of these places were filled with monuments preserving the memory of past deeds, while historians often took care to locate great events within them.

In and near the city, the holders of various offices and the meetings of senate and people were tied, by custom or by law, to specific places. As we saw in chapter 2, the Temple of Jupiter Best and Greatest on the Capitol was closely associated with the consuls, who entered office and made vows upon their departure from the city at the temple and, if successful, completed their triumphs by returning there. The complex formed by the *curia* and the *comitium* in the northwest corner of the forum, where the city's main processional route, the *sacra via*, began its ascent to the Capitol, was for long Rome's functional core.[1] The *curia* was a substantial building, while the *comitium* was an enclosure, open to the air, that separated the *curia* from the forum and served as its avenue of approach: Livy (45.24.12) calls it the *curia*'s vestibule. The interior of the *comitium* formed a circle of about fifty meters in diameter and with steps like a theater. A speakers' platform, the *rostra*, and the *graecostasis*, where foreign ambassadors waited for admittance to the senate, separated the *comitium* from the forum itself. The *curia*, across the *comitium* from the *rostra* and the *graecostasis*, divided this circle into two wings or *cornua*. Magistrates often placed their tribunals to each side of the *curia*'s entrance.

This complex provided the primary venue for interactions between magistrates, senate, and people. The *curia* was the senate's chief meeting place, although senators sometimes met in the Capitoline temple or, when meeting with commanders who could not enter the city without surrendering their commands, in the temples of Apollo or Bellona in the *campus Martius*, just outside the city's encircling fortifications.[2] Citizens met in *contiones*, gatherings in which speeches were made, information imparted, or edicts proclaimed; at the *comitium*; in the *area Capitolina* in front of Jupiter's temple; or in the *circus Flaminius* on the *campus Martius*. Voting assemblies organized by centuries met in the *campus Martius*. Until the third quarter of the second century, when voting by tribes shifted to the southern *campus Martius* (when under a consul or praetor) and to the Temple of Castor in the southeastern corner of the forum (when under a tribune), the primary location for tribal assemblies was the *comitium*.

The *comitium* and *curia* did more than frame interactions between magistrates, the senate, and the populace at large. Urban praetors usually

The Augurs and Their Spaces

established their tribunals in the *comitium*.³ Messengers or ambassadors arriving in the city expected to find a praetor there, praetors summoned the senate to hear reports or receive delegations in the *curia*, and praetors, if the senate decreed it, would make an announcement to the crowd from the *rostra*. Because of its connection with the urban praetors, the *comitium* played a central role in litigation. On occasion, it also witnessed punishments and even mass executions.⁴ At other times, the *comitium* provided the venue for prominent rites, such as the sacred dances of the Salii or the *regifugium* under the direction of the *rex sacrorum*.⁵ The *rostra* and the forum also provided the venue for the funerals of members of the Roman elite who had reached high office, events that were very much celebrations of the family's glorious past.⁶

These places, along with many others, also played a prominent role in public cult. The worship of the gods was closely connected to specific times and places.⁷ Priests and officials performed rites at temples, altars, shrines, groves, and springs that were devoted to the cult of particular gods on certain days as set out in the city's civic calendar, and they staged festivals and games at designated times and places. By the last decades of the third century, most of the cult places that received the direct attentions of Roman magistrates and priests were within Rome's walls or immediately beyond them, although a scattering of others might be found at slightly greater distances. Within and immediately outside the city, temples, like other prominent structures and spaces, were not distributed evenly. From the late fourth century, virtually all of the new dedications in the city were in two of its four regions, the Palatina and the Collina, while outside its limits the preferred locations were largely adjacent to them, especially in and around the *circus maximus*, the Aventine, and later the *campus Martius*. The reasons for this distribution are unclear, but it probably rests on concentrations of preexisting sacred sites or associations and the most important public spaces and routes.⁸

THE AUGURS AND THEIR DISCIPLINE

Some priests were responsible for the cult of a single god, but a few operated much more widely, shaping in the process much of Rome's public life—most notably, the pontiffs, the augurs, and the *decemviri* (later, the *quindecemviri*) *sacris faciundis*. For present purposes, the augurs are the most important, for as custodians of the auspices, the rites of divination that ought to precede all public acts, they had a close connection to the perceived legitimacy of these actions. From as far in the past as we can see, the success of Rome's chief magistrates was associated with their auspices, while, from at least as early as the opening decades of the second century, Roman writers linked the auspices and the college of augurs with Rome's foundation.[9] In *On Divination* (1.2.3), Cicero notes that Romulus founded the city through the auspices, his successors had employed augurs, and, after the expulsion of the kings, no business at home or abroad (*nec domi nec militiae*) had begun without them. Roman writers, moreover, often associated the foundation of the augural college with either Romulus or Numa Pompilius, Rome's second king and supposedly the originator of most of its central cultic practices.[10]

Like so many institutions thought to derive from Rome's earliest years, the history of the augurs and their discipline is obscure. Augustan inscriptions set out lists of augurs that reach back at least as far as the early fifth century, but Livy records with any consistency only the deaths of augurs and the selection of their replacements from circa 300.[11] Much later, historians and antiquarians told tales of Attus Navius, supposedly a great augur of the age of L. Tarquinius Priscus, Rome's fifth king.[12] At some point, a statue honoring him was erected in the *comitium*, perhaps circa 300, when images of Rome's kings were probably placed on the Capitol and others representing Pythagoras and Alcibiades were set up in the *comitium*.[13] The augurs possessed secrets, which they were not to write down, most notably the hidden name of Rome and its tutelary deity, which had to be spoken in the *augurium salutis* to prepare the way for prayers for the safety of the Roman people.[14]

Evidence for augural practices and concepts comes primarily from works of the late republic and early empire, some written by augurs, but they are largely preserved in fragments. As a college, the augurs possessed texts, some undoubtedly old, but their collections appear to have contained lists of members, accounts of the performance of some rite, prayers, and specific opinions on some matter at issue, not broad and systematic expositions of doctrine. As a result, written works would have existed within a context of oral tradition and commentary, which might shift over time and with circumstances. In his dialogue *On Friendship* (*De amicitia* 7), set in 129, one of Cicero's speakers asserts that the augurs met monthly to discuss augural matters (*commentandi causa*). Much of our evidence consists of brief statements without context, explanation, or definition, a feature of many priestly opinions as well as juristic ones. Conflicts, differences of opinion, and changes over time are largely invisible.

When we can see matters with some clarity, a situation that probably reaches back in some form into the third century, a firm distinction was made between the *auguria* and the *auspicia*. The former consisted of acts that the augurs performed themselves, most notably the inauguration of persons, places, and certain ceremonies; the latter contained those rites of divination that magistrates performed in order to secure divine approval for their own actions. The augurs, as a college, sometimes issued retrospective judgments on whether the official had done so properly, usually when the subsequent actions had not turned out well, but also when others had challenged an official's right to act. When the augurs found a flaw, a *vitium*, they declared the magistrate's action, and all that derived from it, to be without divine sanction and dangerous to the republic.

For the augurs, time, place, and direction were crucial to their discipline and its divinatory rites. In their roles as priests and as members of a college, they were closely tied to Rome and its environs. Magistrates might take the auspices in the city and abroad, but, while augurs, like other priests, did serve away from Rome in other roles—after all, many also held magistracies—they functioned as augurs and as members of a college only in Rome and its immediate vicinity.[15] There, augurs generally were present during official actions where they might offer their advice and, if necessary, announce that they had detected unfavorable signs (*obnuntiationes*), a task that they are known to have performed in popular assemblies, in certain festivals, and in the conscription of citizens, all operations that took place only at Rome.[16] In their rites, augurs sought to match signs, spaces, and outcomes, and they often did so in a fashion that connected the performance explicitly to the topography of Rome itself, linking the validity of public acts to prominent features in and around the city and serving, if only indirectly, to keep crucial operations near the center. The augurs were closely connected with the *auguraculum* on the *arx*, although they also possessed spaces, whose uses are much less well known, on the Palatine and on the western slopes of the Quirinal.[17] The topographical features of Rome and its immediate hinterland also figured in their formulas. According to Cicero (*ND* 3.52), the augurs opened their ceremonies with an invocation of the Tiber and other nearby rivers. Augural rites were tailored to place.

THE AUGURS AND THEIR *TEMPLA*

In the first set of laws in *On the Laws* (2.20–21), Cicero gives to the augurs a number of essential tasks: to observe the auspices; to preserve the augural discipline; to inaugurate priests and the safety of the people; to warn magistrates and the senate of the wrath of the gods; to observe lightning in the fixed *regiones* of the sky; to keep free and unobstructed the *urbs*, the *agri*, and the *templa*; and to declare certain acts to be unjust and ill-omened.[18] These tasks were closely associated with the construction and the maintenance of a number of boundaries. In this section, we are primarily concerned with the auspices and the definition of *templa*, the spaces necessary for their performance as well as the proper places for a range of other official activities.

First, one must clearly distinguish between the impetrative and the oblative auspices. In the former, a magistrate requested divine approval for a task that he would direct in person on the same day at or near the place of auspication. If unsuccessful, the augurs held that Jupiter had barred the action only on the day in question and that it was perfectly acceptable to ask the same question on another day—and, indeed, to keep on asking it until a positive response was secured. The oblative auspices, on the other hand, consisted of signs that appeared between the original rite and the completion of the act and, when observed, necessarily brought the action to a halt. As might be expected, the impetrative auspices exhibit greater regularity.[19]

The impetrative auspices were associated with the definition of fields, known as *templa*.[20] Auspication by observing the flight of birds from a high place is the best-known form. Varro (*LL* 7.6–8) preserved and commented on the apparently archaic formula augurs used to define the spaces in which they would seek signs from the *auguraculum* on the *arx*, the only place where the rite can be said with any certainty to have been performed.[21] As we shall see in chapter 5, the officiant looked to the east over the forum and the city and defined a visual field, known as a "*templum* on the land" (*in terra*), to organize the search for signs. The antiquarian L. Cincius mentions an archaic practice, supposedly deployed when the Latin communities still had a collective existence separate from Rome, in which the flight of birds, when observed from the Capitol, determined who would command a joint Roman and Latin force.[22] Livy claims that in 437 a Roman dictator, who had pitched his camp not far from the confluence of the Tiber and the Anio, looked back on the *arx*, five or six kilometers away, for the augurs' signal that the birds had proven favorable before entering battle.[23] The historicity of this account, of course, is far from certain, but, at the very least, the anecdote reveals that Livy or his source linked this form of the auspices with the *arx* and with command. Taking the auspices by observing the feeding of chickens (*ex tripudiis*), which was in more fully historical periods the dominant mode away from Rome, was once oblative and became impetrative.[24] Could this shift have been a response to the increasing distance from the city of Roman operations?

Other *templa* were rectangular enclosures clearly defined on the ground. One form, known as a "lesser *templum*" (*minus templum*), may have marked the limits of certain augural spaces until more permanent boundaries or structures could be erected, or it may have been established in the camps, which contained spaces known variously as *auguratoria* or *templa*, where commanders took the auspices for a limited range of activities.[25] At present, however, another form is of greater interest. The augurs themselves, acting under the direction of a magistrate, created a *templum* that was a permanent enclosure, a *locus inauguratus*, through rites of inauguration in which they set the lines that separated the space from its surroundings, an action denoted by the verb *effari*, and then purged it of unwanted spiritual influences, an act signified by *liberare* (to free). *Effari* is an old word: Cicero (*De or.* 3.153) considered it old-fashioned and best suited for poetry and cult formulas. It belonged to a series of related words—*fari, praefari, fas, nefas, fastus, nefastus*, and *fatum*—that involved speech that both declares something to be real and creates the reality.[26] Thus, *fatum*, fate, is spoken by a god or the gods and sets out future occurrences; *fas* or *nefas* are things declared to be proper or improper; *praefari* (to say before) denotes prayer formulas intended to establish suitable conditions for a subsequent prayer or the performance of a rite. The act *effari*, then, signifies the creation of a space by setting lines defined by words (and probably by gestures as well), so that the lands outside the enclosed space count as *effatus*. (The *pomerium*, Rome's urban boundary, was an inaugurated zone, although not a *templum*, and the augurs referred to lands outside it as *ager effatus*.) Cicero requires his augurs to "keep free and unobstructed the *urbs*, the *agri*, and the *templa*," which may imply some continuing responsibility to maintain these spaces. *Templa* in camps, where augurs were not present in their priestly role, would not have been inaugurated and were suitable only for a limited range of activities.

Inaugurated *templa* served a variety of public and sacred purposes. When followed by dedications, which required the actions of magistrates and the cooperation of pontiffs, they became the sites for temples, altars, and shrines. Other *templa* encompassed all or parts of places of assembly.[27] The *ovile*, where the centuriate assembly met on the *campus Martius*, was such a place, although it is unclear whether the augural enclosure encompassed the entire space or only the presiding magistrate's tribunal. The complex formed by the *curia* and the *comitium* exhibits a similar uncertainty. The *curia* and the *rostra* clearly were *templum*, but scholars differ over whether the *comitium* was one as well, as is likely, or only a restricted space with a concentration of separate *templa*. Rome's augural boundary, as we shall see in the next section, was an augural representation of the fundamental contrast between town and country. In much the same fashion, rites of inauguration—and the belief that such rites had occurred even in the distant past—recognized and rendered more explicit the special nature of the city's most prominent places and structures.

In general, *templa* provided a stage for the performance of certain essential activities. Those associated with temples and shrines provided the locus for continuing cult. In addition, Roman magistrates often used the high podia of temples—and the *comitium* and *rostra*—to address crowds or perform other public acts, and they were required to summon meetings of the senate within a *templum* and under a roof. Varro cites two *commentarii*—accounts of the performance of some act—that illustrate the link. In the first (*LL* 6.86–87), the censor went by night to a *templum* and took the auspices in order to conduct the *lustrum* that closed the census. When successful, he instructed a herald (*praeco*) to summon the people, first in the *templum* and then from Rome's walls, which also had augural associations. When the people had assembled on the *campus Martius*, the two censors cast lots to determine who would conduct the ceremony. The successful censor then defined another *templum* on the *campus Martius* for the rite. In the second account (*LL* 6.91–2), which sets out a prosecution, the prosecutor first took the auspices in a *templum* and notified a consul or a praetor of the successful result. A herald then summoned the accused from the walls, while a hornblower (*cornicens*) signaled from the doorway of the accused and again on the *arx*. At this point, the prosecutor summoned other magistrates and the senate to give their opinions in the *templum*.

In this way, *templa* provided the necessary spatial frame for significant public actions, and the process of entering or leaving signaled their beginning or end. Livy (45.12.9–12) claims that one of the consuls of 168 neglected to take the auspices when he entered the *templum* to announce the day for his legions to assemble, so that the augurs, when consulted, declared the proclamation of his edict to be a *vitium*. Flaws regarding the use of *templa* could also serve retrospectively to explain failures. According to Livy (41.18.8–9), the consuls of 176, who were campaigning together against the Ligures, decided to split the army and take different lines of approach to the enemy. To match routes to consuls, they cast lots in the camp. One consul performed the rite properly for he was within the *templum*. The other consul, however, died in the ensuing battle, a development that the augurs later explained by noting that he had apparently cast his lot into the urn while outside the enclosure. Livy (3.17.1) represents a consul of 460 as turning from consulting the senate to conferring with the tribunes of the plebs—that is, as shifting from one act to another—by leaving the *curia* and entering the *comitium*. In 204 ambassadors from Locri in southern Italy, having exhausted the senate's patience, were instructed to leave the *templum*.[28] In his account of a meeting between King Eumenes and the senate to discuss rewards for his participation in the war against Antiochus III, Livy (37.52.9–53.1) depicts the king as leaving the *templum* when they failed to reach agreement, whereupon the senate dispatched a praetor to bring him back into it to clarify a point.

When we begin to see their contents with greater clarity, the texts of laws, edicts, and decrees proclaimed their origins through links with actions by named magistrates, some collectivity, and a particular place and time. The earliest surviving edict, issued in *Hispania Ulterior* in 190 or 189, identified the issuing official, L. Aemilius the *imperator*, and the time and place where he proclaimed it: in the camps on the twelfth day before the kalends of February.[29] Just a few years later, the *senatus consultum de Bacchanalibus* of 186 announces at its beginning the names of the two consuls who had summoned the senate, the time and place of the session—the nones of October in the temple of Bellona—and the names of three witnesses to the meeting.[30] Yet another senatorial decree, issued to the people of Thisbae in Greece in 170, identified its source in a meeting presided over by the praetor Q. Maenius in the *comitium* on the seventh day before the ides of October.[31] Other inscriptions of the second century set out the same basic form.[32] Toward its end, when the earliest laws preserved in inscriptions also appear, the elements become more elaborate, identifying the year by the names of its consuls and not just the day and month.[33] These texts reveal a desire, perhaps a growing desire, to locate normative statements in a specific official enactment performed at an identifiable time and place.

With the exception of *templa* in the camps, where only a limited range of actions could be performed, the practice of linking official actions to inaugurated *templa* was almost certainly limited to Rome and its environs. A late antique Vergilian commentator claims that the augurs were only able to inaugurate "among the ancestral dwelling-places" (*in patriis sedibus*).[34] In the mid-first century, Varro (*LL* 5.47) noted that the augurs went out from the *arx* along the *sacra via* when they set out to perform inaugurations. Now, the augurs performed rites of inauguration for priests, for *templa*, and also for various ceremonies that did not possess fixed dates and thus may have needed divine permission for their performance. If Varro's augural processions involved the inauguration of *templa*, as is probable, such spaces are unlikely to have been located very far from the city, although it remains uncertain whether there was a fixed outer limit. In any case, the augurs built these spaces by moving out from a clear center to the site of their activity, much as consuls did when they departed from the Capitol for their *provinciae*. The future *templum* was the focal point of their proposed activity, which it did not encompass, for their actions included the *arx* and the route to the future *templum*.

Here, the construction and dedication of new temples, which required, or came to require, the definition of *templa* to hold them, provide a good indicator. Rome and its vicinity contained a wide range of sacred sites: temples, altars, sacred groves, places for the performance of recurring festivals, and sanctuaries associated with various priesthoods and priestly colleges. From the beginning of the sixth century, the ruling elite began to construct monumental temples either in existing sacred places or in newly defined ones, and after a hiatus for most of the fifth century, the practice resumed again early in the fourth and accelerated later in the century. Literary sources set out the foundations of a large number of temples, some of which can be associated with specific material remains, while others can be located only approximately.[35] Most were within Rome's urban boundary, but from the opening decade of the third century new foundations outside the city but certainly or probably within a mile of it make their appearance.[36] Only two exceptions are known with any certainty: Sp. Carvilius Maximus (cos. 293) dedicated a temple to Fors Fortuna at the sixth milestone of the *via Campana*, and almost a century and a quarter later, C. Cicereius dedicated a temple on the *mons Albanus*.[37] The first represents one of the earliest of the known extra-urban dedications, which may indicate that any rule had not yet solidified. C. Cicereius, however, dedicated his temple, which he had vowed as praetor in 173, where he also had celebrated his triumph after the senate had denied him one at Rome, so that it remains possible that his dedication, like his triumph, was outside the limits of the senate's authority.[38] At the very least, Roman practice reveals a desire to keep the cult of the gods close to Rome.

The augurs, then, attributed considerable significance to certain topographical features in Rome and in its immediate vicinity. In their inaugurations, they constructed in practice a shallow ring around Rome in which they prepared sites for the conduct of public and sacred business in a way that had the effect of keeping crucial operations close to the city. Dio (41.43) reports that the consuls who in 48 had joined Pompey at Thessalonike set aside a plot to serve as an augural *templum* so that the senate and the citizenry might properly meet there to choose their successors.[39] In the event, however, they did not conduct elections, for they considered themselves unable in some way to enact the necessary curiate law. Rome remained the center of its empire in part because it was the proper place for a range of interactions with the city's gods and thus of primary importance for securing the polity's success in its endeavors.

THE AUGURS AND ROME'S BOUNDARIES

In the first set of laws in *On the Laws* (2.20–21), Cicero gives to the augurs the responsibility to keep free and unobstructed the *urbs*, the *agri*, and the *templa*.[40] Like *templa*, which had clear limits, the *urbs* and the lands outside it were separated, and to some degree defined, by a line drawn between them. Although earlier fortifications had covered parts of the city, Rome's encircling walls, built early in the fourth century, provided the most visible line of demarcation. Rome's gates served, practically, ceremonially, and symbolically, as points of entry or departure from the city: distances along Roman roads were calculated from them; magistrates departing for their provinces were escorted with ceremony to one of the gates; prominent Romans returning to the city were often met at the gates or just outside them by friends, dependents, and well-wishers; commanders entering the city in triumph did so through a special gate, the *porta triumphalis*.[41] In *On the Nature of the Gods* (3.94), one of Cicero's speakers proclaims the importance of the pontiffs' declaration of Rome's walls as *sanctus* in securing its safety, while Festus (p. 358 L) holds that certain ritual books, *libri rituales*, contained instructions for rites to sanctify gates and walls. The word *sanctus* had strong augural associations. At core, *sacer* and *sanctus* have the same root, but they came to be associated with two priestly colleges, the former with the pontiffs, and the latter with the augurs.[42] In this sense, an inaugurated place was a *locus sanctus*.

The second boundary was in many ways the most important of the lines that separated Rome from its hinterlands. Unlike the walls, which have left clear traces, much about the *pomerium* remains obscure, including its course and its age. Citing works on the auspices by Roman augurs, one of whom was Cicero's contemporary, M. Valerius Messalla, Aulus Gellius (*NA* 13.14.1–7) defines the *pomerium* as "the space within *ager effatus* designated by the augurs along the whole circuit of the city outside the walls, marked off by fixed boundaries and forming the limits of the urban auspices." By the late republic, if not earlier, its course was defined by stone markers.[43]

Rome's *pomerium* occupied a central place in two contexts. In the first, which can be detected as early as the first half of the second century and possibly as early as the late fourth century, the ritual that created a new *pomerium*, and supposedly had created others in the more distant past, served as the defining moment in the establishment of a kind of settlement known as an *urbs*, a class that *urbs Roma* shared with other Latin cities and some of its own colonies. In this context, historians and antiquarians made Romulus the creator of Rome's *pomerium*, the feast of the Parilia the day that he did so, and the Palatine the space that his boundary enclosed (see chapter 5).

The *pomerium* also separated the city proper, the *urbs*, from its hinterland, its *ager*, forming in the process the complementary pair, *urbs* and *ager*, that was central to augural thought and delimiting those institutions deemed proper for the urban core. In this way, the augurs made explicit the contrast, which would be clearest in the more urbanized regions of Italy, between a center, which contained the places and structures most essential to the polity's political and cultic life and which often was fortified, and the surrounding lands from which it drew its sustenance. In its role as urban boundary, the *pomerium* played a role in the tribal organization of the census, and for this reason some writers linked the line to Servius Tullius, Rome's sixth king, who supposedly had instituted it. Four tribes were urban—that is, they were located within the *pomerium*—while the rest were located outside *urbs Roma* and beyond its course.

To further complicate matters, Roman writers, and Greek authors of works on Roman history and antiquities, often connect the *pomerium* with the city's walls.[44] The supposed link between Rome's urban boundary and its encircling fortifications was established through an etymology that linked *pomerium* to *murus* through an intermediary *moerium*, although there was some disagreement over whether the first syllable ought to be derived from *post* (behind) or from *pro* (in front of), which placed the *pomerium* on different sides of the wall;[45] Livy (1.44.4–5) has it both ways, interpreting the word as signifying the tract on both sides of the wall. This lack of certainty about the relationship between Rome's urban boundary and its walls by authors resident in the city is disconcerting. In any case, Rome's *pomerium* certainly did not follow the walls through their entire length, for the Aventine and possibly the *arx* on the Capitol were within the fortifications but outside the augural boundary.[46] The augur M. Valerius Messalla, Cicero's contemporary, sought to explain the Aventine's exclusion from the *pomeria* of Servius Tullius, Sulla, and Caesar by noting that Remus had taken the auspices from the hill, which had thus become ill-omened;[47] he did, however, note that others had proposed different explanations. If, as is likely, the *pomerium* is genuinely old, from the middle of the fourth century its line would not have fully matched the city's fortifications or its built-up area.

Because of its associations with Servius Tullius, who supposedly ruled in the sixth century, many view the *pomerium* as a fossilized boundary, perhaps originally apotropaic in function, that preserved the physical limits of archaic Rome despite the great growth of the city in the succeeding centuries.[48] In this, it joins other supposedly fossilized boundaries, such as the one allegedly revealed in the festival of the *Septimontium*, older than the *pomerium*, and Rome's original territory, the *ager Romanus antiquus*.[49] Whenever the *pomerium* was established, in later periods it certainly was far from being a fossil. In the third, second, and first centuries, it was used to define and organize many civic functions and, as we shall soon see, it was also central to the spatial definition of certain magisterial powers and to the rites of the auspices.

In addition to the walls and the *pomerium*, some have also suggested that a line drawn one mile from the *urbs* also functioned as an augural limit. As we shall see in chapter 6, this boundary had a long life in Roman law, and as we have just seen, it may also have kept new temples, altars, and shrines close to the city. Indeed, a ring of sacred sites may have marked its location along major routes from the city.[50] For some, moreover, the line also restricted meeting places of the senate and popular assemblies, the powers of the tribunes of the plebs, and a citizen's right to appeal against magisterial coercion, but much of this is questionable. It must be stressed, however, that, while Varro (*LL* 5.143) and Aulus Gellius (*NA* 13.14.1) link the urban auspices to the *pomerium*, no source explicitly gives an augural significance to this more distant limit. The choice of location for new temples and altars involved magistrates and senators, who may have had the greater role in the matter than the augurs, who only inaugurated the site.

IMPERIUM AND THE POMERIUM

Rome's chief magistrates were closely associated with the concepts of *imperium* and *auspicium*.[51] Some view the original *imperium* as the undivided power of Rome's kings, which would be dispersed under the republic over magistracies and priestly colleges, while others suggest that it once stood only for the ability to command armies. For later periods, many hold that *imperium* came in two broad forms, one limited to the *urbs* and called *domi* (at home) and the other for operations, primarily military in nature and outside the *pomerium*, known as *militiae* (on campaign). This sharp spatial distinction between two forms of *imperium* is probably an illusion, although the exercise of *imperium* did take different forms in the city and away from it.

First, however, an argument seeking to remove considerations of place from the exercise of *imperium* should be addressed. Adalberto Giovannini accepts the existence of two forms of *imperium*, one "at home" and the other "on campaign," but he maintains that the distinction rested on status, leaving both essentially unbounded. Thus, a magistrate's *imperium* was *militiae* when leading citizens assembled in armies and *domi* when dealing with them in their civic roles. In this way, he holds, *imperium* and *auspicium* did not fully coincide, for the *pomerium* separated the urban auspices from the military forms that might be deployed outside it.[52]

At one level, Giovannini rests his argument on the range of meanings of *domi*, which, in addition to any spatial significance, might also denote a condition of peace. Thus, a magistrate's civil functions would embrace all nonmilitary activities wherever Roman citizens might dwell. Still, spatial associations are more common. Here the word may sometimes refer to places other than Rome—when Livy (8.18.4) describes an individual as famous not only at home but at Rome, he uses *domi* to refer to the place from which the person originally came—but more frequently it refers to Rome itself, the common home of all citizens and the location of their governing institutions. Roman writers may have used *domi* and *militiae* to denote the contrast between the city and its various hinterlands, an indication that they viewed activity away from the center primarily through a military lens, but they need not have linked "at home" with any fixed limit. In chapter 6, we will see that a number of lines might serve as boundaries to the city in different circumstances.

In addition, there are the ceremonies involved in taking up commands, which Giovannini views as merely symbolic. Magistrates first took the auspices and then made vows on the Capitol, after which they processed through the city to one of the gates, while, at some point, they and their lictors put on their military cloaks or *paludamenta*. Theodor Mommsen makes the *pomerium* the point of transition, but Giovannini properly notes that no source explicitly links the change in costume with its crossing.[53] That said, Yann Berthelet argues forcefully that the use of words such as *abire* (to go forth), *exire* (to go out), *proficsi* (to set out), or their derivatives shows that the opposition between the domains of peace and war was seen in spatial terms and that the act of leaving the city marked the transition.[54] Indeed, failure to do so properly affected the legitimacy of command.[55] Reentry into the city reversed this process, for it signified the laying down of command, if only for a time. Giovannini's third major point—that citizens' right of appeal too rested on status rather than place—is examined in chapter 6.

Romans did clearly distinguish between a zone suitable for war and its associated operations and one that was not, and the *pomerium* certainly separated them. Higher magistrates took up their commands by leaving the city, and they set them down when crossing the augural limit in the other direction. The senate met outside its course, often in the Temple of Bellona or the Temple of Apollo on the *campus Martius*, when meeting with a commander who had already taken up his command, when receiving ambassadors from states deemed hostile or potentially hostile, or when discussing declarations of war. Tribunes of the plebs sometimes summoned the people to a *contio* at the *circus Flaminius* when a commander wished to address them without surrendering his command. Romans distinguished between assemblies organized by tribes, which met in the *urbs*, and those arranged by centuries as if an army, which met in the *campus Martius*. The jurist Laelius Felix held that the *comitia centuriata* could not gather within the *pomerium*, because it was improper for an army to be commanded (*imperari*) within the *urbs*.[56] Certain rites associated with war also took place outside its limits. The *armilustrium*, a ritual purification of weapons, was staged at the *Armilustrium* on the Aventine, outside the *pomerium* but within Rome's walls. The dichotomy between zones of peace and war is undoubtedly old in some form, and it is probably related to the practice of viewing the polity in certain situations as if an army (see chapter 3).

The act of crossing Rome's augural boundary affected more than military commands. The failure of Ti. Sempronius Gracchus (cos. 163) to conduct in the proper manner the election of his successors serves as a good example.[57] Because of a portent detected during the voting, the senate consulted the *haruspices*, who held that the presiding consul had committed a fault. Himself an augur, Gracchus rejected this claim, but later he discovered his error while reading augural books and reported his discovery to the senate. Cicero, our chief source, presents two versions of the error. In the first (*ND* 2.10–1), Gracchus erred because after he had first placed his augural tent or *tabernaculum* in the gardens of Scipio, probably not far from where he would conduct the assembly, he had reentered the *urbs* to consult the senate but had forgotten to auspicate when crossing the *pomerium* on his return to the *campus Martius*. In the second (*Div.* 1.33), Cicero asserts that Gracchus erred because, after placing his *tabernaculum* but before completing the auspices, he had crossed the *pomerium*. In a third passage (*Div.* 2.74–5), he says only that the fault involved either the placement of the *tabernaculum* or the rules concerning the *pomerium* (*aut de tabernaculum recte capto aut de pomeri iure pontuerunt*), framing the matter as an either/or statement and suggesting that different versions were circulating. Much later, Plutarch (*Marc.* 5) reports another norm: if, after setting the tent outside the city walls to take the auspices, a consul returned to the city before detecting the signs, he must relocate his tent upon his return and begin the process anew. The event may have survived as a literary or rhetorical *exemplum*, where the priestly opinion was less important than Gracchus's sense of duty.

These representations of Gracchus's fault or faults, although they differ in detail, give to the *pomerium* a central role, for all involve the act of crossing it, and all probably made sense in augural terms. In the first, Gracchus failed to auspicate when he crossed the urban boundary on his return to the site of the assembly. According to Festus (p. 296 L), consuls on the way from the city to the *campus* were expected to auspicate when crossing the *amnis Petronia*, not far beyond the *pomerium*. One must auspicate, in other words, when crossing an augural boundary. In the others, movement into the city and across the *pomerium* brought to an end an incomplete auspication, much like a similar movement ended a military command, with the result that an entirely new rite was deemed necessary when the consul returned to the *campus*.

The contrast between the auspices associated with war and those linked to other endeavors finds, or would come to find, another form of institutional expression in certain laws enacted by the curiate assembly (*comitia curiata*). In the middle of the first century, the only time when the practice is visible in any detail, consuls, and presumably praetors as well, tested their auspices, the so-called auspices of investiture, when entering office and at some later date, they put another law before the curiate assembly which would grant them different powers.[58] The *comitia curiata* was supposedly Rome's earliest assembly, but when we can see it in operation, the bulk of Rome's citizens did not participate: its meetings, which took place within the *pomerium*, often, if not always, in the *comitium*, consisted of the thirty lictors who represented the *curiae*, although some augurs also attended.[59] Their failure to secure a curiate law because of obstruction by the tribunes of the plebs, it should be noted, did not prevent the consuls of 54 from exercising their *imperium* and thus their *auspicium* within the *urbs* and even for events slightly outside it as well, for they held the assembly on the *campus Martius* that elected their successors.[60] That said, Roman writers persistently link the law with a magistracy that is "lawful" (*iustus*).[61]

As for the measures themselves, Cicero (*Leg.Agr.* 2.27) asserts that, after the establishment of the centuriate and tribal assemblies, the curiate assembly was maintained only for the sake of the auspices. Late republican authors clearly associated these *leges curiatae* with military command. Cicero (*Leg.Agr.* 2.30) claims that without such a law a consul could not engage in military matters (*attingere rem militarem non licet*). Livy (5.52.15–16) characterizes meetings of the curiate assembly as embracing military affairs (*comitia curiata, quae rem militarem continent*). One of the consuls of 54, himself an augur, who wished to take up a *provincia*, linked his assumption of his assignment to the passage of such a law and sought to find an alternate procedure.[62] These *leges curiatae*, then, were probably connected in some fashion with the ability to perform the auspices needed to take up commands and to auspicate in the field.[63]

Scholars often make a sharp distinction between the urban auspices (*auspicia urbana*), taken within the *pomerium*, and the military auspices (*auspicia militaria*) deployed outside it.[64] But how certain is the existence of a pervasive distinction between two spheres—*domi* and *militia*—separated by an explicit boundary? The *pomerium* clearly served to keep warlike activities outside the city, and in this way it formed the inner limit of a sphere deemed suitable for military action, the outer reaches of which would encompass any region in which Roman armies were active. But other operations were not bound in the same fashion. Tribunes of the plebs might summon *contiones* beyond the *pomerium* at the *circus Flaminius*, while curule and plebeian aediles took charge of festivals with elements on both sides of it, prosecuted offenders before meetings of the *comitia centuriata*, or took care to maintain roads, often at some distance from the city.[65] Like the aediles, higher magistrates presided over rites and festivals with components on both sides of the *pomerium* and supervised the construction of temples and altars inside the *urbs* and just outside it. Indeed, all Rome's officials processed yearly to the Alban Mount for the Latin festival. The *pomerium*, then, was not directly relevant to them, or not relevant in the same way that it was for commanders.

Against this background, we should return to the consuls of 54. For some, their ability to conduct the election of their successors in the *campus Martius* demonstrates that their "urban auspices" were in force outside the *pomerium* and suggests that their powers were actually delimited by a line drawn one mile from the *urbs*. Attempts to detect hard-and-fast rules, however, are complicated by indications that some restrictions may have been customary rather than explicit, that practices may have shifted from time to time, and that clearly expressed norms may have been linked to specific contexts. Some events that took place just outside Rome's walls may have begun within the city, if only occasionally. The different versions of Ti. Gracchus's fault have him begin the process of holding elections within the *urbs* and then crossing the *pomerium*. Elsewhere, we learn that magistrates leaving the city to preside over assemblies on the *campus Martius* were expected to auspicate when crossing a small brook, the *amnis Petronia*, which flowed between the city and the site.[66] Thus, one might envision a series of auspications as presidents moved to the site of the elections, first to cross the *pomerium*, then to pass over the *amnis Petronia*, and finally at the site itself. Livy (5.52.15–16) included meetings of the centuriate assembly among events that could take place only within the *pomerium*, clearly not the case for the actual gathering, while elsewhere (24.7.8; 9.1–2) he recounted an anecdote concerning a consul of 215 that gains its force from the assumption that the consuls returning to Rome to conduct the election of their successors usually entered the city before leaving it again to hold the actual assembly.

Some functions of magistrates with *imperium* may have had implicit constraints rather than formal ones. Operations beginning in the *urbs* may have been restricted to an indeterminate area around the city, especially if they had to be completed within a day. As we saw in chapter 3, however, most consular activities that did not directly involve the command of soldiers—expiating prodigies, presiding over meetings of the senate and public assemblies, granting audiences to foreign ambassadors and envoys of subordinate polities and corresponding with their governments, and issuing edicts that would be disseminated in the city and away—took place very near Rome. The relatively few occasions when consuls also engaged in nonmilitary actions that required their presence away from Rome may have been too widely scattered in time to have produced firm rules.

Ostensibly civil actions away from the city, moreover, may not have been clearly separable from military ones. On occasion, the senate gave to some consul or praetor such an assignment away from Rome—the dispatch of a consul of 173 to separate public and private land in Campania is a good example—but since Livy often presents such operations as tasks to be performed before going to their *provinciae*, only a single departure from the city may have been involved. Would magistrates have taken up their military powers when they left the city, if only to keep open the possibility of going directly to their commands upon completion of a supplementary task?

Curiate laws of the first century, then, gave to magistrates the auspices needed to command armies, but they did not involve other activities, even when they took place beyond the limits of the *urbs*. Romans of the late republic thought that curiate laws were very old, and modern scholars usually agree. A. Magdelain suggests that the authors of our sources did not understand their full significance, while C. J. Smith notes that issues around them probably will never be satisfactorily resolved.[67] Our evidence for the laws, however, largely refers to events in the first century, leaving open the possibility that the consequences associated with such measures shifted over time. A. Dalla Rosa plausibly suggests that the development of the promagistracy led to the assertion that the end of a magistracy only involved the termination of the "urban auspices," a shift that he made a consequence of the first promagistracy, although a later date, when the practice had become more common and more institutionalized, is perhaps more likely.[68] At some point, such a practice received an explicit complement, when popular assemblies granted promagistrates *imperium* for a day so that they might enter the *urbs* in triumph.[69] In 231 C. Papirius Maso celebrated one on his own authority on the *mons Albanus*, beyond the *pomerium* and the need for permission to cross it, a model that others would follow, for we know of at least three more Alban triumphs before Livy's narrative ends.[70]

Some isolated norms may also have served to distinguish between magistrates and promagistrates, although one cannot always say with any confidence whether the rules were genuinely old, were merely customary in the author's own day, or represented a particular position in some controversy. Himself an augur, Cicero made a number of assertions about the auspices in his *On the Nature of the Gods* and *On Divination*, written in the midst of civil war and after decades in which commanders who either were promagistrates or held some extraordinary command overshadowed the holders of regular offices. Twice, he maintains that promagistrates did not possess the auspices at all, and once he proclaims that no action in war was taken without consulting the entrails of sacrificial animals, the sphere of the *haruspices*, while more peaceful projects involved the auspices—yet another version of the distinction between *domi* and *militiae* and undoubtedly to be linked to his assertion that only magistrates possessed the auspices.[71]

For some, Cicero was both rigorous and conservative, a conclusion that rests on the assumption that the principle was old.[72] His assertion, however, cannot be accepted at face value. From the fourth century, magistrates who had continued as promagistrates triumphed, which required that they still possessed *imperium* and *auspicium*. Some promagistrates, however clearly were barred from the honor. As a private citizen given *imperium*, Scipio Africanus was denied a triumph because he had not held a magistracy, a distinction that persisted until Pompey celebrated his victory in Africa.[73] Such a rule cannot be older than grants of *imperium* to private citizens, traceable to the opening decade of the third century, and it may not be older than the decision concerning Africanus, the first such person whose deeds may have been seen as worthy of the honor, although it clearly no longer applied to prominent first-century figures. Cicero's claims, then, may best be viewed in the context of its time and the recent past. Indeed, in works written slightly later, he would suggest that the consuls had the right to take whatever province they wished and that they even had power over those who were not granted to them.[74] Clearly he wished to use the auspices to strength the city and its traditional offices over powerful figures on the margins.

A different set of assertions may reveal broadly similar concerns. In a fragment from an unknown work, Varro maintains that only magistrates might auspicate *ex caelo*, and in the passage as we have it, he also associates the form with the act of returning to "this side of the Tiber," which probably indicates a return to Rome; his contemporary Cicero links signs *ex caelo* with electoral assemblies.[75] Do these assertions reveal a desire to keep a crucial activity near Rome and in the hands of magistrates?

The dichotomy between activities suitable for performance within the *pomerium* and those best kept outside the *urbs* is undoubtedly old, although the terms of the contrast may have shifted. Many of the norms and practices concerning magisterial powers and the *pomerium* appear only in late republican or imperial works, and, although some are undoubtedly older, their origins are uncertain. What emerges with some clarity, however, is that the city itself provided a long-term reference point for conceptualizing the proper activities of magistrates and commanders, even ones that would take place at some distance from Rome, and that their powers were often defined in terms of entering, leaving, or returning to the *urbs*. Although the rule does not involve *imperium*, a provision in the Law on Praetorian Provinces of 100 specifies that quaestors or proquaestors who had received the *provinciae* of Asia or Macedonia could not be prosecuted for misuse of funds until they had returned to Rome.[76]

The Augurs and Their Spaces

The *pomerium* separated *urbs Roma* from a sphere in which war was possible, while another limit, much farther away, marked off the "land of Italy" from Rome's allies and enemies outside the peninsula. Between the two, the augurs established at least one other line that separated the outside world from an inner space. In the first set of laws in his *On the Laws* (2.20–21), Cicero ordains that his ideal augurs ought to "keep free and unobstructed the city, the fields, and the *templa*" (*urbemque et agros et templa liberata et effata habento*).[77] We have already seen how the *pomerium* separated the city, the *urbs*, from the surrounding countryside, its *ager*. But what about his assertion that they were to preserve the *agri* (in the plural)?

According to Varro, Cicero's contemporary, the augurs identified five *agri* and matched them to the appropriate form of the auspices:

> As our public augurs have set out, there are five kinds of *ager*: *Romanus, Gabinus, peregrinus, hosticus, incertus*. *Romanus* is named from Romulus, from whom Rome received its name. *Gabinus* is named from the town of Gabii. *Peregrinus* is land reduced to peace, which is outside Roman and Gabinian, because in these the auspices are kept in one manner. Peregrine is named from *pergendo* [going forth], that is, from *progrediendo* [advancing], for into it the first advance was made from *ager Romanus*. For this reason, *Gabinus* should also be *peregrinus*, but because it has its own auspices, it is kept separate from the rest. *Hosticus* is named from *hostis* [enemy]. *Incertus* is land of which it is unknown to which of the four classes it belongs.[78]

Festus (p. 287 L) sets out only a threefold division into *ager Romanus*, *ager peregrinus*, and *ager hostilius*, which may indicate that for him *ager Gabinus* and *ager incertus* were not significant categories. Note that Varro establishes an etymology for *peregrinus* that places it in the context of movement out from Rome's original core.

In a reconstruction that has been widely followed, Theodor Mommsen saw these augural *agri* as corresponding to the statuses of those who lived within them, just as he also viewed tribes as territories originally formed from the aggregate holdings of their members.[79] Thus, *ager Romanus* signified the land inhabited by Roman citizens, while *ager hosticus* included the lands of communities that were hostile or potentially hostile to Rome. *Ager incertus* was uncertain and undefined. *Ager Gabinus* was not limited to the territory of Gabii, a small town eighteen kilometers to the east of Rome on the road to Praeneste, but also included the *agri* of Latin cities and colonies. *Ager peregrinus*, then, would include the lands of Rome's other allies.

Now, Latin authors used *ager* in a variety of ways, among them fields belonging to some private person or the land in the hands of some ruler or ethnic group. Varro (*LL* 5.32) proclaims that "where Latinus once had his kingdom, the entire *ager* was called *Latinus*, but, when taken in parts, it is named after towns, as *Praenestinus* from Praeneste and *Aricinus* from Aricia." Mommsen's conception of *ager Romanus* can certainly be found in some passages. The Elder Cato (*FRHist* 5 F 46 = Varro *RR* 1.2.7) claims that the *ager Gallicus* between Ariminum and the land of the Picentes was called Roman because it had been distributed to Roman citizens, probably as a result of C. Flaminius's agrarian law of 232. Livy (27.37) reports that in 207 the *haruspices* recommended that a hermaphrodite in Frusino, a town of citizens without the vote about seventy-five kilometers from Rome, should be taken immediately from the *ager Romanus*.

On closer examination, however, Mommsen's interpretation proves untenable.[80] While Roman authors did occasionally use *ager Romanus* to denote the lands inhabited by citizens, who were widely dispersed, rendering the category rather abstract and difficult to define on the ground, they also used the word in a narrower fashion. Varro created an etymology for *peregrinus* that made peregrine lands those into which the Romans first advanced from *ager Romanus*. Thus, his augurs must have placed at least some of the tracts that citizens had come to occupy in another category or categories. In his work *De religione*, the jurist C. Trebatius Testa, another contemporary of Cicero, also distinguishes between Rome's original lands, which he calls its *ager antiquus*, and later additions.[81] In the fragment, Testa asserts that the same rites and practices (*caerimonia moreque*) ought to be used in sacred groves within this core and on captured lands as well, apparently recognizing no difference between them in this regard. Did others think that the distinction ought to have more significant consequences? In his prodigy notices, moreover, Livy sometimes reports portents in the *ager Romanus* as well as other nearby locations, such the *ager Veiens*, the *ager Crustuminus*, Ostia, Tarracina, and the *ager Veliternus*, all occupied by citizens.[82]

If Varro's *ager Romanus* denoted only some inner core around Rome, what were his *ager Gabinus* and *ager peregrinus*? Pierangelo Catalano has suggested, with considerable force, that *ager Gabinus* was limited to the old city of Gabii and its hinterland.[83] Like other places near the city, Gabii occupied an important place in the history, real or imagined, of Roman institutions. By the end of the republic, and for some uncertain time before, it was viewed as the source for certain ritual forms, the *ritus Gabinus*, and costume, the *cinctus Gabinus*. Dionysius of Halicarnassus (*Ant.Rom.* 1.84.5) and Plutarch (*Rom.* 6) hold that Romulus learned the art of augury there. Since Livy (43.13) once referred to the Latin colony of Fregellae as "a peregrine place" (*in loco peregrino*), the augural *ager peregrinus* probably included the lands of both Latin and allied towns.[84] Indeed, since it apparently included all that was not in the core *ager Romanus*, or in *ager Gabinus*, or in the hands of enemies (*ager hosticus*), the category covered lands occupied by citizens, Latins, and allies.

If this reconstruction is correct, the augurs distinguished between Rome's environs (*ager Romanus*), lands that they saw as coming into Rome's power later, whether occupied by citizens, Latins, or allies (*ager Gabinus* and *ager peregrinus*), and the territories of communities that lie outside Rome's order (*ager hosticus*). The use of *peregrinus* to describe lands occupied by citizens, Latins, or allies is not as remarkable as it might appear at first glance. As we have seen, when describing persons, *peregrinus* was often contrasted with citizen, but when describing things or practices, it could denote ones brought more fully into the Roman order.[85] Recall that C. Trebatius Testa described as "captured" lands outside Rome's ancient territory. With respect to *ager peregrinus*, then, the civic status of its inhabitants and the polities in which they lived were not the augurs' primary concerns, which focused instead on the auspices, and thus on magistrates and the acceptability of their activities to the gods, which were not directly determined by the status of those among whom they acted.

When Cicero assigned to his augurs the task of keeping free and unobstructed the *urbs* and the *agri* (in the plural), he probably intended for them to maintain not only the boundary that separated *urbs Roma* from the *ager Romanus* but also a further line that would have separated the *ager Romanus* and perhaps the *ager Gabinus* from the lands outside it, for the outer limits of *ager peregrinus* would not have been clearly definable and, in any case, would have been too far from the city to receive the augurs' attentions. By setting out the auspices that magistrates might use in Latin and allied communities, the augurs found a way for Roman magistrates to act, in accordance with Jupiter's will, in all. In this way, the augurs' categorization of spaces is yet another instance of an attempt to create some overarching order that we have already encountered in the augural and juridical *terra Italia* and in the general use of *peregrinus*.

The augurs, then, created a nested series of spaces that they associated with different auspices: the urban auspices, bound by the *pomerium*; another to be used in *ager Romanus*; those suitable in *ager peregrinus*; and finally the auspices involved in the actual conduct of war. Note that the assemblage formed by *ager Romanus*, *ager pereginus*, and *ager hosticus* represents not only a series of statuses but also their enumeration out from the center, much as Roman legislators would do with their categories (see chapter 6). These spaces also represent movement from the city. For the augurs, entering and leaving their spaces were matters of concern, features that we have already encountered in inaugurated *templa* and with respect to *urbs Roma* itself. Crossing one more distant augural boundary was linked with its own auspices. A late antique grammarian claims that a special form of the auspices, the *pertermine auspicium*, was taken when crossing from the "Roman boundary" (*finis Romanus*) into *ager peregrinus*.[86] Since he linked the crossing of this boundary with the movement into peregrine lands, his "Roman *finis*" must separate *ager peregrinus* from *ager Romanus*. Another form of the auspices, the *auspicium peremnia*, was employed when crossing rivers, for flowing water provided an augural boundary of its own. Livy (23.36.9–10) reports that Q. Fabius Maximus (cos. 215) was delayed in crossing the Volturnus into Campania because he was having difficulty in obtaining positive auspices. Much of Roman government involved increasingly lengthy journeys from the center, and the augurs clearly were concerned with movement across spaces and a magistrate's changing relationship with the center and its gods while doing so. Note that the grammarian presents that act as outbound, that is, as moving into *ager peregrinus* from *ager Romanus*, just as consuls auspicated when crossing the *amnis Petronia* on the way to the *campus Martius*. Except for the return across Rome's *pomerium*, which ended commands, the outward journey was apparently more important than its reverse, if only because an official's primary responsibility lay at its outer limits.

Several passages in Livy's history confirm the existence of an inner zone, with identifiable limits, beyond the city but within the broader area occupied by Roman citizens in the late third and early second centuries. In the first, he (22.15.11) claims that in 216 the dictator Q. Fabius Maximus strengthened the garrison at Tarracina in order to deny Hannibal access by the *via Appia* to the *ager Romanus*; as we have seen in chapter 3, some Roman citizens already lived in tribal clusters well to the colony's south. In the same year, after Hannibal had sent an ambassador to propose peace, the dictator sent a lictor to warn him to leave Roman *fines* before night, a command that implies that the boundary was not very far away.[87] Finally, in 216, because its members were outraged by their demands, the senate sent a lictor to lead Capuan ambassadors out of the city and order them beyond the Roman boundaries (*fines Romani*) that night.[88] A late antique grammarian, one should recall, placed the *auspicium pertermine* at the point where the auspiciant crossed Roman *fines* into *ager peregrinus*.[89]

How old was the augurs' ensemble? Here, the augurs' categories provide the only evidence. *Ager Romanus* and *ager Gabinus* derived their names from specific polities and may be quite old, while *ager hosticus* may once have denoted only non-Roman lands in general, since *hostis* first meant "foreigner" rather than merely "enemy" (see chapter 3). On at least one other occasion, the augurs treated a place away from Rome and its immediate vicinity with some specificity, much as they did with Gabii. At some uncertain point after its foundation in the middle of the fourth century, the augurs made Ostia an *urbs maritima et effata*, associated in some fashion with the Tiber, so that fleet commanders might conduct their operations from it.[90] Ostia regularly served as a base for magistrates conducting naval operations, as opposed to other places that might rarely or intermittently witness the presence of higher officials.

Ager peregrinus, however, is an abstraction, and as an abstraction it can always accommodate expansion. As we have seen, the adjective *peregrinus* probably developed in the middle or late third century where it was used to denote an intermediate category between citizen and enemy or foreign practices that had been brought more fully within Rome's civic order. By creating *ager peregrinus* with its own auspices, the augurs may have recognized the necessity for commanders to pass through the territories of friendly polities before reaching the targets of their operations or to exercise jurisdiction among subordinated peoples, a sign not only of the growing sphere of Roman operations but also of their increasing complexity. Along with *terra Italia*, the use of *peregrinus* indicates that the augural categorization of spaces was ongoing in the third century.

If *ager peregrinus* was the last of the augurs' ensemble, just how early would the augural *ager Romanus* have been? Traces can be found of adjustments that the Romans made to accommodate operations at greater distances from the center, some of which refer to the second half of the fourth century, just the period when Rome's citizens and its armies had begun to spread far from the old core, although their historicity and their proper interpretation is often far from clear. If for any reason—uncertain or negative signs or checks in battle—commanders thought their auspices to be in doubt, they, and not their armies, returned to Rome to start over, a *repetitio auspiciorum*, yet another indication of the close connection of the auspices to Rome and its environs.[91] Livy preserves examples of the practice from the late fourth and the late third centuries—his account of the intermediate years is largely lost—and, as might be expected, the commanders were operating in Campania, against the Marsi and in southern Etruria, and probably in northwestern Samnium, all broadly within western central Italy.[92] A late antique commentator reports that, while magistrates had once returned to Rome for this purpose, as they began to operate at greater distances, they did not wish to leave their armies in order to go to Rome and back, so they designated a place in their area of operation as *ager Romanus*.[93] Note that they created spaces to serve in place of Rome's environs, not the *urbs*, possibly because reentering the city would have ended a command.

At about the same time, the same fiction was sometimes associated with the appointment of dictators. In most instances, a consul made the appointment at Rome, returning to the city if away.[94] On three occasions in the fourth century, however, a consul is said to have appointed a dictator in the camp, apparently in order to avoid breaking off military operations.[95] This shift may not have been without controversy. According to Livy (8.23.13–17), a consul of 327 appointed a dictator in camp, but the augurs declared the act improper. In Livy's account, the priests do not give a reason for their conclusion. Instead, he has the tribunes of the plebs, who were opposing the augurs, proclaim that no augural reason could have existed, for no augur had witnessed the performance of the rite and no report about it had reached them, and then suggest that opposition to a plebeian dictator was the real reason behind their ruling.[96] Livy's lack of clarity about the form of the *vitium* may indicate that he, or his source, did not know it. Could opposition to performing the act away from Rome have been part of the problem?

Appointments during the Second Punic War make the link to an *ager Romanus* explicit. On a least two occasions, consuls returned to Rome to name a dictator.[97] In 210, however, the senate informed a consul in Sicily that his appointment of a dictator in his area of operations was invalid since dictators could not be appointed outside the *ager Romanus*, which was bounded by Italy, and two years later they informed another consul at Capua that, if he could not come to Rome for the elections, he should appoint a dictator within the *ager Romanus* to do so.[98] Recall that our sources use *ager Romanus* in three distinct ways: the territory occupied by

Roman citizens, Rome's immediate vicinity, and a space intended as a substitute for the inner *ager Romanus*. In the case of the consul at Capua in 208, the senate's *ager Romanus* was probably the last of these possibilities, for Capua and its environs almost certainly would have been considered Roman at the time, while a return to Rome's environs would have been virtually the same as a return to Rome.[99] The consul on Sicily clearly appointed his dictator outside of *ager Romanus* in the broadest sense, since citizens did not have their domiciles outside of Italy, but he may have attempted to define an *ager Romanus* in his camp, an act that the senate declared to be improper at that distance.[100] While the practice of defining an *ager Romanus* in such a fashion was probably older, the norm restricting the operation to Italy would have been an artifact of the First or Second Punic Wars.[101]

The creation of such spaces in camps or areas of operations, then, points to the existence or the simultaneous development of *ager Romanus*, in some form, as an augural concept; the augurs, in other words, may have first become concerned with the limits of Rome's core *ager* when its armies had begun to campaign with some regularity far from it. If this is correct, their response would represent yet another instance of an elite concern for the performance of crucial activities or the making of important decisions away from Rome, of which traces, always difficult to interpret, can be found in the fifth and fourth centuries and more securely in the third and second (see chapter 6).

In scholarly debates, the location of these Roman *fines*, the limits of the augural *ager Romanus*, has become intertwined with the matter of the *ager Romanus antiquus*.[102] Writers of the late republic and empire occasionally presented Rome's territory under the kings as a more or less clearly defined space.[103] Some linked these early limits with specific places. Ovid (*Fasti* 2. 679–84) reports that the festival of the *Terminalia* involved a sacrifice at the sixth milestone on the *via Laurentina*, which he appears to have viewed as a remnant of a very early frontier between the Romans and the nearby Laurentes.[104] A few years later, the Greek geographer Strabo (5.3.2) mentions a "place called *Festoi*" between the fifth and sixth milestones on an unnamed road that marked Rome's boundary under Romulus, and he asserts that certain priests, probably the pontiffs, performed a sacrifice there and at several other places because they also marked the same early limit.

Using these sites as a model, some scholars have identified as boundary shrines other places at a similar distance from the city and along the roads that radiated from it: a statue of Mars at the fourth milestone of the *via Appia*; the sanctuary of *Fortuna muliebris* at the fourth milestone of the *via Latina*, which supposedly marked the place where Roman matrons had persuaded Coriolanus to turn back from his march on Rome; the sacred grove of Robigo, who kept disease from Rome's crops, at the fifth milestone of the *via Claudia*; the grove of Dea Dia, whose priests purified Rome's agricultural lands, at the fifth milestone of the *via Campana*.[105]

In this way, then, scholars envision the preservation of yet another fossilized boundary, fixed through cult sites and the festivals that encompassed them, that once marked the outer limits of Rome's territory, just as others view the festival of the *Septimontium* and the *pomerium* as successive archaic limits to the city of Rome. In any case, modern estimates of the age when Rome's civic order was supposedly encompassed within this ring vary from the eighth to the end of the fifth century. For some, an association with Romulus should indicate that the sites marked the outer limits of Rome's territory when it first formed as an organized community, whenever this "event" might be seen as having taken place. For others, the boundary was a creation of some later, but not much later, period, to be determined by assessments of when the polity was large enough, or small enough, to have fit within it.

Adam Ziółkowski has directed strong arguments against viewing these sanctuaries as fossilized representations of Rome's earliest frontier.[106] According to Strabo, certain priests performed at *Festoi* and several other places sacrifices that he calls *ambarouia thusia*, which some scholars view as part of the festival of the *Ambarvalia*, when priests led sacrificial animals around the limits of Rome's territory, frozen in the distant past, with sacrifices at the cult sites that marked its course.[107] A procession around some frontier, even one quite close to Rome, almost certainly would have been far too long to be encompassed within a day, but it remains possible that such a sacrifice might have marked only a few points, leaving the rest untouched and perhaps undefined.[108] Still, Ziółkowski rejects the entire rite, partly because the *Ambarvalia* does not appear on surviving calendars and partly because the word *ambarvalia* appears in our sources, not as a name for some specific occasion, but rather as an adjective characterizing a kind of cult act that might form a part of larger performances.[109] At the same time, and more importantly in the present context, Ziółkowski casts doubt on the liminal nature of many of the supposed boundary shrines, for no surviving text attributes such a function to most of them—their sacred nature, their distance from Rome, and their locations on radial roads are the only indicators. There is, moreover, no firm evidence that any of the places marked a genuinely old boundary, for attributing later practices to the distant past was common in Rome, while the proposed ring around the city is far too regular to mark a plausible frontier.

At core, viewing the *ager Romanus antiquus* and the cult sites that supposedly marked its outer limits as Rome's territory at an early date rests on a certain model for locating extra-urban sanctuaries in archaic Italy. Here, most sacred sites either were in the main settlement or formed a kind of "sacred belt" immediately adjacent to it, while a few were placed much farther away on the frontiers of the polity.[110] In later periods, Rome and its hinterland contained a range of sacred sites, most of which appear to have been in the city or just outside its walls. But Festus (p. 296 L) reports that the *Pomonal*, associated with the deity Pomona and the *flamen Pomonalis*, often thought to be among the most archaic features in public cult, was located in the *ager Solonius* at the twelfth milestone on the *via Ostiensis*, beyond the supposed limits of the *ager Romanus antiquus*. Even in the Greek world, the ultimate source of the model, some supposedly liminal shrines were only toward the frontiers rather than on them, while a few sites might be distributed more widely over the civic territory.

But still, Ovid and Strabo did give a liminal role to the site of *Terminalia* and to *Festoi* and other places that witnessed the *ambarousia thusia*, and some Romans may have thought that the grove of Dea Dia served such a function as well. This grove was the seat of the priestly college of the *fratres arvales*, which Romulus supposedly had founded.[111] The college's rites sought to guard the productivity of Rome's plow lands, its *arvum*, and because of this link between the priesthood and the fields, many have identified the grove with Strabo's *Festoi*; the *arvales*, however, are only known to have performed their rites at the grove of Dea Dia, while Strabo claims that the priests in question performed sacrifices at several places. Excavations at the grove have revealed signs of cult from as early as circa 300, although much remains unexplored. Among the many imperial inscriptions found there, one, recording a performance of A.D. 218, set out the prayer or *carmen* that the *fratres Arvales* recited on the second day of sacrifices.[112] It is archaic or archaizing, apparently composed before the shift from an intervocalic "s" to an "r" in the late fourth century, and its contents are obscure. It had, if only in part, an apotropaic purpose, invoking Mars as guardian of the threshold or *limen*, although scholars are divided over whether the limit in question was Rome's or the shrine's or the grove's.[113] John Scheid points out that the grove occupies the slope of a hill that bars the right bank of the Tiber, and he suggests that this placement confers on it the character of a port of entry into the lands around the city.[114]

That said, any association between the *Terminalia*, the *ambarousia thusia*, and perhaps the grove of Dea Dia with Rome's earliest frontiers is probably a retrospective one. Ziółkowski suggests that the concept of Rome's ancestral core appeared in the first century as part of the antiquarian speculation that was common at the time, largely because we first hear of it in works of this period. But if, as has sometimes been suggested, Strabo drew his information from Polybius's history, which in turn may have rested on the work of Fabius Pictor, the connection between "*Festoi*" and Rome's original *ager* would have been at least as old as the late third century.[115] Recall that Livy attributed references to Roman *fines* to the last decades of the third century, and he records concerns over Rome's core *ager* in the fourth.

Where, then, were the outer limits of the augural *ager Romanus*? Accepting that the space was genuinely old, Adam Ziółkowski, whose chief concern was to show that the *ager Romanus antiquus* was not Rome's earliest frontier, proposed two possibilities: either Rome's territory at the end of the monarchy (i.e., a very early boundary, but not the earliest) or "the one mile wide belt around the city walls created for the sake of the *comitia centuriata* and within which the *tribunicia potestas* was operative."[116] Varro, one should recall, claimed that the *ager Romanus* and the *ager Gabinus* shared the same auspices, which should indicate that they abutted to the east of Rome. If this limit marked the Roman *fines*, then Gabii's own limits would have come within a mile of Rome, which is unlikely. But what about other routes away from the center? Ovid and Strabo linked the sites for the *Terminalia* and the places where the pontiffs performed certain liminal rites with Rome's frontiers under Romulus, much as Varro did with his augural *ager Romanus*. Given this similarity, it is possible, although uncertain, that they did actually mark portions of the augural boundary. After all, Livy's claim (23.6.7–8) that the senate ordered the ambassadors of the Campani to leave the city and cross the Roman *fines* by night implies that they were not very far away.

INSIDE AND OUTSIDE

Over time, the augurs established a nested series of spaces that took on its developed form in the third century. Within the city and near to it, they created under the supervision of magistrates inaugurated places that served to frame important activities. They also built out zones from the city, bounded by the *pomerium*, the outer limits of their *ager Romanus*, the territories that had come into Roman hands, and finally the lands of their enemies and the frequent scene of military operations. In this way, augural practice was but a specific instance of a broader tendency to build zones around Rome or occasionally other centers as well, which we have encountered informally in the distribution of statuses and official roles and in the acknowledgment of prodigies and will later encounter with greater formality in laws, edicts, and decrees. Like the early significance of *provincia*, these augural zones concerned magistrates and their ability to act and move legitimately rather than the peoples or polities encompassed within them. *Terra Italia*, with its boundaries at the Aesis and Arnus Rivers, constituted a still larger zone, although its augural consequences are uncertain.

These spaces and zones, moreover, were connected to a valuation in which the inner was preferred or emphasized over the outer, a feature that we will later encounter in Roman legislation as well. In the small spaces, *templa*, that the augurs constituted in and about Rome, they performed the operations of a *liberatio* and an *effatio*, which defined their limits and removed unwanted spiritual influences from their interiors; later operations might impose a law or laws on these spaces. (Although they were not *templa*, the clearings at the center of sacred groves were more important than the woods that surrounded them and separated them from the outside world, and they too might be regulated by laws.)[117]

Although the *urbs* was not a *templum*—profane activities did take place in it—the *pomerium* excluded matters relating to war, and magistrates, priests, and the senate might prohibit others in certain circumstances: the Twelve Tables, for example, barred burials within the *urbs*, while on a number of occasions during the first century priests of Isis and cult places dedicated to her were ordered removed from the *urbs* or even the Capitol.[118] A purification of the *urbs* (*lustratio urbis*) was one of the most common rituals used to expiate prodigies, while other rites, such as that of the *Argei*, closely connected to the four urban regions, performed the same broad function in different contexts.[119] Special powers, moreover, might be attributed from time to time to religious functionaries within it: Pliny (*HN* 28.13) claims that the Vestals might fix the feet of runaway slaves there. (By the late republic, if not earlier, Roman legislators thought that some of these rules were appropriate to other settlements as well: the authors of the *lex coloniae Iuliae Genetivae* banned burials from within "boundaries of the town where the plow was led around," while decurions, augurs, and pontiffs were to have their domiciles within the *urbs* or within a mile of it unless they had received a special exemption.)[120] The pontiffs' sanctification of Rome's walls was thought to help ensure the city's safety, while priests expressed the opinion that the underworld gods ought not be summoned within the walls during the *ludi Taurei*.[121]

The same practice persisted on a larger scale away from the city. Some scholars suggest that the limits of the augural *ager Romanus* possessed an apotropaic function, just as Rome's walls and its *pomerium* may have done; we have already seen how decrees used it as reference point when driving undesirable persons away from the city. *Terra Italia* provides a clearer example. By 225, if not earlier, Rome's allies within its bounds were organized for military purposes in the *formula togatorum*. By the last decade of the third century, *terra Italia* and the *formula togatorum* had received an implicit complement outside the peninsula in the *formula amicorum, sociorum*, or *sociorum et amicorum*, which listed individuals and polities outside of Italy that had the right for their representatives in Rome to be introduced into the senate and to receive public lodging (see chapter 3). The differing treatment of allies inside and outside peninsular Italy is clearly reflective of a qualitative difference.

Terra Italia also appears in language attributed to edicts and decrees of the last decades of the third century, in which it emerges as a kind of special space. On two occasions during the Second Punic War, Livy (25.7.1–4; 27.28.3) attributes to senatorial decrees the temporal restriction that their provisions were to be in force "as long as the enemy was in the land of Italy" (*donec hostis in terra Italia esset*). For 205, he (29.10) reports that the *decemviri sacris faciundis*, after consulting the Sibylline Books, declared that "whenever a foreign foe should bring war on the land of Italy, he could be driven from Italy and punished if the Idaean Mother were brought to Rome from Pessinus." Later, he (38.47) has Cn. Manlius Vulso (cos. 189) tell the senate that he should receive a triumph because he had "left everything this side of the Taurus range more peaceful than the land of Italy." In the earliest surviving use of the term, the Elder Cato too uses it while describing a foreign intrusion.[122] When the augurs defined *terra Italia*, they may have thought, or hoped, that military operations would largely, if not entirely, be conducted beyond its limits.

Some Romans sought to link the boundaries separating these spaces, creating, if only in the imagination, an overarching order that focused on the city. When Cicero (*Leg.* 2.20–21) assigns to his augurs the task of keeping free and unobstructed the *urbs* and the *agri* (in the plural), he probably intended for them to maintain the boundary that separated *urbs Roma* from the *ager Romanus*, but also a further line that would have separated the *ager Romanus* from the lands outside it. The dictator Sulla extended the *pomerium*, utilizing a supposedly ancient privilege that those who had expanded the frontiers of Italy might also do the same to Rome's own *pomerium*, probably a reference to the movement of the limits of *terra Italia* from the Aesis to the Rubicon.[123] Plutarch (*Rom.* 11) claims that Romulus founded Rome first by drawing a circle around the *comitium*, the interior of which was circular in form, and then by plowing a furrow at a greater distance from the same center, which would become the *pomerium*.

Connections could also be made that were grander in scale. Romans customarily translated the Greek *oikoumenē*, which had no intrinsic shape—it was defined by the contrast with nomads (*nomades*) who followed a different way of life—by *orbis terrarum* (circle of lands), which possessed not only an implicit shape but also the possibility of a center. Varro (*LL* 5.143) links through a contrived etymology an *urbs*, whose connection with the plowing of a furrow around it he had just described, with *orbis* (circle) and *urvum* (curved), and stresses that it lies within the *pomerium*. Writing a generation later, Ovid (*Fasti* 2.683–84) asserts that other nations have fixed boundaries, but for Rome the *urbs* and the *orbis* are the same. In a fragment from an unknown work, Varro identifies the *orbis terrarum* as the vault of the heavens and the lands encompassed beneath them as defined by an observer creating a *templum* in order to observe the heavens for signs, a rite that may have been performed only at Rome.[124] In this case, the words *orbis terrarum* would quite literally constitute a "circle of lands" around the auspiciant, and perhaps around Rome as well, which may provide its original meaning. At the very least, one can detect a persistent tendency to image Rome in terms of a series of circles drawn around it.

Roman writers often depicted their order in terms of a contrast between the city and regions under its power, and they frequently represented official activity in terms of official journeys away from Rome and returns to the city. Roman practice also constructed, if only implicitly and informally, a series of irregular zones around Rome, constituted in part by official activity and in part by the spatial distribution of statuses. The augurs established a more explicit and formal version of the same broad practice. Cult was closely connected to places, and the activities that were most relevant to the Roman order were concentrated in and near the city. Here, the augurs sanctified certain places that were essential to the performance of crucial public activities and set rules that kept them close to the city. They also drew clear lines around Rome—the *pomerium*, the limits of the augural *ager Romanus*, and *terra Italia*—in which the inner zone was emphasized over the outer. The priests do not appear to have felt the need to construct further limits outside of peninsular Italy. The outermost of these limits, moreover, was distant from the others, creating denser lines nearer the center, while the innermost, the *pomerium*, had the most significant associations. These augural spaces primarily affected magistrates and their powers and movements and were not directly concerned with those who might live within them. At the same time, the augurs were especially concerned with the implications of crossing these boundaries, giving special emphasis to the outward journey. In the following chapters, we will see the same broad pattern in other spaces.

FIVE

Sciences of the Center

The senate assigned to magistrates polities or regions against or in which they were to conduct certain operations, forming spaces from their subsequent activities Magistrates and their assigned tasks also provided the lens through which other spaces in Rome and abroad might be viewed and created. In the city, prominent places gave to officials and priests orientations that placed them in some relationship with Rome's gods. Away from Rome, officials applied similar principles to a range of other spaces that they would create, and in the process they also established clear centers surrounded by more or less clearly defined zones, much as the augurs had done with Rome.

TEMPLA, THEIR ORIENTATIONS, AND THEIR DIVISIONS

In chapter 4, we surveyed the range of spaces that were designated *templa*. The use of the same word for so many spaces obscures that fact that they were, in many ways, not very much alike. Some were fields of vision; others were clearly defined enclosures on the ground. Inaugurated *templa* were rectangular in form, but the *templum in terra* was roughly triangular, with the auspiciant at the apex. Creators of some *templa* stood on the margins of the space they were creating, while those who established others stood at the center. At the most basic level, all *templa* were bounded spaces that were intended to frame an official actor and his legitimate actions. Many, if not all, were also linked by an abstract system of internal organization and orientation, one that the Romans would also impose on a still broader range of spaces.

Templa of all forms were linked to the perspectives and the persons of the priests or magistrates who created them and of the functionaries who would continue to use them. The antiquarian Varro provides the bulk of our evidence for the fields of vision that auspicants created when they left their *tabernacula*. In his *On the Latin Language* (LL 7.6–10), he discusses a number of meanings for *templum* for which he also provided an etymology. In the process, he mixes poetic uses with augural ones, for his interest was the word and not augural practice.[1] After beginning with a line from Ennius's *Annales* referring to the *templa* of the heavens, Varro announces that *templum* is used in three ways—"by nature" (*ab natura*), "by auspicating" (*ab auspicando*), and "by likeness" (*ab similitudine*)—and goes on to link the first with the heavens (*in caelo*), the second with "on the land" (*in terra*), and the third with "under the land" (*sub terra*).[2] Varro then quotes verses to illustrate each of the three. Next, Varro turns to the *templum* "in the heavens," but before examining this segment, we should first consider the *templum in terra*—that is, the field of vision created to observe the behavior of birds and the earthly enclosure from which it was formed.

Varro and Livy both describe the creation of the necessary visual field from the *arx*, the only place the rite is known to have been performed. In Livy's account (1.18.6–10) of the supposed inauguration of Rome's second king, Numa Pompilius, the future king sat in the *auguraculum* facing south, while the augur who would take the auspices sat next to him facing east.[3] Then, looking out over the city and the surrounding fields, the priest marked out the lines (*regiones*) that defined the outer limits of his space to the left and to the right. Next, he fixed in his mind some landmark far in front of him on the horizon. In *On the Latin Language* (7.6–8), Varro sets out the formula that the augurs used to create this space, a text that is certainly fairly old, for its language is obscure and archaic.[4] In it, the auspicant first identifies a tree to his left and pronounces it to be the boundary between the *templum* and the "wild" (*tescum*) and then does the same to his right. Varro explains the formula as first establishing the outer limits by identifying the trees that defined them and then subdividing the space by lines (*regiones*) created by a glance. In Livy's account, the auspicant also identifies a point directly in front of him which would have divided the space into two halves. In addition, although it is less certain, the *pomerium*, which crossed this field of vision, probably provided another limit to the field of vision, dividing it into two registers, one connected with low-flying birds and the other with high-flying ones.[5] At the end of the second century, the augurs required the removal of the upper story of a senator's house because it obstructed their lines of sight; in 100 C. Marius built his votive temple to Honos and Virtus on the Velia without a podium so as not to obstruct their view.[6]

An installation at another city broadly confirms this reconstruction. Near the end of the second century, the allied polity at Bantia on the margins of Lucania and Apulia reorganized its civic life on the model of Rome, in the process replacing scattered settlements with a more nucleated core. Its citizens created a charter for their city now known as the Oscan Law of Bantia.[7] In it, the framers set out rules for magistrates, assemblies, trials before the people, and private litigation, all in formulas that were near to Latin. The charter of the nearby Latin colony of Venusia may have provided the model.[8]

Slightly earlier, Bantia's elite also constructed a rectangular enclosure for taking the auspices, about nine meters from east to west and eight from north to south, that was clearly oriented toward the cardinal directions.[9] A seat for the officiating augur or magistrate lies just outside the enclosure, in the middle of and parallel to its western side. Nine stone markers, arranged in three parallel rows of three, aided in the construction of the field of vision. Two rows define the northern and southern limits of the enclosure; the contents of their inscriptions, which guided the interpretation of signs, are obscure. The third row runs from east to west across the center; its easternmost marker bears the name of Jupiter, the central one names *Sol*—that is, the sun—and the westernmost carries the name of a local divinity. The location of the auspiciant's seat, along with the fact that the inscriptions on the markers can only be read from the west, clearly demonstrates that he was marginal to his *templum*. In this way, then, the augural enclosure at Bantia eliminates the possibility, if only for this form of enclosure, that the person taking the auspices sat at the center of the space he was creating, a position that many scholars have held.[10]

In his fuller discussion of the augurs and the heavens, Varro begins with an etymology for *templum* that connects it with *intuiti* (gazed on), thus making the heavens the first *templum*; cites a verse from Ennius's *Annales* that calls the sky the great *templum* of Jupiter; and then quotes another by the late third-century poet Naevius depicting the heavens as a hemisphere bounded by the vault of the sky.[11] The antiquarian (*LL* 7.7) then notes that the four parts (*partes*) of this *templum* are the left to the east, the right to the west, the front (*antica*) to the south, and the back (*postica*) to the north. Here, his nomenclature implies a southward orientation to the observer, a matter to which we will return shortly.

Jerzy Linderski holds that this celestial *templum* was not augural and suggests that the augurs required the delimitation of a more restricted field to frame the search for signs. Since those performing the rite rushed out of their *tabernacula* and divided the space in front of them, such a *templum* would have contained only a portion of the heavenly vault, the margins of which would have been defined by the horizon and the officiant's restricted field of vision. Since persons taking the auspices were to be still, moreover, the person taking the auspices clearly occupied a position that was marginal to the space he was observing. More recently, R. Taylor takes Naevius's hemisphere literally as half of a sphere, not just a portion of one.[12] Since an observer cannot take a marginal position with respect to the vault of the heavens, he suggests that auspicants occupied the center of their space, for him the chief matter at issue, and proposes that they either rotated around the center to view the various quadrants or had an attendant observe the spaces behind them, despite requirements that persons taking the auspices be still or that they personally observe signs.

When Varro set out the parts of the celestial *templum*, did he intend the vault of the heavens or some more restricted field of vision? The antiquarian links the fourfold organization explicitly to the heavens that he has just illustrated with verses from Naevius and Ennius: they are the four parts of "this *templum*" (*eius templi partes quattuor*). Elsewhere, in a passage that is examined later in this chapter, Varro asserts that the Etruscan *haruspices* also divided into four parts by two axes the *orbis terrarum*. The practice of viewing the sky as a hemispherical vault is also observable in other republican authors.[13]

Varro's divisions of the heavens, then, apply most directly to the vault of the sky. If this interpretation is correct, we do not know how the augurs organized the search for signs *ex caelo* or if they defined some more restricted *templum* to do so. The Etruscan *haruspices* did acknowledge certain obscure correspondences between spaces that they projected on the heavens and others that they imposed on the livers of sacrificial animals, although neither would have looked very much alike. In the second of his codes in *On the Laws* (3.43), Cicero claims that the augurs' knowledge of the divisions of the heavens (*partes caeli*) made possible the conduct of public business. Here, he probably means that they should be familiar with the significance of the various regions of the vault of the heavens and their implications for the interpretation of the meanings of signs detected within at least some augural spaces. In some fashion, *templa* were in correspondence with the heavens.

The word *templum* also serves to characterize enclosures firmly marked on the ground: spaces for sortitions or for observing the feeding of chickens—that is, the auspices *ex tripudiis*, the dominant form away from Rome—and more permanent inaugurated spaces that might contain temples, altars, or other prominent structures. Scattered passages indicate that these spaces too involved the same, or similar, rules of orientation and division. As we shall soon see, there are signs that right and left were significant when observing the feeding of chickens. Orthogonal axes, moreover, did form, or come to form, part of inaugurated *templa*. The Augustan historian Dionysius of Halicarnassus (*Ant.Rom.* 4.59.2–61.4) imagines the *templum* that would hold Jupiter's Capitoline temple as defined by its outer limits and by four quadrants within them.[14] Some late republican and early imperial authors claim that a *stella*, formed by two orthogonal lines, was put at the entrance to all such places, with the words *antica* (in front) and *postica* (behind) inscribed on it, while contemporary inscriptions recording the dedication of temples indicate that the dedicator confirmed the space's defining *regiones*.[15]

Unlike *templa* for observing the flight of birds, those forming spaces on the ground sometimes did so from their centers. In Cicero's depiction (*Div.* 1.31) of the performance by Attus Navius of an *augurium stativum*, a rite intended to determine the location of some object, the legendary augur stood in the middle of a vineyard facing south and divided it into four parts and then asked for signs in order to identify the quadrant in which the largest cluster of grapes was to be found so that he might fulfill a vow. Similarly, Roman surveyors, whose practice resembled the augural organization of spaces rather closely, also constructed their boundaries from a single central point, as we shall see in the following section. Finally, in a passage that is unfortunately corrupt, a scholiast writing on Vergil's *Aeneid* describes a commander sitting on his augural seat in his *tabernaculum*, freeing from their cage the chickens for the auspices and placing them around his seat (*circum sellam suam*) and then, after silence had fallen, pronouncing a formula that included a request for a good omen from the left (*sinisterum solistimum*).[16] The scholiast depicts the commander as sitting openly in the presence of his army (*coram exercitu*) whose divisions he notes in the invocation in a formula that may have developed before the Social War since it includes soldiers of the Latin Name.

The augurs clearly favored eastward and southward orientations. Thus, Varro named the *templum* that was the heavens from the perspective of an observer facing toward the south, the same perspective that Cicero gives to the legendary augur Attus Navius when performing the *augurium stativum*. The inscriptions on the stones in the augural enclosure at Bantia reveal both southward and eastward orientations, as does Livy, who has Numa face south for his inauguration and the augur who was to inaugurate him face east. In the grid that was formed in this fashion, the distinction between left and right was primary. In the first century, if not earlier, Jupiter was viewed as looking from the north toward the south. Since the left was deemed more fortunate, the eastern side would have been the luckier. At the same time, the north was thought to be stronger than the south. Thus, the most favorable sign was in the northeastern quadrant, while the most unfavorable one sign was in the northwestern. As Cicero (*Div.* 2.82) notes, a single quadrant might be both "right" and "left," almost certainly because of the differing orientations of god and auspiciant. Jupiter and the official taking the auspices were marginal to their space.

In augural *templa*, either god and auspiciant shared the same perspective—that is, both looked to the south—or their lines of sight were at right angles. The recurring rites at altars or temples that were constructed within *templa* added yet another perspective, for celebrants looked toward the structure, its *cella*, and its cult statue, which might be seen as looking back. Festus/Paulus (pp. 244–45 L) gives to the heavens an orientation from north to south and notes that, because of this, the parts of the temple were named according to an eastward orientation, the same combination of celestial and human orientations found in the *templum* from the *arx* or in the *auguraculum* at Bantia. For Vitruvius (4.5.1–2), temples should be constructed, if possible, so that the structure and the cult statue faced the west, in order that those who sacrifice and pray at the altar in front of the temple might look toward it, its statue, and the eastern portion of the heavens. Hyginus Gromaticus (p. 136.13–17 Campbell), a writer of the first or second century of the empire, notes that architects at first had held that temples should face to the west, but later they reversed the preferred orientation since the world was illuminated from the east. The three temples in the Largo Argentina in the *campus Martius*, constructed between the late fourth and the late second centuries in a place where the topography gave to builders considerable freedom, all share a common orientation, with their porches and thus their cult statues facing east. P. Servilius, who probably was an augur and jurist as well as a consul in the middle of the first century, linked the parts of a temple to the orientation of the worshipers. He claims that the portion of a temple that lies behind the door—that is, within the *cella*—was the temple's rear part, which implies that its porch and the altar constituted the front.[17] He went on to state that the portion in front of "us" was called *antica* while that behind us was *postica*—note that he puts his observer in the center of the space—and for this reason, we say that *antica* is to the right and *postica* to the left.

Against this background, it must be stressed that the Roman practice regarding divinatory spaces and temples linked them not only to the cardinal directions and the divine order but also to the perspectives—and, thus, the persons—of Roman magistrates and priests who were also oriented by them. Livy's Numa and Cicero's Attus Navius faced to the south, the same perspective as Jupiter's. Varro (*LL* 7.6–10) gave *templum* an etymology that linked it to the act of gazing upon the heavens. Vitruvius (4.4.1–2) linked the orientation of temples with the direction toward which those performing rites ought to look. At the same time, the officiant certainly occupied a significant location with respect to the auspices *ex avibus*—that is, the *auguraculum* on the *arx*—and they may have done so in other performances as well. When defining their *agri*, the augurs were clearly concerned with magistrates' increasing distance from the city of Rome, but when constructing their *templa*, the chief concern involved properly placing magistrates and their activities with respect to the gods and the larger cosmic order.

Another aspect of *templa* is the link with laws that were to govern the use of their interiors. By the middle of the first century, when the earliest preserved examples are found, records of temple dedications in some towns and citizen colonies, which imitated Roman practices in a number of ways, identify the official who had dedicated the temple, along with the year and the day that he had done so, and set out the prayer in which the dedicator had set, or had taken note of, the *templum*'s defining lines or *regiones* that he was apparently pointing out at the time.[18] Thus, the local magistrates who dedicated a shrine at Furfo announced that they were doing so "by these laws and by these *regiones*," as did others at the citizen colonies of Narbo Martius in A.D. 11 or 12 and Salonae in A.D. 137. The inscriptions, moreover, went on to specify the laws in question, often quite detailed, which identified activities that were permitted or forbidden within the enclosures. Some proclaimed the laws governing the temple of Diana on the Aventine to be valid in their temples as well.[19]

In fact, *templa* of all kinds appear to have been associated with laws, *leges*. When an auspicant defined his visual field, he announced at the same time, in verbal forms appropriate to laws and prayers, the action that he was contemplating and the sign or signs that he hoped to see if it were proper (*fas*) for him to proceed. Temples too had their own laws, given at the time of dedication. Indeed, Festus (p. 204 L) finds it noteworthy that the temple of Ops had no known law. Some temples accumulated laws over time.

Livy (7.3) reports an "ancient law, inscribed in antique letters and words," that required whomever was *praetor maximus* on the ides of September to drive a nail next to the *cella* of Minerva in the Capitoline temple, a rite that he claims was revived because of plague in the fourth century.[20] Laws of the late third and early second centuries from Latin colonies applied rules to sacred groves in much the same manner.[21]

The *comitium* too possessed its laws, and from an early date, for rules relevant to the space can be found in the Twelve Tables. Today, the laws survive only in fragments preserved in juristic and antiquarian works. Although the collection was supposedly composed in the middle of the fifth century, the language of the fragments represents a later Latin, while the conditional clauses vary in form from second- and first-century practice. Beginning with Sex. Aelius Paetus (cos. 198), the Twelve Tables began to attract commentary, while antiquarians such as L. Aelius Stilo later in the century focused on obscure words, an indication that portions were already difficult to interpret. The Elder Pliny (*HN* 34.20) claims that the Twelve Tables were inscribed on a bronze plaque placed on the *rostra*, and, while he attributes it to the Decemvirs in the fifth century, the renovations of the *comitium-curia* complex in the fourth century provide a more likely context. Perhaps this represents the origins of the surviving form of the text. If so, its relationship to the original code is uncertain.[22]

The surviving portions of the Twelve Tables set out a long series of specific infractions and their consequences in order to guide those who would actually judge cases, and in the midst of these rules one also finds clauses that set out how litigation was to proceed. Thus, "if they (*i.e.* the contesting parties) do not agree, they are to present their case in the *comitium* or the forum before midday. They are to finish bringing action together, both present"; "after midday, he (*i.e.* the presiding official) is to confirm the suit to the one present"; "if both are present, sunset is to be the last time (*i.e.* for judgement)"; "on three successive *nundinae*, he (*i.e.* the plaintiff) is to produce him (*i.e.* the defendant) in the *comitium*."[23] Other clauses provide for casting the guilty "from the rock" or selling them "beyond the Tiber" (*trans Tiberim*) while another required that, in cases where the accused's civic status was at stake, the assembly that condemned him had to be well attended.[24]

At a basic level, then, the Twelve Tables sets out how officials and citizens were to conduct themselves in certain important matters within a particular place. It should come as no surprise, then, to find that the complex was adorned with texts of the laws that were to apply within it, just as was the case with temples and altars. At some point, which Pliny (*HN* 34.20) links with its promulgation, the Twelve Tables was inscribed on a bronze plaque affixed to the *rostra*, a structure that bore the name only from circa 338, which may provide a more probable date. By the end of the fourth century, other laws were added as well. Cn. Flavius, curule aedile in 304, placed on the *comitium* a calendar of *dies fasti* along with the *legis actiones*, setting out the days on which the enclosure could be used for a certain purpose and how those coming forward must proceed.

The elaboration of laws about the *comitium* and official actions within it did not cease with these measures. Varro (*LL* 6.5) holds that the Twelve Tables defined the last part of the day, its *suprema*, and the point at which the day's litigation must end, at sunset, but a *lex Plaetoria*, probably of the third century, declared that litigation should end when the urban praetor announced the end of the day in the *comitium* and also ordained that the praetor might have two lictors with him when he administered justice.[25] Thus, the inscriptions recording the Twelve Tables and the *ius Flavianum*, and perhaps the *lex Plaetoria* as well, were placed on the enclosure that they regulated and, by regulating it, shaped in turn crucial interactions between magistrates and citizens and between citizen and citizen. As we shall see in chapter 6, other laws might be linked to spaces built on different principles.

The prologue to Plautus's *Poenulus*, probably first performed in the 190s, reveals a broadly similar practice.[26] In the first two of its three broad parts, the speaker or *prologus* parodies a number of public acts in order to introduce his summary of the plot or *argumentum* of the play. First, he identifies himself as a commander (*imperator*), although of actors, not of soldiers. Then, he issues orders to his herald and an edict to the *curatores ludorum*, the lictors, and to the audience telling them where to sit and how to behave, instructing them as if he were a magistrate addressing an assembly. His words parallel the forms of a magisterial edict. Then, after completing his edict and reminding the audience of his *imperium*, the *prologus* announces (ll. 46–49): "Now I wish to revert again to the plot, so that you might be as well informed as I am. I shall now define its *regiones*, *limites*, and *confinia*; in this matter, I have been made *finitor*" (*Ad argumentum nunc uicissatim uolo remigrare, ut aeque mecum sitis gnarures. eius nunc regiones, limites, confinia determinabo: ei rei ego finitor factus sum*). Slightly later (l. 60), he gives the plot a clear place, the stage on which the play was about to be performed (*locus argumentost suom sibi proscaenium*). The *finitor's regiones*, *limites*, and *confinia*, then, define the stage, which would limit in turn the play.

In his edict, Plautus's *imperator* parodies the words of magistrates, and it is likely that his *finitor* does too. The primary meaning of the words *determinare regiones* is the formal definition of a space; they are often used to describe an augur's setting of the defining lines of his *templum* by word and by gesture.[27] His *finitor* proclaims in the future tense his intention to mark out his boundaries. In the first century and later, as we have seen, the dedicator of a temple or altar defined his space verbally and then set out the laws that would govern it. The opening part of the verbal formula, preserved in a number of inscriptions, partially replicates the words of Plautus's *finitor*, for both announce their intention, in the future tense, to perform a certain action: "When I will give and dedicate this altar to you today, I will give and dedicate it by these laws and by these *regiones*, which I will say openly here today."[28] This ritual definition of a space, moreover, was closely connected with the proclamation of the rules that were to govern it. Here, the third of the prologue's sections, which recounts the play's plot, almost certainly serves to set out the rules that were to govern the theatrical space.

The development of these practices is difficult to set out in stages and place chronologically. After all, the creation of a *templum* imposed an abstract system on a variety of spaces intended for a range of uses, and the category may have extended from just a few forms to include more possibilities. In practice, the orientations of some temples are varied, as one might expect with enclosures firmly traced on the ground rather than projected through the imagination on the heavens or on the landscape. According to Vitruvius (4.5.12), architects might give temples an actual orientation that differed from the ideal if street plans or the local topography required it. Their orientation, then, may sometimes have been created by the conventions of the rite. Indeed, Dionysius of Halicarnassus (*Ant.Rom.* 4.59.2–61.4) sets out a tale, placed in the reign of Rome's last king, that rests on the assumption that the location and orientation of a space were set in part by the consensus of the participants in the rite that created it. It remains possible, however, that some sacred places were older than some of the practices surrounding *templa*, if only in the form in which we later encounter them.

As we shall see in the next section, Varro held the fourfold division of the *templum in caelo* to be an Etruscan invention. The history of the *haruspices* and their art is at least as obscure as that of the augurs.[29] Here, the fourth century appears to have been crucial, as it so often was in Rome, although the degree of innovation or continuity remains obscure.[30] Visual representations of *haruspices*, their emblems, and their divinatory practices appear at this time. In the following century, monuments reveal the existence of books on haruspicy, although little can be said about their contents.[31] From the third century, if not earlier, the Roman senate consulted Etruscan *haruspices* about the significance of prodigies, usually involving lightning, thunder, and monstrous births, and from some uncertain point lesser-ranking *haruspices* aided Roman magistrates by interpreting signs in the organs of sacrificial animals. P. Nigidius Figulus, a senator active in the middle of the first century, claimed that Etruscan experts held that their interpretations of certain signs affecting the Roman polity were valid only in Rome and its environs.[32] For the *haruspices*, as well as the augurs, the significance of signs was connected to the places where they were detected.

Like the augurs, the *haruspices* too imposed the same basic structure on different spaces, although in a way that differed from Roman practice. For Cicero (*Div.* 1.47) and Pliny (*HN* 2.142–44), the *haruspices* imposed a sixteenfold order on the heavens by first quartering a space and then quartering each of the quadrants again. The *haruspices* also projected a broadly similar organization onto the livers of sacrificial animals. The so-called bronze liver of Piacenza, fabricated around 100, is the best preserved and most detailed of the model livers that were used to teach the techniques.[33] It is not divided into quadrants. Instead, its fabricators divided its rim into sixteen subspaces that correspond to the regions of the heavens, while they gave to its center twenty-four more and to its reverse two. The *haruspices* associated each of the sixteen marginal subspaces with a different deity or group of deities, enabling them to identify the gods or gods who might be dissatisfied. Viewing the heavens and the liver as in correspondence was old, and its roots lie far beyond Italy: the seventh-century Assyrian king Assurbanipal boasted of his skill in learned debates about the matter.[34] At best, Roman practice was a variation of the Etruscan, although both had more distant predecessors.

Rome's early practice, of course, is obscure. Certain concepts, such as *urbs*, *ager*, and the *pomerium* that separated them may well be quite old, although little can be said about their original significance.[35] Some have suggested that the *templum*, if only in the sense of a rectangular sacred space oriented toward the east and set aside for purposes of cult, has Indo-European roots.[36] At the same time, Rome almost certainly existed in a kind of "sacred landscape" from an early date. Hills or mountains, such as the Capitol, the Palatine, and the more distant *mons Albanus*, long figured in cult and probably in worldview as well, while temples and sacred sites were concentrated in and near the city. Rome's topography may have been at least as important as any more abstract system in setting the observer's orientation from the *arx*, for the *templum*'s main axis ran south of east, rather than directly east, following the *sacra via* through the *forum* and toward the *mons Albanus*, occasionally visible from the *arx*.[37] Indeed, lines of sight linking sacred mountains appear to have been significant in central Italy.[38]

One aspect of the set of practices around *templa* may point to a later origin for certain elements or to a later extension to a greater range of spaces. The origins of the *curia-comitium* complex, each later a *locus inauguratus*, lie at the end of the seventh century. Archaic Rome also possessed a range of sacred sites that included temples, altars, and sacred groves, some of which may have been quite old as sacred places, in existence before monuments were built within them and, in some instances, even before the city itself. The construction of new temples, however, became much less frequent in the fifth century, and it did not resume until early in the fourth or become common until the beginning of the third century. Now, augurs inaugurated *templa* to prepare spaces for temples and altars, but, if new projects ended for several generations, would the rite have survived the hiatus? The steady increase in dedications from the fourth century may have provided the necessary context for the development of the practice or its elaboration.

Sometimes our sources report events that did not follow later norms. Within the limits of our knowledge, the centuriate assembly usually met on the *campus Martius* in a *templum* called the *saepta* or the *ovile* at the site of the later *saepta Iulia*. For an earlier period, however, a few gatherings outside Rome's walls reportedly met at seemingly unconventional locations, which, while sacred, may not have been *templa*: in 385 or 384, the trial of M. Manlius Capitolinus took place in the *lucus Petelinus*, a sacred grove near the *forum Boiarum*; four decades later, a dictator put a law to a vote in the same place; in 287 the dictator Q. Hortensius proposed and carried a law in the *Aesculetum*, a sacred grove along the Tiber near the future *circus Flaminius*.[39] Groups of Latin communities, we are told, met in groves on the Alban Mount or near Aricia, while some Roman *curiae* shared names with groves.[40] Like *templa*, sacred groves were separated from the external world, for the word *lucus* denotes the clearing at the grove's center and not the woods surrounding it.[41]

The complex formed by the *curia* and the *comitium* is perhaps the clearest case, although much remains obscure and contentious. It formed a cluster of *templa*, for the *curia*, the *comitium*, and the *rostra* are each described as *templa* at various times.[42] The officials who laid out the circular *comitium*, probably in the last decades of the fourth century, supervised the fifth of the site's building phases.[43] The first *curia* and *comitium* formed part of the grand project that drained, leveled, and paved the Roman *forum* in the last quarter of the seventh century. The complex, then, represents one of the innermost and most central of Rome's public spaces from the city's formative period. The fourth phase is usually associated with C. Maenius, consul in 338 and censor in 318, because of his connection to monuments linked to it. Those who laid out the first stage established the basic form that later remodelers and restorers would preserve, although the *comitium* did grow in size. In the first four phases, the *comitium* was rectangular in form, so that the fifth circular *comitium* may mark, in some fashion, a departure.

The common layout of the first four stages of the complex is certainly consistent with its identification as a *templum*. Its builders and remodelers gave to it a clear north-south orientation, set by the *curia* itself, which faced directly to the south over the adjacent *comitium*. In this way, it is clearly distinguished from the forum to its front, the orientation of which was determined by the terrain and ran from the northwest to the southeast. Thus, magistrates presiding from the front of the *curia* would have faced south over the *comitium*, a preferred augural direction. At the same time, each of the *comitium*'s sides faced one of the cardinal directions. For some, the construction of the circular *comitium* demonstrates that the enclosure either never was a *templum* or had just ceased to be one. Despite changes to the *comitium*'s interior, however, the builders of the circular enclosure maintained the essential relationships, for their *curia* also looked directly to the south over the *comitium*, which they placed within a rectangle with sides facing the cardinal directions.[44]

The orientation of the *comitium* and those who acted in it was, or came to be, linked to attempts to coordinate activities to the movements of the sun. As we have seen, the Twelve Tables used sunrise, sunset, and perhaps noon to establish chronological limits to phases in the process of litigation within the enclosure. The Elder Pliny (*HN* 7.212) connects these rules to the use of the complex as a kind of sundial: in the past, a consul's attendant (*accensus*) announced the coming of midday from the *curia* when he saw the sun between the *rostra* and the *graecostasis*, and he proclaimed day's end when the sun went down from the *columna Maenia* to the prison or *carcer*. This practice, he holds, continued into the first years of the First Punic War, when a series of sundials took over the role, only to be replaced in turn by a water clock in 159 to make it possible to ascertain the hours on cloudy days. A late republican jurist reports in a work on legal actions that praetors ordered their assistants (*accensus*) to call out the third and ninth hours as well, although their connection, if any, to litigation is unknown.[45] In some fashion, then, the sun and its movements were deemed relevant to the activities that took place within the complex.

At present, however, our chief concern is the relationship between the use of the complex in this fashion and its building phases. Pliny uses the *rostra*, the *graecostasis*, and the nearby *columna Maenia* and *carcer* as points of reference, which links the practice to structures and monuments associated with the fourth building phase, when they were established, or to the fifth, when their use continued. In other words, our most direct evidence applies to the period between circa 338, when the monuments in question were established, and the early years of the First Punic War, when Pliny claims that the practice ended. Some scholars, however, take the Twelve Tables' references to sunrise, noon, and sunset to indicate that the *comitium* was already used in such a fashion over a century earlier.[46] One should note, however, that Pliny holds that, while sunrise and sunset were mentioned in the Twelve Tables, noon was added to the rules only "after a few years": the preserved rule that set noon as a limit may be a later interpolation. Sundials would be of little use in detecting sunrise and sunset alone. Two Greek cities also associated sundials with places of assembly. Around the beginning of the Peloponnesian War, the astronomer Meton erected one in the Pnyx at Athens, then the assembly's meeting place, while a few decades later, the tyrant Dionysius placed a sundial "below the acropolis and the Pentapyla" in a place suitable for addressing crowds.[47] A Roman use of the *comitium* as a sundial in the middle of the fifth century would have been remarkably early.

One can find signs, then, that a rectangular form and an orientation to the cardinal directions that emphasizes the north-south axis may well have been important from an early date, all features that are consistent with the identification of the *comitium* as a *templum* but do not prove it. The interest in the divisions of the day may indicate a concern for the sun's movements, which would provide an east-west line. If so, the complex's use as a sundial from the late fourth century may indicate that it and the magistrates who acted within it were viewed as in harmony with the structure of the cosmos. Does the shift of voting place to the southeast part of the forum in the second half of the second century indicate that this vision had lost its force?

ROME AND ITS COLONIES

Greek and Roman writers report the foundation of colonies in virtually every period. In practice, however, little can be said with any confidence about the historicity of the earliest examples or about what the act of colonization may have meant in the seventh, sixth, fifth, and early fourth centuries.[48] Matters become clearer from the middle of the fourth century and most visible in the late third and second centuries, when the foundation of colonies was a characteristic practice of Roman imperial expansion in peninsular Italy and the Po Valley.

Third- and second-century colonies came in two basic forms that differed in status, in size, and in the complexity of their institutions. Latin colonies were fully developed polities, and they received at the start a substantial number of settlers: reported examples range from twenty-five hundred to more than six thousand adult males. For long, citizen colonies were markedly smaller. The few surviving notices for foundations from the fourth century through the 190s mention only three hundred *coloni*. Beginning with the 180s, a few reports note foundations with two thousand adult male settlers. These larger citizen colonies may have been an innovation of this decade when the foundation of Latin colonies was coming to an end, although such a clear transition may be only an illusion that rests on the failure of our sources to provide numbers for many settlements.[49] That said, citizen colonies founded before the Second Punic War were along the coast and generally at harbors, and excavated sites thus far have been small. The apparent shift from Latin colonies to larger citizen ones almost certainly implies a different ideal of the relationship between the new polity and Rome.

By the last decades of the third century, if not earlier, colonies of both kinds were enshrined in lists. From at least as early as 225, Roman magistrates and the senate organized the military contributions of Latins and other allies within peninsular Italy in the *formula togatorum*. During the Second Punic War, thirty polities composed the Latin Name (*nomen Latinum*), and later authors would identify all of them as colonies and give them foundation dates, some as early as the fifth century;[50] Praeneste and Tibur, it should be noted, were in Latium, but ranked as allies after 338. Twenty-three of these polities were founded in the 116 years between the foundation of Cales in 334, the first after Rome had achieved complete dominion over the Latins, and the outbreak of the war with Hannibal. Between the end of the Second Punic War and 167, Roman magistrates founded four or five more as well.[51]

The situation with respect to citizen colonies is less clear. In the Second Punic War, citizen colonies claimed, or were able to claim, that their citizens possessed an exemption from service in the legions, and it seems likely that there would have been a list of such colonies and that each would have had a list of its citizens. At that time, ten settlements were deemed citizen colonies; in one case, Ostia, writers gave it a foundation date in the regal period, although they gave others dates in the late fourth and third centuries.[52] Between the end of the Second Punic War and 167, when Livy's history fails, Roman magistrates founded fifteen more.[53]

As an operation, the establishment of new communities was associated with its own magistracy, colleges of *triumviri coloniae deducendae*; no founding college established both citizen and Latin settlements, which may indicate that the processes were thought to differ in fundamental ways. In books 21 to 45, which cover the years from 218 to 167, Livy, our chief source, invariably named the members of each of the founding colleges, but his practice in the first decade is more irregular. He (3.1.6; 4.11.5–7) and Dionysius of Halicarnassus (*Ant. Rom.* 9.59.2) identify the triumvirs who allegedly founded colonies at Antium and Ardea in the fifth century, although their claims are difficult to assess. Livy (8.16.4) provides the names for the triumvirs who settled Cales in 334, the first of the Latin colonies founded after the Latin War, while Festus (p. 458 L) identifies the commissioners who established Saticula in 313. Elsewhere, Livy often asserts that some triumvirate had founded a colony in the fourth and early third centuries without naming the members.[54] Of these, the college that supposedly founded Sinuessa and Minturnae in 295 is the first to be associated with citizen colonies. Does the lack of names indicate that Livy only assumed their presence?

This simple dichotomy and these straightforward identifications almost certainly make Roman practice appear more regular than it probably was. Roman commanders occasionally made other arrangements on their own authority. In the late third and second centuries, we catch glimpses of such settlements in Sicily and in Spain.[55] In Italy, traces are much sparser, but the practice may lie behind Polybius's identification (3.40) of Mutina as a colony (*apoikia*) in 218, although it did not become one formally until 183. On at least one occasion, the senate authorized the formation of a settlement that bore some similarities to a citizen colony without being one: Livy (32.7.3) reports that in 199 the senate instructed the censors to install three hundred settlers at a camp (*castrum*) where they also arranged for the collection of harbor dues.

At present, however, our primary concern lies with formal settlements and the ways in which the responsible magistrates went about their tasks.[56] Triumvirs had to recruit settlers and lead them to the scene, where they established an urban core and the institutions appropriate to their settlement, and survey and assigned land for the settlers. At the most basic level, the founders of Latin polities dealt with a larger number of settlers, which required the creation of more plots, and they had to establish more elaborate institutions of government, suitable for fully developed polities, whose officials raised their own troops, sometimes conducted military operations on their own initiative, and performed their own censuses. For long, colonial institutions are more visible in Latin colonies than in citizen ones, perhaps because communities of only three hundred adult males would have required little in the way of formal structures.

Scholars have suggested that the Romans intended their colonies to resemble the metropolis in crucial ways and that they had this goal in mind from an early, if rather indeterminate, age. In the first century, the organization of new colonies clearly imitated Rome's. New settlements often possessed *capitolia*, temples shared by Jupiter, Juno, and Minerva, just like the Capitoline temple in Rome, while the law that was to regulate Caesar's colony at Urso in Spain gave to the town's pontiffs and augurs privileges like those possessed by Roman priests.[57] At the Augustan citizen colony of Puteoli, a grove of Libitina was used for funerals and it seems to have been quite intentionally modeled after a grove of Libitina at Rome used for the same purpose.[58] From a different perspective, late republican and early imperial authors made Romulus an exemplary figure for the founders of colonies and for some of the critical techniques. At a general level, the development of some fully realized plan at an early date does appear unlikely given the Romans' reluctance to create overarching systems. The state of the evidence, however, presents a more fundamental problem, since it generally derives from later stages in a colony's history, leaving obscure what the founders instituted, for successful foundations might change over time.

The clearest evidence of colonial constitutions is to be found in scattered inscriptions, often honorific or dedicatory in nature and inscribed generations after the foundation, that record the titles of specific persons. Thus, it masks changes and fails to reveal the complete range of magistracies and priesthoods as they existed at any one time. By assembling the scattered evidence from Latin colonies, one finds the full range of Roman, or possibly Latin, titles—dictators, censors, consuls, praetors, aediles, quaestors, and tribunes of the plebs—although colleges sometimes differed in number from their Roman analogues, while no single colony need have possessed them all. Officials possessing the same title, moreover, may not always have had the same functions as their Roman analogues: an inscription from Latin Venusia (*ILLRP* 699) records the construction of a road by a local tribune of the plebs. Citizen colonies had fewer titles: *duumviri, praetores,* or *duumviri praetores;* aediles; decurions; pontiffs and augurs. Here too, changes may have occurred over a city's history.

But what about the triumvirs' organization of spaces? For long, modern scholars have sought some clear and persistent pattern made manifest at the foundation. Here, Cosa, which Roman magistrates founded on an uninhabited site in 273, often serves as the model.[59] Its founders, we are told, replicated on the hill that their town would occupy much of Rome's public and sacred topography, forming quite explicitly a little Rome. More recent studies, however, have questioned the claim.[60] In some cases, founders appropriated existing structures for their purposes. In addition, the material remains often make it difficult to establish the identities of certain structures or of the deities who received cult at temples and altars, while their supposed Roman analogues often remain undiscovered. Many of the most prominent structures and spaces, moreover, were constructed or expanded later in a colony's history, leaving the original organization of spaces and structures obscure.

That said, from a fairly early date some Romans and colonists did make overt analogies between prominent elements in Rome's and a colony's spatial organizations, if only informally. An early third-century inscription from Cales reveals a district named after the Esquiline at Rome, and other inscriptions, though possibly not as early, reveal similar practices in other Latin colonies.[61] Colonial triumvirs were members of Rome's ruling elite, who would have possessed some ideas about the features that were appropriate to a new urban order. One might expect, then, that Roman arrangements, or more generally Latin ones, served as models. These ideas would for long have been limited and perhaps mutable, focusing on but a few practices and representing only part of what would become the political and religious life of the city. Paul Zanker suggests that founders followed Roman models more in certain individual structures, most notably *capitolia* and *comitium-curia* complexes, than in overall plan and that they installed in their new settlements an abstract and idealized version of their Roman prototype.[62]

Colonies, it must be stressed, were nucleated settlements. That is, they possessed a clear urban core, surrounded by fortifications and including the house plots of at least some of the settlers and the spaces and structures necessary for the new polity's public and sacred life. The central act in founding a Latin colony—and, from an uncertain point, a citizen colony as well—involved the ritual definition of this core through the establishment of a local equivalent of Rome's *pomerium*, an act that served as the defining moment in the establishment of an *urbs*.[63] Two imperial authors, Dionysius (*Ant.Rom.* 1.88) and Plutarch (*Rom.* 12), make the ritual plowing of a furrow, the *sulcus primigenius* or primeval furrow, around the site of Rome the central act in its foundation, and they identify the day that the rite was performed—April 21, the festival of the Parilia—as Rome's foundation day. Much earlier, the Elder Cato claims that founders (*conditores*), with their heads partly covered by their togas according to the Gabine rite (*ritus Gabinus*), marked out polities (*ciuitates*) by yoking together a bull and a cow and plowing a furrow that defined where the walls were to be built, lifting up the plow around the locations for the gates.[64] The authors who preserved Cato's opinion, it should be noted, understood his *civitates* to mean *urbes*, while the reference to the Gabine rite points to Roman practice. Slightly earlier, Ennius linked Romulus's successful auspication with the act of plowing.[65] A relief honoring a founder of the Latin colony at Aquileia, now in the National Archeological Museum there, may be nearly contemporary with its foundation, depicts the rite.

A century after Cato wrote his account, Varro (*LL* 5.143) describes much the same performance, which he attributes to Rome's colonies, other Latin cities, Rome itself, and cities deemed ancestral to Rome, such as Lavinium, the seat of the Penates and the place where Aeneas first settled in Italy. First, he links the rite to the foundation of towns (*oppida*) in Latium and to their *pomeria*. Then, after setting out etymologies for *urbs* and *pomerium* that emphasize the supposed ties between them, he notes that Rome and Aricia used stones to mark their *pomeria*. Next, he adds that all of Rome's colonies were called *urbes* by "ancient authors" because they had been founded in the same way that Rome had been. Varro, then, thought the practice both old and common to all Latin cities, including Rome and its colonies. He even creates what amounts to a genealogy linking Latin colonies to Rome and Rome and other older Latin cities to Lavinium. Cato seems to have made most, if not all, of the same associations.

What was the age of the rite and when was it first associated with Rome's own foundation? How early, in other words, had Romans made explicit links between Rome and its colonies in this fundamental feature of spatial organization? Here, the evidence is at best indirect. Rome and at least some of its colonies possessed clear foundation days, which later writers would link to the ritual plowing of a furrow around the future city. Cicero (*Sest.* 131) witnessed the annual celebrations of the Latin colony of Brundisium (244) when he landed in Italy while returning from exile.

From scattered references, we also know the foundation days of three more Latin polities: Saticula (313), Placentia (218), and Bononia (189).[66] In the last decade of the third century, Fabius Pictor gave to Rome a clear birthday: the feast of the Parilia.[67] If the link between the rite and the foundation day were made at these early dates, this complex of practices may reach back into the last decades of the fourth century, early in the Roman process of expansion. At the very least, the common possession of such a date demonstrates that links were being formed between the metropolis and its offspring in at least one element of their "foundings."

With respect to citizen colonies, the earliest surviving accounts of the rite apply to settlements of the first century, although the practice may be older.[68] One passage in the *lex Ursonensis* refers to the "the boundaries [*fines*] of a town or of a colony, where [a line] shall have been drawn around by a plow."[69] Some rules governed by the Roman *pomerium* also applied to this line. Urso's law and the Twelve Tables barred burying the dead within the city or town, while an inscription from the citizen colony of Puteoli records a public contract (*lex locationis*) that prohibits anyone from carrying a dead body "into the town" (*in oppidum*).[70] The Extortion Law of 123 prohibited service on juries to those without dwellings in *urbs* Roma or within a mile of it, while Urso's charter contains a similar provision for colonial magistrates, priests, and decurions.[71] Still, the framers of Urso's law did not call the line a *pomerium* or the town an *urbs*, perhaps an indication that the boundary of the urban core of citizen colonies, which were not autonomous, possessed a different significance.

But what about the new city's structures and public and sacred spaces? Here, we begin to detect from the middle of the fourth century, a tendency toward orthogonal town planning, which was already old in the Greek world. In Italy, the Etruscans even deployed it in their new city of Felsina, founded in the Po Valley at the end of the sixth century. From circa 350, Roman officials began to follow a modified version of the practice in some of their colonial foundations. At Ostia, the colony's founders established a walled enclosure of approximately 194 by 126 meters to serve as the urban core, and they organized its interior in rectangular blocks that were defined in turn by two main orthogonal roads that met at the town's forum and were aligned with its four gates.[72] The founders of the citizen colonies of Minturnae (295) and Pyrgi (middle of the third century), both on the same small scale, followed a similar pattern.[73] The instruments—the surveyor's cross (*stella*) or the more complex *groma*, along with measuring rods, the *pertica* and the *decempeda*—favored the creation of right angles and

Sciences of the Center

straight lines.[74] But Roman practice goes beyond a simple technological determinism, for the Greeks, who used the same basic instruments, did not organize their urban cores or their field systems by clear orthogonal axes as the Romans did.[75]

Early practice in Latin colonies is less clear, if only because they were larger and were often located in high places, difficult of access and easy to defend, restricting the ability to impose a clear overall plan. Some of the earlier foundations possessed a forum along one or more major routes and with direct access to at least one gate.[76] The founders of Ariminum (268) organized their colony's urban core by two orthogonal axes that met in the forum and left by four gates, just as the founders of earlier citizen colonies had done. Many of the magistrates who founded later colonies followed the same basic practice, although, owing to the uncertainties involved in finding and interpreting material remains, it is sometimes difficult to determine whether these orthogonal main roads too were directly aligned with the gates.

From the last decades of the fourth century, the founders of Latin colonies also focused on an official core that followed the pattern of Rome's forum and its adjacent *curia* and *comitium*. In Fregellae, founded in 328, a *curia* and a *comitium* were built at the time of foundation. At first, its *comitium* was rectangular in form, as was its Roman model at the time, but, by the end of the third century, Fregellae's *comitium* was refashioned according to the contemporary Roman pattern. In the colonies of Alba Fucens (303), Cosa (273), Paestum (273), and Aquileia (181), on the other hand, the complexes that were installed at their foundation featured a circular *comitium*. Indeed, it is possible that *comitia* in the new style appeared first in colonies and then in Rome.[77] The late second-century Oscan Law of Bantia, a local measure that imitated Roman practice and possibly the law of the nearby Latin colony of Venusia, requires certain oaths to be sworn in the *comitium* by light of day and ordains that those who failed to attend the local census were to be flogged there, practices that are known for the analogous place in Rome.[78] The presence of a *comitium* may indicate that the founders of Latin colonies were thought to have established a clearly distinct *populus*, so that their absence from the larger citizen colonies may indicate a fundamental shift in the perceived relationship between Rome and its colonies.

Citizen colonies too had their centers. As we have seen, the towns established at Ostia, Minturnae, and Pyrgi centered on a forum where the axes met, as did the larger citizen colonies that come into view in the second decade of the second century. At Luna, which Roman triumvirs founded in

177, a *capitolium*—that is, a joint temple to Jupiter, Juno, and Minerva—was installed adjacent to its forum at its foundation, which may have been typical for such settlements, although the secure identification of the material remains of such structures is often difficult.[79]

Founders employed similar patterns in surveying the surrounding fields and defining the plots for settlers.[80] Surveying became more regular in the last third of the fourth century. At first, surveyors laid out parallel roads or *limites*, collectively known as *decumani*, that were separated by an interval that varied from project to project. Next, they established lines that crossed the *decumani* at right angles. The result was a series of rectangular modules—known in different configurations as *scamna* or *strigae*—which would in turn be subdivided, although in a less regular fashion, to form the allotments for settlers. Traces have been detected at Cales (founded in 334), Alba Fucens (303), and Cosa (273).

In the middle decades of the third century, surveying became still more formulaic. Surveyors first laid out a broad road, the *decumanus maximus*, which ideally ran from east to west. Then, they defined a north-to-south road that ran perpendicular to the first, the *kardo maximus*. Using these axes as a base, surveyors next established parallel *decumani* and *kardines* by measuring out set distances of twenty *actus* (ca. 708 meters) to each side of the *kardo maximus* and the *decumanus maximus*. The result was a regular grid of paths and roads, separated by a standard distance and intersecting everywhere at right angles, that created square modules or *centuriae*, each of two hundred *iugera*, which would be divided in turn, although with less regularity, to form settlers' plots. Individual projects, it should be noted, sometimes diverged from the ideal either in orientation or in the size of the modules.

Looking down the *decumanus maximus*, ideally toward the east, observers imposed on the grid a terminology that has an obvious resemblance to augural practice. According to Frontinus, an imperial writer on the technique:

> The first origin of *limites*, as Varro has described, is in the Etruscan *disciplina*, because the *haruspices* divided the inhabited world [*orbis terrarum*] into two parts: they called "right" that part which lay to the north and "left" that part of the world that was to the south, looking <from east to> west because the sun and the moon looked in that direction; similarly, some †architects have written that temples should rightly look to the west. The *haruspices* divided the earth with

Sciences of the Center

another line from north to south, and, from the middle, they called the far side of the line *antica*, the near side *postica*. From this basis our ancestors evidently established their system of measuring land. First they drew two *limites*, one from east to west, which they called the *decumanus*, the other from south to north, which they called the *kardo*. So, the *decumanus* divided the land by a "right" and a "left," the *kardo* by a "this side" and a "beyond."[81]

Another imperial author, Hyginus Gromaticus (pp. 134.6–19 Campbell), gives the practice a similar origin, although, as we have seen, the fourfold division of the heavens was more Roman than Etruscan. In its ideal form, then, centuriation was linked to a larger order. Frontinus (p. 8.36–38 Campbell) proclaims that "the *kardo* gets its name because it is drawn from the pivot of the universe. Without doubt the universe turns on the northern part of the earth." In the midst of a lengthy account of the best methods for determining true east, Hyginus (p. 150.19–21 Campbell) notes that *kardo* signifies the hinge of the world and claims as an advantage of his method that the layout of *limites* would match the four parts of the heavens (*caeli partes*).

Orienting the fields involved orienting the surveyors and those who supervised them. Hyginus Gromaticus (p. 136.19–21 Campbell) depicts the first placement of the *groma* in ways that are reminiscent of the auspicant's definition of his *templum*: "When the *groma* had been positioned after taking the auspices, perhaps in the very presence of the founder, they sighted accurately the next sunrise and sent out *limites* in each direction" (*posita auspicaliter groma, ipso forte conditore praesente, proximum uero ortum conprehenderunt, et in utramque partem limites emiserunt*). As was the case with *templa* and temples, the vocabulary of viewing is common in works on surveying. Frontinus (p. 10.6 Campbell) calls the roads that "looked to" (*spectabant*) the east "straight ahead" (*prorsi*) and those running toward the south "transverse" (*transversi*), while Hyginus Gromaticus (p. 136.14–15 Campbell) notes that the phrase "looking to the east" should have the same meaning when applied to boundary paths that it possessed in the orientation of temples. Frontinus and Hyginus Gromaticus certainly were not the only authors to place *limites* in this context. The augur and jurist Ser. Sulpicius Rufus, Varro's contemporary, also assigned *limites* names from this same terminology of orientation, as did Festus/Paulus.[82] The perspectives of the responsible persons, then, would again determine the nomenclature. Siculus Flaccus (p. 126.21–23 Campbell), another imperial author on surveying, suggests that the *limites* of neighboring projects be distinguished by having different orientations; after all, they were the results of different founding acts.

In *templa*, one should recall, the quadrants served to help interpret signs and perhaps order rites, but in centuriation grids, they possessed no overarching significance. But they did play an important role in assigning plots and keeping records by identifying modules and thus the plots within them. By counting the number of *kardines* or *decumani* that intervened between any given *kardo* or *decumanus* and the *kardo maximus* and *decumanus maximus*, surveyors were able to identify individual *centuriae* and record them on a schematic drawing or *forma*.

Many of these spaces were organized by orthogonal axes ideally oriented toward the cardinal directions, but in practice the local topography or the line of certain roads sometimes set different orientations. In 187 the consul M. Aemilius Lepidus laid out the *via Aemilia*, which ran in a nearly straight line, 176 Roman miles long, from Ariminum to Placentia, passing through the urban core of the newly founded colony of Bononia. The triumvirs who soon founded Mutina and Parma used the route to orient their town plans and their centuriation grids, as did the decemvirs of 173, who made viritane assignments in the *ager Gallicus*.[83] Finally, a Gracchan boundary marker (*ILS* 24) allows the *decumanus maximus* in Campania to be identified with the road from Capua to Atella, while the east-west route between Capua and Calatia served as the *kardo maximus*. Hyginus Gromaticus (p. 144.17–22 Campbell) insists that, since *kardo* signifies the hinge of the world, it should not run from east to west.

Assigning a clear chronology to centuriation presents certain problems. Surveying networks that have been detected through aerial surveys are usually dated by their apparent association with known colonial foundations or viritane assignments, although some colonies received later supplements. At the same time, there was no clear and absolute sequence of forms. Frontinus (p. 2.5–11 Campbell) considers the formation of *scamna* or *striga* to be the older form (*more antiquo*), giving as an example the Latin colony of Suessa Aurunca, founded in 313, but later surveyors sometimes measured out modules that varied in their size and regularity or in the orientation of the grid. Centuriation, in other words, was an ideal that allowed for variation. That said, modern surveys have detected traces of field systems with square modules of the appropriate size at Ariminum, founded in 268, and in the colonies and viritane assignments of the late third and second centuries. Unfortunately, the physical traces of centuriation networks do not permit the easy identification of the main axes and thus confirm their existence. Here, a Gracchan boundary marker of 132 (*ILS* 24) provides the earliest certain evidence and a secure terminus ante quem. If centuriation was an innovation of the first half of the third century, it would strengthen the tentative conclusion that the *comitium* of the last decades of the fourth century reflected an intensified desire to orient the acts of prominent officials with a larger order.

As we saw in chapter 3, in some circumstances Romans regarded their polity as if an army and their armies as if cities. Latin colonies too were drawn into this range of associations. In a practice that we first catch sight of in 218, founders divided settlers into infantry (*pedites*) and cavalry (*equites*) and gave to each plots of a different standard size, although Aquileia (181) had a threefold division into *pedites*, centurions, and *equites*.[84] On only three occasions are we informed of the number of *equites*. In two, the three hundred *equites* equal the most common size of the citizen cavalry detachment assigned to a legion, while the third's two hundred match a variant for the legionary contingent. With this in mind, it may be significant that the known numbers of *pedites* are about the same order of magnitude as the infantry detachment of a legion, and even closer if one excludes skirmishers (*velites*). We will examine this matter in greater detail at the end of the following section.

POLYBIUS, THE ROMAN ARMY, AND ITS ENCAMPMENTS

Camps shared features with colonies and *templa*. Here, Polybius's account (6.26–32) of army encampments is our chief source. His description forms part of his extended examination of the Roman constitution, and, as we saw in chapter 3, his depiction of military arrangements is idealizing and probably best represents practice at the outbreak of the Second Punic War. In his account, Polybius (6.26–32) shifts between attributing his description to the camp in which commanders first mobilized their armies and to the encampments that they formed at the end of a day's march, which probably shared a common organization.[85] Reconstructing the layout of camps on the basis of his description has proven difficult, but, for our purposes, a few basic elements are reasonably clear.

When nearing the end of a day's march, commanders sent ahead a military tribune and centurions to examine the site and choose within it the place that provided the best view and was most suitable for issuing orders. There, surveyors erected their *groma* at the future location of the commander's tent or *praetorium*, which surveyors would define by measuring out a square, one hundred feet on each side. The quaestor's headquarters or *quaestorium* and an assembly area or forum, which Polybius calls an *agora*, were immediately adjacent to the *praetorium* but at its front and back. Along one side of this ensemble, they set out the camp's main avenue, which ran between two of the camp's four gates; Polybius (6.27.3) suggests that it should be oriented to give the best access to water and foraging. From this core, surveyors then measured out the straight streets and rectangular blocks, all fixed in size and in number, that would accommodate the tents of the soldiers. Finally, the entire camp would be surrounded by fortifications, most frequently a ditch and a dike (*fossa* and *agger*). When completed, the camp took on a familiar organization. The main avenue ran completely through the rectangular camp and ended at gates on opposite sides of the ensemble. Another major route, at a right angle to the first, set out from the *praetorium* to gates on the other two sides of the camp but did not run completely through it, for the headquarters intervened. Although Polybius did not use the terms, these streets and the *praetorium* allowed the camp to be divided into a front, a back, a left, and a right.[86]

Camps had clear centers, from which roads radiated to the gates. Here, commanders' placed their headquarters, accommodations for the quaestors, a forum in which they might assemble and address their soldiers, and the tents of the military tribunes. This ensemble was surrounded first by the tents of the soldiers and then by the camp's fortifications. In Polybius's description, when two consuls were campaigning together, they did not create a shared core. Instead, each had his own headquarters which was separated by the tents of soldiers from the headquarters of his colleague, although both lie fairly close to the center of the ensemble. Each consul was clearly the commander of his own army, and his camp a stage for his activity.

Polybius does not exhibit much interest in Roman public cult and often left it out of his narrative, but the central areas of the camp also included places for the performance of essential acts. Much later, the author who wrote *On the Measurement of Camps* (*De metatione castrorum*) in the second or third century A.D. holds that altars were established in the innermost part of the *praetorium*, an *auguratorium* was set up on its right side, and a tribunal on its left, so that, having successfully taken the auspices, the commander might address his army properly.[87] Livy (41.18.6–10) confirms that camps contained an altar for sacrifices and a *templum* for taking the auspices and performing sortitions; Festus (p. 249 L) calls the commander's tent a *tabernaculum*, which Cicero (*Div.* 1.33; 2.76) also applies to the tent occupied by a person about to take the auspices; Tacitus (*Ann.* 15.30.1) says that the altar was in front of the *augurale*. A later scholiast asserts that commanders took the auspices in the center of their armies (*coram exercitu*).[88] The central places in the camp, then, set out locations for the performance of official functions in a Roman manner and had done so for some time. As we saw in chapter 4, Roman commanders from the late fourth century created spaces in the midst of their areas of operation where they could perform acts that required special auspices but which in the past had been performed only at Rome.

Camps also resembled cities, including Rome, in the interpretation and expiation of prodigies. Persistent failure to secure favorable auspices or to achieve the successful completion of a sacrifice might be deemed prodigious just like similar occurrences at Rome. Other prodigies concerned the physical structures and the spatial organization of the camp itself. Thus, we encounter lightning striking the central square, the *praetorium*, or the walls. One rather dramatic sign represented a clear violation of the walls of a city or a camp. The more concise notices of this prodigy, in which wolves entered a city, report only the presence of a wolf or identify some place within the city where the animal was detected or the gate through which it had entered. On two occasions, Livy gives the animals a detailed itinerary in which he identifies the gates at Rome through which they entered and escaped and sets out the districts that they traversed. Although most instances come from Rome, the senate also accepted similar events at Capua in 207, in the citizen colony of Minturnae in 133, and in an army encampment.[89]

At another level, analogies occasionally were made between certain acts at Rome and their analogues in the camps. In the central forum, commanders could assemble their soldiers and address them after taking the auspices, much like magistrates did at Rome itself. Texts from the early first century sometimes refer to these gatherings as *contiones*, just as in Rome, and Sulla appears to have used such a gathering to confirm and thus validate his march on the city.[90] Roman authors of the late republic, moreover, occasionally depicted magistrates of the distant past using assemblies of soldiers in their camps as voting assemblies (see chapter 6). The image of a higher magistrate surrounded by his citizen-soldiers may have been sufficient to call to mind other gatherings in Rome, perhaps especially in the *campus Martius*, in which citizens sometimes came together as if an army.

Certain lustral rites provide another link between Rome, its armies, and Latin colonies. To mark the conclusion of the census, the censors summoned the Roman people to meet at dawn on the *campus Martius*, where they assembled in their tribes and centuries for the *lustrum*, the rite of purification that marked the culmination of the *census*.⁹¹ There, one of the censors, chosen by lot, performed the sacrifice of the *suovetaurilia*, in which he conducted around the assembled citizenry a bull, a boar, and a ram, which he sacrificed, and then, behind a standard, he led the citizens in a procession back into the city. Cicero (*Div.* 1.45.102) explicitly links the censors' *lustrum* with the *lustra* by which colonial commissioners formed the citizenry of their colonies and generals purified their armies. We have little direct evidence for colonial *lustra*. With camps, the matter is clearer. During the course of a campaign, generals purified their armies when they first formed them, when they took over an army from another commander, when they merged previously separate forces, when they collected scattered detachments from their winter quarters, when they divided a single army with another commander, and when they regrouped their forces to prepare for battle after a long march.⁹² Magistrates performed these rites—as colonial commissioners probably did too—in a setting analogous to the censors' performance at Rome. Just as the censors performed their rites on the *campus Martius* just outside the *pomerium* and the walls, generals also purified their armies just outside their camps.⁹³ Lustral rites, then, make a fundamental contrast between inside and outside that we have already encountered in an augural context, and they culminated in a formal entry into camp or city.

SPACES AND THEIR CENTERS

From the middle of the fourth century, and more intensively from the middle of the third, commanders and founders began to deploy progressively more formalized ways of building spaces around themselves, their essential functions, and the groups under their authority: commanders constructed camps to organize and shelter their soldiers; founders of colonies built urban cores for the new polity and large-scale field systems to aid in the establishment of settlers' plots. If one examines these spaces, and the *templa* at Rome that shared rules of orientation and elements of internal organization, certain broad principles become apparent.

First, these spaces are clearly separated from the external world, and they exhibit strongly marked centers or focal points that are explicitly associated with the magistrates or priests who created them and sometimes with those who would use them in the future. For some *templa*, auspicants and augurs occupied a marginal position with respect to the spaces that they were creating, delimiting an area to their front, dividing it in quadrants, and naming the resulting divisions—left and right, this side and beyond—from their perspectives. The place or places that they occupied when doing so were themselves significant, most notably the *auguraculum* on the *arx*, the site of the auspices *in terra*. Although the creators of these enclosures oriented them toward the cardinal directions according to the conventions of the rite, prominent features in Rome's setting, such as the *mons Albanus* and the *pomerium*, played important roles. In the *templum in terra*, created from the *arx* to watch for signs revealed through the flight of birds, the auspiciant (and the *arx*) occupied the apex of the resulting triangular enclosure. The space, in other words, depended upon the persons of magistrates and priests and secondarily on the places that they occupied.

In some cases, however, the functionary or functionaries occupied the center of the space they were creating, the point where the orthogonal lines crossed and the four quadrants met, thus establishing a true center. Cicero (*ND*. 2.9) describes the legendary augur Attus Navius defining quadrants around him as he stood in the middle of a vineyard, while Hyginus Gromaticus (p. 136.19–21 C) depicts the first placement of the *groma* as leading to the definition of paths around it (*et in utramque partem limites emiserunt*).

The rites and the nomenclature involved in creating these spaces reveal a clear preference for the counterclockwise over the clockwise and the left over the right.[94] Varro (*LL* 7.7) holds that the parts of the *templum in caelo* were formed from two contrasting pairs, first a "left" to the east and the "right" to the west, and then the "front" to the south and the "back" to the north.[95] The old augural formula for the creation of a *templum in terra* from the *arx* has the auspiciant first pronounce his boundaries to the left and then to the right.[96] When Livy (1.18.6–10) sets out the supposed inauguration of Rome's second king, Numa Pompilius, he has the augur who would take the auspices first set the lines that defined the outer limits of his space to the left and then to the right.

Although they possessed more complicated structures, camps and colonies too had their centers. Roman surveying practices emphasized a single point, the place where the *groma* was first erected, for only in this way could standardized distances and orientations be maintained. The common emphasis on clearly defined major orthogonal axes only reinforced this centrality. In camps, these axes crossed at the location of the commander's *praetorium*, and in many colonies they met in the forum (for citizen colonies) or in the forum and near the *comitium* (for Latin ones), places linked to the continuing exercise of public power and having easy access to the gates and to all parts of the resulting settlement. In camps and in many colonies, moreover, the places occupied, or were close to, the physical center of the settlement. For Polybius (6.41.6), the spot where the tribunes first placed the *groma* was called the *gramma*, while much later, the author of *On the Measurement of Camps* (*De metatione castrorum*) would call it the *locus gromae*, showing it to be sufficiently significant to possess its own name.[97]

In some instances, moreover, founders and surveyors sought to give a common center to urban cores and field systems. When they did so, surveyors used the orthogonal axes that crossed in the forum and left by the four gates to organize the construction of *centuriae* in the fields, a practice that later writers would regard as ideal. Hyginus Gromaticus (p. 142.12–13, 31–36 Campbell) recommends that surveying begin near the town and, if possible, even within it; he holds that having the axes leave through four gates, the practice in camps, is the "most beautiful arrangement" (*ratio pulcherrima*), noting that "the *groma* is set up at the crossroads [*in tentrantem*] where men can assembly as in a forum.

Rome too might be seen as having its own center, although its locus might shift from context to context. In 20, when he was exercising a general supervision of the roads in Italy, Augustus erected the "golden milemarker" (*milliarium aureum*) "under the temple of Saturn at the head of the *forum Romanum*" (*sub Saturni aede in capite Romani fori*), which bore inscriptions setting out the distances to the major cities of the empire and thus established the place as the center of Rome's order.[98] For certain projects, the *arx* provided the necessary focal point. When Augustus established the fourteen regions of his expanded Rome, he gave to them a formal order, which the so-called Marble Plan of Rome reveals.[99] On this map, Rome's layout is defined with respect to the *arx* that lies at its center and from which a number of routes radiate to the margins. Of these, the most important runs directly to the map's upper edge, setting out the course of the sacred way (*via sacra*) within the limits of the city and the *via Latina* just outside and replicating the line of sight that the augurs established when taking the auspices from the *arx*.[100] The regions were numbered in sequence along this route and then along other radial roads, moving out from the city along each road and then from road to road in a counterclockwise fashion around the *arx*.

Almost two and a half centuries earlier, the tribal system that emerged circa 244 was organized according to similar principles. The thirty-one rural tribes possessed an official order that was determined by their positions with respect to the city and probably the roads that radiated from it as well (see chapter 3). They began with the Romilia, slightly west of Rome's south and adjacent to the city, followed by the Voltinia and Volturia along the *via Ostiensis* and then proceeding counterclockwise around Rome; once again, tribes were enumerated from the city to the farthest in each direction. Lily Ross Taylor has suggested that the order of these tribes was linked to the procession of the *Ambarvalia* around Rome's original territory, the *ager Romanus antiquus*, which the *fratres Arvales* supposedly led from their grove of Dea Dia south of the city.[101] As we saw in chapter 4, however, the festival may be a scholarly fiction. Recall that when augurs created their *templum* from the *arx* the preferred orientations were to the east and south. In practice, the eastward line was oriented to the southeast of the Capitol in the direction of the *mons Albanus* and followed, more or less, the course of the *via Latina* as it made its way there.[102] If the eastward axis followed the *via Latina* to the southeast, then the *via Ostiensis* would correspond, if only roughly, to the southern, or more properly, southwestern axis.

In addition to setting focal points and centers, Romans also exhibited a marked tendency to imagine or to establish zones out from some central point, a feature that we have already encountered in the augural boundaries around Rome, its *ager*, and the land of Italy. In *templa*, magistrates and augurs established a clear distinction between inside and outside by setting firm boundaries separating the enclosure from the external world. In colonies, the forum was surrounded by the house plots of at least some of the settlers and then the walls, which firmly separated it from the external world. In Latin colonies this line provided the local *pomerium* and in citizen ones it set the town's *fines*; both served as reference points for concentrating in the center certain activities while excluding undesirable ones. In some cases, as we shall see in chapter 6, Roman legislators might imagine a further limit, one mile from the town's boundary, just as they projected around Rome. Beyond the town lay the plots of the settlers, while still farther away one would encounter the limits to a colony's civic territory, the limits of its magistrates' jurisdiction and its laws.[103] Surveyors assisting army commanders did much the same, establishing a clear official core that was surrounded by the tents of the soldiers and then the fortifications. The consuls of 192 constructed an oath for their soldiers that required them to foreswear robbery within ten miles of the army, creating a zone of law within the larger sphere of war.[104]

The *sententia* Minuciorum of 117 exhibits the same broad practice, although without a strongly nucleated urban core. The two senatorial legates whom the senate had dispatched to resolve a boundary dispute between the Genuates of Genua and the Langenses Viturii recorded their decision on an inscription erected on the scene.[105] In it, the envoys defined an inner core that contained the fields of the Langenses by establishing its outer limits, which followed the courses of rivers and streams until one of four markers indicated a shift to another watercourse. Outside this inner core, the legates established another zone, largely concentric with the first, containing public land, the outer limits of which they defined by setting the locations for fifteen markers. When identifying the location of each set of markers, the legates, from the perspective of an observer facing to the south from the center of the innermost space, noted first a marker roughly to his south and then began to identify the remainder by proceeding in a counterclockwise manner.

Of our three remaining examples, two are possibly antiquarian reconstructions and the other a long poem. Livy (1.32.5–14) set out the fetial procedure for demanding compensation preparatory to declaring war by recounting an instance that he placed in the reign of Ancus Marcius, Rome's fourth king. When the Roman ambassador who was sent to demand redress reached the borders of the opposing community, he addressed it with the phrase "Hear, Jupiter; hear, borders [*fines*]" and then recited Roman demands.[106] He then repeated the words, with appropriate modifications, when he crossed the borders, when he encountered the first citizen of the hostile polity, when he entered the gates in its fortifications, and finally in its forum, thus moving across zones to the innermost space. In his life of Romulus, the Greek biographer Plutarch (*Rom.* 11), who sometimes used Roman antiquarian sources, made the *comitium* Rome's center. He and the Augustan poet Ovid (*Fasti* 4.820–24) claim that Romulus first dug a sacrificial trench or pit into which the colonists cast offerings before plowing the furrow around Rome. Plutarch, however, asserts that the trench was excavated in a circle around the *comitium*, itself circular in form; that it was called the *mundus*; and that when Romulus subsequently plowed the furrow in the founding rite, he formed yet another circle around the common center. His account presents many problems. It does not accord well with the little that is known about the *mundus*, and it does not easily fit other tales that located Romulus's city on the Palatine. His rite, moreover, is otherwise unattested, although the *comitium* did possess some centrality in Latin colonies. If it was not entirely a speculative reconstruction, the central role that Plutarch gives to the *comitium* may best fit this context. Almost two centuries earlier, the poet Lucretius, when proclaiming the boundless condition of the universe in his *On the Nature of Things* (*De rerum natura* 1.951–87), claims that wherever one stands, the most distant line one can draw around the observer is insufficient to encompass the totality of things. Here, one should recall that the Romans came to use the phrase "circle of lands" (*orbis terrarum*) to denote the inhabited world.

As we saw in chapter 4, the augurs created a range of spaces in and around the city of Rome to frame magisterial important actions and then built zones around this center. When constructing camps and colonies, Roman magistrates and their attendants established places to perform actions that otherwise would have been performed at Rome. At the same time, they tended to create spaces with clearly defined focal points or even centers, often established by setting orthogonal axes, which were associated with the actions either of the responsible magistrates or of their colonial successors, and they sometimes built out zones from such a center. As we shall see in chapter 6, constructing spaces around such a point, when combined with concerns over distance and occasionally direction from the center, permeate Roman forms of organizing space.

SIX

LAWS, DECREES, EDICTS, AND THEIR SPACES

As was the case with the augurs, the framers of laws, edicts, and decrees also sought to define spaces and connect them to the actions of magistrates, to groups of people, or to certain norms. When constructing such measures, one should recall, magistrates might seek to address a single situation that would pass after having been properly addressed, they might attempt to establish processes and norms that would be in force for the foreseeable future, or they might focus on a particular controversy. When setting out their proposed rules, moreover, they put them in a particular language, suitable for their proclamation in assemblies of various kinds, that would properly define crucial matters, requiring the creation of verbal formulas which might be appropriated by others. In the process, broadly similar concerns were expressed in several ways at different times.

MAGISTRATES, LAWS, EDICTS, AND SPACES

Spatial considerations permeated Roman laws, edicts, and decrees. Some connected colonial triumvirs and agrarian decemvirs to the formation of colonies or the installation of settlers in a town or towns or in the *ager* or *agri* of one or more polities. Magistrates with the proper authorization or status might construct or dedicate specific altars and shrines.[1] Still others permitted or instructed some magistrate to sell or lease tracts of public land. From the second and first centuries, inscriptions survive recording laws and decrees that regulated some aspect or aspects of the relationship between a specific community, in Italy and beyond, with Rome: a long series of second-century decrees along with the first century *lex Antonia de Termessibus* and the *lex de insulo Delo* provide sufficient examples.[2]

These tasks, along with others, often required the demarcation of boundaries on the scene. Thus, augurs under the direction of magistrates inaugurated the spaces that would hold altars and temples, two praetors in 197 defined the limits of their *provinciae* of Nearer and Farther Spain, and magistrates or legates defined the bounds of subordinate polities in conflict with their neighbors. The crucial task of defining the limits of Roman public property was usually associated with consuls, praetors, and censors. The senate dispatched a consul to Campania in 173 to separate public and private lands and an urban praetor in 165 to purchase private property that intruded into public land. Outside of Italy, legates sometimes separated lands liable to tribute from those that were free of the burden.[3] From late in the second century, inscribed markers survive that identify the responsible magistrate, his office, the source of his authority, and perhaps the nature of the limit.[4] Laws, tracts of land, and the official responsible for their definition and regulation were intertwined.

Some operations required the establishment of a network of boundaries. Dionysius of Halicarnassus (*Ant.Rom.* 8.73.3), in a passage probably owing more to first-century practices than to the fifth century where he placed it, has a speaker in a debate over a proposed agrarian law recommend that ten of the leading senators be chosen to fix the limits of public land, mark them with inscribed stones, and lease a portion and sell the rest. Colonial commissioners, as we have seen, instituted a range of different boundaries: between the urban core and its surrounding *ager*, between the plots to be assigned to different persons, between the lands to be distributed among the colonists and those reserved as public land, and between the lands subject to a colony's jurisdiction and those beyond it. Victorious generals, with the retrospective approval of the senate or a popular assembly, made complicated settlements at the end of a major war, declaring some lands public and rewarding individuals and polities with others. Here, the elimination of the polity of the Campani during the Second Punic War was the first such example since the fall of Veii; it was followed by settlements at the end of the Macedonian monarchy in 167, the destruction of Carthage in 146, and the reorganization of the territory of the former kingdom of Pergamum in the 120s.

On still other occasions, magistrates and senatorial legates set limits, if only partial, to other polities. In chapter 2, we saw how groups of senatorial legates might declare certain limits beyond which potentially hostile states could not go. In 168 the senate sent five legates to resolve a boundary dispute between the allied city of Pisae and the recently established colony of Luna; it instructed a proconsul in 134 to mark the boundary between Ateste and Vicentia; and in 117 it sent two legates to fix the limits between the Genuates and the Veturii Langenses.⁵ An imperial inscription (*ILS* 5947) mentions that a consul of 115 had marked the boundaries of a town on Sardinia and recorded the result on a bronze plaque. In most, if not all, of these instances, Roman intervention was sparked by petitions from those concerned, as we saw in chapter 2 a common feature in Rome's management of its empire.

The seemingly close connection between identifiable magistrates or groups of legates and a tract of land that they had delimited in some fashion is made clearer by an associated practice. As we have seen, the word *lex* could signify a formal enactment by a popular assembly, which was characterized by certain linguistic practice, but it could also denote a set of rules imposed on some group or space by a magistrate empowered to do so, in which the same linguistic norms were also in force.⁶ When an auspiciant defined the limits of his field of vision in order to take the auspices, he proclaimed the signs that he wished to see within them if his proposed action was proper. The dedicators of temples and altars linked the structures and the *templum* that contained them with the laws that were to govern them. Magistrates who sold or leased tracts of land proclaimed the terms of the contracts in the same fashion. Colonies too had their own laws. A second-century inscription from Aquileia honors a triumvir who gave the colony its laws.⁷ The so-called Oscan Law of Bantia, a local measure, enacted at the end of the same century, that imitated Roman practice and probably the law of the nearby Latin colony of Venusia, requires certain oaths to be sworn in the *comitium* by light of day and ordains that those who failed to attend the local census were to be flogged there, practices that are known for the analogous place in Rome.⁸ The *lex coloniae Iuliae Genetivae*, which regulated Caesar's colony at Urso in Spain, is the best-known measure of the kind.⁹

In these instances, magistrates or legates defined the limit of some space and imposed rules on it. In the range of spaces set aside in such a fashion, norms applied within their limits, leaving the external world largely or entirely beyond their reach. In this way, legal practice resembled augural techniques, where an inner space was emphasized over an outer one. Many of the spaces in question might be small, as would be the case with temples, while others would encompass entire polities or groups of polities, where the officials often worked with existing arrangements. Still, attempts to regulate spaces and polities were not part of generally applicable administrative activities. Instead, as was the case with extra-urban *provinciae*, which were long aimed at trouble spots, magistrates sought to match rules and actions to spaces to meet specific problems or exploit certain opportunities. The next section turns to spaces defined in a different manner.

THE CITY AND ITS LIMITS

Roman legal practice tended to emphasize Rome over other regions in which its citizens might live, sometimes by specifying rules that applied only within its bounds and sometimes by using it as an essential reference point. Public life, of course, was most intense in the city, where the senate and popular assemblies met and most public cult acts were performed, and where magistrates entered office and performed many, if not all, of their functions. Many measures applied only to Rome and its immediate vicinity because the offices, institutions, and practices that their authors sought to direct or regulate only operated within it: elections of magistrates, meetings of the senate and popular assemblies, and the regulation of certain public events. Measures of broader applicability, moreover, often included quite specific instructions for events in Rome. In general, the framers of these norms appear to have been more concerned with the city than with other places and with regions close to Rome than with those at a greater distance.

Writers of legal formulas occasionally defined the scope of their measure's application in terms of various boundaries around the city. The Twelve Tables, for example, banned burials within the *urbs* and thus within the *pomerium*. Slightly farther, a line drawn one mile from the urban limit occupied a prominent place in many normative statements. Scholars have given this line a role in the regulation of crucial Roman offices and institutions, suggesting that it constrained the powers of tribunes of the plebs, a citizen's right to appeal from magisterial oppression (*provocatio*), and the ability of officeholders to summon meetings of the senate and popular assemblies. This limit, defined in terms of distance from the *urbs*, did form in certain circumstances a clear boundary. As we saw in chapter 4, the dedication of all, or nearly all, new temples from the fourth century lie within it, while certain altars, temples, or shrines marked its location along major roads.

The existence of a formal rule limiting sessions of the senate and gatherings of the centuriate and tribal assemblies to this space is less certain. In practice, magistrates summoned the senate and popular assemblies to meet at places within the line, but the locations deemed suitable by custom and augural practice and of sufficient size to contain the gathering were all within it. Roman laws and decrees, moreover, often were put forward to resolve specific conflicts, rather than proclaim broad general principles. On three occasions in the surviving portions of his history—one each in the fifth, fourth, and third centuries—Livy reports gatherings in camps that conducted elections or approved legislation, and these warrant further examination. Camps, one should recall, centered or came to center on spaces that might be likened to the forum, while occasions within them in which magistrates instructed or exhorted their troops were sometimes called *contiones*. The historicity of these episodes may be doubted, but it is nevertheless instructive to see how Livy framed opponents' objections.

Arranged from earliest to latest, the episodes become progressively less detailed. In the first episode (3.20.6–7), the tribunes of the plebs sought to block an attempt by the consuls of 460 to have the augurs inaugurate a *templum* at Lake Regillus in which they hoped to summon an assembly in accordance with the auspices but away from the tribunes and their powers of obstruction. The tribunes believed that such an assembly would vote as the consuls wished since the right of appeal did not extend more than a mile from the city (*neque enim prouocationem esse longius ab urbe mille passuum*) and any tribune who might attend would be subject to the power of the consuls just like everyone else (*et tribunos, si eo ueniant, in alia turba Quiritium subiectos fore consulari imperio*). In the second (7.16.7–8), he claims that one of the consuls of 357 enacted a law in his camp with his soldiers playing the role of citizens. The tribunes of the plebs took exception to his act and sought to make it a capital offense to "call away" an assembly from Rome. The verb that Livy uses to describe the offense, *sevocare*, was also used to describe occasions, which again bore a capital penalty, when a magistrate took control of an assembly away from a tribune. The last of the three sets out the senate's response to a letter from Spain, where, as a result of the deaths of the proconsuls in battle in 211, the soldiers had elected their own commander, who, according to Livy (26.2), had identified himself in the letter as propraetor. The senators rejected the title because it had not been authorized by senate and people and because they deemed it improper that such decisions with their necessary auspices be taken in the camps, and they soon decided to send a commander of their own to Spain.

For present purposes, note that Livy does not give as objections to such gatherings, to which he did attribute some controversy, any assertion that proper assemblies must take place within a set distance from Rome. With respect to the earliest episode, the only one involving a specific limit, he associates a line drawn one mile from the *urbs* with *provocatio*. In the second, he bases objections on the fact that the assembly in the camps was held at some indeterminate distance from the city and perhaps the tribunes of the plebs. In the final example, his senate bases its objections on the inability to take the necessary auspices in camps. Recall that Dio (41.43) claims that the reason Pompey and his supporters abandoned their plan to hold elections in Thessalonike in 48 was not the distance from Rome but rather their inability to inaugurate the necessary *templum* there. The chief norms that served to keep meetings of the senate and popular assemblies close to Rome may have been primarily augural in nature, linked to auspices that must be performed in *urbs Roma* and to inaugurations that were limited to a zone in and around it that was restricted but not necessarily formally defined. Note, however, that Livy's augurs of 460 were not limited in their inaugurations in such a fashion. Does this indicate that the rites and rules delimiting them were later restrictions or formalizations?

Limitations also applied to the power of the tribunes and the issue of *provocatio*. As we have just seen, Livy (3.20.6–7) asserts that the right of appeal against a consul's threat to impose summary punishment did not extend more than a mile from the city. Dio (51.19.6) reports that when Octavian was given the tribunician power for life in 30, he was also assigned the duty to aid those who called upon him for assistance within the *pomerium* and up to a mile beyond it, commenting, probably incorrectly, that no earlier tribunes had possessed this power.

Scholars have generally accepted that a limit drawn around the *urbs* one mile beyond the *pomerium* once did serve to define the outer limits to such appeals.[10] Romans clearly linked the power to punish without restraint with the ability to command armies. As we have seen in chapter 4, the assumption of military command involved movement out of the city during which the commander put off his civic garb and put on his military cloak. In the same operation, the ability of higher magistrates to impose floggings and capital punishment was expressed symbolically when his lictors placed axes in the bundle of rods that made up their *fasces*, an indication of their greater powers in this regard. *Provocatio* may have begun as a kind of self-help, in which the person about to be sanctioned called upon bystanders for assistance, and thus it would have been limited to the city, if only in practice. Andrew Lintott suggests that these appeals received legal expression only with a *lex Valeria* of circa 300.[11] The ability to successfully appeal, moreover, was linked, again probably only in practice, to the powers of intercession of the tribunes of the plebs, which also was restricted to Rome in some fashion.

If so, certain laws of the second century mark a clear shift. The shadowy *leges Porciae*, one of which may be attributed to the Elder Cato, protected Roman citizens from flogging, even when away from the city or on military service.[12] The Extortion Law of 123 gave *provocatio* as a reward for noncitizens after successful prosecutions, which may mean that it too applied away from the city.[13] According to Plutarch (*C. Gracch.* 9), M. Livius Drusus, tribune of the plebs in 122, proposed forbidding the flogging of Latins even when on military service. That said, the successful use of *provocatio* away from the city appears to have been rare and those accused may have encountered difficulties in proving their citizenship.[14]

Adalberto Giovannini, however, holds that the right of appeal was always linked to status—whether the target was in a civil context or a military one—and not place: one of the props of his argument is that the exercise of *imperium* was differentiated by function, not location, which we examined in chapter 4.[15] Thus, citizens who were not serving in one of Rome's armies would have faced no spatial restrictions in their right of appeals, while those who had taken the military oath were fully subject to a magistrate's power. Still, Giovannini does give considerations of space a role, for he suggests that soldiers possessed some protection from a commander's power when they were very close to Rome so that they might take up certain civic functions. For him, Livy's account (3.20.6–7) of the supposed event of 460 concerns that ability of consuls to punish those who were assembled in their armies, for Livy asserts that these magistrates had summoned those who had taken the military oath but had not yet been formally discharged. Although not soldiers in the consuls' army, the tribunes apparently were liable to punishment as if they were.

Livy (24.7.8; 9.1–2) recounted an episode that might be seen in the same terms. When a consul of 215 returned to Rome to conduct the election of his successors, he deliberately avoided entering the city and went directly to the *campus Martius*. In the assembly, when a dispute with a candidate erupted, the consul informed him that his *fasces* still had their axes, since he had not entered the city. The consul, in other words, had not laid down his ability to punish without restraint by entering the city, so that citizens who were not soldiers in the consul's army were supposedly subject to his full power. Note that here Livy made no reference to any formal limit beyond the *pomerium*, which would have changed markedly the anecdote, for the place in which the elections were to be held was within it. In any case, Livy clearly placed the ability to punish in a military context, and he clearly viewed restrictions on these powers as linked in some fashion to Rome.

Livy's accounts of events in 460 and 215, whatever their historical accuracy, link magisterial powers with the *urbs* or a line drawn with respect to it. At the same time, the existence of formal rules protecting participants in meetings of the senate and *contiones* in the *circus Flaminius* and assemblies in the *campus Martius* is less certain. After all, consuls returning to consult the senate or hold elections may rarely, if ever, have sought to threaten senators or voters, who possessed the ability to retaliate when the official left office. Some norms and practices, moreover, may have served a protective function without specific spatial limitations. As we saw in chapter 4, consuls about to preside over the election of their successors sometimes began in the city, where, of necessity, they would not have possessed their military powers.

The right of appeal, of course, was linked with questions of public order, a matter that appears to have become more prominent in the third and second centuries, with differing responses in the city and away from it. For long, the chief sanctions for violations of certain societal norms probably were familial, and magistrates may have been involved only in matters involving treason or major threats to good order. Over time, new circumstances and new norms, some of which may have received formal expression in laws, edicts, and decrees, almost certainly extended magisterial competence in such matters. Early in the third century Roman assemblies began to elect *triumviri capitales*, whose very name links them to capital punishment, and later in the century they began to choose *quinqueviri uls cis Tiberim* ("five men for the farther and nearer sides of the Tiber") as well. In his account of the Bacchanalian conspiracy of 186, the only occasion, in which they can be seen acting, Livy (39.14.3–10) reports that the consuls instructed the *triumviri capitales* to post guards throughout the city and prevent nocturnal gatherings and arson, while each of the *quinqueviri uls cis Tiberim* was to supervise a single region. Theodor Mommsen connected these five regions to the four urban regions plus Trastavere, but his view would leave the Aventine, outside the *urbs* but within the walls, outside their competence.[16] If, as is more probable, the entire space within the walls fell within their jurisdiction, then their *regiones* would not have been the same as the four divisions of the *urbs*, although each may have been the core of a region. In any case, the five *regiones* certainly included the *urbs*, but they were not limited to it or even to the territory within the walls, since at least one *regio* was across the Tiber. The duties of these *triumviri* and *quinquiviri* did not reach very far into Rome's hinterland.

Despite the uncertainties around limits to *provocatio* and meetings of senate and people, a line drawn one mile beyond the *pomerium* did occupy a prominent place in Roman legislation. It first comes clearly into view in the *lex Oppia*, a sumptuary law enacted in 215 at the most dangerous point of the Second Punic War, that barred women from wearing multicolored clothing or more than an ounce of gold or from riding a horse or in a carriage within *urbs Roma* or a mile of it, except for certain religious rites, a limit that also applied to other towns as well.[17] Note the concern for display in or near a town, but not in the countryside, and the assumption that other towns had, like Rome, clearly marked urban boundaries. Macrobius (*Sat.* 3.17.6) reports the passage of another sumptuary law, the *lex Fannia*, probably in 153, which, he says, left unclear whether it applied more broadly or only to the city of Rome, so that another law, the *lex Didia*, was enacted extending it to "all of Italy." For such laws, the implication that the rules applied only in the city may have been the default position.

Even routine operations might be conducted in a fashion that cut off many outside the city. In *On the Latin Language* (6.86–87, 90–95), Varro quotes at length from two documents that probably derive from the late third or second centuries, since they assume the presence of more than one praetor. The first, from "censorial records" (*de censoriis tabulis*), sets out how the censors summoned the citizens to the *lustrum*, the rite that closed the *census*, by having a herald summon them from the walls. The second, a *commentarium anquisitionis*, describes how the people were called together for a trial on a capitol charge. In the first stage, a praetor summoned the accused to a *contio*, first by having his herald issue a summons from the city's walls and then by having a hornblower (*cornicens*) sound his horn at the accused's house and then from the *arx*. On the day of the vote, a trumpeter (*classicus*) sounded his trumpet on the walls, on the *arx*, and at the house of the accused to summon him and the people to an assembly on the *campus Martius*. Varro claims that censors, consuls, dictators, and *interreges* had summoned in this fashion all assemblies organized by centuries, but, in his own day, consuls gave the order to summon the people to an augur, not a herald. This summons was deemed sufficient to assemble the Roman people, although many lived far beyond Rome's walls.

Rules delimited by a line drawn one mile from the *pomerium* had a long life in Rome. The *lex Cornelia* on murderers and poisoners (*de sicariis et ueneficis*) of 81 established a court to investigate actions that unjustly brought death to a citizen or citizens in the *urbs* or within one mile of it and probably another court, which also met in Rome, to address these matters beyond this limit.[18] Much later, the jurist Gaius (4.103–4) distinguishes between courts that rested on magisterial authority and those created by statute and holds that the latter met within *urbs Roma* or the first milestone. We will encounter other examples later in this chapter.

On other occasions, more distant limits might be expressed in similar terms. The closest was a relatively short distance from Rome. According to Livy (27.37.8–10), after the *haruspices* had determined that a certain portent concerned matrons (*matronae*), a curule aedile in 207 issued an edict requiring those who lived in the city or within the tenth milestone of it (*quibus in urbe Romana intraque decimum lapidem ab urbe domicilium essent*) to come to Rome, contribute to the offering, and choose some of their number to participate in the rites of expiation there. Two decades later, the senate used the same boundary, expressed in terms of distance along Rome's radial roads, to delimit tasks given to magistrates. In 180 they ordered the peregrine praetor to investigate poisonings in the *urbs* and within ten miles of it (*quod in urbe propriusue urbem decem milibus passuum esset commissum*) and assigned to another praetor the task of conducting investigations beyond the tenth milestone before going to his *provincia* of Sardinia (*ultra decimum lapidem per fora conciliabulaque C. Maenio, priusquam in Sardiniam prouinciam traiceret, decreta*).[19] In the following year, the senate gave to the urban praetor the task of investigating poisonings within ten miles of Rome.[20]

Other edicts linked magisterial actions with a still more distant line. Livy (25.5.5–7) reports that in 212, in the midst of recruitment problems as a result of losses in the Second Punic War, the senate ordered the establishment of two triumvirates to search the countryside for recruits, one operating on "this side" and the other "beyond the fiftieth milestone" (*alteros qui citra, alteros qui ultra quinquagensiumum lapidum*). Just after the war, he (31.13.2–9) notes that the senate instructed the consuls to compensate certain public creditors with "public lands within the fiftieth milestone" (*agri publici qui intra quinquagesimum lapidem esset*).

The framers of these measures set one, two, or even three zones around the city, for Italy in some form almost certainly provided, if only implicitly, their outer limits. Like the augurs, their zones were densest close to the city, becoming progressively fewer and broader as distance increased. At the same time, defining limits in terms of distances from Rome would have required little knowledge of local conditions and arrangements, even fairly close to the center, and no effort to coordinate with the boundaries of subordinate polities. After all, lines drawn in this fashion evenly around the city would almost certainly not have matched the limits of all the subordinate polities encompassed within them. In this way, then, they resembled the augural categorization of spaces, which concern the legitimacy of magisterial actions more than the status or circumstances of the inhabitants. In 207 the ten-mile limit separated *matronae* who were expected to contribute to the performance of a rite in the city from others, also Romans, who were not, while in 179 it marked the outer limits to the urban praetor's search for poisoners, although malefactors almost certainly could have been found beyond the line if only some official had been instructed to look. Here, both lines defined a core within the broader region of citizens, much as did the walls, the *pomerium*, and the limit placed one mile beyond it. The consuls of 190, it should be noted, constructed a sphere around their commands in similar terms when they required their soldiers to swear that they would not commit robbery within ten miles of the army.[21] Some rules were to apply only in or near the center.

The remaining examples also emphasize Rome and its environs over more-distant regions. For the praetors of 180 and the triumvirs of 212, the tenth and fiftieth milestones served to separate functionaries who were to undertake the same operation, but in different spaces. (As we have seen in chapter 2, the senate required the first praetors sent to Nearer and Farther Spain in 197 to set a boundary separating their commands for much the same reason.) While it is possible that the praetor and the triumvirs who received the inner assignments may have acted in a manner that affected persons broadly over their spheres of activity, the same cannot be said about those who received the outer, for the areas that they impacted must have largely been determined by the routes that they took out of the city.

Two other instances, discussed more fully later in this chapter, illustrate the principle. In 186 the two consuls who received the assignment to seek out Bacchic conspirators away from the city each received their own region, one apparently to Rome's north and the other to its south. We don't know how the former addressed his task, which he finished more quickly than his colleague, but the other consul arranged his operation as a journey along both coasts of Italy. Over half a century later, the commissioners who were chosen to implement the Gracchan reform law of 133 received broad powers in peninsular Italy, but they arranged their operations in a series of forays down one or another of Rome's radial roads (see chapter 3). The legislators set their tasks in terms of boundaries around Rome, but again the officials organized and experienced them in terms of the roads along which they departed from the city.

Because Livy provides the bulk of our knowledge of these lines placed ten and fifty miles from the *urbs*, we cannot say when the practice began or ended, for his second decade and the later books are now lost. The practice of proclaiming boundaries in similar terms did continue, if only occasionally. In 43 the senate decreed that M. Antony, who was besieging Decimus Brutus in Mutina, should withdraw with his army "this side of the Rubicon, which is the boundary of Gaul, provided that he not march nearer than two hundred miles from Rome."[22] And in an opinion preserved in the *Digest*

(1.12.1.4), the imperial jurist Ulpian defined the jurisdiction of the urban prefect as extending out one hundred miles from Rome.

Away from the city, the authors of various measures sometimes used topographical features to define spaces from the perspective of observers based in Rome. As we shall soon see, a decree and a law of 210 matched provisions to reference points such as "beyond the Tiber," "this side of the Liris," and "this side of the Volturnus." In 180 the senate decided that a military tribune who had disbanded his legion in northern Italy prematurely should be banished "beyond New Carthage" and that a letter be sent to the praetor in Farther Spain informing him of the matter.[23] This equation between "beyond New Carthage" and the *provincia* of Farther Spain may indicate that the province was perceived not only as more distant than Nearer Spain but also as farther along the same route that led from Rome to one of the nearer province's chief towns. In the Agrarian Law of 111, a fragmentary passage refers to magistrates leasing "lands beyond Curio," although the significance of the location is now lost.[24]

Antiquarians, historians, and other authors report rules aimed at keeping specific persons, the holders of certain offices, or identifiable classes of people either close to the city, when their presence was deemed desirable, or pushing them away when it was thought undesirable, using norms that might be expressed spatially, temporally, or functionally. Livy (5.49–55) reports that the priest of Jupiter, the *flamen Dialis*, could not spend a night away from the city, while Aulus Gellius (*NA* 10.15.1–32) claims that rules found in certain unnamed books on public priests and in the first book of a work by a Fabius Pictor included a prohibition against the priest sleeping three nights in succession away from his bed. Elsewhere, we learn that tribunes of the plebs should not be absent from the city for more than one night, except for the celebration of the Latin Festival, and that urban praetors should not spend more than two weeks away from Rome.

Norms such as these float vaguely in time, but others can be located in specific contexts. As we saw in chapter 4, the senate on at least one occasion proclaimed that a consul could not appoint a dictator outside of Italy. According to the Livian epitomator (*Per.* 19), the *pontifex maximus* prohibited a consul of 242 from taking up his *provincia* in Sicily because, as *flamen Martialis*, he could not abandon his sacred responsibilities. Toward the end of the Second Punic War, a consul who was also *pontifex maximus* received the Bruttii as his *provincia* because his duties required him to remain in Italy.[25] Livy (37.51) also claims that another *pontifex maximus* prevented the departure of a praetor of 189 who was also *flamen* of Quirinus on similar grounds. (The norm affecting the movements of the *pontifex maximus* was relatively short-lived: according to Livy [*Per.* 59], the departure of P. Licinius Crassus [cos. 132] for Asia to fight against Aristonicus was the first time that a *pontifex maximus* had left Italy.) In the midst of preparations for war against Antiochus III of Syria, a consul forbade senators and the holders of lesser magistracies from going more than a day's journey from Rome, while at a crucial point in the Third Macedonian War, a praetor issued an edict forbidding senators not on public business from going more than one mile from the city.[26]

On other occasions, laws, edicts, and decrees sought to push certain individuals or groups farther away from Rome, much as the senate would later seek to do with M. Antony in 43. In 216 a dictator sent a lictor to warn Hannibal's ambassadors to leave Roman *fines*, the limits of an inner *ager Romanus*, before night;[27] in the same year, the senate sent a lictor to lead Capuan ambassadors out of the city and order them to go beyond the Roman boundary (*finis Romanos*) by that night;[28] in 190 the senate ordered the Aetolian ambassadors to leave the city that day and Italy within fifteen days;[29] in 167 the senate dispatched a quaestor to Brundisium to prevent Eumenes, king of Pergamum, who was in disfavor at the time, from landing in Italy, and sought to secure the passage of a law prohibiting all kings from coming to Rome so that the Pergamene ruler might not appear to have been judged an enemy;[30] an urban praetor in 161 ordered philosophers to leave the *urbs* while a peregrine praetor of 139 expelled Chaldaeans not only from Rome but from Italy as well.[31] These examples, it must be stressed, do not involve expelling persons or groups deemed undesirable from Rome's empire or from the sphere of operations of its magistrates, for the Roman elite certainly viewed regions outside of Italy as within their power.

Still other measures sought to exclude certain persons from Rome's vicinity, but still keep them broadly within western central Italy. The seemingly old institution of *exilium* involved the voluntary departure from Rome to avoid prosecution.[32] In later periods, the place of exile would be an allied polity that was identified in some fashion in laws or treaties. According to Polybius (6.14.8), those leaving Rome for this purpose might take refuge in Neapolis, Praeneste, Tiber, and some other unnamed towns. Livy (26.3.12) reports that one target of prosecution went into exile at Tarquinii, about eighty kilometers away, and in 211 the plebs voted that his residence there was a lawful exile (*iustum exilium*). In the first century, when all the polities of Italy possessed Roman citizenship, exiles left the peninsula entirely.

In the treatment of hostages and prominent prisoners, the Roman elite also seem to have been concerned with keeping them close enough to Rome to be observed but not too close to the center. After the fall of Capua in 211, members of the local elite deemed most responsible for the revolt were imprisoned for a time in the Latin colony of Cales and in nearby Teanum Sidicinum, both not very far north of the Volturnus River, the northern boundary of Campania.[33] The Mauretanian king Syphax in 201, the Macedonian monarch Perseus in 167, and Bituites, king of the Arverni who was defeated in 121, were all consigned to Alba Fucens, a Latin colony less than one hundred kilometers to Rome's east.[34] In 199 Carthaginian hostages were transferred from the Latin colony of Norba, about fifty kilometers southeast of Rome, to the Latin colony of Signia and to Ferentinum, sixty and sixty-five kilometers to Rome's southeast, while others can be found in the following year at the Latin community of Setia, sixty-five kilometers to the south of Rome.[35] In 186 the senate ordered the citizens of the Latin Ardea, thirty-five kilometers south of Rome, to keep a close watch on a supposed leader of the Bacchanalian conspiracy.[36] After L. Aemilius Paullus's triumph for his victory in the Third Macedonian War, Bithys, son of the Thracian king Cotys, was held as a hostage in Carseoli, a Latin colony sixty-eight kilometers to Rome's east.[37] In 167 Gentius, king of the Illyrians, was sent to the Latin colony of Spoletium, 126 kilometers north of Rome, but, when the Spoletini refused to accept him, he was transferred to the allied town of Iguvium, farther to the north.[38]

A more complex example warrants closer examination. In 210, after the failure of Capua's revolt, a senatorial decree and a plebiscite issued a complicated series of instructions for the surviving free Campani, Atellani, Calatini, and Sabitini, who were to be divided into three groups and settled in different spaces.[39] Those who were in Capua when the gates were closed—that is, were present in the city during its rebellion—were to be transferred "beyond the Tiber, but not touching the Tiber," a requirement that was soon made more specific by identifying the areas of settlement as the lands of Veii, Sutrium, and Nepete. The second group, consisting of Campani and citizens of other rebellious Campanian polities who were not in their towns during the revolt, were "to be removed this side of the Liris in the direction of Rome." The last group—those who had joined the Romans before Hannibal had come to Capua—were to be "removed this side of the Volturnus, no one of them to have land or building nearer the sea than fifteen miles."

In effect, the senate created three separate zones each defined by rivers and from the perspective of Rome and perhaps of Capua as well. Those most closely associated with the rebellion were to be moved farthest from their homes, while Rome itself was to separate their new habitations from their old. Those who had demonstrated their loyalty were permitted to reside close to their old residences provided that they did not live near the sea and possible contact with outsiders. At the same time, the outer limits of settlement for the first, and presumably most dangerous group, were less than fifty kilometers from Rome, about one-third the distance to the Liris River, the outer limits of settlement for the intermediate group and on the margins of the innermost space established in the settlement of 338. They were under closer observation from the city. Here, we find asymmetric zones, with the most dangerous being closest although not adjacent to the city and the least dangerous farthest away. No hostage or prisoner was installed at a place within the inner zone created by the settlement of 338, and virtually all were within an outer zone in western central Italy (see chapter 3).

ROME AND ITALY

The establishment of Italy, either the more restrictive *terra Italia* or the less restrictive space bounded by the Alps, served as a complement to Rome within the broader sphere of Roman activity. We have already seen how the "land of Italy" was used in the third century to denote a kind of privileged space and to distinguish between allied and Latin polities within it, whose military contributions were organized through the *formula togatorum*, and communities outside its bounds, whose relationship to the center was less clearly defined. Writing in the middle of the second century, Polybius (6.12–3, 17) envisions the Roman order as three concentric zones: Rome, Italy, and beyond. He sets out the functions of the consuls through a simple dichotomy between their duties when in Rome and when in command of an army. To the senate, however, he gives a more complicated series of tasks: controlling the treasury, including the granting of funds to censors for building projects in Italy; investigating crimes in Italy including treason, conspiracy, poisoning, and assassination; arbitrating disputes between private persons and polities in Italy; and dispatching embassies outside of Italy to settle differences, offer advice, impose ultimata, receive submissions or declare war, and give the appropriate responses to delegations from such polities when they came to Rome. This division was replicated in laws, edicts, and official activities. Indeed, it may have become more marked as new standing courts were established from the second half of the second century and as consuls and praetors came to spend much of their terms in the city, departing to their commands, usually if not always outside of Italy, late in their magistracies in the first.

Before proceeding, however, we should turn to another problem. Some legal and priestly formulas attributed to measures of the third and second centuries link citizens and "[allies] of the Latin Name" (*ciues Romani atque [socii] Latini nominis*) almost as if they were the higher and lower ranks of a single order.[40] Still other formulas expand this core by including allies (*socii*) or modify it to include only Latins and other allies as did the *formula togatorum*, which, as we have seen, applied to Latins and allies within peninsular Italy. Our knowledge of late third- and second-century laws, edicts, and decrees derives primarily, and usually exclusively, from later literary sources, which often leave certain matters obscure. These authors sometimes describe an enactment or a process as covering or promulgated to "Italy" (*Italia*), "all of Italy" (*tota Italia*), or "the *fora* and the *conciliabula*." Scholars have viewed these formulaic phrases in several ways. Some take assertions about Italy at face value and see the associated norms as broadly applicable over the polities of Italy—citizen, Latin, or allied—that is, Italy itself would serve as the outer limit for the application of some norms.[41] Others seek to preserve distinctions between citizens, Latins, and allies and suggest that *Italia* or *tota Italia* covered only citizens within Italy.[42] The phrase "the *fora* and the *conciliabula*" has also been interpreted in various ways. For some, it indicates that certain norms or procedures were in effect only in rural areas inhabited by citizens and that different ones applied to towns or *municipia*.[43] Henrik Mouritsen, however, argues that the phrase represents only one side of the complementary pair "in the city and away from it" that appears in other contexts as *urbs* and *ager* or "at home" (*domi*) and "on campaign" (*militiae*), and thus should not be taken too literally.[44] In practice, the matter may be unresolvable, perhaps because later writers did not understand or deem significant the categories that they encountered in their sources. Roman practice may well have varied from time to time and from measure to measure.

Some normative statements and institutions certainly crossed status divides. The legal functions of the peregrine praetor imply an attempt to draw some noncitizens into a Roman legal framework, if only to a limited degree. Latins were sometimes eligible to serve as colonists, while the measure authorizing the viritane assignment of 173 limited allotments to citizens and Latins, although the latter received smaller plots than the former.[45] The *formula togatorum* brought Latins and Italian allies into a common framework for military service. Some laws affecting private persons explicitly crossed statuses. According to Livy (35.7.1–5), early in the second century Roman creditors sought to evade Rome's usury laws by having allies or Latins, who were not bound by Roman law, serve as formal lenders. Soon after, a tribune of the plebs successfully proposed a law providing that allies and Latins should follow the same law in these matters as Roman citizens. At some point, magistrates in Latin polities gained Roman citizenship, but in a manner that permitted them to retain their position in their community.[46] In the same broad period, some Latins received the right of *provocatio*, hitherto restricted to citizens.

Another practice involved polities adopting certain Roman rules to regulate their own public life or the private activities of their citizens. Imitation of Roman practices probably was fairly old, and some polities may have undertaken it on their own initiative, although it is worthy of note that in 180 the Cumaeans, citizens without the vote, felt it necessary to petition the senate for permission to conduct public sales and form certain contracts in Latin, probably in accord with Roman legal formulas.[47] Cicero (*Balb*. 19–22), our chief source, refers to a practice designated by the obscure phrase "to make *fundus*" (*fundus fieri*) in which Latin polities and citizen communities came to have the right to adopt certain Roman laws, although in some cases the Roman authorities may have exerted pressure in the matter. Although he claims that the Latins had adopted "innumerable laws" in this fashion, the earliest measures that Cicero identifies as having been treated in such a fashion—the *lex Furia* on stipulations and the *lex Voconia* on inheritances—were enacted in 169, while the earliest known use of the practice by allied polities comes in the aftermath of the Social War.[48] Cicero praises his grandfather for keeping Arpinum from adopting Roman ballot laws circa 115. Some have suggested that two sumptuary laws of the middle of the second century, the *lex Didia* and the *lex Fannia*, may have been adopted more widely in such a fashion as well.[49] If these notices reflect the approximate age of the practice, they show that below the level of the narrative sources the ruling elite were beginning to seek more standardization among polities in Italy, although only sporadically and in a few areas of activity.

Magistrates, priests, and the senate certainly did not always respect the boundaries between citizens, Latins, and allies. In the construction of the *formula togatorum*, the Roman authorities required Latin and allied polities within the land of Italy to assess their available manpower, report to Rome, and accept the demand for soldiers that the consuls and the senate might impose on them. In the aftermath of the Second Punic War, the senate required Latin communities that had failed to provide the required soldiers to conduct their own censuses according to Roman norms. Likewise, when the augurs defined their *ager peregrinus*, a category that included the lands of citizens, Latins, and allies, they established a way for Roman magistrates to act in it in accordance with the auspices. The senate occasionally accepted as public prodigies events that took place in Latin and allied communities. Indeed, in 217 the *decemviri sacris faciundis* performed expiatory rites in the *forum* of the Latin Ardea, although none of the year's prodigies are said to have occurred there.[50] In 167 the senate permitted Prusias, king of Bithynia, to sacrifice not only on the Capitol but also at the temple of Fortuna at Praeneste, an allied town.[51] Consuls sometimes set Latin towns, such as Ariminum or Brundisium, and allied polities, such as Arretium and Pisae, as mustering places for their armies. An anecdote from 193 reveals the presence of a prefect, probably a garrison commander, in Pisae, then an important center in Rome's wars with the Ligures.[52]

Against this background, later additions to the categories of citizen, Latin, and ally show that the ensemble, which at one time may have designated the entirety of the Roman order, had come to denote only Rome's order in Italy. The *senatus consultum de Bacchanalibus* of 186 announces that one set of rules, at least, applies to allies (*foederati*), while another provision covers anyone who was a "Roman citizen or of the Latin Name or of the allies" (*ceiuis Romanus neue nominis Latini neue socium*).[53] More than sixty years later, the authors of the Extortion Law of 123 identify as potential victims who might seek redress citizens of Latin towns (the *nomen Latinum*) and of allied polities (*socii*), those who belonged to foreign nations, and whomever was "within the discretion, sway, power, or friendship of the Roman people"; scholars differ over whether Roman citizens too might sue in such a court.[54] Over two decades later, the Law on Praetorian Provinces of 100 gives as its intended beneficiaries "citizens, allies, Latins, and also those of the nations—the Greek *ethnē* undoubtedly serves for the Latin *nationes*—who are friends of the Roman people."[55]

When we turn to the sequences of statuses in the later measures, we find that, like the earlier *formula togatorum* and *formula sociorum et amicorum*, they preserve a distinction between Rome's Italian and non-Italian allies. The Extortion Law of 123's "foreign nations (*exterae nationes*) and whomever was "within the discretion, sway, power, or friendship of the Roman people," and the Law on Praetorian Provinces of 100's "nations that are friends of the Roman people" clearly refer to polities outside of Italy. Indeed, the translator of the Greek version of the law of 100 inscribed at Delphi makes this distinction explicit for he translated the formula "citizens, allies, and Latins" as "Roman citizens, allies from Italy, and Latins."⁵⁶ Later, Festus/Paulus (p. 17 L) defines auxiliaries as forces contributed by "Roman allies of the foreign nations" (*socii Romanorum exterarum nationum*), a definition that appears to form a clear contrast with the Agrarian Law of 111's reference to Latins and allies "from which it is customary to summon soldiers within the land of Italy according to the *formula togatorum*."⁵⁷ In this way, then, the *exterae nationes* are distinguished spatially from the other elements of the formula: *ciues Romani, socii, nominis Latini*.⁵⁸

Citizens and Latins were closely associated with Italy. At any one time, individuals might be dispersed rather widely, especially as Roman power spread in the second and first centuries. But citizens and Latins each possessed their own domiciles, and here Italy comes to the fore. Latin polities were to be found in peninsular Italy and the Po Valley, the only regions in which their founding colonial triumvirates operated. The domiciles of citizens were also restricted to Italy until the last quarter of the second century, when the colony of Iunonia was founded on the site of Carthage. Indeed, when criticizing C. Gracchus's plan for the settlement, Velleius Paterculus (2.7.7) complains that, against custom, its settlers would not be required to return to Italy for the census.

This connection between citizenship and a domicile in Italy finds confirmation in the laws that extended citizenship during and after the Social War. The first, probably carried by L. Iulius Caesar (cos. 90), granted citizenship to those Latin polities and loyal allies, primarily Etruscan and Umbrian, who chose to accept it and was intended to keep their loyalty in the crisis.⁵⁹ The shadowy *lex Calpurnia* of 90 and the *lex Plautia Papiria* of 89 seem to have made only minor extensions of citizenship with the former recognizing the ability of commanders to award citizenship to individuals or small groups for bravery and the latter addressing those who had been added to the roles of an allied community receiving citizenship, had their domiciles in Italy at the time of the law's enactment, and made a declaration to a praetor within sixty days.⁶⁰ In 89 the consul Cn. Pompeius Strabo carried a *lex Pompeia* that was apparently aimed at cutting off disaffection in the Po Valley, where the war was threatening to spread.⁶¹ According to Asconius (*In Pis.* p. 3 Clark), the chief source, the law gave Latin status to the old inhabitants of transpadane Gaul.⁶² This measure, it should be noted, marks the final stage in the evolution of Latin from an ethnic category to a legal one.⁶³ Over the next few years, citizenship was also extended to the members of defeated polities in Italy although the means and the terms remain obscure.⁶⁴ A later law, probably enacted in 42 after the end of the *provincia* of *Gallia Cisalpina* and the incorporation of its communities into Italy, extends some of the procedures of Roman civil law to the region and distinguishes between cases that might be heard locally and those that involved a praetor at Rome.⁶⁵

One should note that the more extensive list of categories of the late second-century laws set out not only a hierarchical series of statuses but also an enumeration of statuses out from the center: Latins, allies, and "foreign nations, or whomever was within the discretion, sway, power, or friendship of the Roman people" in the law of 123; citizens, Latins, allies, and "nations who are friends of the Roman people" in the law of 100. Cicero would deploy a more elaborate version of this practice: in a speech to the pontiffs in 57, he moves from the gods to the senate, the Roman people, all of Italy, the *provinciae*, and finally the *exterae nationes*, while in one of his orations against Catiline in 63, he goes from the senate to the *equites*, the city, the treasury, the revenues of empire, all of Italy, the *provinciae*, and the *exterae nationes*.⁶⁶ John Richardson notes that the *exterae nationes* were not limited to polities encompassed within *provinciae* but are often outside and even beyond, them.⁶⁷ In any case, recall that Varro (*LL* 5.33) described the augurs' *agri* in a sequence defined in terms of movement out from the center, a practice that may mirror the experience of traveling from Rome to more-distant places in its empire.

SOME EXAMPLES

Against this background, we should turn to certain measures or sets of measures that are known, if only in part, through inscriptions and thus preserve more of the original wording. The Bacchanalian conspiracy of 186 represents one of the most problematic episodes in republican history, but our concern is less with its causes than with its suppression.⁶⁸ Livy's narrative (39.8–19) provides the fullest account of the affair and its context, although it is not without problems of its own. He, and perhaps his predecessors as well, clearly reworked what was to be found in their sources for literary effect. This aspect of his narrative is most visible in his description of the origins of the cult and the manner in which it first came to the attention of the authorities, where it resembles a drama with stock characters. While he makes it appear that the authorities were unaware of a cult that supposedly was recently introduced, it certainly was firmly established in Rome and in Italy where it might be found in the polities of citizens, Latins, and allies.⁶⁹

As a result, the factors that led to the cult's repression remain uncertain, although the sense that it was in some ways a polity within the polity may lie at the center. In any case, Livy presents events associated with the cult's ritual performances in the city as leading directly to the senate's response.

The inscription bearing the text now known as the *senatus consultum de Bacchanalibus* provides the best contemporary evidence.[70] The bronze tablet does not preserve a senatorial decree but rather a consular edict that contains clauses from one or more decrees, and it may preserve selections from a more elaborate set of provisions deemed most relevant for its intended audience. The text opens by identifying the magistrates who had called the senate to render an opinion, the day and place where they had met and issued their decree, and the names of three senators who were present and thus able to serve as witnesses. The senate often met at the site of this meeting, the Temple of Bellona just outside Rome's walls, when it discussed matters of war and peace or received ambassadors from hostile or potentially hostile states. The last clause reveals clearly that the intended recipients were the leaders of organized communities, for it instructs them to "proclaim this at a public gathering for a period of not less than three market days [*nundinae*]," have the decree inscribed on a bronze tablet, which should be set up where it could easily become known, and seek to dissolve Bacchic meetings. The inscription ends with the brief notice, perhaps in another hand, "in the *ager Teuranus*," the district in Bruttium in which it was erected.

The rules that were to govern the cult fall into three broad sections, introduced or separated by the words "they decreed" (*censuere*). The first begins with the provision "concerning the Bacchanal," in which "they decreed that the following should be issued to the allies" (*De Bacanalibus quei foederatei esent, ita exdeicendum censuere*). One of the following clauses asserts: "Let no man, whether Roman citizen or of the Latin Name or of the allies" (*ceiuis Romanus neue nominis Latini neue socium quisquam*) attend a gathering of Bacchic women. The section ends with the provision that that those seeking exemptions should approach the urban praetor, who would seek authorization from the senate in a meeting with no fewer than one hundred senators present. The second and third sections end with similar provisions for exceptions. One clause prohibits anyone from holding rites (*sacra*) in public or in private or outside the city (*neue in poplicod neue in preivatod neue extrad urbem*) unless he had approached the urban praetor and through him the senate.

These passages lie at the center of an extended debate about the consuls' and the senate's intended audience and thus the identities of those who were to be bound by the edict's provisions. The edict itself appears to have been addressed "to the allies," while one of its provisions applies to persons who are "Roman citizen or of the Latin Name or of the allies." Some scholars suggest that these phrases indicate that the measure was to be applied broadly across these categories, although not necessarily in the same ways. Livy, it should be noted, depicts decrees and edicts as applying "not only in Rome but in all the *fora* and *conciliabula*" or "in the city and through all of Italy."[71] Others, however, suggest that the Roman authorities would have preserved the distinction between statuses, seeking some other explanation for the apparent presence of Latins and allies.[72] Would the authorities have proceeded in such a legalistic fashion against those who were clearly thought to threaten the state?

At the most basic level, the phrase "in public or in private or outside the city" forms yet another version of the conventional distinction between the city and its hinterlands, although it is expressed in a seemingly atypical manner. The repeated references to the urban praetor and properly attended meetings of the senate, moreover, suggest that the ruling elite may have distrusted local authorities in this matter and may have wished to reinforce the central role of Roman institutions in decision making. While some have seen in these passages a sign that citizens were the primary targets, the practice of settling out matters in Rome more thoroughly and with greater precision than more distant incidents is paralleled in other Roman legislation.

Livy's narrative (39.8–19) is broadly consistent with this picture. After the consul Sp. Postumius Albinus had reported the matter to the senate, it instructed the consuls to investigate, to take care that the witnesses suffer no harm, to offer rewards in order to bring forward other informers, and to search out priests of the cult in Rome and in the *fora* and *conciliabula*, so that they might be at the consuls' disposal. In addition, the consuls also had an edict read out in Rome, with copies dispersed "in Rome and through all of Italy" (*in urbe Roma et per totam Italiam*), forbidding initiates in the rites from holding religious assemblies or performing cult acts.

After this, the authorities turned to more direct actions. The consuls instructed the curule aediles to seek out priests and keep them under house arrest, and they told the plebeian aediles to ensure that no secret rites took place. They instructed the *triumviri capitales* to post guards throughout the city and prevent nocturnal gatherings and arson. Each of the *quinqueviri uls cis Tiberim* was to supervise a single region in or very near the city. The consuls then summoned the citizenry to the *rostra*, where they had the senatorial decree read to the gathering and announced a reward for anyone who brought forward an offender or denounced them in their absence, established a time limit for anyone who had fled to return, and announced that those who failed to come back within this period would be condemned in their absence, although those who were "outside the land of Italy" (*qui tum extra terram Italiam essent*) were granted more time. Finally, they prohibited sales and purchases by fugitives and barred anyone from assisting them.

This marked concern for cultic practices in the city over activities in the countryside is paralleled by a series of events that Livy (25.1.6–12) placed in 213. As a result of the disorder in the countryside because of war in Italy, refugees filled Rome. Crowds of women, we are told, made unconventional sacrifices and pronounced unusual prayers in the forum and on the Capitol, while the sellers of oracles disturbed the populace. The senate chastised the aediles and *triumviri capitales* for failing to suppress these practices, but they were assaulted when they attempted to do so. The senate then gave the task to the urban praetor, who read the decree aloud in an assembly and issued an edict requiring that books of oracles, prayer formulas, and sacrificial procedures should be turned over to him and forbidding sacrifices according to strange or foreign rituals in public or sacred places.

After describing events in the city in 186, Livy changed his focus. Panic, Livy (39.17.4) says, did not stop at the walls or the *urbs* or Rome's *fines* (*nec moenibus se tantum urbis aut finibus Romanis continuit*) but spread through all of Italy (*per totam Italiam*), giving in quick succession boundaries to the city: its fortifications, the *pomerium*, the *fines Romani*, that is, the augural *ager Romanus*, and the limits of Italy. Many sought to flee Rome only to be captured by the guards that the triumvirs had placed at the gates. Livy (39.18) claims that the exodus from the city was so great that the urban and peregrine praetors suspended all private litigation so that the consuls might complete their investigations. The massive departure from the city also forced the consuls to conduct investigations, *quaestiones*, "around the *fora*," because the people who had been denounced either had failed to come forward or could not be found.[73] The consuls were then assigned the task of destroying all centers of Bacchic worship, first in Rome and then in Italy (*ut omnia Bacchanalia Romae primum, deinde totam Italiam diruerent*), except where there was some ancient altar or shrine. Next, the senate issued a decree barring such rites in Rome and in Italy, but permitting those who thought such rites to be essential to petition the urban praetor for permission, which he could grant after consulting the senate in a meeting in which at least one hundred senators were present.

Finally, the two consuls left the city, each to his district (*regio*). One, Q. Marcius Philippus, went to his original command in Liguria after completing his investigations, while the other, Sp. Postumius Albinus, spent his term on a tour of inspection along both coasts of Italy, later reporting that he had found the citizen colonies of Sipontum and Buxentum, established less than a decade earlier, to have been abandoned.[74] Investigations continued outside of Rome for some time. A praetor of 185, who was assigned Tarentum as his command, put down a slave revolt in Apulia and a "conspiracy of shepherds" whose depredations had made roads and public pastures unsafe, and in the following year, while serving as a promagistrate, he reported that he had also detected large numbers of participants in the Bacchanal who were hiding in the area, punishing some himself and sending others to Rome where the peregrine praetor incarcerated them.[75]

In this account, the primary concern was the city and then Italy. The consuls and the senate appear to have been largely indifferent to any manifestations of the cult outside of Italy, even in areas in which Roman magistrates were acting. Indeed, the only provision that affected people outside *terra Italia* gave them additional time to return to Rome to answer charges, presumably for activities nearer to the center.[76] Here, the phrase "beyond the land of Italy" (*extra terram Italiam*) appears as only a vague complement to Italy. A century and a half later, one provision in the *tabula Heracleensis*, compiled when all the polities of peninsular Italy had received Roman citizenship, refers to persons who as a result of their condemnation by a public court at Rome were not permitted to be in Italy.[77]

In the edict, judgments about the acceptability of cult acts at widely scattered places were concentrated in Rome, where the senate was to function as a kind of court. Other measures enacted later in the century made more formal the concentration of certain decisions in the city while establishing the courts that would make them. In the opening decades of the second century, the senate sometimes assigned a consul or a praetor the task of searching out malefactors in some region of Italy, but, by the time that Livy's narrative fails, this practice appears to have largely ended. Instead, from the middle of the century, laws began to establish standing courts, in which selected senators at first served as judges, that met in the city, although the offenses that they addressed might take place at some distance from the center.[78] The earliest of these courts was established in 149 to address attempts by officials to extort money from those among whom they acted.[79] Earlier in the century, magistrates and the senate had occasionally sought to address such matters through procedures that resembled litigation over private disputes, but the desire for some more formal procedure, with perhaps clearer penalties, led to the creation of a formal court dedicated to the matter.

The Extortion Law of 123 is the best-known measure establishing such a court.[80] Of the almost ninety lines that survive in more or less damaged condition, the first three identify those who were permitted to seek restitution, the officeholders against whom they might proceed, and the grounds for bringing actions. Among the potential victims, the framers include persons who possessed a range of statuses. The list of potential targets is damaged, but clauses elsewhere in the law repeat it, in whole or in part: dictator, consul, praetor, *magister equitum*, censor, aedile, tribune of the plebs, *triumvir capitalis*, triumvir for the granting and assigning of lands, tribune of the soldiers of one of the first four legions, and the son of any of the magistrates who had been listed, provided that his father be a senator.[81] This portion of the law, it should be noted, involved no spatial qualifications since offenses could take place wherever officials, senators, or their sons happened to be.

The remaining lines, the vast majority, set out in great, but often obscure, detail how trials were to be conducted in Rome. Some identify whom the praetor in charge of the court might accept as plaintiffs, while others provide for appointing or repudiating a patron. The supervising magistrate was to choose 450 judges whose names he was to have read aloud at a *contio* and have inscribed in black letters on a white tablet, along with the names of their fathers, their tribes, and their *cognomina* (ll. 12–18). When choosing the panel that was actually to decide a case, he was to swear in the presence of the people that he had done so lawfully and see that these judges swear oaths "before the *rostra* facing the forum" and take care that their names are read aloud in a *contio* and displayed in the forum where they can be read from the ground (ll. 35–38). Certain decisions are to be announced in a *contio* in front of the *rostra* (l. 42). One long section (ll. 49–52) describes the ballot boxes in which judges were to deposit their ballots and how they were to do so: their arms are to be uncovered, but their fingers are to obscure the letters indicating their decisions. In cases of conviction, a list of the goods that were to be distributed was to be displayed in the forum where it could be read from the ground (ll. 66–67).

A few clauses link norms to broader spaces. When the praetors chose their judges, they must choose men between thirty and sixty years of age, who do not hold or ever have held one of the magistracies subject to the law and must not be a father, brother, or son of a senator. To this list of qualifications, the framers appended other criteria: they must have their domicile in *urbs Roma* or within a mile of it, and they must not be overseas (*trans mare*). The chief considerations, then, were a domicile in or very near the city along with physical presence in Italy. A badly damaged clause instructs praetors to order the search, either for plaintiffs or for witnesses, "in the land of Italy in the towns, *fora*, and *conciliabula*," with the possible exception of places in which *praefecti iure dicundo* were present.[82] The framers of a measure aimed at improper actions over the broad sphere of Roman activity focused primarily on the city itself and a zone of up to a mile from it and secondarily, but much more vaguely, on Italy.

The practice of linking official actions with occasions and spaces in the city of Rome was a common feature in legislation from the last quarter of the second century. The Latin Law of Bantia was enacted in the last decades of the century, but because of its fragmentary condition, its identification is unknown: a law on murderers and poisoners enacted at some point between 129 and 111 or a law of Saturninus later in the century, possibly his *lex de maiestate*, are among the possibilities.[83] The bronze tablet bearing the text was probably associated with the allied town of Bantia because the Oscan Law of Bantia was inscribed slightly later on its reverse. Despite its appearance in an allied town, the surviving sections focus very much on Rome. Certain individuals, presumably those who had been condemned under the law, were to be excluded from Rome's public life. They were not "to wear in public, in the light of day, the *toga praetexta*," any magistrate who "shall hold an assembly or *concilium* was not to allow him to cast a vote," and, although this is less certain, those holding a *census* were to leave him outside the tribes and centuries but liable for the payment of tribute. After these provisions, the text sets out instructions for the praetor to appoint *recuperatores* to conduct trials. Finally, the text instructs the holders of a long range of offices—dictator, consul, praetor, *magister equitum*, censor, aedile, tribune of the plebs, quaestor, *triumvir capitalis*, triumvir for granting and assigning land, and judges chosen according to the law itself—to swear oaths that they would obey its provisions in front of "the temple of Castor, openly, before the light of day, facing the forum, and they are to swear within the same five days, in the presence of the quaestor, by Jupiter and the gods." Those swearing the oath were to take care that their acts were recorded in public records in the presence of the urban quaestor. In the slightly later Roman *lex Cornelia* on quaestors (*de XX Quaestoribus*), the consuls were required to post the names of those whom they had chosen to be their messengers (*viatores*) and heralds (*praecones*) on a specific section of the walls of the temple of Saturn.[84] Recall that the Twelve Tables had located certain actions in the *comitium*.

An example from the first century is more substantial. The *Tabula Heracleensis*, found near the city of Heraclea in southern Italy, where it probably was erected in the middle of the century, records either substantial portions of a law or, more probably, excerpts from a number of measures.[85] When it was put together, Roman citizenship had been extended over Italy and the senate, and popular assemblies had begun to regulate local government in various ways. The surviving portions contain a long series of clauses intended to govern certain activities in Rome and in colonies, *municipia*, and prefectures in Italy. Despite the appearance of the text at some distance from the center, half of the preserved sections refer only to Rome and certain events within it. Most apply to a space defined as *urbs Roma* and within a mile of it, a limit occasionally modified by notices that a provision applied only to areas of continuous habitation within the outer limit. One section prohibits the use of carts within this space, but grants exceptions to the Vestal Virgins, the *rex sacrorum*, and the *flamines* and also for triumphs and for games (ll. 62–65). Still other clauses regulate the care of public spaces and public porticoes and the erection of stages and platforms for games within the same limits (ll. 68–72, 77–79).

Other provisions define in some detail responsibility for public roads. Before examining them in detail, however, we should review what little is known about the responsibility for maintaining Rome's great roads. Consuls and occasionally praetors built the routes leading from Rome, but they do not appear to have been involved in maintaining or improving them, the burdens of which would only have increased with the number of roads and the ever greater distances that they traversed.[86] On occasion, magistrates or private individuals were given or assumed the task of repairing or improving all or part of a specific route. Livy (10.47.4) reports that early third-century aediles paved the *via Appia* from Rome's gate to Bovillae eighteen kilometers away, while two late third- or early second-century mile markers reveal aediles repairing sections of the *via Ostiensis* and the *via Appia*. First-century examples report an urban quaestor, a tribune of the plebs, and even a private citizen who had been given supervision of a specific road or some segment of it.[87] According to Suetonius (*Aug*. 30), Augustus personally undertook in 20 to rebuild the *via Flaminia* to Ariminum and assigned the rest of the roads to persons who had been honored with triumphs, asking them to use the money that they had acquired in war to pave them.

On other occasions, the task of maintaining or repairing roads was assigned on a different principle. According to Plutarch (*CGrach.* 6.3; 7.1), Gaius Gracchus carried laws setting out rules for constructing and perhaps maintaining roads, which Mommsen thought had created a general supervision of these routes.[88] A *lex Visellia*, in effect by 68, may have provided for appointments to take care of roads in the city.[89] And Dio (54.8) notes that Augustus, in addition to assigning routes to particular persons, also took charge of roads around (*peri*) Rome. In the collection from Heraclea, the curule and plebeian aediles were to divide among themselves the supervision of public roads in the four *partes* of *urbs Roma* and within a mile of it, treating them as if they formed a single college.[90] Property owners in areas of continuous habitation were to maintain the roads adjacent to their properties in accordance with the edicts of the magistrates to whom their region had been given (ll. 20–23). The *pomerium* and a line drawn one mile from it also defined the duties of two colleges of minor magistrates: *IVviri* who were to clean roads in the *urbs* and *IIviri* who were to do so outside the *urbs* but within a mile of it.[91] Decades earlier, the framers of the Agrarian Law of 111 took note of a small group of magistrates given supervision of a larger space—*IIviri* who were to keep free and unobstructed public roads on public lands within *terra Italia*—and they took care to preserve the public nature of lands occupied by the otherwise unknown *viasii* and *vicani* who were to maintain certain public roads with the same broad limits.[92] Outside of Italy, different practices were followed.

In contrast, the remaining provisions on the *Tabula* are more general and abstract. Most rules that were to apply in colonies, *municipia*, and *praefecturae*, and occasionally in *fora* and *conciliabula* as well, concern eligibility for office and for membership in the local senate. One extensive portion (ll. 135–41) provides instructions for the highest magistrates in a colony, *municipium*, or prefecture when a censor was conducting the census at Rome. Here, the primary concern was that local officials conducted the count according to norms that the censor had proclaimed at Rome, that they act within a set period of time, and that they preserve the results locally and deliver copies to the censor in Rome.

The *senatus consultum de Bacchanalibus*, the Extortion Law of 123, and the Latin Law of Bantia focus, sometimes primarily, on the city of Rome, where they set out procedures for seeking exemptions from certain rules or adjudicating cases. Regions beyond the city, even when they served as the locus for the events in question, figure much more vaguely, if at all. To some degree, this distinction probably represents the limits of the knowledge of magistrates and the senate, but it also should reflect the greater control that they might exercise in the city and their greater concern for arrangements there. We have seen how the Extortion Law of 123 used *terra Italia* to define the limits of some task given to the urban praetor. In Livy's depiction of the senatorial decrees of the Bacchanalian conspiracy, "outside the land of Italy" appears only as the possible locus in which some of the accused who had domiciles closer to the center might be found.

Our final examples concern measures that required magistrates to make decisions and arrangements away from Rome. In the past, when laws or decrees had authorized it, magistrates had distributed land to settlers in colonies or viritane assignments or set the boundaries to tracts of land and sold or leased portions within it. The law put forward by Ti. Sempronius Gracchus when he was tribune of the plebs in 133 was much more wide ranging. This measure aimed at addressing specific circumstances, some of which would prove fleeting. When he took office, Roman commanders in the war against the slaves on Sicily had proved unsuccessful, the rebellious slaves and their leaders appeared to be winning, and the revolt threatened to spread to the Italian mainland.[93] Appian (*BC* 1.7–9) and Plutarch (*TG* 8), our chief sources for the reform and its context, claim that Gracchus wished to address several related problems: the spread of large estates with servile workforces; the resulting displacement of the poor, leading to a decline in the manpower available for military service; and the ongoing war against the slaves on Sicily, which demonstrated the dangers of large concentrations of slaves.[94] The reality of such a manpower shortage is, and has been, the focus of vigorous debate on the economy and demography of Roman Italy, but members of the ruling elite contemporary with the reform also thought, on grounds that are uncertain, that citizens were not producing a sufficient number of children while the dangers of a rebellion of slaves would have been clear to the major participants.[95] The tribune had the assistance of prominent men when constructing his measure. Among those known to have had a role were some of the most prominent jurists of the day—his father-in-law Ap. Claudius Pulcher, consul in 143 and censor in 136; P. Mucius Scaevola, consul in 133, the year of the reform; P. Licinius Crassus, a former praetor and father-in-law of Tiberius's younger brother Gaius—who may have been the source of the measure's most innovative features.

At the center of their law, the reformers placed a special college of magistrates, using an established form, the commissions of three that had in the past founded colonies, but they gave them broader powers and a more complicated task. At the most basic level, these triumvirs were to implement a rule *de modo agrorum* (on the size of fields) that limited holdings of public lands—that is, lands captured from Rome's enemies but not yet distributed, sold, or leased—to five hundred *iugera* and established a maximum to the number of animals that might be pastured there; the tribune may have increased the former in the face of opposition, but this is less certain. The law's framers appropriated this provision from earlier legislation, but with a crucial modification. Our sources report only one such measure, supposedly enacted in 367 and usually known as the *lex Licinia*, with the same restrictions as Gracchus's law. Appian (*BC* 1.7–9) and Plutarch (*TG* 8), our chief sources for the reform and for the earlier law, give both the same context and purpose—to limit large estates, so that the poor might cultivate the excess and raise more children. Scattered prosecutions from the end of the fourth to the early second century seemingly confirm the existence of an early law, although its purpose probably was different, for large estates worked by slaves were probably not a problem at this early date.

The framers of the law of 133 did change one crucial feature of the earlier measure. Gracchus and his allies applied their limits to public lands, and Appian and Plutarch claim that its model did the same. Other authors, however, assert that the Licinian law covered "holdings" or "possessions." Indeed, a strong argument can be made that the *lex Licinia agraria* was a kind of sumptuary law and that it applied to all lands that some person might cultivate.[96] The authors of the law of 133, then, probably narrowed the focus of their predecessor's measure. Rules *de modo agrorum*, moreover, were enforced by aedilician prosecutions and punished with fines, but the law of 133 required the confiscation of surplus lands and their subsequent assignment to citizens and perhaps Latins as well.

Clauses in the Agrarian Law of 111, enacted, in part, to address problems that had arisen as a result of the implantation of the law of 133, reveal the spatial limits to the triumvirs' task and powers. Decrees and laws had long created triumvirates to install colonists in the territory or territories of a specific community or communities. These *triumviri* were to act over a much broader space, which was qualified by an abstract legal category. In the law of 111, the triumvirs' sphere of operation is set out repeatedly with the formulaic phrase "whatever public land of the Roman people there was in the land of Italy in the consulship of P. Mucius and L. Calpurnius, apart from that land, whose division was excluded or forbidden according to the statute or plebiscite which C. Sempronius, son of Tiberius, tribune of the plebs, proposed..."[97]

The Agrarian Law of 111, the bulk of which survives on fragments of a bronze plaque, was apparently enacted to deal with difficulties that had arisen as a result of the activities of this triumvirate and another that founded the colony of Iunonia at Carthage.[98] This focus is reflected in the law's organization, which also rests on older and more established categories. The first forty-odd lines address lands within *terra Italia*, the sphere of operations of the *triumviri lege Sempronia*. A slightly longer segment addresses problems in Africa and ends with a few cryptic phrases addressing lands in the territory of Corinth, which also fell to a Roman army in 146. Shortly after the transition from one sphere to another, a point that cannot be exactly determined because of the fragmentary nature of the text, the framers (l. 49) mentioned lands or places "outside the land of Italy" (*extra terra Italia*). Although the context of the phrase is uncertain, it does demonstrate that in at least some matters a distinction between inside and outside *terra Italia* was deemed relevant.

In the clauses addressing matters in Italy, the law's authors confirmed or modified some of the triumvirs' arrangements and provided for situations in which allotments and other tracts had been inherited or sold or when sales of public revenue had resulted in conflicts with public contractors, *publicani*. Here, the details are often very obscure, partly because of the fragmentary nature of the text but also because of the frequently convoluted language in which the provisions were expressed. The framers, however, clearly envisioned the resolution of disputes as taking place within the processes normally available to citizens. One clause (ll. 9–10) prohibited attacks on its provisions by bringing matters to the senate or to a *iudicium*. Those who claimed that their possession had derived from sale or inheritance or who asserted that they had been improperly ejected from their lands were to come before persons who had jurisdiction before the law (ll. 16–18). Other disputes were to be placed before a consul or praetor who should appoint judges, *recuperatores*, to hear the matter. Status too had its place. Some provisions applied only to citizens, while others included Latins and allies as well, instructing that *recuperatores* should be appointed for them too.

Outside the land of Italy, the law's authors faced different problems and proposed different solutions. The *lex Rubria*, enacted in 123 or 122, provided for the creation of triumvirs, *triumviri lege Rubria*, to found the colony of Iunonia on the site of Carthage, the first known instance when a colonial law and its triumvirate were directed to found a settlement outside of Italy.[99] After the completion of the project, another measure repealed the *lex Rubria* while permitting colonists within the legal limits, which the triumvirs had apparently exceeded, to retain their allotments.[100] Provisions in the law of 111 reveal a range of disputes connected to the ways that the triumvirs conducted their operations: some of the land belonging to free communities had been sold or perhaps distributed in colonial allotments; some promised allotments had not in fact been made (ll. 66–67); some allotments had been mistakenly reassigned (ll. 63–65); more allotments had been made than the colonial law allowed (ll. 58–61); some colonists had not received their allotments; and some *stipendiarii* may have been imperfectly regulated (ll. 77–78).

When the law's framers set out instructions dealing with lands in the region, they divided responsibilities between officials operating in Rome and magistrates on the scene. Thus, some lands might be sold publicly in Rome at some time in the future (ll. 48 and 75); a praetor was to arrange certain matters in Rome (l. 83); the urban praetor was to sell certain public lands (ll. 73 and 74); and the quaestor who held the treasury in Rome as his *provincia* was to record certain private sales (l. 46). A few passages require or prohibit some action by current or future magistrates without clearly specifying where these actions were to take place. Thus, line 53 requires some praetor to perform some uncertain action within twenty-five days of the issuance of an edict by the law's own duumvirs, an action they are to perform within two days of their election and thus at Rome. Lines 70–72 prohibit any magistrate or promagistrate from changing, or any senator for voting to change, the ways certain revenues were to be collected, while lines 87–89 forbid any magistrate, promagistrate, or holder of *imperium* from leasing out the collection of certain revenues on terms other than those that the censors of 115 had established. The last two provisions, it should be noted, are rather generic and are written rather broadly to prohibit any attempt by any official or the senate to change the law's arrangements.

While seeking to clarify the legal status of various tracts and to resolve the many disputes that followed the foundation of Iunonia, moreover, the law's authors assigned responsibility for investigating and settling these conflicts to members of a special commission that the measure itself created specifically for the tasks that they were to perform in Africa and in the *ager Corinthus*. In Africa, these duumvirs were to identify lands that officials had sold; examine the colonial allotments at Carthage; give equivalent tracts of undistributed land to individuals who purchased lands that had been assigned to another, to colonists who had not received their allotments, and to purchasers of lands that had been determined to be part of a colonial allotment; compensate individuals and communities that had lost lands improperly; and identify lands that were still public or had been turned to certain special purposes. Note that their areas of responsibility—the environs of Carthage and of Corinth—were widely dispersed. Apparently, the law's framers granted greater importance to the contrast between the land of Italy and the outside world than they did to the distance between the focal points of their duumvirs' activities.

In the process of setting out their tasks, the framers' law also provided a clear schedule for certain activities. The duumvirs were to issue an edict about some matter within 2 days of their election; a praetor was to perform some act that is now obscure within 25 days of the edict; a praetor was to register certain contracts and revenues within 120 days of the Ides of March; the duumvirs were to resolve disputes in Africa arising out of the actions of some obscure *decemviri lege Livia* within 150 days of their election; they were to resolve disputes surrounding the actions of the founders of Iunonia within 250 days of the law's enactment.[101]

In the aftermath of the Gracchan reform, laws seeking to provide for the distribution of land to citizens or veterans continued as a fairly common form of legislative activity. Laws carried by Q. Appuleius Saturninus, when tribune of the plebs in 103 and 100, proposed to give lands to Marius's veterans in Gaul, Sicily, Achaea, Africa, and Macedonia, although it is unclear whether many were actually installed.[102] According to Appian (*BC* 1.35), M. Livius Drusus (tr. pl. 92) proposed a law seeking to establish colonies in Italy and Sicily. In the aftermath of civil war, the dictator Sulla began the largest of these operations, although in the irregular circumstances of the time, he may not have sought an authorizing law. In any case, his settlements appear to have been heavily concentrated in Etruria, Umbria, Latium, and Campania, the regions closest to Rome and long a core area of Roman activity.[103]

Our final example is more wide ranging than the law of 133, but it too maintained a sharp contrast between Italy and the rest of Rome's empire. The details of the proposed agrarian law put forward by P. Servilius Rullus (tr. pl. 63), apparently a complex measure, are known only through Cicero's attacks on it, a very uncertain source.[104] Rullus's measure centered on the creation of a special college of ten magistrates, who were to be elected by a complicated procedure that imitated the one used in choosing a new *pontifex maximus*.[105] They were to possess the auspices for founding colonies and a *pullarius* to assist them, "just as the *triumviri lege Sempronia* had."[106] Each was to be assisted by ten men of equestrian status who would serve as surveyors, *finitores*, thus enabling actions at many more places in much the same fashion as contemporary legislators established broad commands for Pompey.[107]

If the proposal had been enacted and implemented, these decemvirs would have sold public lands, placed contracts to collect certain revenues, purchased tracts for distribution, founded colonies, and made viritane assignments. In Cicero's depiction of the measure, Rullus set forth extensive instructions, sometimes identifying areas and potential sources of funds precisely and at other times in a more general manner. To raise money, for example, he ordered to be sold all things not yet sold among those whose sale the senate had authorized in 81; those lands, places, and buildings outside Italy that had become public in 88; and the property that would be confiscated by Pompey, who was then campaigning in the East, along with certain public revenues identified by name.

The revenue raised in this fashion was to finance the installation of settlers on plots within Italy. The decemvirs were to purchase lands in Italy at whatever price the owners set.[108] Claiming to quote the exact words of the proposed law, Cicero (*Agr.* 1.6.17) asserts that it instructed the decemvirs to settle *coloni* in whatever colonies and *municipia* they wished and to assign them lands wherever they wanted. In his own voice, he indicated that this was to take place in Italy. Elsewhere (*Agr.* 1.6.20–1; 2.28.72), he holds that the measure ordered that five thousand settlers be installed at Capua and in the nearby *campus Stellas*. Funds from widely scattered sources, dispersed over the broad sphere of Roman activity, were to be used to fund operations in Italy or some restricted parts of it.

AT THE END OF THE REPUBLIC

The republican practice of imagining and regulating the Roman order in terms of zones constructed around a center reached its culmination during the reign of Augustus, Rome's first emperor. Near the end of his life, he composed his *Res Gestae*, which set out how he wished to be remembered, and in the will that the younger Drusus read aloud to the senate in the first meeting after his death in A.D. 14, he instructed that the text be inscribed on bronze and displayed in front of his mausoleum in the *campus Martius* at Rome.[109] Today, its contents are known through three different copies found in three cities in the province of Galatia: one, in Ancrya, contains both Latin and Greek texts; the second, at Pisidian Antioch, is only in Latin; the third, at Apollonia, only in Greek. The means by which the text was disseminated and the significance it was thought to possess are controversial. Some suggest that instructions from Rome ordered that copies be placed throughout Rome's empire, but others propose that the concentration of known examples in a single province points to some local initiative, by either the governor or the provincial assembly.[110] The Greek and Latin versions differ, perhaps to capture the attention of different audiences, most notably by simplifying geographic and institutional terms.

One persistent theme is Rome's rule over the *orbis terrarum*, which is connected directly and explicitly to the achievements of Augustus much like earlier writers had linked the same claim to the deeds of Sulla and Pompey or like still earlier functionaries had tied Rome's *fines* to the victories of its commanders. The heading of the Latin version announces the intention to set out the deeds by which Augustus "made the *orbis terrarum* subject to the *imperium* of the Roman people and of the expenses that he incurred for *res publica* and the Roman people." In the third chapter, Augustus summarizes his achievements over the course of his career:

> I have often conducted wars by land and sea, civil and foreign, across the *orbis terrarum*, and as victor I was merciful to all citizens who asked for pardon. As for foreign peoples, those whom I could safely pardon, I preferred to preserve rather than destroy. There have been roughly 500,000 Roman citizens under oath of allegiance to me. Considerably more than 300,000 of these I have settled in colonies or sent back to their towns after they had completed their terms of service, and to all of them I allotted pieces of land or else gave them money as the rewards for their service. I have captured 600 ships excluding those smaller than triremes.[111]

In the remainder of the text, Augustus proclaims that his power runs from Gades in Spain to the mouth of the Elbe and then goes on to note that embassies from India reached him in Spain.[112] The connection between the power of Rome—and of Augustus—and the *orbis terrarum* was common in Augustus's time and the recent past. The poet Ovid claims that "the expanse of the city of Rome and the world is the same."[113]

Despite Augustus's claims about his achievements in the broader world, the bulk of the *Res Gestae*, at least twenty of its thirty-five chapters, remains entirely or largely focused on Rome, in much the same manner in which the framers of Roman laws focused on procedures in Rome and in its public and sacred spaces. Victories over foreign peoples are transformed into events in Rome:

> Twice I have celebrated triumphal ovations and three times I have driven triumphal chariots and I have been hailed twenty-one times as victorious general, although the senate voted me more triumphs, from all of which I abstained. I deposited the laurel from my *fasces*

in the Capitoline temple, in fulfillment of the vows that I had taken in the war. On account of affairs successfully accomplished by land and sea by me or through my deputies under my auspices, the senate fifty-five times decreed that thanksgiving should be offered to the immortal gods. Moreover, the days during which thanksgiving has been offered by decree of the senate have amounted to 890. In my triumphs nine kings or king's children have been led in front of my chariot. I had been consul thirteen times at the time of writing, and I was the holder of tribunician power thirty-seven times.[114]

In later chapters, we read of still other offices and honors awarded by the senate, priests, and people in Rome, including a long series of priesthoods—*pontifex maximus*, augur, *quindecemvir sacris faciundis, VIIvir epulonum, frater arvalis, sodalis Titius*, and fetial—whose functions, of course, were performed only in and about the city. In addition, he revised three times the list of senators and conducted three censuses, dedicated or restored numerous temples, altars, shrines, and public buildings, distributed money to the people of the city, and displayed animals from Libya in Roman performances. Throughout the text, one encounters the conventional oppositions and distinctions: *urbs* and *orbis terrarum*; "all Italy" (*tota Italia*); citizens versus foreign nations (*externae nationes*).

The focus on Rome was not merely a matter for texts. In 20, Augustus erected the "golden milemarker" (*milliarium aureum*) in the Roman *forum* at the base of the Capitol, and he had inscribed on it the names of the major cities of the empire and their distances from Rome. Within Rome and Italy, he supervised reforms that created a more regular and thorough administrative order. For long, Rome and its population had expanded beyond the *pomerium* and the four regions that were contained within it. To encompass this larger Rome, he extended the formal limits of the city for several miles beyond its augural boundary, and to serve as the most basic unit of government, he organized and regulated formal neighborhoods, *vici*, 265 in number.[115] These neighborhoods were encompassed within fourteen new regions, each under the supervision of a praetor, an aedile, or a tribune of the plebs.[116] Rome, then, continued to possess an administrative density that was unparalleled in other regions of its empire.

The urban regions possessed a formal order, which the Marble Plan of Rome reveals.[117] On this map, Rome's layout is defined with respect to the *arx*, which lies at its center and from which a number of routes radiate to the margins. Of these, the most important runs directly to the map's upper edge, setting out the course of the Sacred Way (*via sacra*) within the older limits of the city and the *via Latina* just outside and replicating the augurs' line of sight when taking the auspices from the *arx*.[118] The regions were numbered in sequence along this route, the lower numbers closer to the center, followed by the others while going in a counterclockwise direction around the *arx*. This method of ordering the urban regions, it should be noted, follows the much earlier enumeration of the thirty-five tribes, perhaps sharing a common center although favoring a different orientation.

At the same time, Augustus also divided Italy beyond the newly expanded limits of Rome into eleven regions that again were numbered according to their relationship to the course of the *via Latina*.[119] As Werner Eck notes, Italy remained virtually unaffected by this reform, for the approximately four hundred Italian towns and cities were almost completely self-governing.[120] Beyond Italy was the sphere of military commands, *provinciae*.

Conclusion

From as far in the past as we can see, Romans viewed their political order spatially through the lens provided by their city and its magistrates. They represented the history of their polity in terms of the deeds of exemplary figures, most of whom were magistrates; they linked institutions and the public and sacred structures and spaces in which they met and acted with their supposed creators; and they connected Rome's empire with its most successful commanders. Laws, edicts, and decrees exhibit great concern for the proper duties of magistrates, the tasks to which they ought to devote themselves while in office, and their movements away from Rome. Indeed, many spaces were constructed through magistrates who had been given tasks that involved, more or less directly, the performance of operations with respect to them.

The city of Rome provided the core around which the polity had coalesced and from which it had expanded and would continue to expand. Its persistent importance was firmly rooted in the experience of members of the ruling elite and had several modes of expression. Magistrates entered office in the city, where the assemblies that chose them and the senate that instructed them met, and many spent their terms in or near Rome. Commanders of armies left the city with great formality, and they sometimes returned to it in triumph. Magistracies, the senate, and popular assemblies were linked to specific places in and around Rome. Roman historians often set out their histories through accounts of exemplary figures who acted in these spaces, which came to be filled with monuments to the deeds of political figures of the past. Finally, members of the elite spent much of their adult lives in Rome when they were not away on public service. In this way, the city and its public spaces occupied a prominent and ongoing place in their lives.

Rome and its environs also occupied an important place in the city's public cult, which insured the success of the polity and its projects. In Rome, as in other communities in the ancient Mediterranean world, the worship of the gods was closely linked to particular places and times, some of which, such as Jupiter's Capitoline temple, possessed considerable symbolic importance. The *decemviri sacris faciundis*, the pontiffs, and the *haruspices* often sought to divert the gods' anger, revealed in signs that might take place far from Rome, by proposing rites of expiation, most of which were to be performed in the public spaces and sacred structures of their city. The augurs attributed great significance to the city, establishing its most prominent boundary, using topographical features in and around Rome as aids in interpreting the signs detected in the rites of divination that proceeded all important public acts, and developing procedures that enabled magistrates to act legitimately at great distances from it. At the center of their discipline was the construction of spaces formed on a number of principles. In and near Rome, the priests inaugurated *templa* that served to frame a range of magisterial and priestly activities, place them in the proper relationship with Rome's gods, and keep them near the city. *Templa* had quite specific orientations, which in theory were linked to the heavens but in practice were connected to the perspectives of the magistrates or priests who had established them or to those who would use them in the future. Away from Rome, army commanders and the founders of colonies placed analogous spaces in their camps and settlements.

Yet another index of the city's continuing importance is the steady concentration of certain activities in or near Rome, to prevent some functionaries from moving too far from it, or to push undesirable persons and activities to some greater distance from the core. Some rules were augural in nature, others were expressed in the formulaic language of laws and decrees, and still others were contained in norms that were supposedly customary. In the second and first centuries, moreover, one can detect persistent efforts to concentrate in Rome important judgments about the behavior of Roman magistrates, subordinate polities, or their inhabitants.

Rome was also the center of a polity whose citizens, allies, and armies were widely dispersed around it. Its ruling elite largely saw their city's empire in terms of its power over peoples or polities, not over territories; they did not connect their city's sphere of operations with firm boundaries; and, until the first century, they did not see any need to govern broadly the many communities that might be encompassed within them. This view of empire did not lead to the establishment of clear and firm limits to Roman power. Instead, Romans identified "the boundaries of the Roman people" (*fines populi Romani*)" with the most-distant points commanders and their armies had reached, while in the first century some Romans linked their city's power to the inhabited world, the *orbis terrarum*.

Although the ruling elite viewed their polity's empire in terms of power over peoples, not control over territories, they attempted to match officials and tasks or groups of people and norms to subordinate polities or spaces, large and small, clearly or vaguely defined, creating in effect islands within the broader sphere over which Roman magistrates and armies operated. The senate and popular assemblies assigned to consuls and praetors their armies and enemies, and they sometimes instructed them to search out malefactors among some group of polities or within certain broad limits. Colonial triumvirs and agrarian decemvirs were to found their settlements in the lands of named communities. On a smaller scale, the duumvirs who were to dedicate temples or arrange for their construction were matched to the places in or near Rome in which they were to carry out their assignments; censors and quaestors arranged in Rome for the sale or lease of tracts whose boundaries had been defined by other magistrates who had been sent to the scene for the purpose. Laws, senatorial decrees, and magisterial edicts might be aimed at a particular polity or they were to be in force within some clearly identified limits. This method of regulation, it must be stressed, did not create broad administrative spaces but rather addressed specific problems or opportunities.

The Roman elite also possessed other ways of setting or imagining spaces. Much of Roman government consisted of the regular movement of magistrates, citizens, armies, and the representatives of subordinate polities to and from Rome. Members of the ruling elite would have experienced their city's empire largely through events in Rome and journeys to and from more distant assignments. Exits and reentries, moreover, provided clear points of reference for conceptualizing prominent aspects of the powers of the city's major magistrates, the commanders of its armies. At the same time, citizens exercised many of the privileges of citizenship or performed its duties by traveling to Rome for assemblies, the great rites of public cult, and for a long time the census and the *dilectus* as well.

Rome's radial roads, the construction of which began in the fourth century, gave form to many of these journeys. In addition to easing the movement of magistrates, citizens, ambassadors, and armies, they also provided the spatial framework for a range of official activities. Certain routes were closely linked to specific allies, enemies, and theaters of operations. Triumvirs and decemvirs founded colonies and made viritane assignments along them in order to make them more secure, and they sometimes used the road as the basis for field surveys or the formation of streets within the urban core. On other occasions, officials who were expected to act more broadly organized the implementation of their tasks into separate forays down major routes from the city. At other times, spheres of official activity or groups of citizens who were the target of some enactment were defined specifically in terms of distances along these routes. Thus, magistrates might be expected to act within or beyond the first, tenth, or fiftieth milestones from the city, while the tribes over which citizens were distributed were themselves arranged in groups determined by proximity to some road. At the same time, groups and statuses were often enumerated in sequences from nearest to farthest along them. This structural feature of public life—the repeated journeys to and from Rome often channeled by roads which had their origins there—almost certainly would have reinforced views of Rome's centrality.

Indeed, a significant part of the learning of priests and jurists involved journeys of one kind or another. In order to inaugurate new *templa*, augurs processed from the *arx* to the site, which effectively kept such enclosures close to the city. Priests and jurists were especially concerned with movement across these spaces. Entering and leaving *templa* began and ended a range of public and sacred actions, while higher magistrates leaving the city took up powers they later surrendered on their reentry. Magistrates taking up assignments, *provinciae*, away from Rome included within their broad task the routes to and from the focus of their activities, and they sometimes constructed roads leading there. These journeys, during which they kept their powers, would have substantially impeded viewing *provinciae* as clearly defined spaces.

Organizing space in terms of journeys to and from Rome along its radial roads overlapped with yet another way of viewing Rome's empire. The image of the city surrounded by communities and peoples under its authority permeated Roman thinking about the polity and its power. In the third and second centuries, and for some uncertain period before, one can detect a persistent tendency to proclaim a dichotomy between the city and its various hinterlands, some quite distant, and to project zones around the city, more densely near Rome than away. Some of these zones developed gradually and informally as Rome's reach extended ever farther from the city. Other zones, densest nearer to the city, were explicitly defined in laws, edicts, decrees, and priestly or juristic opinions. Thus, the augurs defined spaces, *templa*, that provided the spatial framework for a range of public and sacred activities and kept them in or near the city; they established Rome's most important boundary, the *pomerium*, which defined important magisterial powers; they delimited Rome's core lands, its *ager Romanus*, a short distance beyond, and at a much greater distance; they set the limits to Italy. The priests linked the sequence of zones out from the center with the ability of magistrates to act legitimately in certain matters; the polities encompassed within them were a lesser consideration. Jurists and the framers of laws, edicts, and degrees often followed a broadly similar practice, sometimes even using the same limits. Thus, normative statements applied in the interior of *templa* or within the *pomerium* or *terra Italia*, or they were in force within some space defined in terms of distances down Rome's radial roads. In this way, Rome and its environs and, at a greater distance, Italy take on the appearance of cores within Rome's broad empire. Away from Rome and its environs, the ruling elite often appear to have been largely unconcerned with matching boundaries to realities on the ground.

Perceptions of the polity as a spatial order, then, were set rather firmly from the perspective of residents of Rome, who were more familiar with places closer to the city than farther away while largely experiencing empire through journeys to and from the center. At the same time, across these zones one can detect a persistent valuation of the resulting spaces in which the inner is preferred in some fashion over the outer. The augurs excluded unwanted spiritual influences from their *templa*, while matters associated with war were to be kept out of the *urbs*. Laws set out matters closer to the center more fully than those at a distance. Certain offices were responsible for the maintenance of public order in the city, but similar arrangements were not made for the countryside. Many measures, moreover, applied only in the city, leaving many of Rome's own citizens outside their purview, while others applied within Italy, leaving many of Rome's allies and subordinates outside their scope. Here too, Romans exhibited a marked tendency to list spaces and groups of people in sequences set out from the closest to the most distant.

The practice of viewing and defining spaces in terms of roads to and from Rome or of zones around it made the city the clear center of its empire. Away from the city, magistrates sometimes built other spaces with clear centers, usually the place where they were intending to act or envisioned other officials as acting in the future. Latin and citizen colonies were surrounded by an urban boundary that was analogous to Rome's *pomerium*, they had limits to their civic territory as Rome did, and they sometimes defined limits within this territory in terms of distances from the center, just as at Rome. In other circumstances, the authors of some normative statements might project zones around a camp or some subordinate polity.

Thus, when one looks at the empire as a whole, the reluctance of the ruling elite to create overarching systems or broadly applicable rules becomes clear. Throughout the period covered by this work, they were more concerned about Rome and its environs than with polities and regions at greater distances and with Italy over Rome's transmarine dependencies. Recall that Polybius (1.6.6; 6.50.6) claims that around the time of the Pyrrhic War the Romans began to make war on the rest of Italy as if it belonged to them and that they had intended to rule only Italy but had come to dominate the inhabited world by chance. In his account of the Roman constitution, moreover, Polybius envisioned three broad administrative zones—Rome, Italy, and the rest of Rome's empire—a pattern that would persist until the end of the republic.

Notes

Introduction

1. Finer 1997, 4.
2. For example, Sherwin-White (1973) remarks that Rome entered the Social War as a city-state and left it as a capital.
3. For example, Cornell 1991b; David 1995a, 35–53, esp. 43.
4. See, for example, Lefebvre 1974; Hillier and Hanson 1984; Hirsch and O'Hanlon 1995. For an investigation of ancient Chinese spatial concepts, see M. E. Lewis 2006.
5. Bloch 1998; Bevir and Rhodes 2010, 1.
6. For the office of consul, see Pina Pola 2011 and the articles in Beck, Jehne, and Pina Pola 2011b; for the office of praetor, see Brennan 2000.
7. Stewart (1998) and Bergk (2011) argue that the office of praetor was not firmly distinguished from the office of consul until the addition of the second praetor, but Brennan (2000, chap. 3) holds that the two were distinct from the beginning.
8. For the aediles, see Sabbatucci 1954.
9. For the tribunes of the plebs, see Bleicken 1955; Lobrano 1982; Thommen 1989.
10. For the senate, its membership, and its procedures, see Bonnefond-Coudry 1989; Ryan 1998.
11. See Cornell 2000.
12. See Jehne 2011.
13. For priesthoods, see Beard 1990; Catalano 1974; Scheid 1984; Porte 1989.
14. Mommsen 1887–88; for a recent analysis of his approach, see Jehne 2005. For Mommsen's views on the senate, see Hölkeskamp 2005.
15. Meier 1980.
16. Magdelain 1968, 6ff.; Bleicken 1975, 152–56, 348ff. On the broad and poorly defined nature of the consulship, see Beck, Jehne, and Pina Pola 2011a.
17. See Bleicken 1975, 106, 137.
18. Bleicken 1975.
19. Rüpke 2012.
20. Moatti 1997.

21. Jehne 2012, 406.

22. Scheid 2006; Schiavone 2012. Magdelain (1995, 184) stresses the oral nature of much law until the second century.

23. For the development of the nobility, see Hölkeskamp 1987; for a survey of recent work on its values, see Rosenstein 2006.

24. For the place of spectacle, see H. Flower 2004a; A. Bell 2004; Hölkeskamp 2006a and 2007; for Rome as a theater of power, see Hölkeskamp 2011. For the pervasiveness of public ritual, see Flaig 2003.

25. See Beck, Jehne, and Pina Pola 2011a, 3.

26. See Hay and Lister 2006, 8.

27. For Roman views of their empire, see chapter 2.

28. For Chinese maps, see Hsu 2013.

29. For Roman practice, see Brodersen 2012; Talbert 2013. Brodersen (2004) makes the contrast between Chinese and Roman practice explicit. For Roman conceptions of space in general, see Brodersen 1995; for a different view, Talbert (2010) argues for some administrative use of maps under the empire.

30. For the persistence of local ties, see Patterson 2006a and 2012; Lomas 2012.

31. See Mouritsen 1998.

32. For example, Cornell 1995, 364–68; David 1995a, 35–53.

33. See, for example, Fronda 2010.

34. See, for example, Mouritsen 1998.

35. Thus Rich 2008a. For the institution of *deditio in fidem*, see Hölkeskamp 2004.

36. For the *municipium* and its history, see Bispham 2007; Humbert 1978; Galsterer 1976; Sherwin-White 1973; for the retrospective nature of *civitas sine suffragio*, see Mouritsen 2007.

Chapter 1

1. See Ferrary, 1984, 88 n. 12.

2. Walbank 1957–67, 1:664, suggests that book 6 once contained an extended treatment of public cult, either in the Archaeology or at the very end of the book, which is now lost. Vaahtera (2000) argues that Polybius never actually wrote the promised account.

3. See Brunt 1980a.

4. For its scope, see Cornell et al. 2013, 1:162–78.

5. For local history in general, see Clarke 2008; Rhodes 1990.

6. See Ferrary, 1984.

7. For Ennius, see *Rep.* 1.3, 1.25, 1.30, 1.49, 1.64, 3.6, 5.1, and 6.10; for Cato, see *Rep.* 1.27 and 2.1–3; for Polybius, see *Rep.* 1.34, 2.27, and 4.3.

8. Thus, Rawson 1972. For Cicero as a historian, see Rambaud 1952; Brunt 1980b; Rawson 1972; Cornell 2001. Ferrary (1984) examines in detail the relationship between Cicero and Polybius.

9. See Forsythe 1994.

10. See Cornell et al. 2013, 1:253–55.

11. See Cornell et al. 2013, 1:296–98.

12. For a programmatic statement of the matter, see Livy *praef.* 10; see also Chaplin 2000.

13. See Hickson 1993.

14. Marincola 1997, 17–18.

15. For the tribes, see Dion. Hal. *Ant.Rom.* 4.15.1; for Cassius Hemina, see *FRHist* 6 F 17 and 18 (= Plin. *HN* 32.20 and Macr. *Sat.* 1.16.33); for Gellius, see *FRHist* 14 F 21 (= Dion. Hal. *Ant. Rom.* 2.72.2); for Cato, see chapter 4.

16. For Piso, see Dion. Hal. *Ant.Rom.* 12.9; for Livy, see later discussion in this chapter.

17. See Schaberg 2001, 10.

18. With respect to families, the practice is most visible in aristocratic funerals; see H. Flower 1996.

19. See Rawson 1990; Wiseman 1994b; Sehlmeyer 1999.

20. See H. Flower 2006.

21. For the use of *exempla* in Latin literature, see Rambaud 1952; D'Arms 1972; David 1980; Moore 1989; Chaplin 2000.

22. See Zorzetti 1980; H. Flower 1995; Wiseman 1988; Wiseman 1994c. See also H. Flower 2000 and 2003. For the quote, see H. Flower 1995, 171.

23. See, for example, *ILLRP* 310; 319.

24. For the historical development of the myths around Romulus and Remus, see Wiseman 1995.

25. See Plin. *HN* 33.43. For the difficulties in this passage, see Crawford 1985, pp. 17–24.

26. See *FRHist* 1 F 18 (= Livy 10.37.14); see also Oakley 1997–2005, 4:378–79.

27. See Hölkeskamp 2006b, 481; Timpe 1988.

28. For the relationship between Lavinium, the *mons Albanus*, and magistracies, see Marco Simón 2011.

29. For the curule aediles, see Livy 10.23.11–12; for the coins, see Crawford 1974, pp. 137, and 1985, pp. 30–32; for the *ficus Ruminalis*, see Ovid *Fast.* 2.409–10, and Varro *LL* 5.54.

30. For Romulus's hut, see Balland 1984.

31. For the statues of the kings and Brutus on the Capitol, Evans (1990) places them around 300; Sehlmeyer (1999, 85–86) places the statue of Navius between the end of the sixth century and 300; and Koortbojian (2013, 54) favors the interval between the middle of the fourth century and the middle of the third.

32. See Festus p. 168 L, who connects Attus Navius, Tarquinius Priscus, the change in tribes, and a fig tree in the *comitium*.

33. See Livy 40.51.3.

34. See *FRHist* 9 F 39 (= Plin. *HN* 34.30). For the act, see also *Vir.Ill.* 44.3; for the statue of Sp. Cassius, see also Cic. *Dom.* 101; *Rep.* 2.60; Livy 2.41; Dion. Hal. *Ant.Rom.* 8.69–80; Val. Max. 5.8.2; 6.3.2; Plin. *HN* 34.15. For other instances of the practice, see Cassius Hemina *FRHist* 6 F 43 (= Non. Marc. 548 L); Festus p. 363 L; Cic. *Fam.* 8.14.4; *Att.* 6.9.5.

35. See Feeney 2009, 146; Wilcox 1987, 96.

36. Mommsen 1887–88, 1:101–2, 599, established the interval, but preferred 222; Beck 2005, 409–11, suggests that the shift may have taken place in 218 for military reasons.

37. Dionysius of Halicarnassus (*Ant.Rom.* 6.49.1; 9.25.1; 11.63.1) and Livy (3.8.2; 3.36.3; 3.38.1; 5.9.8; 8.20.3) preserve different dates in the fifth and fourth centuries for entry into office.

38. Livy (37.4.4; 44.37–38) provides dates for eclipses in 190 and 168, which allows the Roman calendar to be compared to modern dating; see also Derow 1973 and 1976.

39. See Fronda 2011.

40. See Rich 2011a.

41. See Phillips 1974, 273; see also Packard 1960.

42. See Rich 2011a and 2005.

43. For Rome as a Greek city, see Momigliano 1971; Gabba 1991, 12–15. Ando 1999 notes some of the distortions that come with viewing Rome as a Greek city.

44. See Momigliano 1971, 22–49. Williams (2001, 94–99) also notes that Polybius exhibits little interest in peninsular Italy beyond Rome.

45. See Polyb. 2.37.10–11; Millar 1987.

46. For such movement in the Seleucid monarchy, see Kosmin 2014, chap. 6.

47. See SIG^3 II, 543.

48. Thus, Levene (1993) summarizes his conclusions at 241–48.

49. See Davies 2004, 22.

50. Hickson 1993, 145.

51. See Rüpke 2007, 117–34; Beard, North, and Price 1998, 114–56.

52. For *superstitio*, often connected with divination and prophecy, see Calderone 1972.

53. See, for example, *ND* 1.61; 2.2; 2.168; 3.5.

54. For comparison, note that the Greek authors of the Lindian chronicle, inscribed in 99, represented the history of a shrine through a series of dedications by famous men and of divine epiphanies, mostly in the distant past; see Higbee 2003.

55. Cic. *ND* 1.60; 2.2–3. See also Cic. *Div.* 1.8.

56. Brisson (2004, 41–55) argues that the dialogue is not about the existence of the gods, which largely goes unquestioned, but rather about their nature and that the basic disagreement is between the Stoic view, which attributes to the gods a distinct nature and purpose, and the more skeptical interpretation, which asserts the limits of rational argument and the superiority of traditional practice.

57. Cic. *ND* 1.113.

58. *ND* 3.5: *Ego uero eas defendam semper semperque defendi, nec me ex ea opinione quam a maioribus accepi de cultu deorum inmortalium ullius umquam oratio aut docti aut indocti mouebit sed cum de religione augitur Ti. Coruncanium P. Scipionem P. Scaevolam pontifices maximos, non Zenonem aut Cleanthen aut Chryisippum sequor habeoque C. Laelium augurem eundumque sapientem quem potius audiam dicentem de religione in illa oratione nobili quam quemquam principem stoicorum cumque omnis populi Romani religio in sacra et in auspicia diuisa sit, tertium adiunctum sit si quid praedictionis causa ex portentis et monstris Sibyllae interpretes haruspicesue monuerunt. harum ego religionum nullam umquam contemnendam putaui mihique ita persuasi Romulum auspiciis Numam sacris constitutis fundamenta iecisse nostrae ciuitatis quae numquam profecto sine summa placatione deorum inmortalium tanta esse potuisset.* In the text, the Loeb translation is used with modifications.

59. See, for example, Pease 1920–23, 12–13; Momigliano 1984, 209; Linderski 1982; Santangelo 2013, chap. 1.

60. See Beard 1986, 35.

61. See Schofield 1986, 51–53, 56. For a different view, see Santangelo 2013, chap. 1.

62. See M. Flower 2008, chap. 2.

63. Cic. *Div.* 1.12; 1.34; 1.109.

64. Cic. *Div.* 1.24–28.

65. Cic. *Div.* 1.85: *Nec uero quicquam aliud adfertur cur ea quae dico diuinandi genera nulla sint, nisi quod difficile dictu uidetur quae cuiusque diuinationis ratio, quae causa sit. Quid enim habet haruspex, cur pulmo incisus etiam in bonis extis dirimat tempus et proferat diem? Quid augur cur a dextra coruus a sinistra cornix faciat ratum?* In the text, the Loeb translation is used with modifications.

66. See North 2000, 39.

67. See, for example, Plaut. *Asin.* 259–61; *Aul.* 4.3.1.

68. For Pictor, see *Div.* 1.43; for Accius, see *Div.* 1.43–45; for Decius Mus, see *Div.* 1.51; for the games, see *Div.* 1.55.

69. See *Div.* 1.2; 1.12; 1.15; 1.16; 1.23; 1.86; 2.27; 2.46. See also Schofield 1986, 62.

70. Thus, Schofield 1986, 62.

71. Cic. *Div* 2.28; 70–71; 75.

72. Thus, Scheid 2003, 182–86; Rüpke 2007, 122–26.

73. See Santangelo 2013, chap. 4.

74. See Beard 1998; Linderski 1985; North 1998; Scheid 1990b; Scheid 1994; Scheid 1998.

75. See, for example, Cic. *Brut.* 55; 60; 72; *Dom.* 136.

76. See Scheid 1999.

77. The pontifical annals have generated a vast literature, primarily because they are often thought to have provided much of the evidence for Roman historiography. For a survey of what is known about them and their relationship to historiography, see Frier 1999; Cornell et al. 2013, 1:141–59.

78. See *FRHist* 5 F 80 (= Gell. *NA* 2.28.4–7); see also Cic. *De or.* 2.51–53; *Leg.* 1.6; Serv. *auct. Ad Aen.* 1.373.

79. See Jacobs 2010.

80. For Scaevola's and Varro's opinions, see Aug. *CD* 4.27.31; 6.5–12; 7.5–6; Tertullian *Ad nat.* 2.1.8–15. For a survey of some modern views on this "tripartite theology," see Lieberg 1973.

81. Rüpke 2007, 134; see also Beard, North, and Price 1998, 149–56.

82. See Linderski 1982, 32 (= Linderski 1995, 478).

83. See Rüpke 2007, 12–13.

84. See Rawson 1985, 233–49; Sehlmeyer 2003.

85. See Stevenson 2004.

86. See Clarke 2008.

87. For sacrifices on a *dies ater*, see Gell. *NA* 4.6.6–10; D'Ippolito 1994, 42–44; Catalano 1960, 57–58, 332–33, 352–53, 380; Michels 1967, 65–66; Latte 1960, 69ff., 102. For the rules on sacrificial animals and family *sacra*, see Pliny *HN* 8.51.77; Cic. *Leg.* 2.21.52.

88. For Servilianus's *responsum*, see Macrob. *Sat.* 1.16.25; for Scaevola's, see Cic. *Leg.* 2.21.52.

89. For these works, see Schiavone 2012, 154–95.

90. See Scheid 2006, 20. Magdelain (1995, 184) stresses that the written texts drew their efficacy from the spoken formula and that rules were systematized only during the second century.

91. Heurgon 1964.

92. Festus pp. 276–77 L.

93. Gell. *NA* 13.14.5–6.

94. The earliest mention of such laws is in Cassius Hemina (*FRHist* 6 F 16 and 17 = Non. Marc. 829 L and Plin. *HN* 32.20); for the *ius Papirianum*, see Pomponius Ench. in D. 1.2.2.2; Dion. Hal. *Ant.Rom.* 3.36.4; Festus p. 260 L. On the *leges regiae* in general, see Mantovani 2012.

95. Momigliano 1990, 59.

96. See, for example, Ferrary (1984, 90), who suggests that the tendency to assign origins of institutions to the regal period emerged during the Gracchan conflict, which increased the need for legitimacy provided by primordial origins.

97. Rawson 1985, 233–49.

98. Wallace-Hadrill 2008, chap. 5.

99. Rüpke 2007, 12, 58–60.

100. Stevenson 2004, 121.

101. For early laws, see Ampolo 1983.

102. For the linguistic peculiarities of *leges*, see Magdelain 1978, 23–54; for a *lex* as a ritual text, see Magdelain 1978, 12–22.

103. Cic. *Leg.* 1.15; 1.20; 2.23; 3.4; 3.12.

104. Schofield 1991, 69.

105. Crawford 1989.

106. The *rogatio Servilia agraria* of 63 defined certain attributes of its decemvirs by reference to the triumvirs established by the *lex Sempronia agraria* of 133, and it set out the manner of their election with a reference to the way that a *pontifex maximus* was chosen; see Cic. *Agr.* 2.7.18; 2.12.31. In the *lex Ursonensis*, clauses liken the rights of Urso's pontiffs and augurs to those of other colonies, and certain privileges of the colony's pontiffs to those of Roman pontiffs; see Crawford 1994, no. 25, chaps. 66 and 103.

107. Note, however, that the Law of Praetorian Provinces of 100 does attempt to justify its provisions; for the measure, see Crawford 1994, no. 12. From the first century, "motivation clauses" sometimes can be found in senatorial decrees, where they serve to explain policy; see Potter 1999.

108. For the form, see Crawford 1994, pp. 7–19.

109. See Appel 1909; Norden 1939, 91–106; Magdelain 1978; Hickson 1993; Hickson 2007; Magdelain 1995, 67–111; Courtney 1999, 8–9; E. Meyer 2004, 44–72.

110. See E. Meyer 2004, 44.

111. Cic. *Leg.* 2.8.19.

112. Cic. *Leg.* 3.6.

113. Cic. *Leg.* 3.3.9.

114. See Gabba 1988; Crawford 1994, pp. 395–96.

115. Cic. *Leg.* 3.7; Crawford 1994, no. 25, chap. 71.

116. Cic. *Leg.* 3.10.

117. Crawford 1994, no. 25, chap. 66.

118. For the development of the structure of legislation, see Crawford 1994, pp. 7–8, and Rawson 1978. See Crawford 1994, pp. 395–99, for the organization of Urso's law.

119. For the influence of philosophical concerns, see Dyck 2004, 12–15.

Chapter 2

1. For the acts involved in entering office, see Lintott 1999, 9–16; Pina Polo 2011, 13–20.
2. On the use of the lot and personal agreement, see Stewart 1998. For a different view of the lot, see Rosenstein 1995.
3. J. S. Richardson 2008, 23.
4. For the *formula togatorum*, the census, and conscription, see chapter 3.
5. See Marco Simón 2011; for the festival itself, see Smith 2012.
6. For the years between 218 and 167, and for an uncertain period before and after, Livy puts the expiation of prodigies among the necessary preparations for the consuls' departure; see Rich 2011a. Some scholars have suggested instead that prodigies were expiated as they occurred, but Pina Pola (2011, chap. 2) and Satterfield (2012) defend Livy's representation.
7. Rüpke (1990, 45–46) properly notes that the "auspices of departure" is a modern construct and that acts of auspication, which were valid for a single day, would not have secured divine approval for an entire campaign. Still, magistrates wishing to take up their commands did auspicate when leaving the city, an essential part of the process. Vervaet (2014, 319–20 n. 62) suggests that the "auspices of departure" are better seen as the "auspices of the assumption of military command," so that if one failed to auspicate properly the legitimacy of one's command would be impaired.
8. Feldherr 1998, 9–10.
9. For Roman conceptions of empire, see the subsequent discussion in this chapter; for movement and divination, see chapter 4.
10. For the triumph, see Bonfante Warren 1970; Versnel 1970; Itgenshorst 2005; Itgenshorst 2006; Beard 2007; Bastien 2007; Rüpke 2012, chap. 5; Lange and Vervaet 2014.
11. See Pittenger 2008, 25–31; Vervaet 2014, chap. 4.
12. Livy 40.50.5–6; 41.28.8–9.
13. See Östenberg 2009.
14. See Eckstein 2006.
15. See Austin and Rankov 1995.
16. Feldherr 1998, 9–12.
17. For the accord, see Polyb. 2.13.3–4. For its date, see Hoyos 1998, 156–58.
18. See Kunze 2011.
19. Polyb. 9.27.5.
20. See Laffi 2012; Gargola 1995, 52–58, 103–6.
21. Gargola 1995, 575–78.
22. Livy 25.7.5–6.
23. For these *duumviri*, see Orlin, 1997, 147–58, 172–78.
24. See Jehne 2009.
25. For Nuceria and Accerrae, see Livy 24.3; for the Cumaeans, see Livy 40.42.13.
26. For Pisa, see Livy 45.13.10–11; for Ateste and Genoa, see *CIL* I.2, 636; I.2.584; see also Scuderi 1991.
27. For supplements, see Livy 31.49.6; 37.46.10–11; 43.17.1.
28. For these Greek embassies and their successes, see Ferrary 2009.

29. Livy 21.25.1; 26.9.6; 37.57.1–2; 40.18.4–5.
30. Livy 22.55.4–5.
31. Livy 22.58.9.
32. Livy 39.23.3.
33. See Jehne 2011.
34. For roads and the landscape, see Laurence 1999.
35. See Patterson 2006b, 191–93. For colonization in general, see chapter 5.
36. Janni 1984.
37. For the *dilectus*, see chapter 3; for groups defined by distance, see chapter 6.
38. See Gargola 1995, 158–61.
39. See Nicolet 1991, 30–31.
40. See Derow 1979; Kallet-Marx 1995, 18–29. For a different emphasis, see J. S. Richardson, 2008, 10–62.
41. See J. S. Richardson 2008, 10–62. The concept will also be examined in chapter 4.
42. For the link between *imperium* and *auspicium*, see Vervaet 2014, 23–26.
43. See J. S. Richardson 2008, chaps. 2 and 3.
44. See chapters 4 and 6.
45. Livy 39.27.
46. Livy 38.38.1–17.
47. *Rhet. Her.* 4.13; see also J. S. Richardson 2008, 55–57.
48. Cic. *Cat.* 3.26; *Balb.* 6.16; see also *Balb.*13.
49. See J. S. Richardson 2008, 74–76. For imperial examples, see Plin. *NH* 6.120; 12.19; 12.98. I wish to thank John Rich for the references.
50. See chapter 3.
51. For the imperial practice, see Talbert 2010.
52. Livy 38.41.3.
53. Livy 34.10.5.
54. Livy 37.57.1–6.
55. Catalano (1978, 493) stresses the importance of keeping separate the boundaries of Rome's immediate hinterland, which, as we shall see in chapter 4, are sometimes called the "Roman *fines*" (*fines Romani*), and the limits of Rome's power, the "*fines* of the Roman people" (*fines populi Romani*).
56. For Pompey's claim, see Diod. Sic. 40.4; for other examples, see Cic. *Mur.* 22, *Prov. cons.* 29, *Phil.* 5.48; 13.14; Pliny, *Ep.* 8.6.6, *Paneg.* 55.4.
57. Gruen (1984, 283–85) accepts that these passages reflect early second-century decisions, which others have doubted, but he suggests that the *haruspices*' responses "amount to nothing more than mechanical repetition of the old formulas." Gruen, and those who have doubted the historicity of the passages in question, rests his position on the failure of the Romans to incorporate additional territories under their direct government as a consequence of victory, and it is for this reason that he assumes the opinion must be a relic of a time when Romans customarily did so. As we have seen, however, Romans did not limit their power to areas under their firm control. The victories in question would extend Rome's *fines* because they would produce new and more distant subordinates.
58. Livy 31.5.7; 36.1.1–4.

59. Brennan (2000, 95) suggests that the commander at Tarentum was a propraetor, apparently because he believes that the fourth praetor must have been stationed on Sardinia, for he holds elsewhere that their presence was required by law (see my subsequent discussion).

60. See Livy 33.27.1–2; 37.3–4.

61. This was the distribution among entering praetors in half of the years from 197 to 167: it was the original disposition in 196 (Livy 33.25–26), 194 (Livy 34.43), 193 (Livy 34.55–56), 192 (Livy 35.20–21), 188 (Livy 38.35–36), 186 (Livy 39.3), 184 (Livy 39.38–39), 182 (Livy 40.1), 179 under *lex Baebia* (Livy 40.35–6), 176 (Livy 41.15–16), possibly 174—the text has lacunae (Livy 41.21), 173 (Livy 42.1), 172 (Livy 42.10), and 167 (Livy 45.16). In 179 and 177 only four praetors were chosen under the terms of the *lex Baebia* of 180. In 180 and 175 the list of praetorian provinces is partial or missing.

62. For assignments in Italy, see Livy 37.1–2; 37.50–51; 38.35–36; 38.42; 39.30; 39.41; 40.18; 40.20; 41.8–9.

63. Livy 39.38–39; 40.37; 40.43; 41; 42.1; 42.8–9; 45.16.

64. See Brennan 2000, 146–50.

65. Livy *Per.* 20; 32.27.

66. See Brennan 2000, 182–90; Ferrary 2008; contra J. S. Richardson 2008, 17–25.

67. Livy 27.22.5–6: *prorogatum et L. Veturio Philoni est ut pro praetore Galliam eandem prouinciam cum iisdem duabus legionibus obtineret quibus praetor obtinuisset. Quod in L. Veturio, idem in C. Aurunculeio decretum est ab senatu, latumque de prorogando imperio ad populum est qui praetor Sardiniam prouinciam cum duabus legionibus obtinuerat.*

68. Livy 35.20.8–10: *praetores deinde prouincias sortiti, M. Fuluius Centumalus urbanam, L. Scribonius Libo peregrinam, L. Valerius Tappo Siciliam, Q. Salonius Sarra Sardiniam, M. Baebius Tamphilus Hispaniam citeriorem, A. Attilius Serranus ulteriorem. Sed his duobus primum senatus consulto, deinde plebei etiam scito permutatae prouinciae sunt: Attilio classis et Macedonia, Baebio Bruttii decreti.*

69. J. S. Richardson 2008, 18–21.

70. See Oakley 1997–2005, 2:660–61.

71. See Brennan 2000, 169–72; see also J. S. Richardson 1986, 110–12.

72. For an example, see Livy 10.15–22.

73. See Livy 8.23.10–2. For the prorogations of this period, see Brennan 2000, 73–75. Hölkeskamp (1987, 136–40) finds the purpose of prorogation in the combination of a desire to ensure continuity in command in a continuing operation and a wish not to block access to office by iterations. Brennan (2000, 75) sees only the military explanation. Note that prorogations also increased the number of commands and thus the number of potential theaters of operation.

74. For arrangements in these years, see Brennan, 2000, 76.

75. See Brennan 2000, 80–83.

76. See *Inscr. Ital.* 13.1, 72–73.

77. See *ILS* 1 = *ILLRP* 309.

78. Brennan 2000, 85–86.

79. See Brennan (2000, 86–87), who also suggests (88–89) that peregrine praetors were first assigned to Sicily and that later events pulled them back to the mainland,

but here there is no evidence. Briscoe (2012) argues that the post's primary purpose was to make available a second praetor in Italy while the consuls were in Sicily.

80. See Brennan 2000, 86–87; Hoyos 2003, 13.

81. See Brennan 2000, 72–73. For the functions of the early praetors, see Brennan 2000, 58–78.

82. For Sicily, Macedonia, and Asia, see the tables in Brennan 2000, 701–16. For the Spanish assignments, see J. S. Richardson 1986, 184, 192–93. Africa is sometimes said to have become a regular assignment in the aftermath of the Third Punic War, but see Gargola 2016.

83. See Brennan 2000, 242.

84. See Brennan 2000, 398–400.

85. See Brennan 2000, 365–71.

86. For the precedence of consuls, see Vervaet 2014, chap. 5; for legislation, see my discussion in chapter 6; for the auspices, see my chapter 4.

87. See Vervaet 2014, 216–23.

88. See Gargola 1995, chap. 8.

89. See the examples in J. S. Richardson 2008, 84.

90. J. S. Richardson 2008, 94–95. The passages in question are Caes. *BG* 1.45.2; 7.77.16.

91. For the Augustan nature of the *formula provinciae*, see J. S. Richardson 2008, 117–45; Lintott 1993, 28–29. For the empire as a collection of provinces, see Talbert 2004.

92. For the significance of *provincia*, see Lintott 1981, 54; J. S. Richardson 1986, 5–10; J. S. Richardson 2008, 12–49. Bertrand (1989) argues that assignments always had territorial implications, although *provincia* denoted the task and not the place where it was to be performed.

93. Ferrary 2008.

94. For Sicily, see Dahlheim 1977, 12–73; for the Spanish provinces, see J. S. Richardson 1986, 72–80; for Macedonia and Asia, see Kallet-Marx 1995, 11–41; 97–122.

95. Drogula 2015, 254–55.

96. Kallet-Marx 1995, chap. 1.

97. See Kallet-Marx 1995, chap. 4.

98. For designation by armies, see, for example, Livy 21.63; 23.32.1–2; 23.32.2.

99. For designation by opponents, see, for example, Livy 24.44.1; 31.6.1; 37.50.1–5.

100. Sall. *Iug.* 27.3; 35.4; 43.1; 62.10; 73.7; 82.2; 82.3; 84.1; 114.3.

101. For the consul of 218, see Livy 21.17.1 and 6; for the praetor of 192, see Livy 35.20.10; for the consul of 190, see Livy 37.1.10; for the consul of 189, see Livy 37.50.1.

102. Livy 23.32.19; 25.3.2; 25.3.4 (At 25.20.3, Livy refers to the same praetor buying grain "from Etruria" [*ex Etruria*]); Livy 26.28.4–6; 27.22.5; 27.22.13.

103. Livy 28.10. 4–5.

104. Livy 31.6.2; 32.1.7.

105. Livy 39.8.

106. Livy 39.29.8–9; 39.41.5; 40.19.10; 40.37.4; 40.42.1–4; 40.43.2–3.

107. Livy 25.3.2; 25.3.4.

108. Livy 27.25.10; 25.20.5–6; 35.20–1; 35.41.7; 37.50.13.

109. Fronda 2010, 55–57.

110. Livy 36.2.7.
111. See Livy 24.44.3; 27.7; 30.1; 32.1.
112. Livy 33.43; 38.35–36; 39.2.
113. Livy 27.22.2.
114. Livy 39.29.8–9; 39.41.
115. Livy 24.7.9; 24.44.4.
116. Livy 32.28.11; for this boundary, see also J. S. Richardson 1986, 77–78.
117. See J. S. Richardson 2008, 29.
118. See Livy 40.37.4; 40.43.2.
119. For the text with commentary, see Crawford 1994, no. 12. For the translators, see Crawford 1994, p. 234, but note that Ferrary (1977) argues for Greek translators.
120. Cnidos Copy, column III, lines 28–41, and Delphi Copy, block B, lines 8–27.
121. For the letters, see Delphi Copy, block B, lines 8–27.
122. For the soldiers, see Cnidos Copy, column II, lines 12–31. Crawford (1994, p. 259) suggests that the recent victory of T. Didius had made the soldiers superfluous.
123. See Cnidos Copy, column IV, lines 5–30.
124. Cnidos Copy, column III, lines 22–27.
125. See Lintott 1993, 23; J. S. Richardson 2008, 45. Bertrand (1989), however, argues that assignments always had territorial implications, although *provincia* denoted the task and not the place where it was to be performed. J. S. Richardson (2008, 46) also notes that the reference to Lycaonia occurs just after a citation of a provision in the *lex Porcia* prohibiting magistrates or promagistrates from leaving their *provincia*, which was probably intended to assert that going to Lycaonia was not the same as leaving *provincia Asia*.
126. For the route and debates about its date, see Kallet-Marx 1995, 347–49. Polybius (34.12.8–10) gives the terminal points.
127. See Cnidos Copy, column IV, lines 5–30.
128. For Cato's opinion, see *ORF*³ frag. 223; Astin (1978, 120) takes the passage as a sign of Cato's strict adherence to rules and procedures. For the Law of 100, see Crawford 1994, no. 12, Cnidos Copy, column IV, lines 31–39.
129. For spatial limitations on magisterial jurisdiction, see chapter 6.
130. Livy 30.1.1–8; 30.24.1–4.
131. Livy 41.7.7.
132. Livy 43.1.10–11.
133. See Pittenger 2008; Vervaet 2014, chap. 4; Lundgren 2014; Rich 2014.
134. Livy 34.10.1–6; see also Pittenger 2008, 75–76.
135. The significance of "under another's auspices" is reasonably clear: since Helvius had received troops from the current commander, Ap. Claudius Nero, he could be seen as Nero's subordinate and thus under his auspices. The identification of "another's *provincia*" is complicated by difficulties in identifying the site of the battle, which must be "in" Farther or Nearer Spain; for discussions of the problems, see Versnel 1970, 178; J. S. Richardson 1986, 182–83; Stewart 1998, 90–93.
136. See *ORF*³ frag. 223.
137. *Inscr. Ital.* 13.1: 79, 552, 338.
138. For a detailed study of his operations—and of Livy's account of them— see Pittinger 2008, 213–30. For yet another example of such a debate, see Livy 27.35.10;

43.6, where C. Claudius Nero (cos. 207) justified leaving his *provincia* "against Hannibal, the Brutti and Lucani" to join his colleague, whose assignment was "Gallia against Hasdrubal," by saying that a commander should not be restrained by the limits of his own *provincia* to fight against the enemy prescribed by the senate.

139. Livy 38.45.3.

140. For the date, see Crawford 1994, p. 260.

141. References to the law can be found in the Law on Praetorian Provinces of 100 (Crawford 1994, no. 12, Cnidos Copy, column III, lines 1–15) and in the *lex Antonia de Termissibus* of 72 (Crawford 1994, no. 19, column II, line 16). For the connection between the two references, see Crawford 1994, p. 260.

142. For the provisions of Sulla's law, see Giovannini 1983, 91–97. Mommsen (1887–88, 1:57) held that Sulla's law broadly reformed provincial government, but Giovannini (1983, 73–101) shows this to be an illusion.

143. See Cnidos Copy, column III, lines 22–27, the source of the translation.

Chapter 3

1. See Harris 2007.

2. Although scholars are in broad agreement that Cato sought to establish a common framework, students of the scattered fragments differ markedly about its nature; see Gotter 2009; Williams 2001, 48–58; Jefferson 2012; Chassignet 1987; Forsythe 2000.

3. For the painting, see Varro *RR* 1.2.1. Scholars disagree over whether the painting was of a map or an allegorical figure. Williams (2001, 37, 129), who views the image as a map, notes the connection between it and Italy as a geographic and political entity.

4. See Fronda 2010.

5. For a discussion of this passage, see Fronda 2010, 27–28.

6. For *terra Italia*, see Catalano 1978, 534–37.

7. For *terra Etruriae*, see Serv. auct. Ad Aen. 1.2, and the "Prophesy of Vegoia" (p. 256.34 Campbell); for C. Gracchus's speech, see Gell. *NA* 11.10; for Scipio's, see Gell. *NA* 4.18.3. Gellius reports that the speech was still in circulation in his own day, although some denied its authenticity.

8. Catalano 1978, 509–10.

9. For the law of 111, see Crawford 1994, no. 2, line 21.

10. For the passage's links to Fabius Pictor, see De Ligt 2012, 41–42.

11. See Salmon 1982, 169–70; Lo Cascio 1991–94.

12. See Marshall 1968; Bowman 1990; Raggi 2001; Valvo 2001. Burton (2011, 82–83) notes that *socii* and *amici* were often interchangeable in literary texts and inscriptions and thus regards the lists as identical.

13. See Catalano 1978, 534–37; Harris 2007, 307.

14. For the games, see L. R. Taylor 1934; Gagé 1955; Brind'Amour 1980; Poe 1984; Hall 1986; Russo 2008; Forsythe 2012, chap. 4.

15. See Ps.-Acron 5.8 (Keller I 471).

16. Zosimus 2.5–7; Phlegon *Macr.* 37.5.2–4 (= *FGH* 257 F 37 V).

17. Russo 2012, 46.

18. L. R. Taylor 1934, 108–11.

19. For the Twelve Tables, see Crawford 1994, II, *tab*. II.2: *status dies cum hoste*. For the meaning of *hostis*, see Stewart 1998, 184–95; Zack 2012.

20. See, for example, Plaut. *Merc*. 635; *Pseud*. 1231; see also Mommsen 1887–88, 3:598; Stewart 1998, 185–86.

21. See Mouritsen 2007. For earlier views, see Sherwin-White 1973, 39–58; Humbert 1978.

22. See Bispham 2007.

23. Mommsen 1887–88, 3:231–32; Pinsent 1954; Bispham 2007, 13–31.

24. See Pinsent 1954, 163; Bispham 2007, 13–16.

25. Sherwin-White 1973, 40–41, 291.

26. See Crawford 1994, no. 2, line 31. For a discussion, see Bispham 2007, 76–87.

27. Bispham (2007, 11) notes: "The progress of municipalization meant that concern for these vital areas [i.e. membership in the tribes and centuries of the Roman census] which had once been the prerogative of the Roman state, gradually shifted to the domain of the *municipia*" and that "the ongoing decentralization of power, financial autonomy, organizational duties, and jurisdiction are a crucial outcome of the municipalization of Italy after the Social War."

28. Festus p. 126 L; Gell. *NA* 16.13.6–7.

29. Festus p. 126 L; Paulus's epitome confirms the reconstructed passages. For the identity of "Servius the son," see Bispham 2007, 22.

30. Bispham 2007, 29.

31. Bispham 2007, 28.

32. Galsterer 1976, 15–24.

33. Morley (1996, 83) describes this space as the region with the easiest access to Rome for persons and goods.

34. For the increasing importance of the tribes, see Cels-Saint-Hilaire 1995; Lo Cascio 2001.

35. The fundamental study of the tribes and their locations is L. R. Taylor 1960. For the earliest tribes, see also Rieger 2007. For doubts about the chronology of the earliest tribes, see most notably, Alföldi 1964, 296–318; Cels-Saint-Hilaire 1995.

36. Mommsen 1887–88, 3:161–62, 163.

37. Fraccaro 1935.

38. L. R. Taylor 1960, 10.

39. Livy 8.14.4; 38.36.7–9.

40. Festus/Paulus (p. 121 L) claims that the Maecia was named for a camp, while Livy (6.2.8) reports a Volscian camp near Lanuvium, which he calls *ad Meciam*; see L. R. Taylor 1960, 53–54. For the connection between Scaptia and *urbs Scaptia*, see Festus p. 464 L; Pliny (*HN* 3.38) lists Scaptia among the lost towns of Latium; see also L. R. Taylor 1960, 54–55.

41. For Cures Sabini and the Sabines, see L. R. Taylor 1960, 59–65; for Formiae, Fundi, and Arpinum, see Livy 38.36.7 and L. R. Taylor 1960, 93, 307.

42. See Shatzman 1975, 12–18.

43. See, for example, Cic. *Leg.Agr*. 2.79; Varro *LL* 5.56.

44. L. R. Taylor 1960, 69–78; contra Rieger (2007, 597–610), who views the order as hierarchical, not spatial, but see J. Linderski's afterword to the 2013 reprint of L. R. Taylor 1960, 366–68.

45. Crawford 2002. For an examination of the ways that the enfranchisement of the Italians after the Social War may have affected the system, see Crawford 2010.

46. See L. R. Taylor 1960, 89–90; Crawford 2002, 1134–35.

47. See L. R. Taylor 1960, 89–90; Crawford 2002, 1134–35.

48. See Crawford 2002, 1131.

49. For the road to Bovillae, see Livy 10.47.4; for the road to Ostia, see *ILLRP* 449; for the *via Appia* near Tarracina, see *ILLRP* 448.

50. See Livy 45.14.9; 45.44.7; Val. Max. 5.1.1.

51. As Pina Pola (2011, 6) explicitly notes.

52. Here, Pina Pola (2011) has assembled the evidence.

53. Brennan (2000) calls this the "localization" of the urban praetor.

54. See Cicero *Agr.* 2.30.82–3; Gran. Lic. pp. 8–9 Criniti. For earlier efforts in the regions, see Livy 42.1.6–12; 42.9.7; 42.19.1–2.

55. For colonial commissions and their members, see Gargola 1995, 58–63. It remains uncertain whether these triumvirs possessed *imperium*. Livy (34.53.1–2) claims that two triumvirates chosen in the same year had *imperium* for three years (*His deducendis triumuiri creati, quibus in triennium imperium esset*), but elsewhere (32.29.4), he gives to one commission a magistracy with a term of three years (*Tresuiri deducendis iis, per triennium magistratum haberent*). Some triumvirs led their colonists into situations where fighting was taking place.

56. See Festus p. 262 L.

57. See Galsterer 1976, 27–33; Linderski 1979; Knapp 1980; Bispham 2007, 95–100.

58. See Knapp 1980, 34–36. He lists some unnamed places in the *ager Picenus*, Amiternum, Atina, Aveia, Casinum, *forum Claudii*, Fulginia, Peltuinum, and Statonia, near Saturnia.

59. Some scholars suggest that the creation of these prefectures continued after the Second Punic War as Rome settled its citizens in new areas. The *Book of Colonies* (*Liber coloniarum*, p. 164 Campbell) identifies eight places in Lucania as *praefecturae*: Volcei, Paestum, Potentia, Atina, Consilinum, Tegianum, Grumentum, and Velia. But the compiler of the *Liber coloniarum*, active in the fourth century A.D., combined texts of various ages, the most fundamental of which were assembled under Augustus and Tiberius; see Campbell 2000, xl–xliv. He, and perhaps the authors of the underlying texts as well, was primarily interested in boundaries and was largely indifferent to the legal statuses of towns and perhaps unreliable when setting them down; see Campbell 2000, xl–xliv, 401–2; Sherwin-White 1973, 209; Knapp 1980, 36 n. 87. (For a defense of the document's accuracy with regard to Gracchan land assignments, see Roselaar 2009.) After all, Paestum, the supposed seat of a praefecture, was a Latin colony until the Social War. Note that the *Liber coloniarum* connects these *praefecturae*, if only by juxtaposition, with Gracchan lands assignments much later in the second century. Brunt (1971, 280–81) suggests that these Lucanian *praefecturae* were intended to be judicial centers for the Gracchan colonists.

60. For the prefecture and assimilation, see, for example, Humbert 1978, chap. 9. For the difficulties in imposing Roman legal practices, see Mouritsen 2007, 152 n. 43. Frederiksen (1984, 268) suggests that while communities of Roman citizens were later thought to be under Roman law, in earlier stages Rome had sought to develop working

relationships rather than to impose its own law completely. For Cumae, see Livy 40.42.13; for Arpinum, see Cato *FRHist* 5 frag. 35.

61. Knapp 1980, 35.
62. See Livy 40.50.2; 41.27.5–12; 42.3.1–11.
63. The literature on prodigies is great. For more recent studies, see MacBain 1982; Rosenberger 1998; Rasmussen 2003; Rosenberger 2005; Rosenberger 2007; Engels 2007; Santangelo 2013.
64. See Engels 2007, 221–35.
65. See, for example, Livy 21.46.1; 23.36.
66. Livy 21.62.1–11; 22.1.8–20; 27.4.11–15.
67. Livy 41.13.3.
68. Obseq. 21.
69. Cic. *Verr.* 1.4.108; Val. Max. 1.1.1; see also Spaeth 1996, 73–79.
70. See, for example, Livy 27.37.8–10; 37.3.6–7; 41.21.11–13; 43.13.7–8; 45.16.5–6.
71. Livy 38.36.4; 40.19.1–5.
72. Livy 40.37.1–3.
73. See Mazurek 2004, 151–52.
74. Livy 27.11.1–6; 27.37.
75. For 200, see Livy 31.12; for 142, see Obseq. 22; for 132, see Obseq. 27a; for 119, see Obseq. 34; for 98, see Obseq. 47; for 97, see Obseq. 48; for 95, see Obseq. 50; for 92, see Obseq. 53. For the significance of the number twenty-seven, see Forsythe 2012, 44–46.
76. Mommsen (1853) argues that prodigies reported from Latin or allied polities must have occurred on Roman public lands there and then uses the reports to locate places where Rome possessed such lands, a position that Ruoff-Väänänen (1972) and Dart (2012) largely follow. Rawson (1971a) suggests that reports from noncitizen polities indicate that our lists are not strictly limited to Roman public prodigies, but also include private signs or ones pertaining to other places.
77. Rosenberger 2005, 240.
78. MacBain, 1982, 114–15; Rosenberger 2005, 235–57. For a year-by-year list of prodigies and expiations, along with the sources for them, see Rasmussen 2003.
79. Most of the few occasions in which our sources identify the source of reports specify that pontiffs and temple attendants or *aeditui* informed magistrates of signs in sacred structures in Rome itself; see Livy 40.19.2; 43.13.4–5; Gell. *NA* 4.6.2. Livy (34.45.8) also claims that the people of the Latin colony of Hadria, much farther way, informed magistrates of a prodigy.
80. Livy's reports of prodigies from Capua with the year of their occurrence can be found at 22.1.8–20 (in 217); 27.11.1–6 (in 209); 27.23.1–4 (in 208); 27.37.1–15 (in 207); 30.2.9–13 (in 203); 32.9.2–4 (in 198); 34.55.1–5 and 35.9.3–5 (in 193); 40.45.3–3 and 40.59.6–8 (in 179); 41.9.4–8 and 41.13.1–3 (in 173). Reports from Campania are in 41.9.4–8 and 41.13.1–3 (in 177) and in 41.21.5–13 and 41.28.2 (in 174). Note that the senate accepted most of these prodigies within two decades of the end of Capua's rebellion, which may have made the city a source of unease.
81. Anagnia's notices are in 211, 210, 204, 203, 169, and 167 (Livy 26.23.4–6; 27.4.11–15; 29.11; 30.2.9–13; 43.13.3–8; 44.18.6–7; 45.16.5–6); Reate's are from 212, 211, 190, 182, 179,

and 169 (Livy 25.7.7–9; 26.23.4–6; 37.3.1–6; 40.2.1–4; 40.45.3–5; 40.59.6–8; 43.13.3–8; 44.18.6–7).

82. Caere's reports are in 218, 216, 208, 206, and 174 (Livy 21.62; 22.36.6–9; 27.23.1–4; 28.11.1–7; 41.21.5–13; 41.28.2); Frusino's are in 207, 203, 202, 200, and 197 (Livy 27.37.1–15; 30.2.9–13; 30.38.8–10; 31.12.5–10; 32.29.1–2); the Sabines's are in 216, 214, 200, 196, and 174 (Livy 22.36.6–9; 24.10.6–11.1; 31.12.5–10; 33.26.7–9; 41.21.5–13; 41.28.2); Tarracina's are in 213, 210, 206, 204, and 179 (Livy 24.44.7–9; 27.4.11–15; 28.11.1–7; 29.10.4–8; 29.11; 40.45.35; 40.59.6–8); Veii's are in 207, 198, 174, 173, and 169 (Livy 27.37.1–5; 32.9.2–4; 41.21.5–13; 41.28.2; 42.2.3–7; 43.13.3–8; 44.18.6–7).

83. Aricia's reports are in 216, 213, 202, and 193 (Livy 22.36.6–9; 24.44.7–9; 30.38.8–10; 34.55.1–5; 35.9.3–5); Amiternum's are in 218, 213, 192, and 191 (Livy 21.62; 24.44.7–9; 35.21.2–5; 36.37.2–6); Cumae's are in 212, 208, 202, and 169. (Livy 25.7.7–9; 27.23.1–4; 30.38.8–10; 43.13.38; 44.18.6–7). The five towns with three prodigies are Antium in 217, 206, and 203 (Livy 22.1.8–20; 28.11.1–7; 30.2.9–13); Formiae in 199, 197, and 192 (Livy 32.1.10–14; 32.29.1–2; 35.21.2–5); Minturnae in 207, 191, and 169 (Livy 27.37.1–15; 36.27.2–6; 43.13.3–8; 44.18.6–7); Privernum in 209, 200, and 173 (Livy 27.11.1–6; 31.12.5–10; 42.2.3–7); and Velitrae in 202, 199, and 198 (Livy 30.38.8–10; 32.1.10–14; 32.9.2–4).

84. Seven were Latin colonies (Alba Fucens, Ardea, Cales, Suessa Aurunca, Fregellae, Setia, and Spoletium), and seven were citizen colonies (Tarracina, Antium, Sinuessa, Minturnae, Puteoli, Volturnum, and Saturnia).

85. For the use of *Sabini* to denote the residents of Cures Sabini, see L. R. Taylor 1960, 59–66; 59–66; Brunt 1969; Humbert 1978, 234ff.

86. Livy 21.62.5; 22.1.8.

87. Livy 25.7.7–9.

88. Livy 32.1.10–14.

89. Livy 22.1.8–20; 22.9.1–5.

90. Livy 26.11.10; 26.23.5.

91. Livy 24.10.6–11.1.

92. Livy 32.1.10–14; 32.9.2–4; 33.45.6–8; 35.21.2–5; 41.9.4–8; 41.13.1–3; 41.21.5–13; 41.28.2; 42.4.3–4; 42.20.

93. For the censors, see Suolahti 1963.

94. In the fourth century, Rome may have borrowed from Campania the practice of formally defining an elite whose claim to leadership was based on military service on horseback; see Massa-Pairault 1995.

95. Livy (1.43) and Dionysius of Halicarnassus (*Ant.Rom.* 4.16–18) provide similar descriptions of the centuriate organization, which they attribute to Servius Tullius, probably following a common source through different intermediaries; see Cornell 1995, 179–90. Livy notes that the later census differed from the earlier, because it had only seventy centuries of the first class, so that there would be one century of *seniores* and one of *iuniores* for each of the thirty-five tribes that existed after circa 244. Cicero (*Rep.* 2.22.39–40; *Phil.* 2.82) reveals that the number of tribes remained constant despite the shift. The arrangements that Livy and Dionysius describe, if not an idealizing fabrication, fit best the late fourth or early third century, for they set out the qualifications for each class in monetary terms, most probably a development of a period when the Roman state began to become monetized; see Crawford 1985, 17–24.

96. See Cels-Saint-Hilaire 1995; Lo Cascio 2001.

97. See Prosdocimi 1995; Prosdocimi 1996; Carandini 1997, 348–54; Smith 2008, 200–201. For a different view of the dichotomy between military and civil aspects of the polity, see Mitchell 1990.

98. For the *census* as a rite, see Pfeilschifter 2002, 440–64.

99. See Humm 2005, 153–55.

100. For the senators' seating privileges, see Livy 34.54.4–8; for the juries, see chapter 6.

101. For voting assemblies as a public ritual, see Hopkins 1991, 492–95.

102. Strabo 5.2.3; Gell. *NA* 16.13.7.

103. For *iuratores*, see Plaut. *Trin.* 87; *Poen.* 55–8; Livy 39.44.2; for *curatores*, see Varro *LL* 6.86; Festus p. 51 L; pp. 358–59 L.

104. For the text, see Crawford 1994, no. 24, lines 142–56; Crawford (1994, pp. 388–89) also notes that census records had been kept by tribe, but the clause apparently envisions them kept by town, which he sees as a step in the process by which tribes were superseded by the Augustan regions.

105. See Cic. *Pro Clu.* 41; 125; see also Moreau 1994.

106. See, for example, Lintott 1999, 117; Lo Cascio 1999a and 1999b.

107. Livy 29.15.

108. Livy 38.28.4; 38.36.5–6.

109. Additional evidence for decentralization is slight and even more indirect. Under the empire, municipal officials known as *quattuorviri quinquenalles* counted the citizens in most towns, but a few cities, such as Caere, Suessula, and Treba, used the title of censor, a peculiarity that some have seen as a sign that they performed the census themselves before the Social War; see Brunt 1971, 40–41; Ilari 1974, 81–82; Moatti 1993, 73–74. For a discussion, see also Bispham 2007, 337–64. Others hold that these local censors may only have counted and ordered their towns' own citizens for local offices and functions; see, for example, Lo Cascio 1999a and 1999b.

110. See Gell. *NA* 5.19.15–16; Brunt 1971, 39.

111. See Sumner 1970, 70–71; Keppie 1984, 19–20.

112. For Rome, see Livy 22.36; for Tibur, see Livy 22.11; for Praeneste, see Livy 23.17; for Cales, see Livy 23.31; for Sinuessa, see Livy 23.32.

113. For Arminium, see Livy 31.11; 34.5; 41.5; for port of Luna, see Livy 34.8; for Arretium, see Livy 35.3; for Brundisium, see Livy 36.3; 37.4; 42.18; for Pisae, see Livy 40.26; 41.5.

114. Rawson 1991, 35.

115. Most notably, Rawson 1991, 35–37; see also Salvatore 1996, 5–29.

116. See A. von Premerstein, *RE* IV, col. 726, s.v. *commentarii*.

117. See Salvatore 1996, 11.

118. For the use of plurals, see Rawson 1991, 37.

119. Brunt (1971, 625) characterized Polybius's source as antiquarian largely because it did not fit his view of conditions in the second century, on the apparent assumption that "antiquarians" were primarily concerned with outdated practices. Elizabeth Rawson (1991, 35–35) held that the source could not be antiquarian because she thought that any work that Polybius might have used in the 150s would have been too

early—elsewhere she regards antiquarianism as a development of the Gracchan age—and suggests a handbook as a possible alternative to *commentarii*, although she does not address the nature of the proposed distinction.

120. Vaahtera (2000, 259) suggests that Polybius did use Cato's treatise as his source. For the treatise, see Astin 1978, 184–85. For the classes of infantry and the camp guards, see Festus p. 298 L; Festus/Paulus p. 299 L; for the auspices, see Festus p. 236 L.

121. See Gargola 2004 and 2005.

122. See, for example, Livy 29.24.14; 35.2.4; 42.31.2; 44.21.8. Keppie (1984, 64–65) suggests that these figures are in error, perhaps the result of an assumption that each of a legions' sixty *centuriae* had one hundred men.

123. M. Bell 1965; Rawson 1991, 37–48.

124. Keppie 1984, 64.

125. Astin 1978, 37.

126. Rawson 1971b, 13–31.

127. Rawson 1991, 37–48.

128. Brunt 1971, appendix 19.

129. Livy 2.28.5; 2.29.2; 3.10.1; 3.11.1; 3.29.2; 3.69.6–7; 4.26.12; *Per* 14; 34.56.9–11; 43.14.2; Varro *apud* Non. p. 28 L; Val. Max. 6.3.4; Varro *apud* Gell. *NA* 11.1.4.

130. See, for example, Livy 32.26.5–14; 34.56.11–12; 41.5.1–12; 43.9.7.

131. For conscription by dictators, see Livy 22.11 (217); by consuls, see Livy 31.9 (200); 34.56 (193); 40.36–41 (180); 41.14 (176); 41.21 (175); 42.1 (173); 42.32–35 (171); 43.14 (169); 44.21 (168); *Per.* 48; 55; by praetors, see Livy 41.5 (178); 42.18 (172); 42.27 (172); 43.2 (171).

132. See, for example, Livy 25.3; 25.31.5; 42.32–35; 43.14.3–15.1.

133. See Crawford 2002, 1125–35.

134. For Murena, see Cic. *Mur.* 20 /42, who notes that Murena's generosity in the levy won him many friends.

135. Vaahtera (2000, 258) notes that Cincius's oath included the possibility of delay over unfavorable omens, just as Polybius did when setting out the oaths that conscripts took to reassemble at the designated time and place.

136. See Plaut. *Merc.* 3.3.8.0; Cic. *Mil.* 25, 67; *Att.* 7.21.1.

137. See, for example, Humbert 1978, 323.

138. See Mouritsen 1998, 48–52.

Chapter 4

1. See David 1995b, 373. Humm (1999, 633) notes that the *comitium* was long the chief place for voting by tribes, and it once may have been the only locus for such votes.

2. For the meeting places of the senate, see Bonnefond-Coudry 1989, 25–197.

3. In special circumstances, the urban praetor might take up position elsewhere in the city; see, for example, Livy 23.32.

4. For examples, see Livy 22.57; 24.20; 25.7; 28.28; 40.29; Polyb. 1.7.

5. See Ovid *Fasti* 2.685ff; Festus/Paulus p. 346 L; see Scullard 1981, 81–82.

6. See Polyb. 6.53.1–54.5; H. Flower 1996.

7. See Lipka 2009, 11–30.

8. See Ziółkowski 1992, 271–3. Muccigrosso (2006) argues that most temples were located in these regions not for any "religious" reason but because they were the prime spaces for political display.

9. For Rome's foundation, see Ennius 1.47 Skutsch. On this passage, see also Linderski 2007a. For the link between magistrates' *imperium* and their *auspicium*, see Vervaet 2014; Berthelet 2015.

10. See, for example, Livy 1.18.6; Dion. Hal. *Ant.Rom.* 3.70–71.

11. For the fragments, see *ILS* 9338.3 (= *CIL* VI, 1976); *ILS* 9338.4 (= *CIL* VI, 32318); see also Vaahtera 2002. J. Rüpke (2008) suggests that the lists of augurs only began circa 300 and that the college probably began around this time as well, but this goes beyond the evidence.

12. See, for example, Livy 1.36.6.

13. Livy (1.36.5) and Pliny (*HN* 34.21–3) attribute the statue to Tarquinius Priscus. For the statues of Pythagoras and Alcibiades, see Pliny *HN* 34.26. Sehlmeyer (1999, 85–86) places the statue of Navius between the end of the sixth century and 300; J. Evans (1990) places all the statues circa 300; M. Koortbojian, (2013, 54) favors the interval between the middle of the fourth century and the middle of the third.

14. See Linderski 1985, 221 (= Linderski 1995, 510).

15. Linderski (1986, 2192) stresses that augurs did not accompany commanders in the field.

16. Linderski 1986, 2198–99.

17. For the *auguraculum* on the Quirinal, see Varro *LL* 5.5.2; for the *auguratorium* on the Palatine, see *ILS* 317. For the *auguraculum* on the *arx*, see Festus/Paulus p. 17 L. Festus pp. 14–15 L refers to a sacrifice that the augurs made on the *arx*.

18. For a discussion of this passage, see Linderski 1986, 2148–51, 2156–58.

19. Festus (pp. 316–17 L), probably following the Augustan antiquarian Verrius Flaccus, places augural signs in five broad categories: "from the heavens" (*ex caelo*), "from birds" (*ex avibus*), "from sacred dances" (*ex tripudiis*—e.g., the movements of feeding chickens and other animals), "from quadrupeds" (*ex quadrupibus*), and "from ill-omened events" (*ex diris*). The first two constituted the impetrative auspices, the last two the oblative, while the category *ex tripudiis* included both.

20. See Varro *LL* 7.6. On *templa* in general, see Catalano, 1960, 248–319; Catalano 1978, 467–79; Linderski 1986, 2256–96.

21. The augurs also possessed an *auguraculum* in the *collis Latiaris* on the western slopes of the Quirinal, a location that provided a clear prospect over the *campus Martius*, much as the better-known example on the *arx* did for the forum. Coarelli (1981) suggests that the two *auguracula* once corresponded to the two forms of popular assembly, one of which met outside of Rome on the *campus Martius*, while the other met inside the city.

22. Festus pp. 276–77 L. Oakley (1997–2005, 1:340–41) observes that this passage, which Festus says to be from a work on consular powers, almost certainly means that the consuls were candidates for the command. Ziółkowski (2011) suggests that the augurs, not the consuls, actually auspicated.

23. Livy 4.17–8. Ogilvie (1965, 561) points out that the *arx* would not have been visible from the Roman camp. Still, while Livy clearly envisioned that the dictator

could see the *arx*, the use of messengers over the short distance that separated the Capitol from the camp would certainly have been feasible.

24. For the transition from oblative to impetrative, see Linderski 1986, 2156. For the formula of the *auspicium ex tripudiis*, see Cic. *Div.* 2.71–72.

25. Festus p. 146 L; Serv. *auct. Ad Aen.* 4.200; Linderski 1986, 2274–78.

26. See Bettini 2008.

27. See Humm 2014.

28. Livy 29.19.

29. See *ILLRP* 514.

30. See *ILLRP* 511.

31. See SIG^3 II, 646. For other meetings in the *comitium*, see SIG^3 II, 674 (c. 140); SIG^3 II, 688 (135).

32. See *ILLRP* 512 (*senatus consultum de Tibertinis* of midcentury); *ILLRP* 513 (early first century). For edicts, see *ILLRP* 514 (189); *ILLRP* 513 (early first century).

33. See, for example, *ILLRP* 513; 517 (the *sententia Minuciorum* of 117).

34. See Serv. *auct. Ad Aen.* 3.20. Catalano (1978, 473 n. 119) identifies the phrase with the augurs' *ager Romanus*; see also Catalano 1960, 182, 387ff.

35. For temples and their locations, see Ziółkowski 1992; Pietilä-Castrén 1987.

36. See Ziółkowski 1992, 268–96.

37. Ziółkowski 1992, 38–39.

38. For the triumph, see Livy 42.216–17; for the dedication, see Livy 45.15.10. For the connection between the two events, see Brennan 1996, 336 n. 79.

39. Catalano (1978, 500) notes that the space was intended to be a *locus inauguratus*.

40. For a discussion of this passage, see Linderski 1986, 2148–51, 2156–58.

41. For the gates as starting points for the roads, see Plin. *HN* 3.66; for praetors and the gates, see Festus p. 276 L; for ceremonial returns, see Lacey 1998.

42. For the meaning of *sanctus*, see Rives 2012, 169–72. Pontiffs and augurs, it must be stressed, sometimes exhibited concern for the same spaces, although the augurs' may have been conceptually prior, for they inaugurated *templa* that pontiffs would later make sacred through rites of dedication. As we shall see later in this chapter, the pontiffs may have performed rites at places the augurs thought to mark the limits of the *ager Romanus*.

43. See Varro *LL* 5.143; Livy 1.44.4–5.

44. See, for example, Plut. *QR* 27.

45. See, for example, Varro *LL* 5.145, who placed the *pomerium*, or rather the *postmoerium*, "back of the wall" (*post murum*). Antaya (1980) suggests that the *pomerium* originally had no contact with the walls and instead bore some meaning like "outer boundary" or "outer measurement."

46. Magdelain (1977, 89) suggests that the Capitoline hill and the forum remained outside the structure of the urban tribes, but at 94ff., he argues that only the *arx* was outside the *pomerium*. Recently, Sandberg (2009) argues that the presence of a late republican shrine to Isis on the Capitol shows that it was outside the *pomerium* because foreign deities could not receive cult within the *urbs*, a proposed rule that itself is controversial.

47. Gell. *NA* 13.14.

48. For the so-called City of the Four Regions, see Thomsen 1980, 212–37; Cornell 1995, 202–3.

49. For the Septimontium, see Festus/Paulus p. 459 L; for the *ager Romanus antiquus*, see the discussion later in this chapter.

50. See Colonna 1991.

51. For recent studies on the significance of *imperium*, see Drogula 2007; Vervaet 2014, chap. 1; Berthelet 2015, 186–200; Drogula 2015. The origin of the view that there was a strict dichotomy between two forms of *imperium* is sometimes attributed to Theodor Mommsen (1887–88, 1:61–75), but he used *domi* and *militiae* to denote not two forms of *imperium* but rather the two spheres in which *imperium* might be deployed. (I wish to thank John Rich for the observation.) More radically, Drogula (2007) suggests that *imperium* signified only the power to command armies, while other areas of magisterial activity were under their *potestas*.

52. Giovannini 1983, 29, 54–56.

53. See Mommsen 1887–88, 1:63–64; Giovannini 1983, 16–19; Pina Pola 2011, 215–17.

54. Berthelet 2015, 190–91.

55. Livy 21.63.7–9; 41.10.7; 41.12–13.

56. Gell. *NA* 15.27.4.

57. The chief sources are Cic. *Nat.D.* 2.11–12; 2.35; 2.40; *Div.* 1.33; 2.74–75; Gran. Lic. 28.25; Plut. *Marc.* 5.

58. Magdelain (1968, 17–20), Humm (2012, 73–81), and Pina Pola (2011, 17) hold that the predecessors of the consuls-to-be enacted the curiate law. But Vervaet (2014, 340–43), van Haeperen (2012, 90–95) and Berthelet (2015, 119–27) demonstrate that the new consuls carried their own laws.

59. For the thirty lictors, see Cic. *Leg.Agr.* 2.31; for the presence of three augurs at one assembly, see Cic. *Att.* 4.17.2; Vervaet 2014, 332 n. 94. Livy 5.52.15–16 includes meetings of the *comitia curiata* among occasions that could take place only within the *pomerium*. Varro *LL* 5.155 identifies the *comitium* as the meeting place of the *comitia curiata*.

60. Berthelet 2015, 109.

61. Vervaet 2014, 320–21.

62. Cic. *Fam.* 1.9.25.

63. See, with different formulations, Smith (2008, 217–23), Vervaet (2014, 316), and Berthelet (2015, 119).

64. See, for example, Vervaet 2014, 82–83 n. 47. For Jörg Rüpke (1990, 32 n. 29 and 43 n. 98), the concept of the urban auspices best fits circumstances in the mid-first century, when concern over the powers of magistrates was widespread. He properly notes that the authors making the claim probably shared a common source, which he suggests was antiquarian rather than augural in nature, despite Gellius's claims to have followed a work *de auspiciis* by an unnamed augur. While some rules probably took explicit form in the first century, the contrast between spaces inside and outside the *pomerium* undoubtedly was old and certainly had long possessed implications for auspication.

65. For prosecutions, see Varro *LL* 6.90–95; for roads, see *ILLRP* 448; 449; 463.

66. Festus p. 296 L.

67. Magdelain 1964; Smith 2008, 221.

68. Dalla Rosa 2011, 248–49.

69. See Rich 2014, 210.

70. See Brennan 1996, 315–37. These triumphs were not without controversy; see Lange 2014.

71. For the distinction between magistrates and promagistrates, see Cic. *Nat.D.* 2.9; *Div.* 2.77–78; for the dichotomy between war and peace, see Cic. *Div.* 1.95.

72. See, for example, Giovannini 1983, 60; Hurlet 2006, 161–64.

73. Berthelet (2015, 157–68) rightly stresses the necessity of distinguishing between promagistracies that began with tenure in a magistracy, those in which private citizens were granted *imperium*, and those in which promagistrates received their *imperium* by a process of delegation.

74. Cic. *Att.* 8.15.3; *Phil.* 4.4.9.

75. See Non. Marc. p. 131 L: *eo die cis Tiberim redeundum est, quod de caelo auspicari ius nemini sit praeter magistratum.* Catalano (1960, 474) and Humm (2012, 68 n. 50) use Varro's claim that only magistrates might auspicate *ex caelo* as evidence that only magistrates could auspicate. For electoral assemblies, see Cic. *Div.* 2.74.

76. Crawford 1994, no. 12, Cnidos copy, column III, lines 1–15.

77. For a discussion of this passage, see Linderski 1986, 2148–51, 2156–58; see also Dyck 2004, 303–9.

78. Varro *LL* 5.33: *Ut nostri augures publici disserunt, agrorum sunt genera quinque: Romanus, Gabinus, peregrinus, hosticus, incertus. Romanus dictus unde Roma ab Rom<ul>o; Gabinus ab oppido Gabi<i>s; peregrinus ager pacatus, qui extra Romanum et Gabinum, quod uno modo in his seru<a>ntur auspicia; dictus peregrinus a pergendo, id est a progrediendo: eo enim ex agro Romano primum progrediebantur: quocirca Gabinus quoque peregrinus, sed quod auspicia habet singularia, ab reliquo discretus; hosticus dictus ab hostibus; incertus is, qui de his quattuor qui sit ignoratur.*

79. See Mommsen 1887–88, 1:598 n. 4. More recently, Zack (2012, 97–107) also seeks to link Varro's *agri* to the civic statuses of their inhabitants.

80. See Catalano 1978, 494–97; Rüpke 1990, 30–35.

81. For Testa's opinion, *see* Serv. auct. *Ad Aen.* 11.316.

82. See, for example, Livy 27.37.6; 28.11.1ff.; 30.38.8; 41.9.5; 41.21.11–12; 44.18.6.

83. See Catalano 1978, 494–95.

84. See Catalano 1978, 409–17.

85. See chapter 3.

86. Marius Victorinus, *Ars grammatica* 4.42: *pertermine dicitur auspicium quod fit cum de fine Romano in agrum peregrinum transgrediuntur.* De Martino (1973, 2:17ff,) notes that these auspices must be connected to Varro's *genera agrorum*. Dahlmann (1976, 170ff.) notes the parallels between the dichotomies between Roman and peregrine lands and between land and water, each with their own auspices for crossing, the *auspicium pertermine* and the *auspicium peremnia*.

87. Livy 22.58.9.

88. Livy 23.6.7–8. Livy, it should be noted, expressed doubt about the episode because the Campanian ambassadors supposedly made demands similar to those made by the Latins before the Latin War (see Livy 8.5; 8.7), but even a fabricated episode might make reference to a real limit.

89. See Marius Victorinus, *Ars grammatica* 4.42.

90. See Serv. *auct. Ad Aen.* 1.13: *Ostiam vero ideo veteres consecratum esse voluerunt, sicut Tiberim, ut si quid bello navali ageretur, id auspicato fieret ex maritima et effata urbe, ut ubique coniunctum auspici, ut Tiberis, cum colonia esset.* The foundation of Ostia in the middle of the fourth century, the creation of *duumviri navales* several decades later, the establishment circa 268 of quaestors in charge of the fleet, or the beginning of large-scale naval operations in the First Punic War provide possible contexts.

91. For examples, see Livy 5.17.3; 5.31.7; 5.52.9; 6.5.6.

92. See Livy 8.32.4; 10.3.6; 23.19.3–5; *ILS* 53; see also Festus p. 326 L; Serv. *Ad Aen.* 2.178.

93. Serv. *auct. Ad Aen.* 2.178; see also Catalano 1978, 501–2. For instances in the late fourth and early third centuries, see Livy 8.30.2; 8.32.4; 10.3.6; Val. Max. 2.7.4; 3.2.9.

94. See, for example, Livy 7.19.9–10.

95. Livy 7.21.9; 8.23.13–17; 9.38.13–14.

96. For discussions of the passage, see Jahn 1970, 87–89; Rilinger 1976, 21; Hölkeskamp 1987, 117–18; Loreto 1993, 61.

97. See Livy 22.57.8–9; 23.22.10–11.

98. See Livy 27.5.14–19; 27.29.5.

99. Thus De Libero 1994, 311–12; Zack 2012, 80 n. 63.

100. One incident has often been cited as an example of such an *ager Romanus* away from Rome and even outside of Italy. According to Valerius Maximus (2.7.4), one of the consuls of 252 "passed by Messana" on Sicily to repeat his auspices after a failed attack on the Lipara islands. For some, this passage indicates that the commander intended to repeat his auspices at or near Messana, but for others it only shows that the consul passed by the place on his way back to Italy; see Konrad 2008. To add to the difficulty, the Romans may have considered Messana to be part of Italy at the time because the Mamertines, who came from the peninsula, occupied the place; see Russo 2012; contra: Valvo 1997, 10–19, and Prag 2006.

101. Zack 2012, 79 n. 60, places it between the end of the First and the beginning of the Second Punic War.

102. See, for example, Carla 2015.

103. Varro (*apud* Aug. *CD* 4.29); Dion. Hal. *Ant. Rom.* 2.74.4–5; 3.36.6; Plut. *Numa* 16.1; *QR* 15.

104. For the *Terminalia*, see Scullard 1981, 79–80.

105. See, for example, Alföldi 1964, 296–97; Quilici Gigli 1978; Scheid 1987, 583–95. Some, including Quilici Gigli, identify the shrine of Dea Dia with Strabo's "place called *Festoi*"; for counterarguments, see Scheid 1990a, 98–100.

106. Ziółkowski 2009.

107. See, for example, Scullard 1981, 124–25.

108. Ziółkowski 2009, 126.

109. Ziółkowski 2009, 123–27.

110. For Italian practice, see Castagnoli 1984; Edlund 1987.

111. For the college, see Scheid 1990.

112. *CIL* VI, 2104.

113. For example, Scheid (1990a, 616–23), who follows, with some modifications, the reconstruction of Norden (1939, 115), holds that the threshold is Rome's, while Latte

(1960, 65 n.2) links it with the shrine or grove. Ziółkowski (2009, 113–17) notes that Norden made his link between the hymn and Rome's boundaries while assuming that the *fratres Arvales* led the procession of the *Ambarvalia* around Rome's ancient frontier. Still, the prayer is apotropaic and it remains unclear why the claim that the *carmen* was to ward off evil from the priests is more plausible than the assertion that it was intended to protect Rome.

114. See Scheid 1987, 591.

115. Ziółkowski 2009, 124. For him, Strabo's use of the present tense to describe the sacrifices at *Festoi* suggests that the rites were recently established. Strabo, however, often displays little concern for chronological procession, using "now," "recently," and "in our time" very broadly and even adopting chronological expressions from the source or sources that he was following; see Pothecary 1997; Clarke 1999, 255–60; Pothecary 2002.

116. Ziółkowski 2009, 125.

117. As Scheid (2003, 74) notes.

118. For the Twelve Tables, see Crawford 1994, no. 40. X.1; for Isis, see Versluys 2004.

119. See Ziółkowski 1999.

120. See Crawford 1994, no. 25, chap. 73 and 91.

121. Festus s.v. *Ludi Taurei*.

122. For Cato, see *ORF*³ xlviii, frag. 147 (= Gell. *NA* 2.6.7 = Macrob. *Sat.* 6.7.10): *cumque Hannibal terram Italiam laceraret atque vexaret*; see also Valerius Antias in Gell. *NA* 3.8.1: *Cum Pyrrhus rex in terra Italia esset et unam atque alteram pugnas prospere pugnasset satisque agerent Romani et pleraque Italia ad regem descivisset, tum Ambraciensis quispiam Timochares, regis Pyrri amicus.*

123. Keaveney (2005, 159) takes this "right" as regal in origins; see also Keaveney 1983, 71–72. Italy, however, was not a political concept this early.

124. For Varro's use of *orbis terrarum*, see Frontinus p. 8.23–33 Campbell.

Chapter 5

1. For a discussion of this section of Varro's work, see Linderski 1986, 2261–69.

2. P. Regell (1881, 605) connects Varro's second category only with the observation of birds, leaving out other forms of auspication, a suggestion that Linderski (1986, 2261 n. 453) rejects.

3. For an examination of the passage, see Linderski 1986, 2256–96.

4. Norden (1939, 3–106, 281–86) provides the best reconstruction of the formula, which is corrupt in the manuscripts. To describe this formula, Varro (*LL* 7.6) uses the phrase *concepta verba*, which draws its meaning from a contrast with *certa verba*, a distinction that also appears in legal formulas. *Certa verba* denotes those formulas that are fixed and unchanging, while *concepta verba* denotes formulas that may be tailored to specific circumstances, although they may be unchanging for those circumstances.

5. See Linderski (1986, 2279), who suggests that Livy's phrase *prospectu in urbem agrumque capto* distinguishes between the *prospectus in urbem*, which embraces the city, and the *prospectus in agrum*, which constitutes the *tescum*. He also tentatively

accepts the suggestion of Valeton (1889–90, 18: 246–63) that the *pomerium* divided the visual field into two registers. Berthelet (2015, 198 n. 300) notes that these uses apply only to the auspices from the *arx*.

6. For the house, see Cic. *Off.* 3.66; for the temple, see Festus p. 466.36–68.3 L.

7. For the Oscan text, see Crawford 1994, no. 13; for its date, see Crawford 1994, pp. 274–75.

8. See Crawford 1994, p. 273; Torelli 1999a, 114.

9. See Torelli 1966 and 1969. Torelli first placed the structure after the Social War, when Bantia became a *municipium*, but he has since placed it before the Social War; see Torelli 1999a, 114–15.

10. Torelli (1966) suggested that the auspiciant sat on the middle marker in the middle row, but he later (1969) moves this functionary to the margins. More recently, R. Taylor (2000) suggests that auspiciants at Bantia sat on the central post of the middle row, so that the enclosure would surround him. But, as Linderski (1986, 2260) properly notes, these markers, which vary in diameter between 29 and 34 centimeters, are too narrow to serve as seats.

11. Varro *LL* 7.7. Ennius's verse is *Annales* 541 Skutsch; Naevius's is unassigned.

12. See R. Taylor 2000, 20–22.

13. See Jocelyn 1967, 254.

14. For an investigation into augural terminology and practices in Greek writers, see Vaahtera 2001.

15. For the *stella*, see Festus p. 476 L: *stellam significare ait Ateius Capito laetum et prosperum, auctoritatem secutus P. Servili auguris [stellam], quae ex lamella aerea adsimilis stellae locis inauguratis infigatur*; Dolabella p. 224, lines 1–3 Campbell: *quare per aedes publicas in ingressus antiqui fecerent crucem, ANTICA et POSTICA? quia aruspices secundum aruspicium in duabus partibus orbem terrarum diviserunt; una parte ab oriente ad occidentum, alia a meridian in septentrionem.* Prosdocimi (1991) argues that there was no similarity between the augurs' *stella* and the surveyors,' since the latter had the shape of a cross, while the former, he suggests, was rectangular, with the corners forming points that were starlike. But see the comments of Dolabella.

16. Schol. Verg. Veron. Aen. 10.241: *Ut in exercitu [prius quam acies instrueretur, is, penes que]m imp[erium auspice]umque erat, in tabernaculuo in sella [se]dens auspicabatur, coram exercitu pullis e cavea liberatis [positisque in lo]cum circum sellam suam [dicebat]: obnuntiato a[ugurium bon]um [sinisterum solisti]mum, quisqu[is vestrum viderit] tripudi[a cum]ulata. silentio deinde facto residebat et dicebat: equites et pedites nomenque Lati[num, contuberna]les, cincti armati paludati, [quicunque in haec castra et hoc bellum me ducem vestrum] estis secuti, [nunc augurium] dum sinisterum solistimum quisquis vestrum vider[it, taceto.] deinde il[le augurio] nuntiato diceba[t iterum: ergo Di], uti placet, a legionibus invocentur faciantque, quod iis imperabitur [milites] imp[eriumque] fidemque m[eam servent, quod con]ducat salutareque siet, viros voco, proelium ineant. Deinde exercitu in aciem educto iterum [ibi auspicaba]tur, interim ea mora utebantur, qui testamenta in procinctu facere volebant.*

17. See Festus/Paulus pp. 244–45 L. Linderski (1986, 2289 n. 568) suggests that the augur P. Servillius is to be identified with the P. Servilius who was consul in 48 B.C.

18. See, for example, *ILLRP* 508 (middle of the first century): *L. Aienus L.f., Q. Baebatius Sex.f. aedem dedicarunt Iovis Liberi Furfone a.d. III idus Quinctileis L. Pisone, A. Gabinio co(n)s(ulibus)mense Flusare [i.e., a local month] comulateis olleis legibus, illeis regionibus...; ILS* 112 (A.D. 11 or 12): *Numen Caesaris Aug(usti) p(atris) p(atriae)! Quando tibi hodie hanc aram dabo dedicaboque, his legibus hisque regionibus dabo dedicaboque, quas hic hodie palam dixero, uti infimum solum huiusque area titulorumque est; ILS* 4907 (A.D. 137): *L. Aelio Caesare II P. Coleio Balbino Vibullio Pio cos. VII idus Octobres, C. Domitius Valens IIvir i.d., praeunte C. Iulio Severo pontiff. Legem dixit in ea uerba quae infra scripta. Hisce legibus hisce regionib. sic, uti dixi, hanc tibi aram, Iuppiter optime maxime, do dico dedicoque....*

19. In addition to the temples at Narbo and Salonae, Ariminum too had a temple governed by the laws of the temple of Diana; see *CIL* XI, 361. Ando (2008, 114–15) suggests that while the law may have had considerable symbolic force in the late republic and under the empire, few, if any, of the residents of these places may have actually known its provisions.

20. For a discussion of the passage and the rite, see Foresti 1979; Oakley 1997–2005, 2:74–75.

21. See *ILLRP* 504; 505; and 506.

22. See Crawford 1994, pp. 556–75, for the problems in establishing and ordering the fragments. For the language, see Crawford 1994, p. 557.

23. See Crawford 1994, no. 40, I.7; I.8; III.5; III.6, the source of the translation.

24. See Crawford 1994, no. 40, VIII.12; III.7; IX.6.

25. Censorinus *De die natale* 24.3.

26. For the prologue's structure, see Gargola 2004. Jocelyn (1969) suggests that the prologue, as we have it, is the work of several authors, although it was fixed during the first third of the second century.

27. For the use of *determinare regiones* to describe the definition of a *templum*, see Valeton 1892–98, 20: 370–73.

28. Thus, *ILS* 112: *quando tibi hodie hanc aram dabo dedicabo, his legibus hisque regionibus dabo dedicaboque, quas hic hodie palam dixero.* For other examples, see *ILS* 4907; *CIL* I.2.756; III.1933; X.3513.

29. For Etruscan practice, see Weinstock 1946; Weinstock 1950; and Weinstock 1951; Turfa 2012; Santangelo 2013, chaps. 4 and 5.

30. See Massa-Pairault 1985; Turfa 2006.

31. See Bonfante 2006.

32. Figulus's opinion is reported in John Lydus (*De ostentis* 38); see also Turfa 2012, 25. For the context of Lydus's work, see Maas 1992.

33. See van der Meer 1979 and 1987.

34. Cited in M. A. Flower 2008, 49–50.

35. J. Vaahtera (1993) suggests that the oldest Roman spatial categories were the *pomerium*, the *templum*, and the sacred grove or *lucus*.

36. See, for example, Dumézil 1970, 314–16; Woodard 2006, 243–44.

37. See L. Richardson 1978; Coarelli 1981, 178–80.

38. See De Cazenove 2005, 68–69.

39. For the trial, see Livy 6.20.10–11; Plut. *Cam.* 36.6–7; for the legislative assembly, see Livy 7.41.3–8; for Hortensius and his law, see Plin. *HN* 16.37.

40. See Palmer 1969, 33–42. Note also that Livy (3.54.14–15; 3.54.10–12) reports two voting assemblies in 499, both under the presidency of tribunes of the plebs, in the *prata Flaminius*, the meadow that was the *circus*'s predecessor.

41. Scheid 2003, 74.

42. Varro, in Gell. *NA* 14.7.7, identifies both the *curia* and the *comitium* as *templa*. For the *rostra* as a *templum*, see Livy 2.56; Cic. *In Vat.* 24. (Note that the earliest form of the *rostra* was apparently erected in the middle of the fifth century, although it would not have received its name until some point after its reconstruction in the last third of the fourth century.) For a discussion, see Berthelet 2015, 249–58; Humm 2014, 315–45.

43. For the complex and its stages, see Coarelli 1983–85, 1:119–60; 2:11–21; Humm 1999. P. Carafa (1998) proposes a markedly different reconstruction. His *comitium* is roughly triangular in form and is separated from the *curia* by a long stairway and by the *sacra via*. As Humm (1999) and Mouritsen (2001, 19 n. 7) note, Carafa's reconstruction leaves unexplained the *cornua* of our sources, which also placed the *curia* and *comitium* in close proximity, permitting easy movement between them, and it leaves without parallel the standardized *curia-comitium* complexes of Latin colonies.

44. Humm (1999, 634–37) suggests that the rectangular form and the orientation of the sides toward the cardinal directions indicate that the *comitium* was a *templum* from its origins; contra: Vaahtera 1993, 107–16. Vaahtera (113) does show that the phrase *in licium*, found in Varro's accounts of summoning citizens to the census and to voting assemblies, refers to a *locus licio saeptus*, that is, a *templum*.

45. For the opinion, see Varro *LL* 6.89.

46. Crawford (1994, p. 595) holds, on the basis of the Twelve Tables, that the *comitium* was used as a sundial throughout the fifth and fourth centuries; see also Santoro 1991.

47. See Gibbs 1976, 94; Hannah 2003, 53; Clarke 2008, 306. For Syracuse, see also Plut. *Dion* 29.2. Barton (1994) suggests that Meton's attempt to reform the Athenian calendar circa 432 was based on Babylonian methods, then becoming known in the Greek world.

48. For an overview, see Torelli 1999b; Patterson 2006b.

49. See Bispham 2006.

50. Livy 27.9 gives the total. The thirty are Signia, Norba, Ardea, Circeii, Setia, Sutrium, Nepet, Cales (334), Fregellae (328), Luceria (314), Saticula (313), Suessa Aurunca (313), Pontiae (313), Interamna (312), Sora (303), Alba Fucens (303), Narnia (299), Carseoli (298), Venusia (291), Hadria (280s), Cosa (273), Paestum (273), Ariminum (268), Beneventum (268), Firmum (264), Aesernia (263), Brundisium (244), Spoletium (241), Placentia (218) and Cremona (218).

51. The Latin colonies were Thurii Copia (193), Vibo Valentia (192), Bononia (189), Aquileia (181), and perhaps Luca, which Velleius Paterculus (1.15.2) makes such a colony, although scholars disagree over his accuracy.

52. Livy (27.38.4) lists seven who applied for an exemption from conscription in 207: Ostia, Alsium (247), Antium (328), Tarracina (329), Minturnae (295), Sinuessa (295), and Sena Gallica (280s), the only one not on the coast of Latium and southern Etruria. To these one should add Castrum Novum (264), Pyrgi (late 240s), and Fregenae (245). For the chronology of the colonies, see Salmon 1969, chap. 4.

53. According to Asconius (p. 3 Clark), Placentia was Rome's fifty-third colony, a figure that certainly included both Latin and citizen foundations and one that may be correct if Asconius mistakenly thought that the number applied to Placentia's foundation in 218 and not its reinforcement in 190. The Latin colonies were Thurii Copia (193), Vibo Valentia (192), Bononia (189), Aquileia (181), and perhaps Luca. The citizen colonies were: in the 190s, Volturnum, Liternum, Puteoli, the *castrum* of Salernum, Sipontum, Buxentum, Croton and Tempsa: in the 180s and 170s, Potentia (184), Pisarum (184), Saturnia (183), Mutina (183), Parma (183), Graviscae (181) and Luna (177). In a letter to the people of Larisa in Thessaly in 215, Philip V of Macedon asserts that the Romans had sent out almost seventy colonies, a claim that is even more difficult to match with known foundations; see *SIG* II^3, 543; 26.

54. Livy 5.24.4; 6.21.4; 9.28.7–8; 10.21.7–10.

55. For settlements in Spain, see App. *Ib.* 38.115 (Italica); Livy *Per.* 41 and Festus p. 86 L (Gracchuris); Strabo 3.2.1 (Corduba); Livy *Per.* 55 (Valentia).

56. For the process, see Gargola 1995, chap. 4.

57. For the law from Urso, see Crawford 1994, no. 25.

58. For the law regulating Puteoli's grove, see *AE* (1971) 88; Hinard and Dumont 2003. Bodel (1986) argues that the grove at Latin Luceria was also funerary and in the same tradition as the groves at Rome and Puteoli.

59. See Brown 1980. For the problems with this approach, see Fentress 2000a. At Paestum and some other colonies, founders or colonists appropriated existing buildings and cults, incorporated some of the previous residents either as citizens or as *incolae*, and adopted some local customs; see Crawford 2006. Bradley (2006) argues that Rome and its colonies were open to outsiders., while Bispham (2006, 75) suggests that the inhabitants of a colony may have possessed multiple identities rather than strictly Roman or Latin ones.

60. For a more detailed critique, see the articles in Stek and Pelgrom 2014.

61. For Cales, see *ILS* 8597; on the date and the context, see Bispham 2006, 87; for the evidence from other colonies, see Mouritsen 2004.

62. Paul Zanker 2000.

63. For the plowing of the furrow as the founding act, see Eckstein 1979.

64. See *FRHist* 5 F 66a (= Serv. *Ad Aen.* 5.755); *FRHist* 5 F 66 b (= Isid. *Etym.* 15.2.3).

65. Ennius *Ann.* 95–96 Skutsch: *Conspicit inde sibi data Romulus esse propritum / auspicio regni stabilita scamna solumque.* See also Skutsch 1986, 236–38.

66. For Saticula (313), see Festus p. 458 L; for Placentia (218), see Asconius *Pis. P.* 3 Clark; for Bononia (189), see Livy 37.57.7.

67. See Cornell et al. 2013, 3:23–24.

68. See Cic. *Phil.* 2.100–4; *Att.* 14.20–21.

69. See Crawford 1994, no. 25, chap. 73.

70. For the Twelve Tables, see Crawford 1994, no. 40, table X.1: *hominum mortuum in urbe ne sepelito neue urito*; for Urso's law, see Crawford 1994, no. 25, chap. 73; for the law from Puteoli, see *AE* (1971) 88.

71. For the Extortion Law, see Crawford 1994, no. 1, lines 13 and 17; for Urso's law, see Crawford 1994, no. 25, chap. 91: *domicilium in ea col(onia) oppido propriusue it oppidum p(assus) (mille) non habebit annis (quinque) proxumis.*

72. Von Hesberg 1985; Lackner 2008, 135–38. For the colony's date, see Bispham 2000; Zevi 2002.

73. Brandt 1985.

74. See M. T. Lewis 2001 and 2012.

75. See Martin 1956, 122.

76. For the plans, see the relevant entries in Lackner 2008.

77. See Mouritsen 2007.

78. See Crawford 1994, no. 13, lines 2 and 10.

79. See Bispham 2006, 93.

80. For the development of the techniques, see Hinrichs 1974; Chouquer and Favory 1991; Schubert 1996. For the republican surveyors, see Takács 2013, 13–24.

81. Frontinus p. 8.23-33 Campbell: *Limitum prima origo, sicut Varro descripsit, a[d] disciplina[m] Etrusca[m]; quod aruspices orbem terrrarum in duas partes diuiserunt, dextram apellauerunt, <quae> septentrioni subiacere<t>, sinistram quae a meridiano terra<e> esse<t> <ab oriente ad> occasum, quot eo sol et luna spectaret, sicut quidam †carpiunt architecti delubra in occidente<m> recte spectare scripserunt. aruspices altera[m] linea[m] a septentrione ad meridianum diuuserunt terram, <et> a me[ri]dia[no] ultra antica, citra postica nominauerunt. Ab hoc fundamento maiores nostri in agrorum mensura uidentur constituisse rationem. primum duo limites duxerunt; unum ab oriente in occasum, quem uocauerunt decimanum; alterum a meridiano ad septentrionem, quem cardinem appelauerunt. decimanus autem diuidebat agrum dextra et sinistra; cardo citra et ultra.*

82. Festus p. 262 L; *Posticam lineam in agris dividendis Ser. Sulpicius appellavit ab exori<ente sole>*; Festus/Paulus p. 263 L: *Postica linea in agris dividendis ab oriente ad occasum spectat*; p. 265 L: *Prorsi limites appellantur in agrorum mensuris, qui ad orientem derecti sunt.*

83. See Dilke 1971, 146–47; Regoli 1984.

84. According to Asconius *Pis.* p. 3 Clark, Placentia (218) received 6,000 *pedites* and 200 *equites*; Livy (35.9.8–9) reports that Copia (193) received 3,000 *pedites* and 300 *equites*; he (35.40.5) also claims that Vibo (192) had 3,700 infantry and 300 cavalry and (37.57.8) that Bononia (189) too had *pedites* and *equites* although he does not give their numbers; According to Livy 40.34.2, Aquileia had 3,000 *pedites* and an unspecified number of centurions and *equites*.

85. For reconstructions, see Salvatore 1996; Dobson 2008, 47–121. For the commonalities between marching and mustering camps, see Salvatore 1996, 5–29. In his account, Polybius claims that the camp he was about to describe would contain a consul, his two legions, and allies, and he placed the headquarters near the camp's outer margins. At the end, however, he (6.32) describes how camps with two consular armies and thus four legions were set out: back to back, so that the two headquarters were almost adjacent and between the two armies. He then notes that when the two armies were encamped separately—that is, in groups of two legions—each headquarters was placed more centrally, which is not the location that Polybius first gives. Perhaps the easiest way of resolving this problem is to assume that Polybius's source described a camp containing two consular armies, where the central squares would have been virtually adjacent, and that Polybius described the camp for a single army by dividing the larger camp in half, correcting inaccuracies later; Salvatore 1996, 5–29.

86. For the directions, see Dobson 2008, 70–71.

87. *De metatione castrorum* 11 Grillone.

88. Schol. Verg. Veron. Aen. 10.241.

89. Livy 3.29.9; 21.46.1–3; 27.37.1–15; 32.29.1–2; 33.26; 41.9; Orosius 4.4.1–4; Obseq. 13; 43; 49; 52; 63; 69; Plin. *HN* 16.132; Dio 39.15; 40.17.1; 43.2.1; 46.33; App. *BC* 4.4.

90. See, in general, Pina Pola 1995.

91. See Mommsen 1887–88, 2:332–33; Wiseman 1969. For the *lustrum*, see Mommsen 1887–88, 2:412–31; Ogilvie 1961; Piéri 1968, 77–98.

92. See, for example, App. *BC* 4.88–89; *Iber.* 19; Dio 47.38.4; Hirtius *BG* 8.52.1; Livy 3.22.3–4; 23.35.5; 38.12.2–10; 38.37.8; 41.18.6; Plut. *Brut.* 39; *Caes.* 43; Tac. *Ann.* 15.26.

93. Dio 47.38.4 and Plut. *Brut.* 39 both claim that a location outside the camp was customary.

94. For the preference for left over right, see Liou-Gille 1991; Aretini 1998, 74–98, but see also Linderski 2007a, 9 n. 18. Salway (2012) shows the pervasiveness of the counterclockwise organization of spaces in later periods.

95. Varro *LL* 7.7. Note, however, that elsewhere Varro apparently had the auspiciant first go the right and then to the left; see Frontinus *De limitibus* p. 8. 23–29 Campbell.

96. Varro *LL* 7.8.

97. For the *locus gromae*, see Hyg. 12 Grillone.

98. For the *milliarium aureum*, see Dio 54.8.4; Plut. *Galba* 24.4; Plin. *HN* 3.66; Tac. *Hist.* 1.27; Suet. *Otho* 6.2.

99. For the plan, see Rodriguez-Almeida 1981.

100. For the importance of the routes and the shrine on the Alban Mount, see Salway 2012, 219.

101. L. R. Taylor 1960, 69–78. Coarelli 2003 makes the same suggestion.

102. See L. Richardson 1978; Coarelli 1981, 178–80.

103. Several clauses in the *lex Ursonensis* mention the colony's frontiers; see Crawford 1994, no. 25, chap. 77: ... *intra eos fines, qui colon(iae) Iul(iae) erunt*; chap. 78: ... *intra eos fines, qui colon(iae) dati erunt*; chap. 98: *qui in ea colon(ia) intraue eus colon(iae) fin<e>s domicilium praediumue habebit*. ... Siculus Flaccus (p. 102. 8–9 Campbell) proclaimed that surveyors established "the *regiones* within the *fines* of which there is the free power of *ius dicendi* and *ius coercendi*" for the magistrates of individual colonies. In 168 the senate dispatched ambassadors to resolve a boundary dispute between Pisae and the colony at Luna; see Livy 45.13.10–1.

104. See Gell. *NA* 16.4.6.

105. See *CIL* I^2 584 = V 7749; Crawford 2003, on which the present discussion is based.

106. For a discussion, see Rich 2011b, 199–204.

Chapter 6

1. For conflicts over the ability to dedicate a temple and for laws attempting to regulate it, see Tatum 1993; Orlin 1997, 166–67 n. 13.

2. For many examples from the Greek East, see Sherk 1969; for the *lex Antonia de Termissibus* and the *lex de insula Delo*, see Crawford 1994, nos. 19 and 22.

3. See, for example, *IG* VII.413.

4. See, for example, *ILS* 9376: *C. Caninius C. f. pr. urb. de sen. sent. poplic. ioudic.*
5. Livy 45.13.10–11; *CIL* I.2.638; I.2.584. For further measures, see Scuderi 1991.
6. See Magdelain 1978, 23–54.
7. *AE* (1996) 685.
8. Crawford 1994, no. 13, lines 2 and 10.
9. Crawford 1994, no. 25.
10. For examples, see Lovisi 1999, 204–8, 213–17; Berthelet 2015, 191–94.
11. Lintott 1999, 33–34; see also Lintott 1972, 228–31. For a different view of *provocatio*'s origins, see Cloud 1998.
12. See Lintott 1972, 249–53.
13. See Crawford 1994, no. 1, lines 78–79. Lintott (1972, 251) suggests that the right would only have been valuable away from Rome.
14. Jehne 2002; Hölkeskamp 2011, 174.
15. Giovannini 1983, 26.
16. Mommsen 1887–88, 2:611.
17. For the *lex Oppia*, see Livy 34.1.
18. For the law and what is known of its provisions, see Crawford 1994, no. 50.
19. See Livy 40.37.4. A little later, at 40.43.2, he describes the second province as *de veneficiis longius ab urbe milibus passuum*.
20. Livy 40.44.6.
21. For the oath, see Gell. *NA* 16.4.6.
22. Cic. *Phil.*6.3.5.
23. See Livy 40.41.10.
24. See Crawford 1994, no. 2, line 21.
25. Livy 28.38.
26. Livy 36.3.3.
27. Livy 22.58.9.
28. Livy 23.6.7–8. Livy, it should be noted, expressed doubt about the episodes because the Capuans made demands similar to those made by the Latins before the Latin War (see Livy 8.5; 8.7), but the fact that an earlier author might express his anecdote in terms of such a limit is still significant.
29. Livy 37.17.
30. Polyb. 30.19.1–7; Diod. Sic. 31.7.1; Livy *Per.* 46.
31. For the expulsion of philosophers and rhetors, see Gell. *NA* 15.11.1; for the expulsion of Chaldaeans, see Val. Max. 1.3.3; for a discussion of these two passages, see Brennan (2000, 128–29), who also suggests that "the city praetors divided responsibility for tasks of this sort on the basis of location . . . , depending on whether the senate wished that the offensive parties be run out of Rome (as was the brief of the *pr. urb.* of 161) or from Italy as a whole (the *pr. per.* 139)."
32. See Sherwin-White 1973, 34–35, 126, 182; Kelly 2006, 65–67.
33. Livy 26.14.
34. Livy 30.45; 45.42; *Per.* 61.
35. Livy 32.2; 32.26.
36. Livy 39.19.2.
37. Livy 45.42.

38. Livy 45.43.
39. Livy 26.34.6–10.
40. See Sherwin-White 1973, 100.
41. See, for example, De Libero 1994.
42. See Mouritsen 1998, 48–52; Galsterer 1976.
43. See, for example, Humbert 1978, 361–64.
44. See Mouritsen 1998, 48–52.
45. For Latins as colonists, see Gargola 1995, 64–65; for the viritane assignments, see Livy 42.4.3–4.
46. See Sherwin-White 1973, 111.
47. Livy 40.42.13.
48. For the laws, see Elster 2003, 371–80.
49. See Lintott 1990.
50. Livy 22.1.
51. Livy 45.44.
52. Livy 34.56.1.
53. See discussion in the following section.
54. See Crawford 1994, no. 1, line 1: *[quoi socium no]minisue Latini exter//arumue nationes, quoiue in arbitratu dicione potestate amicitiau[e populi Romani*. Venturini (1979, 52ff.) and H. D. Meyer (1980, 145–46) argue that Roman citizens were included, while Lintott (1992, 110) argues against; Crawford (1994, p. 95) suggests that the evidence does not permit a firm conclusion.
55. See Crawford 1994, no. 12, Cnidos Copy, column II, lines 1ff.
56. See Crawford 1994, no. 12, Delphi Copy, block B, line 6: . . . *politai Romaion su[mmakhoi] te ek tes Italias, Latinoi* . . .; see also Crawford 1994, p. 259.
57. See Festus/Paulus p. 17 L; Varro *LL* 5.90; Crawford 1994, no. 2, line 21.
58. See Catalano 1978, 540–42; Venturini 1979, 52ff.; Lintott (1992, 111) is dubious. Crawford (1994, p. 95) says that "*exterarumue nationum*, like *nominisue Latini*, form a subset of the *socii* of Rome" and cites for the purposes of comparison Cicero's phrase (*Div. in Caec. 66*): *ab exteris nationibus, quae in amicitiam populi Romani dicionemque essent, iniurias propulsare*. But his interpretation leaves out of consideration Rome's non-Latin but Italian allies, unless one views *externae nationes* as only a legal category that denotes allied polities who are not Latin.
59. For a detailed discussion, see Bispham 2007, 162–72.
60. See Sherwin-White 1973, 151–52; Bispham 2007, 172–73; see also Cic. *Pro Archia Poeta* 7.
61. See Williams 2001, 120–21; Bispham 2007, 173–75.
62. See Asconius *In Pis* p. 3 Clark.
63. See Catalano 1978, 515.
64. See Bispham 2007, 175–87.
65. See Crawford 1994, no. 28.
66. Cic. *Dom.* 89: *si dis immortalibus, si senatui, si populo Romano, si cunctae Italiae, si provinciis, si exeris nationibus* . . .; 2 *Cat.* 25: *omissis his rebus quibus nos suppeditamur, eget ille, senatu, equitibus Romanis, urbe, aerario, vectigalibus, cuncta Italia, provinciis omnibus, exteris nationibus.*

67. J. S. Richardson 2008, 86–89.

68. See Beard, North, and Price 1998, 92–98. The literature on the Bacchanal and its repression is immense. See, for example, North 1979; Pailler 1988; Montanari 1988; Gruen 1990.

69. As Beard, North, and Price (1998, I, 93–94) note, references in the plays of Plautus show that the cult was widely practiced before its repression; see also Pailler 1988, 229–38; Gruen 1990, 150–52. For its distribution in Italy, see Pailler 1988, 275–303.

70. For the text, see *CIL* I2.581 (= *ILS* 18).

71. See Livy 39.14.7: *non Romae modo sed per omnia fora et conciliabula conquiri; ...in urbe Roma et per totam Italiam edicta mitti*; 39.18.7: *Romae primum, deinde per totam Italiam*; 39.18.8: *ne qua Bacchanalia Romae neve in Italia essent*. De Libero (1994) demonstrates that such phrases often, if not always, denote all the statuses of Italy.

72. Thus, Mommsen (1887–88, 1:249 n. 3) suggests that the *foederati* were not Roman allies but rather those who had taken oaths as participants in the cult. Other interpretations focus on the supposed legal status of the place, Tiriolo in Bruttium, where the inscription was found. By 186, the Brutti had lost the status of ally as a result of their rebellion in the Hannibalic War, and much of their territory became Roman public lands. With this in mind, Pailler (1988, 290) suggests that the apparent allies were only former allies who had been degraded as a result of their rebellion in the Hannibalic War, while De Cazenove (2000) suggests that the polity that received the text was located on Roman public lands that had been attributed to the newly founded Latin colony of Vibo Valentia and thus had received the status of ally through them.

73. Livy 39.18.2.

74. Livy 39.20.1; 39.23.3.

75. Livy 39.29; 39.41.

76. Livy 39.17.

77. See Crawford 1994, no. 24, lines 117–18.

78. For the organization of the standing courts, see Mantovani 1989.

79. See Lintott 1993, 98–107.

80. For its text, see Crawford 1994, no. 1.

81. Crawford 1994, no. 1, lines 2, 8, and 16.

82. See Crawford 1994, no. 1, line 31.

83. For the text, see Crawford 1994, no. 7; for the murder court, see Lintott 1978; for the law of Saturninus, see Crawford 1994, pp. 197–99. Ferrary (1979, 106–7) argues that the measure is not an extortion law.

84. For the law, see Crawford 1994, no. 14, lines 38 to the end.

85. For the text, see Crawford 1994, no. 24; for the text as a collection, see Crawford 1994, pp. 358–59.

86. Pina Pola (2011, 136–42) sets out what is known about the magistrates responsible for building public roads.

87. *ILLRP* 465; 465a; Plut. *Caes.* 5.

88. See Mommsen 1887–88, 2:670.

89. See *ILLRP* 465a.

90. For the text, see Crawford 1994, no. 24, lines 24–28. Lott (2004, 32 and 89) links these four *partes* to the urban regions, but he does not comment on the extension beyond the *pomerium*. He also suggests that this provision is tralatician and dates from the middle of the fourth century, when the college of curule aediles began, but the only evidence pertains to the first century.

91. See Crawford 1994, no. 24, lines 20–21: *quae viae in urbem Rom(am) propriusve u(rbem) R(omam) p(assus) m(ille) ubei continente habitabitur sunt erunt, quoius ante aedificium earum quae viae erunt, is eam viam arbitratu eius aed(ilis),quoi ea pars urbis h(ac) l(ege)obvenerit, tueatur*; line 50: ... *IIIIvir(ei) vieis in urbem purgandeis, IIvir(ei) extra propriusve urbem Rom(am) passus <m(ille)>* ... Crawford (1994, p. 382) interprets the phrase *extra propriusve urbem Rom(am) passus <m(ille)>* as "a clumsy way of expressing 'outside and within a mile of the city of Rome.'"

92. See Crawford 1994, no. 2, lines 28, 11–13. For a discussion, see Bispham (2007, 69–71), who suggests that the practice may reach back to the fourth century, but in earlier periods *terra Italia* could not have supplied its outer bounds.

93. Rich (2007, 155–66) justly notes that developments on Sicily provide the necessary context for the Gracchan law of 133.

94. See Gargola 2008.

95. For an overview of the debate over Roman demography, see De Ligt 2012.

96. See Rich 2008b; Roselaar 2010, 112.

97. See, for example, Crawford 1994, no. 1, line 3: *quei ager publicus populi Romanei in terra Italia P. Muucio L. Calpurnio co(n)s(ulibus) fuit, extra eum agrum, quei ager ex lege plebeiue sc(ito), [quod C. Sempronius Ti. f. tr(ibunus) pl(ebis) rogauit, exceptum cauitumue est nei diuideretur.*

98. For the text with translation, commentary, and bibliography, see Crawford 1994, no. 2. For the connection between the law and the triumvirates, see Lintott 1992, 48–49.

99. For the provisions of the *lex Rubria*, see Gargola 1995, 164–66; for the contents of earlier colonial legislation in Italy, see Gargola 1995, 52–58.

100. For the retention of allotments, see line 60 of the law; see also Lintott 1992, 253–54.

101. See Crawford 1994, no. 2, lines 52, 53, 70–74, 77–78, 78–82.

102. For his laws, see Auc. *Vir.Ill.* 73.1; 73.5; Livy *Per.* 69; Plut. *Mar.* 29. Brunt (1971, 577–80) notes that there is little evidence for actual settlements in Africa.

103. See Brunt 1971, 300–12.

104. For some attempts to reconstruct the law, see Afzelius 1940; Jonkers 1963; Ferrary 1988. For the identification of quotations from the law in Cicero's text, see Ferrary 1988; Crawford 1994, no. 52.

105. Cic. *Agr.* 2.7.18; 2.8.20.

106. Cic. *Agr.* 2.2.12.31.

107. For the surveyors, see Nicolet 1970; Gargola 1995, 186–87; Takács 2013, 13–24.

108. Cic. *Agr.*2.23.62–27.72.

109. For the *Res Gestae*, see Cooley 2009, the source of the translations in the text.

110. See Cooley 2009, 18–22.

111. RGDA 3.1–2: *[b]ella terra et mari c[ivilia ex]ternaque toto in orbe terrarium s[aepe gessi], victorque omnibus v[eniam petentib]us civibus peperci. exte[rnas gentes,*

quibus tuto [ignosci pot]ui[t, co]nservare quam excidere ma[lui.] millia civium Roma[no]rum [sub] sacramento meo fuerunt circiter [quingen]ta, ex quibus dedu[xi in coloni]as aut remisi in municipia sua stipen[dis emery]tis millia aliquant[o plura qu]am trecenta, et iis omnibus agro a[dsignavi] aut pecuniam pro p[raemis mil]itiae dedi. naves cepi sescen[tas praeter] eas, si quae minore[s quam trir]remes fuerunt.

112. See Cooley 2009, 36.

113. See Ovid. *Fast.* 2.684: *Romanae spatium est urbis et orbis idem.*

114. Aug. RG 4.1–4: *[bis] ovans triumphavi et tri[s egi] curulis triumphos et appella[tus sum v]iciens et semel imperator, [decernente pl]uris triumphos mihi sena[t]u, qu[ibus omnibus su]persedi. l[aurum de f]asc[i]bus deposui in Capi[tolio, votis quae] quoque bello nuncupaveram [sol]utis. ob res a [me aut per legatos] meos auspicis meis terra ma[rique] e pr[o]spere gestas qui[nquagiens et q]uinquiens decrevit senatus sup[lica]ndum esse dis immortalibus, dies a[utem, pe]r quos ex senatus consulto [s]upplicatum est, fuere DC[CCLXXXX in triumphis meis] ducti sunt ante currum meum reges aut r[eg]um lib[eri novem. Consul f]ueram terdeciens cum [scrib]a[m] haec, [et eram se]p[timum et t]ricen[simu]m tribunicae potestatis.* (Cooley's text and translation.)

115. For the *vici*, see Lott 2004.

116. See Dio 55.8; *ILS* 3616; 3619; 3772; for the urban regions, see Nicolet 1991, 195–97.

117. For the plan, see Rodriguez-Almeida 1981.

118. For the importance of the routes and the shrine on the Alban Mount, see Salway 2012, 219.

119. For the regions of Italy, see Thomsen 1947, 15–144; Nicolet 1991, 203.

120. Eck 2003, 80.

Bibliography

Afzelius, A. 1940. "Das Ackerverteilungsgesetz des P. Servilius Rullus." *C&M* 3:214–35.
Alföldi, A. 1964. *Early Rome and the Latins*. Ann Arbor.
Ampolo, C. 1983. "La storiografia su Roma arcaica e i documenti." In *Tria corda: Scritti in onore di Arnaldo Momigliano*, edited by E. Gabba, 9–26. Como.
Ando, C. 1999. "Was Rome a *Polis*?" *CA* 18:5–54.
———. 2008. *The Matter of the Gods: Religion and the Roman Empire*. Berkeley.
Antaya, R. 1980. "The Etymology of *Pomerium*." *AJP* 101:184–89.
Appel, G. 1909. *De Romanorum precationibus*. Giessen.
Aretini, P. 1998. *A destra e a sinistra. La orientamento nel mondo classico*. Pisa.
Astin, A. E. 1978. *Cato the Censor*. Oxford.
———. 1988. "Regimen morum." *JRS* 78:14–34.
Austin, R. J. E., and N. B. Rankov 1995. *Exploratio: Military and Political Intelligence in the Roman World from the Second Punic War to the Battle of Adrianople*. London.
Balland, A. 1984. "La casa Romuli au Palatin et au Capitole." *REL* 62:57–80.
Baltrusch, E. 1989. *Regimen morum: Die Reglementierung des Privatlebens der Senatoren und Ritter in der römischen Republik und frühen Kaiserzeit*. Munich.
Barton, T. 1994. *Ancient Astrology*. London.
Bastien, J.-L. 2007. *Le triomphe romain et son utilization politique aux trois derniers siècles de la République*. Rome.
Beard, M. 1986. "Cicero and Divination: The Formation of a Latin Discourse." *JRS* 76:33–46.
———. 1990. "Priesthood in the Roman Republic." In Beard and North 1990, 19–48.
———. 1998. "Documenting Roman Religion." In Moatti 1998, 75–102.
———. 2007. *The Roman Triumph*. Cambridge, MA.
Beard, M., and J. North, eds. 1990. *Pagan Priests: Religion and Power in the Ancient World*. Ithaca.
Beard, M., J. North, and S. Price. 1998. *Religions of Rome*. Cambridge.
Beck, H. 2005. *Karriere und Hierarchie. Die römische Aristokratie und die Anfänge des cursus honorum in mittleren Republik*. Berlin.

Beck, H., A. Duplá, M. Jehne, and F. Pina Pola. 2011a. "The Republic and Its Highest Office: Some Introductory Remarks on the Roman Consulate." In Beck, Duplá, Jehne, and Pina Pola 2011b, 1–15.

Beck, H., A. Duplá, M. Jehne, and F. Pina Pola, eds. 2011b. *Consuls and Res Publica: Holding High Office in the Roman Republic.* Cambridge.

Bell, A. 2004. *Spectacular Power in the Greek and Roman City.* Oxford.

Bell, M. 1965. "Tactical Reform in the Roman Republican Army." *Historia* 14:404–22.

Bergk, A. 2011. "The Development of the Praetorship in the Third Century." In Beck, Duplá, Jehne, and Pina Pola 2011b, 61–74.

Berthelet, Y. 2015. *Gouverner avec les dieux. Autorité, auspices et pouvoir, sous la République romaine et sous Auguste.* Paris.

Bertrand, J.-M. 1989. "À propos du mot *provincia*: Étude sur les modes de élaboration du langue politique." *Journal des savants,* 191–215.

Bettini, M. 2008. "Weighty Words, Suspect Speech: *Fari* in Roman Culture." *Arethusa* 41:313–75.

Bevir, M., and R. A. W. Rhodes 2010. *The State as Cultural Practice.* Oxford.

Bispham, E. 2000. "Mimic? A Case Study in Early Roman Colonization." In *The Emergence of State Identities in Italy in the First Millenium,* edited by E. Herring and K. Lomas, 157–86. London.

———. 2006. "*Coloniam deducere:* How Roman Was Roman Colonization during the Middle Republic?" In Bradley and Wilson 2006, 73–160.

———. 2007. *From Asculum to Actium: The Municipalization of Italy from the Social War to Augustus.* Oxford.

Bleicken, J. 1955. *Das Volkstribunat der klassischen Republik.* Munich.

———. 1975. *Lex Publica: Gesetz und Recht in der römischen Republik.* Berlin.

Bloch, M. E. F. 1998. "What Goes without Saying: The Conceptualization of Zafimaniry Society." In *How We Think They Think: Anthropological Approaches to Cognition, Memory and Literacy,* edited by M. E. F. Bloch, 22–38. Boulder, CO.

Bodel, J. 1986. "Graveyards and Groves: A Study of the *Lex Lucerina*." *AJAH* 11:1–133.

Bonfante, L. 2006. "Etruscan Inscriptions and Etruscan Religion." In *The Religion of the Etruscans,* edited by N. T. de Grummond and E. Simon, 9–26. Austin.

Bonfante Warren, L. 1970. "Roman Triumphs and Etruscan Kings: The Changing Face of the Triumph." *JRS* 60:49–66.

Bonnefond-Coudry, M. 1989. *Le sénat de la république romaine de la guerre d'Hannibal à Auguste.* Rome.

Bowman, D. 1990. "The Formula Sociorum in the Second and First Centuries BC." *CJ* 85: 330–36.

Bradley, G. 2006. "Colonization and Identity in Republican Italy." In Bradley and Wilson 2006, 161–87.

Bradley, G., and J.-P. Wilson 2006. *Greek & Roman Colonization: Origins, Ideologies & Interactions.* Swansea, 2006.

Brandt, J. R. 1985. "Ostia, Minturno, Pyrgi: The Planning of Three Roman Colonies." *ActaAArtHist,* ser. 2, 5:25–87.

Bremer, F. 1896. *Iurisprudentia antehadrianae quae supersunt.* Leipzig.

Brennan, T. C. 1989. "C. Aurelius Cotta praetor iterum (*CIL* I², 610)." *Athenaeum* 67:467–87.

———. 1996. "Triumphus in Monte Albano." In *Transitions to Empire: Essays in Greco-Roman History, 360–146 B.C., in Honor of E. Badian*, edited by R. W. Wallace and E. M. Harris, 315–37. Norman, OK.

———. 2000. *The Praetorship in the Roman Republic*. Oxford.

Brind'Amour, P. 1980. "Le origine des jeux séculaires." In *ANRW* 2.16.2:1334–417.

Briscoe, J. 2012. "Notes on the Function of the Peregrine Praetor in the Republic." *Latomus* 71:996–99.

Brisson, L. 2004. *How Philosophers Saved Myths: Allegorical Interpretation and Classical Mythology*. Translated by C. Tihanyi. Chicago.

Brodersen, K. 1995. *Terra cognita: Studien zur römischen Raumverfassung*. Hildesheim.

———. 2004. "Mapping (in) the Roman World." *JRS* 94:183–90.

———. 2012. "Cartography." Chapter 4 in *Geography in Classical Antiquity*, by D. Dueck, 99–110. Cambridge.

Broughton, T. R. S. 1951–83. *The Magistrates of the Roman Republic*. 3 vols. Atlanta.

Brown, F. 1980. *Cosa: The Making of a Roman Town*. Ann Arbor.

Brunn, C., ed. 2000. *The Roman Middle Republic: Politics, Religion, and Historiography, c. 400–133 B.C.* Rome.

Brunt, P. A. 1969. "The Enfranchisement of the Sabines." In *Hommages à Marcel Renard*, 121–29. Collection Latomus 102. Brussels.

———. 1971. *Italian Manpower*. Oxford.

———. 1980a. "On Historical Fragments and Epitomes." *CQ* 30:477–94.

———. 1980b. "Cicero and Historiography." In Philias kharin. *Miscellanea di studi classici in onore di E. Manni*, edited by P. Salmon, 1:311–40. Rome.

Burton, P. 2011. *Friendship and Empire: Roman Diplomacy and Imperialism in the Middle Republic (353–146 BC)*. Cambridge.

Calderone, S. 1972. "Superstitio." In *ANRW* 1.2:377–96.

Campbell, B. 2000. *The Writings of the Roman Land Surveyors: Introduction, Text, Translation and Commentary*. London.

Cancik, H. 1985–86. "Rome as Sacred Landscape: Varro and the End of Republican Religion in Rome." *Visible Religion* 4–5:250–65.

Carafa, P. 1998. *Il comizio di Roma dalle origine all età di Augusto*. Rome.

Carla, F. 2015. "*Pomerium, fines* and *ager Romanus*. Understanding Rome's First Boundary." *Latomus* 74:599–630.

Carandini, A. 1997. *La nascita di Roma: Dei, lari, eroi, uomini all'alba di una civiltà*. Turin.

Castagnoli, F. 1984. "Il tempio romano: Questioni di terminologia e tipologia." *PBSR* 52:3–20.

Catalano, P. 1960. *Contributi allo studio del diritto augurale*. Vol. 1. Turin.

———. 1974. "La divisione del potere in Roma (a proposito di Polibio e Catone)." In *Studi in onore di Giuseppe Grosso* 6:667–91. Turin.

———. 1978. "Aspetti spaziali del sistema giuridico-religioso romano. Mundus, templum, urbs, ager, Latium, Italia." In *ANRW* 2.16.1:440–553.

Cels-Saint-Hilaire, C. 1995. *La république des tribus: Du droit de vote et des ses enjeux aux débuts de la République romaine (495–300 av. J.-C.)*. Toulouse.

Chaplin, J. 2000. *Livy's Exemplary History*. Oxford.

Chassignet, M. 1987. "Cato et l'imperialisme romain au II s. av. J.-C. d'apres les *Origines*." *Latomus* 46:285–300.

Chouquer, G., and F. Favory 1991. *Les paysages de l'antiquité: Terres et cadastres de l'occident romain, IVe s, avant J.-C. / IIIe s. après J. C.* Paris.

Clarke, K. 1999. *Between Geography and History: Hellenistic Constructions of the Roman World*. Oxford.

———. 2008. *Making Time for the Past: Local History and the* Polis. Oxford.

Cloud, J. D. 1998. "The Origin of Provocatio." *RPh* 72:25–48.

Coarelli, F. 1981. "La doppia tradizione sulla more di Romulo e gli *auguracula* dell'*arx* e del Quirinale." In *Gli Etruschi e Roma: Atti dell'incontro di studio in onore di Massimo Pallottino: Roma, 11–13 dicembre 1979*, 173–88. Rome.

———. 1983–85. *Il foro romano*. 2 vols. Rome.

———. 2003. "Remoria." In *Myth, History, and Culture in Republican Rome: Studies in Honour of T. P. Wiseman*, edited by D. Braund and C. Gill, 46–55. Exeter.

Colonna, G. 1991. "Acqua Acetosa Laurentina, l'ager Romanus antiquus e i santuari del I miglio." *Scienze dell'Antichità* 5:209–32.

Cooley, A. E. 2009. *Res Gestae Divi Augusti: Text, Translation, and Commentary.*, Cambridge.

Cornell, T. J. 1991a. "The Tyranny of the Evidence; a Discussion of the Possible Uses of Literacy in Etruria and Latium in the Archaic Age." In *Literacy in the Roman World*, edited by J. Humphrey, 7–33. Journal of Roman Archaeology Supplementary Series 3. Ann Arbor.

———. 1991b. "Rome: The History of an Anachronism." In *City-States in Classical Antiquity and Medieval Italy*, edited by A. Molho, K. Raaflaub, and J. Emlen, 53–69. Ann Arbor.

———. 1995. *The Beginnings of Rome: Italy and Rome from the Bronze Age to the Punic Wars (c. 1000–264 BC)*. London.

———. 2000. "The *Lex Ovinia* and the Emancipation of the Senate." In Brunn 2000, 69–89.

———. 2001. "Cicero on the Origins of Rome." In *Cicero's Republic*, edited by J. G. F. Powell and J. North, 41–56. Bulletin of the Institute of Classical Studies Supplement 76. London.

Cornell, T. J., E. Bispham, J. W. Rich, and C. J. Smith 2013. *The Fragments of the Roman Historians*. 3 vols. Oxford.

Courtney, E. 1999. *Archaic Latin Prose*. Atlanta.

Crawford, M. 1974. *Roman Republican Coinage*. Cambridge.

———. 1985. *Coinage and Money under the Roman Republic: Italy and the Mediterranean Economy*. London.

———. 1989. "Aut sacrom aut poublicom." In *New Perspectives in the Roman Law of Property: Essays for Barry Nicholas*, edited by P. Birks, 93–98. Oxford.

———. 1990. "Origini e sviluppi di sistema provinciale romano." In *Storia di Roma: II: Il impero mediterraneo. I: La repubblica imperiale*, edited by G. Clemente, F. Coarelli, and E. Gabba. 91–121. Turin.

———, ed. 1994. *Roman Statutes*. Bulletin of the Institute of Classical Studies Supplement 64. London.

———. 2002. "Tribus, tessères et regions." *CRAI* 146:1125–35.

———. 2003. "Language and Geography in the *Sententia Minuciorum*: *Corpus Inscriptionum Latinarum* I^2 584 = V 7749." *Athenaeum* 91:204–10.

———. 2006. "From Poseidonia to Paestum via the Lucanians." In Bradley and Wilson 2006, 59–72.

———. 2010. "Community, Tribe and Army after the Social War." In *Le tribù romane: Atti della XVIe Rencontre sur l'épigraphie (Bari 8–10 ottobre 2009)*, edited by M. Silvestrini, 97–101. Bari.

Dahlheim, W. 1977. *Gewalt und Herrschaft: Das provinziale Herrschaftssystem der römischen Republik.* Berlin.

Dahlmann, H. 1976. "Zu Varros antiquarisch-historischen Werken, besonders den Antiquitates rerum humanarum et divinarum." In *Atti del Congresso Internazionale di Studi Varroniani*, 1:163–76. Rieti.

Dalla Rosa, A. 2003. "Ducto auspicioque: Per una riflessione sui fondamenti religiosi del potere magistratuale fino all'epoca augustea." *SCO* 49:185–255.

———. 2011. "Dominating the Auspices: Augustus, Augury, and the Proconsuls." In *Priests and State in the Roman World*, edited by J. H. Richardson and F. Santangelo, 243–69. Stuttgart.

———. 2014. *Cura et tutela. Le origini del potere imperiale sulle province proconsulari.* Stuttgart.

D'Arms, J. 1972. "Pro Murena 16 and Cicero's Use of Historical Exempla." *Phoenix* 26:82–84.

Dart, C. 2012. "The Address of Italian Portents by Rome and the *Ager Publicus*." *AC* 81:111–24.

David, J.-M. 1980. "*Maiorum exempla sequi*: L'*exemplum* historique dans les discours judiciaires de Cicéron." In *Rhétorique et histoire: L'exemplum et l'modèle de comportement dans le discours antique et medieval*, edited by J.-M. David, 67–86. MEFRA (Moyen âge) 92.

———. 1995a. *The Roman Conquest of Italy.* Translated by A. Nevill. Oxford.

———. 1995b. "Le tribunal du préteur: Contraintes symboliques et politiques sous la République de le début de l'Empire." *Klio* 77:371–85.

Davies, J. P. 2004. *Rome's Religious History: Livy, Tacitus and Ammianus on their God.*, Cambridge.

De Cazenove, O. 2000. "I destinari dell'iscrizione di Tiriolo e la questione del campo d'applicazione del senato consulto *de Bacchanalibus*." *Athenaeum* 88:59–69.

———. 2005. "Mont et citadelle, temple et *templum*. Quelques réflexions sur l'usage religieux des hauteurs dans l'Italie républicaine." *ARG* 7:63–82.

De Libero, L. 1994. "Italia." *Klio* 76:301–25.

De Ligt, L. 2012. *Peasants, Citizens and Soldiers: Studies in the Demographic History of Roman Italy, 225 BC—AD 100.* Cambridge.

De Ligt, L., and S. Northwood, eds. 2008. *People, Land and Politics: Demographic Developments and the Transformation of Roman Italy, 300 BC–AD 14.* Leiden.

De Martino, F. 1973. *Storia della costituzione romana.* 2nd ed. Naples.

Derow, P. S. 1973. "The Roman Calendar, 190–168 B.C." *Phoenix* 27:345–56.

———. 1976. "The Roman Calendar, 218–191 B.C." *Phoenix* 30:265–81.

———. 1979. "Polybius, Rome, and the East." *JRS* 69:1–15.

Dilke, O. A. W. 1971. *Roman Land Surveyors: An Introduction to the Agrimensores.* New York.

D'Ippolito, F. 1994. *I giuristi e la città: Ricerche sulla giurisprudenza romana della repubblica.* 2nd ed. Naples.

Dobson, M. 2008. *The Army of the Roman Republic: The Second Century BC, Polybius and the Camps at Numantia, Spain.* Oxford.

Drogula, F. 2007. "*Imperium, Potestas,* and the *Pomerium* in the Roman Republic." *Historia* 56:419–52.

———. 2015. *Commanders and Command in the Roman Republic and Early Empire.* Chapel Hill.

Dumézil, G. 1970. *Archaic Roman Religion.* Translated by P. Krapp. Chicago.

Dyck, A. 1998. "On the Interpretation of Cicero, *De Republica.*" *CQ* 48:564–68.

———. 2004. *A Commentary on Cicero,* De Legibus. Ann Arbor.

Eck, W. 2003. *The Age of Augustus.* Oxford.

Eckstein, A. 1979. "The Foundation Day of Roman *Coloniae.*" *CSCA* 12:85–97.

———. 2006. *Mediterranean Anarchy, Interstate War, and the Rise of Rome.* Berkeley.

Edlund, I. E. M. 1987. *The Gods and the Place: Location and Function of Sanctuaries in the Countryside of Etruria and Magna Graecia (700–400 B.C.).* Stockholm.

Eigler, U., U. Gotter, N. Luraghi, and U. Walter, eds. 2003. *Formen römischer Geschichtscreibung von den Anfängen bis Livius: Gattungen—Autoren— Kontexte.* Darmstadt.

Eilers, C., ed. 2009. *Diplomats and Diplomacy in the Roman World.* Mnemosyne Supplements 304. Brill.

Elster, M. 2003. *Die Gesetze der mittleren römischen Republik: Text und Kommentar.* Darmstadt.

Engels, D. 2007. *Das römische Vorzeichenwesen (753–27 v. Chr.). Quellen, Terminologie, Kommentar, historische Entwicklung.* Stuttgart.

Evans, J. D. 1990. "The Statues of the Kings and Brutus on the Capitoline." *Opuscula Romana* 18:99–105.

Feeney, D. 2009. "Time." In *The Cambridge Companion to the Roman Historians,* edited by A. Feldherr, 139–51. Cambridge.

Feldherr, A. 1998. *Spectacle and Society in Livy's History.* Berkeley.

Fentress, E., ed. 2000a. *Romanization and the City; Creations, Transformations, and Failures. JRA* Supplementary Series 38. Portsmouth, RI.

———. 2000b. "Introduction: Frank Brown, Cosa, and the Idea of a Roman City." In Fentress 2000a, 1–24.

Ferrary, J.-L. 1977. "Recherches sur la législation de Saturninus et de Glaucia, I." *MEFRA* 89:619–60.

———. 1979. "Recherches sur la legislation de Saturninus et Glaucia, II." *MEFRA* 91:83–134.

———. 1984. "L'archéologie du *De Re Publica* (2, 2, 4–37; 63): Cicéron entre Polybe et Platon." *JRS* 74:87–98.

———. 1988. "Rogatio Servilia Agraria." *Athenaeum* 66:141–61.

———. 2008. "Provinces, magistratures et lois: La creation des provinces sous la République." In *Die römischen Provinzen. Begriff und Gründung,* edited by I. Piso, 7–18. Cluj-Napoca.

———. 2009. "After the Embassy to Rome: Publication and Implementation." In Eilers 2009, 127–42.

———, ed. 2012. *Leges publicae. La legge nell'esperienza giuridica romana.* Pavia.

Finer, S. E. 1997. *The History of Government from the Earliest Times.* Oxford.

Flaig, E. 2003. *Ritualisierte Politik: Zeichen, Gesten und Herrschaft im alten Rom.* Göttingen.

Flower, H. 1995. "*Fabulae Praetextae* in Context: When Were Plays on Contemporary Subjects Performed in Republican Rome?" *CQ* 45:170–90.

———. 1996. *Ancestor Masks and Aristocratic Power in Roman Culture.* Oxford.

———. 2000. "The Tradition of the *Spolia Opima*: Marcus Claudius Marcellus and Augustus." *CA* 19:34–64.

———. 2003. "Memories of Marcellus: History and Memory in Roman Republican Culture." In Eigler, Gotter, Luraghi, and Walter 2003, 39–52.

———. 2004a. "Spectacle and Political Power in the Roman Republic." In Flower 2004b, 322–43.

———, ed. 2004b. *The Cambridge Companion to the Roman Republic.* Cambridge.

———. 2006. *The Art of Forgetting: Disgrace and Oblivion in Roman Political Culture.* Chapel Hill.

Flower, M. A. 2008. *The Seer in Ancient Greece.* Berkeley.

Foresti, L. A. 1979. "Zur Zeremonie der Nagelschlagung in Rom und in Etrurien." *AJAH* 4:144–56.

Forsythe, G. 1994. *The Historian L. Calpurnius Piso Frugi and the Roman Annalistic Tradition.* Lanham, MD.

———. 2000. "Roman Historians of the Second Century BC." In Brunn 2000, 1–11.

———. 2012. *Time in Roman Religion: One Thousand Years of Religious History.* London.

Fraccaro, P. 1935. "'Tribules' ed aerarii.' Una ricerca di diritto pubblico romano." *Athenaeum* 11:150–72.

Frederiksen, M. 1984. *Campania.* Edited by N. Purcell. Rome.

Frier, B. 1999. Libri Annales Pontificium Maximorum: *The Origins of the Annalistic Tradition.* 2nd ed. Ann Arbor.

Fronda, M. P. 2010. *Between Rome and Carthage: Southern Italy during the Second Punic War.* Cambridge.

———. 2011. "Polybius 3.40, the Foundation of Placentia, and the Roman Calendar (218–217 BC). *Historia* 60:425–57.

Gabba, E. 1988. "Reflessioni sulla Lex Coloniae Genetivae Iuliae." In *Estudios sobre la Tabula Siarensis*, edited by J. Gonzales and J. Arce, 157–68. Madrid.

———. 1991. *Dionysius and the History of Archaic Rome.* Berkeley.

Gagé, J. 1955. *Recherches sur les jeux séculaires.* Paris.

Galsterer, H. 1976. *Herrschaft und Verwaltung im republikanischen Italien: Die Beziehungen Roms zu den Italischen Gemeinden vom Latinerfrieden 338 v. Chr. bis zum Bundesgenossenkrieg 91 v. Chr.* Munich.

Gargola, D. 1995. *Lands, Laws & Gods: Magistrates and Ceremony in the Regulation of Public Land in Republican Rome.* Chapel Hill.

———. 2004. "The Ritual of Centuriation." In Konrad 2004, 123–49.

———. 2005. "Hyginus Gromaticus and Frontinus on the Installation of *Limites*: Ritual, Law, and Legitimacy." In *Concepts, pratiques et enjeux environnementaux dans l'Empire romain*, edited by R. Bedon and E. Hermon, 125–52. Caesarodonum 39.

———. 2008. "The Gracchan Reform and Appian's Representation of an Agrarian Crisis." In De Ligt and Northwood 2008, 487–518.

———. 2016. "Was There a Second-Century *Provincia Africa?*" *Historia*. Forthcoming.
Gibbs, S. L. 1976. *Greek and Roman Sundials*. New Haven.
Giovannini, A. 1983. *Consulare Imperium*. Basel.
Gotter, U. 2009. "Cato's *Origines*: The Historian and His Enemies." In *The Cambridge Companion to Roman Historians* edited by A. Feldherr, 108–22. Cambridge.
Gruen, E. 1984. *The Hellenistic World and the Coming of Rome*. Berkeley.
v. 1990. *Studies in Greek Culture and Roman Policy*. Leiden.
Hall, J. F., III. 1986. "The *Saeculum Novum* of Augustus and Its Etruscan Antecedants." In *ANRW* 2.16.3:2564–89.
Hannah, R. 2003. *Greek and Roman Calendars: Constructions of Time in the Classical World*. London.
Harris, W. V. 2007. "Quando e come l'Italia divenne per la prima volta Italia? Un saggio sulla politica dell'identità." *Studi storici* 48:301–22.
Hay, C., and M. Lister. 2006. "Introduction: Theories of the State." In *The State: Theories and Issues*, edited by C. Hay, M. Lister, and D. Marsh, 1–20. Basingstoke.
Heurgon, J. 1964. "L. Cincius et la loi du *clavus annalis*." *Athenaeum* 42:432–37.
Hickson, F. V. 1993. *Roman Prayer Language: Livy and the Aeneid of Vergil*. Stuttgart.
Hickson Hahn, F. V. 2007. "Performing the Sacred: Prayers and Hymns." In *A Companion to Roman Religion*, edited by J. Rüpke, 235–48. Oxford.
Higbee, C. 2003. *The Lindian Chronicle and the Greek Creation of Their Past*. Oxford.
Hillier B., and J. Hanson 1984. *The Social Logic of Space*. Cambridge.
Hinard, F., and J.-C. Dumont 2003. *Libitina: Pompes funèbres et supplices en Campanie à l'époque d'Auguste*. Paris.
Hinrichs, F. T. 1974. *Die Geschichte der gromatischen Institutionen: Untersuchungen zu Landverteilung, Landvermessung, Bodenverwaltung und Bodenrecht im römischen Recht*. Wiesbaden.
Hirsch, E., and M. O'Hanlon, eds. 1995. *The Anthropology of Landscape: Perspectives of Place and Space*. Cambridge.
Hölkeskamp, K.-J. 1987. *Die Entstehung der Nobilität: Studien zur sozialen und politischen Geschichte der römischen Republik im 4. Jhdt. v. Chr*. Stuttgart.
Hölkeskamp, K.-J. 2004. "*Fides—deditio in fidem—dextra data et accepta*: Recht, Religion und Ritual." In *Senatus Populusque Romanus: Die politische Kultur der Republik—Dimensionen und Deutungen*, by K.-J. Hölkeskamp, 105–35. Stuttgart.
Hölkeskamp, K.-J. 2005. "Ein 'Gegensats von Form und Unhalt.' Theodor Mommsens Konzept des republikanischen 'Senatsregiments'—Hindernis oder Herausforderung?" In Nippel and Seidensticker 2005, 87–129.
———. 2006a. "Rituali e ceremonie 'alla romana': Nuove prospettive sulla cultura politica dell'età repubblicana." *Studi storici* 47:319–63.
———. 2006b. "History and Collective Memory in the Middle Republic." In Rosenstein and Morstein-Marx 2006, 478–95.
———. 2007. "Pomp und Prozessionen: Rituale und Zeremonien in der politischen Kultur der römischen Republik." *Jahrbuch des historischen Kollegs*, 35–72.
———. 2011. "The Roman Republic as Theatre of Power: The Consuls as Leading Actors." In Beck, Duplá, Jehne, and Pina Pola 2011b, 161–81.
Holland, L. 1961. *Janus and the Bridge*. Rome.

Hopkins, K. 1991. "From Violence to Blessing: Symbols and Rituals in Ancient Rome." In *City-States in Classical Antiquity and Medieval Italy*, edited by A. Molho, K. Raaflaub, and J. Emlen, 479–98. Ann Arbor.

Hoyos, D. 1998. *Unplanned Wars: The Origins of the First and Second Punic Wars*. Berlin.

———. 2003. *Hannibal's Dynasty: Power and Politics in the Western Mediterranean, 247–183 BC*. London.

Hsu, Hsin-Mei Agnes 2013. "Structured Perceptions of Real and Imagined Landscapes in Early China." In Raaflaub and Talbert 2013, 43–63.

Humbert, M. 1978. *Municipium et civitas sine suffratio. L'organisation de la conquête jusqu'à la Guerre Sociale*. Rome.

Humm, M. 1999. "Le Comitium du forum romain et la réforme des tribus d'Appius Claudius Caecus." *MEFRA* 111:625–94.

———. 2005. *Appius Claudius Caecus. La République accomplie*. Rome.

———. 2012. "The Curiate Law and the Religious Nature of the Power of Roman Magistrates." In Tellegen-Couperus 2012, 57–84.

———. 2014. "Espaces comitiaux et contraintes augurales à Rome pendant la période républicaine." *Ktèma* 39:315–45.

Hurlet, F. 2006. *Le Proconsul et le prince d'Auguste à Dioclétien*. Bordeaux.

Ilari, V. 1974. *Gli italici nelle strutture militari romane*. Milan.

Itgenshorst, T. 2005. *Tota illa pompa: Der Triumph in der römischen Republik*. Göttingen.

———. 2006. "Roman Commanders and Hellenistic Kings: On the 'Hellenization' of the Roman Triumph." *Ancient Society* 36:51–68.

Jacobs, J. 2010. "Traces of the Omen Series *Summa izbu* in Cicero, *De divination*." In *Divination and Interpretation of Signs in the Ancient World*, edited by Amar Annus, 317–39. Chicago.

Jahn, J. 1970. *Interregnum und Wahldiktatur*. Kallmünz.

Janni, P. 1984. *La mappa e il periplo: Cartografia antica e spazio odologico*. Rome.

Jefferson, E. 2012. "Problems and Audience in Cato's *Origines*." In Roselaar 2012, 311–26.

Jehne, M. 2002. "Die Geltung der Provocation und die Konstruktion der römischen Republik als Freiheitsgemeinschaft." In *Geltungsgeschichten: Über die Stabilisierung und Legitimierung institutioneller Ordnungen*, edited by G. Melville and H. Vorländre, 55–74. Cologne.

———. 2005. "Die Volksversammlungen in Mommsens 'Staatsrecht,' oder: Mommsen als Gesetzgeber." In Nippel and Seidensticker 2005, 134–42.

———. 2009. "Diplomacy in Italy in the Second Century." In Eilers 2009, 143–70.

———. 2011. "The Rise of the Consular as a Social Type in the Third and Second Centuries B.C." In Beck, Duplá, Jehne, and Pina Pola 2011b, 211–31.

———. 2012. "Statutes on Public Powers and Their Relationship to *mos*." In Ferrary 2012, 405–28.

Jocelyn, H. D. 1967. *The Tragedies of Ennius*. Cambridge.

———. 1969. "Imperator histricus." *YClS* 21:96–123.

Jonkers, E. J. 1963. *Social and Economic Commentary on Cicero's De Lege Agraria Orationes Tres*. Leiden.

Kallet-Marx, R. 1995. *Hegemony to Empire: The Development of the Roman* Imperium *in the East from 148 to 62 B.C.* Berkeley.

Keaveney, A. 1983. "Sulla and the Gods." In *Studies in Latin Literature and Roman History*, edited by C. Deroux, 3:44–79. Brussels.
———. 2005. *Sulla: The Last Republican*. London.
Kelly, G. P. 2006. *A History of Exile in the Roman Republic*. Cambridge.
Keppie, L. 1984. *The Making of the Roman Army from Republic to Empire*. Norman, OK.
Knapp, P. C. 1980. "Festus 262 L and *Praefecturae* in Italy." *Athenaeum* 58:14–38.
Konrad, C., ed. 2004. *Augusto augurio: Rerum humanarum et divinarum commentationes in honorem Jerzy Linderski*. Stuttgart.
———. 2008. "*Ager Romanus* at Messana?" *CQ*, n.s., 38:349–53.
Koortbojian, M. 2013. *The Divinization of Caesar and Augustus: Precedents, Consequences, Implications*. Cambridge.
Kosmin, P. J. 2014. *The Land of the Elephant Kings: Space, Territory, and Ideology in the Seleucid Empire*. Cambridge, MA.
Kunze, C. 2011. "Carthage and Numidia, 201–149." In *A Companion to the Punic Wars*, edited by D. Hoyos, 395–411. Oxford and Malden, MA.
Lacey, W. K. 1998. "Returning to the City." In *Ancient History in a Modern University: Proceedings of a Conference held at Macquarie University, 8–13 July 1993 to mark twenty-five years of the teaching of ancient history at Macquarie University and the retirement from the Chair of Professor Edwin Judge*, edited by T. W. Hillard, R. A. Kearsley, C. E. V. Nixon, and A. M. Nobbs, 1:276–80. Grand Rapids, MI.
Lackner, E.-M. 2008. *Republikanische Fora*. Munich.
Laffi, U. 2012. "Legge agrarie e coloniarie." In Ferrary 2012, 429–61.
Lange, C. H. 2014. "The Triumph Outside the City: Voices of Protest in the Middle Republic." In Lange and Vervaet 2014, 67–81.
Lange, C. H., and F. J. Vervaet, eds., 2014. *The Roman Republican Triumph: Beyond the Spectacle*. Rome.
Latte, K. 1960. *Römische Religionsgeschichte*. Munich.
Laurence, R. 1999. *The Roads of Roman Italy: Mobility and Cultural Change*. London.
Lefebvre, H. 1974. *La production de l'espace*. Paris.
Le Gall, J. 1976. "Evocatio." In *L'Italie préromaine et la Rome republicaine: Mélanges offerts à J. Heurgon*, 1:519–24. Collection de l'école française de Rome 27. Rome.
Levene, D. S. 1993. *Religion in Livy*. Leiden.
Lewis, M. E. 2006. *The Construction of Space in Early China*. Albany.
Lewis, M. T. 2001. *Surveying Instruments of Greece and Rome*. Cambridge.
———. 2012. "Greek and Roman Surveying and Surveying Instruments." In Talbert 2012, 129–62.
Lichtfield, H. 1914. "National *Exempla Virtutis* in Roman Literature." *HSCPh* 25:1–71.
Lieberg, G. 1973. "Die 'theologia tripertita' in Forschung und Bezeugung." In *ANRW* 1.4:63–115.
Linderski, J. 1979. "*Legibus praefecti mittebantur*." *Historia* 28:247–50. Reprinted in Linderski 1995, 143–46.
———. 1982. "Cicero and Roman Divination." *PP* 12–38. Reprinted in Linderski 1995, 458–64.
———. 1985. "The *Libri Reconditi*." *HSCPh* 89:207–34. Reprinted in Linderski 1995, 496–523.
———. 1986. "The Augural Law." In *ANRW* 2.26.3:2146–312.

———. 1993. "Roman Religion in Livy." In *Livius: Aspeckte seines Werkes*, edited by W. Schuller, 53–70. *Xenia* 31. Konstanz. Reprinted in Linderski 1995, 608–25.
———. 1995. *Roman Questions: Selected Papers*. Stuttgart.
———. 2007a. "Founding the City: Ennius and Romulus on the Site of Rome." In Linderski 2007b, 3–19.
———. 2007b. *Roman Questions II: Selected Papers*. Stuttgart.
Lintott, A. W. 1972. "Provocatio. From the Struggle of the Orders to the Principate." In *ANRW* 1.2:226–67.
———. 1978. "The *quaestiones de sicariis et veneficiis* and the Latin *lex Bantina*." *Hermes* 106:125–38.
———. 1981. "What Was the *imperium Romanum*?" In *G&R* 28:53–67.
———. 1990. "Electoral Bribery in the Roman Republic." *JRS* 80:1–16.
———. 1992. *Judicial Reform and Land Reform in the Roman Republic: A New Edition with Translation and Commentary of the Laws from Urbino*. Cambridge.
———. 1993. *Imperium Romanum: Politics and Administration*. London.
———. 1999. *The Constitution of the Roman Republic*. Oxford.
Lipka, M. 2009. *Roman Gods: A Conceptual Approach*. Leiden.
Liou-Gille, B. 1991. "*Dexter* et *sinister* et leurs equivalents." *Glotta* 69:194–201.
Lobrano, G. 1982. *Il potere dei tribuni della plebe*. Milan.
Lo Cascio, E. 1991–94. "I *togati* della 'formula togatorum.'" *Annali dell'Istituto Italiano per gli studi storici* 12:309–28.
———. 1999a. "The Population of Roman Italy in Town and Country." In *Reconstructing Past Population Trends in Mediterranean Europe*, edited by J. Bintliff and K. Shonias, 161–71. Oxford.
———. 1999b. "Popolazione e risorse agricole nell'Italia del II secolo a.C." In *Demografia, sistemi agrari, regime alimentare nel mondo antico*, edited by D. Vera, 217–45. Bari.
———. 2001. "Il *census* a Roma e la sua evoluzione dall'età 'serviana' alla prima età imperiale." *MEFRA* 113:565–603.
Lomas, K. 2012. "The Weakest Link: Elite Social Networks in Republican Italy." In Roselaar 2012, 197–213.
Loreto, L. 1993. *Un'epoca di buon senso. Decisione, consenso e stato a Roma tra il 326 e il 264 a.C.* Amsterdam.
Lott, J. B. 2004. *The Neighborhoods of Augustan Rome*. Cambridge.
Lovisi, C. 1999. *Contribution à l'étude de la peine de mort sous la République romaine (509–149 av. J.-C.)*. Paris.
Lundgren, C. 2014. "Rules for Obtaining a Triumph: The *ius triumphandi* Once More." In Lange and Vervaet 2014, 17–32.
MacBain, B. 1982. *Prodigy and Expiation: A Study of Religion and Politics in Republican Rome*. Collection Latomus 177. Brussels.
Maas, M. 1992. *John Lydus and the Roman Past*. London.
Magdelain, A. 1964. "Note sur la loi curiate et les auspices des magistrates." *RHD* 42:198–203. Reprinted in Magdelain 1990, 307–11.
———. 1968. *Recherches sur l'imperium: La loi curiate et les auspices d'investiture*, Paris.
———. 1977. "Le pomerium archaïque et le mundus." *REL* 54:71–109.
———. 1978. *La loi à Rome: Histoire d'un concept*. Paris.

———. 1990. *Jus, imperium, auctoritas. Études de droit romain.* Rome.
———. 1995. *De la royauté et du droit de Romulus à Sabinus.* Rome.
Mantovani, D. 1989. *Il problema d'origine dell'accusa popolare.* Padua.
———. 2012. "Le due serie di leges regiae." In Ferrary 2012, 283–92.
Marco Simón, F. 2011. "The *Feriae Latinae* as Religious Legitimation of the Consuls' *Imperium.*" In Beck, Duplá, Jehne, and Pina Pola 2011b, 116–32.
Marincola, J. 1997. *Authority and Tradition in Ancient Historiography.* Cambridge.
Marshall, A. J. 1968. "Friends of the Roman People." *AJP* 89:39–55.
Martin, R. 1956. *L'urbanisme dans la Grèce antique.* Paris.
Massa-Pairault, F.-H. 1985. "La Divination en Étrurie: Le IVe siècle, période critique." In *La divination dans le monde étrusco-italique* (Actes de la Table Ronde, 23 Février 1985), edited by Ch. Guittard, 1:56–115. *Caesarodonum* suppl. 52.
———. 1995. "'*Eques Romanus—Eques Latinus*' (Ve–IVe siècle)." *MEFRA* 107:33–70.
Mazurek, T. 2004. "The *Decemviri sacris faciundis*: Supplication and Prediction." In Konrad 2004, 151–68.
Meier, C. 1980. *Res publica amissa: Eine Studie zu Verfassung und Geschichte der römischen Republik.* 2nd ed. Wiesbaden.
Meyer, E. 2004. *Legitimacy and Law in the Roman World: Tabulae in Roman Belief and Practice.* Cambridge.
Meyer, H. D. 1980. "Der Civis Romanus als Kläger im Repetundenprozess." In *Studien zur antike Sozialgeschichte. Festschrift F. Vittinghof,* edited by W. Eck, H. Galsterer and H. Wolff, 145–46. Cologne.
Michels, A. K. 1967. *The Calendar of the Roman Republic.* Princeton.
Millar, F. 1987. "Polybius between Greece and Rome." In *Greek Connections: Essays on Culture and Diplomacy,* edited by A. T. Koumoulides, 1–18. Notre Dame, IN. Reprinted in F. Millar, *Rome, the Greek World, and the East,* vol. 3: *The Greek World, the Jews, and the East,* edited by H. M. Cotton and G. M. Rogers, 106–35. Chapel Hill.
Mitchell, R. E. 1990. *Patricians and Plebeians: The Origins of the Roman State.* Ithaca.
Moatti, C. 1993. *Archives et partage des terres dans le monde romaine (IIe siècle avant Ier siècle après J.-C.* Paris.
———. 1997. *La raison de Rome. Naissance de l'esprit critique à la fin de la République (IIe–Ier siècle avant Jésus-Christ).* Paris.
———, ed., 1998. *La mémoire perdue: Recherches sur l'administration romaine,* Rome.
Momigliano, A. 1971. *Alien Wisdom: The Limits of Hellenization.* Cambridge.
———. 1984. "The Theological Efforts of the Roman Upper Classes in the First Century B.C." *CP* 79:199–211.
———. 1990. "The Rise of Antiquarian Research." In *The Classical Foundations of Modern Historiography,* by A. Momigliano, 54–79. Berkeley.
Mommsen, T. 1853. *Epistula de Romanorum prodigiis ad Ottonem Jahnium.* Berlin.
———. 1887–88. *Römisches Staatsrecht.* Vols. 1 and 2, 3rd ed.; vol. 3, 1st ed. Leipzig.
Montanari, E. 1988. *Identità culturale e conflitti religiosi nella Roma repubblicana.* Rome.
Mantovani, D. 1989. *Il problema d'origine dell'accusa populare.* Padua.
Moore, T, 1989. *Artistry and Ideology: Livy's Vocabulary of Praise.* Frankfurt am Main.
Moreau, P. 1994. "La memoire fragile: Falsification et destruction des documents publics au Ier siècle av. J.-C." In Nicolet 1994, 121–47.

Morley, N. 1996. *Metropolis and Hinterland: The City of Rome and the Italian Economy 200 B.C.–A.D. 100*. Cambridge.
Mouritsen, H. 1998. *Italian Unification: A Study in Ancient and Modern Historiography*. Institute of Classical Studies Supplement 70. London.
———. 2001. *Plebs and Politics in the Late Roman Republic*. Cambridge.
———. 2004. "Pits and Politics: Interpreting Colonial *Fora* in Republican Italy." *PBSR* 72:37–67.
———. 2007. "The *Civitas sine suffragio*: Ancient Concepts and Modern Ideology." *Historia* 56:141–58.
Muccigrosso, J. 2006. "Religion and Politics: Did the Romans Scruple about the Placement of Their Temples?" In *Religion in Republican Italy*, edited by C. Schultz and P. Harvey Jr., 181–206. Cambridge.
Nicolet, C. 1970. "Les *finitores ex equestri loco* de la loi Servilia de 63 av. J.-C." *Latomus* 29:72–103.
———. 1980. *The World of the Citizen in Republican Rome* Translated by P. S. Falla. London.
———. 1991. *Space, Geography, and Politics in the Early Roman Empire*. Ann Arbor.
———, ed. 1994. *La mémoire perdue: À la recherche des archives oubliées, publiques et privées de la Rome antique*. Paris.
Nippel, W., and B. Seidensticker, eds. 2005. *Theodor Mommsens langer Schatten. Das römische Staatsrecht als bleibende Herausforderung für die Forschung*. Hildesheim.
Norden, E. 1939. *Aus altrömischen Priesterbüchern*. Lund.
North, J. 1979. "Religious Toleration in Republican Rome." *PCPhS* 25:85–103.
———. 1990. "Diviners and Divination in Rome." In Beard and North 1990, 49–71.
———. 1998. "The Books of the *Pontifices*." In Moatti 1998, 45–63.
———. 2000. *Roman Religion*. Greece & Rome, New Surveys in the Classics no. 30. Oxford.
Oakley, S. 1997–2005. *A Commentary on Livy Books VI–X*. 4 vols. Oxford.
Ogilvie, R. M. 1961. "Lustrum Condere." *JRS* 51:31–39.
———. 1965. *Commentary on Livy, Books 1–5*. Oxford.
Orlin, E. 1997. *Temples, Religion, and Politics in the Roman Republic*. Leiden.
———. *Foreign Cults in Rome: Creating a Roman Empire*. Oxford.
Östenberg, I. 2009. *Staging the World: Spoils, Captives, and Representations in the Roman Triumphal Procession*. Oxford.
Packard, J. 1960. "Official Notices in Livy's Fourth Decade: Style and Treatment." Ph.D. dissertation, University of North Carolina at Chapel Hill.
Pailler, J. -M. 1988. *Bacchanalia: La répression de 186 av. J.-C. à Rome et en Italia*. Rome.
Palmer, R. E. A. 1969. *The King and the Comitium*. Wiesbaden.
———. 1974. *Roman Religion and Roman Empire*. Philadelphia.
Patterson, J. 2006a. "The Relationship of the Italian Ruling Classes with Rome: Friendship, Family Relations and Their Consequences." In *Herrschaft ohne Integration? Rom und Italien in republikanischer Zeit*, edited by M. Jehne and R. Pfeilschifter, 139–54. Frankfurt am Main.
———. 2006b. "Colonization and Historiography: The Roman Republic." In Bradley and Wilson 2006, 189–218.
———. 2012. "Contact, Co-operation, and Conflict in Pre-Social War Italy." In Roselaar 2012, 215–26.

Pease, A. S. 1920–23. *M. Tulli Ciceronis De Divinatione Libri Duo*. Urbana, IL. Reprinted, Darmstadt, 1963.

Pfeilschifter, R. 2002. "Die Brüchigkeit der Rituale. Bemerkungen zum Niedergang der römischen Zensur." *Klio* 84:440–64.

Phillips, J. E. 1974. "Form and Language in Livy's Triumph Notices." *CP* 69:265–73.

Piéri, G. 1968. *L'histoire du cens jusqu'à la fin de la république romaine*. Paris.

Pietilä-Castrén, L. 1987. *Magnificentia publica: The Victory Monuments of the Roman Generals in the Era of the Punic Wars*. Helsinki.

Pina Pola, F. 1995. "Procedures and Functions of Civil and Military 'Contiones' in Rome." *Klio* 7:203–17.

———. 2011. *The Consul at Rome: The Civil Functions of the Consuls in the Roman Republic*. Cambridge.

Pinsent, J. 1954. "The Original Meaning of Municeps." *CQ* 4:158–64.

Pittenger, M. 2008. *Contested Triumphs: Politics, Pageantry, and Performance in Livy's Republican Rome*. Berkeley.

Poe, J. P. 1984. "The Secular Games, the Aventine, and the *Pomerium* in the Campus Martius." *CA* 3:57–81.

Porte, D. 1989. *Le prêtre à Rome: Les donneurs de sacré*. Paris.

Pothecary, S. 1997. "The Expression 'Our Times' in Strabo's Geography." *CPh* 92:235–46.

———. 2002. "Strabo, the Tiberian Author: Past, Present and Silence in Strabo's 'Geography.'" *Mnemosyne* 55:387–438.

Potter, D. S. 1999. "Political Theory in the *Senatus Consultum Pisonianum*." In *The Senatus Consultum de Cn. Pisone Patre: Text, Translation, Discussion*, edited by C. Damon and S. Takacs. Special issue, *AJP* 120:65–88.

Prag, J. R. W. 2006. "Il miliario di Aurelius Cotta (*ILLRP* n. 1277): Una lapide in Contest." In *Guerra e pace in Sicilia e nel Mediterraneo antico (VIII–III sec. a. C.); Atti del convegno*, 2:733–44. Pisa.

Prosdocimi, A. L. 1991. "La 'stella' del templum augurale e la 'stella' dei gromatici: Una stella augurale di Alba Fucens." *PP* 46:37–43.

Prosdocimi, A. L. 1995. "Populus Quiritium Quirites, I." *Eutopia* 4:15–71.

———. 1996. "Curia, Quirites e il 'Sistema di Quirino' (Populus Quiritium Quirites, II)." *Ostraka* 5:243–319.

Quilici Gigli, S. 1978. "Considerazioni sui confine del territorio di Roman primitive." *MEFRA* 90:567–75.

Raaflaub, K., and R. J. A. Talbert, eds., 2013. *Geography and Ethnography: Perceptions of the World in Pre-modern Societies*. Oxford.

Raggi, A. 2001. "Senatus consultum de Asclepiade Clazomenio sociisque." *ZPE* 135:73–116.

Rambaud, R. 1952. *Cicéron et l'histoire romaine*. Paris.

Rasmussen, S. W. 2003. *Public Portents in Republican Rome*. Rome.

Rawson, E. 1971a. "Prodigy Lists and the Use of the *Annales Maximi*." *CQ* 21:158–69. Reprinted in Rawson 1991, 1–15.

———. 1971b. "The Literary Sources for the Pre-Marian Army." *PBSR* 39:13–31. Reprinted in Rawson 1991, 34–57.

———. 1972. "Cicero the Historian and Cicero the Antiquarian." *JRS* 62:33–45. Reprinted in Rawson 1991, 245–71.

———. 1978. "The Introduction of Logical Organization in Roman Prose Literature." *PBSR* 46:12–34. Reprinted in Rawson 1991, 324–51.
———. 1985. *Intellectual Life in the Late Roman Republic*. Baltimore.
———. 1990. "The Antiquarian Tradition: Spoils and Representations of Foreign Armour." In *Staat und Staatlichkeit in der frühen römischen Republik*, edited by W. Eder, 157–73. Stuttgart. Reprinted in Rawson 1991, 582–98.
———. 1991. *Roman Culture and Society*. Oxford.
Regell, P. 1881. "Die Schautempla der Augern." *Jahrbb. f. Class. Philol.* 123:597–637.
Regoli, E. 1984. "Centuriazione e strade." In *Misurare la terra: Centuriazione e coloni nel mondo romano*, 106–7. Modena.
Rhodes, P. J. 1990. "The Atthidographers." In *Purposes of History: Studies in Greek Historiography from the Fourth to the Second Centuries B.C.*, edited by H. Verden, G. Schapens, and E. de Keyser, 73–82. Leuven.
Rich, J. 2005. "Valerius Antias and the Construction of the Roman Past." *BICS* 48:137- 61.
———. 2007. "Tiberius Gracchus, Land and Manpower." In *Crises and the Roman Empire, Proceedings of the Seventh Workshop of the International Workshop Impact of Empire, Nijmegen, June 20-24, 2006*, edited by O. Hekster, G. de Klejn, and D. Slootjes, 155–66 Leiden.
———. 2008a. "Treaties, Allies and the Roman Conquest of Italy." In *War and Peace in Ancient and Medieval Italy*, edited by P. de Souza and J. France, 51–75. Cambridge.
———. 2008b. "*Lex Licinia, Lex Sempronia*: B. G. Niebuhr and the Limitation of Landholding in the Roman Republic." In De Ligt and Northwood 2008, 519–75.
———. 2011a. "Structuring Roman History: The Consular Year and the Roman Historical Tradition." *Histos* 5:1–43.
———. 2011b. "The *Fetiales* and Roman International Relations." In *Priests and the State in the Roman World*, edited by J. H. Richardson and F. Santangelo, 199- 204. Stuttgart.
———. 2014. "The Triumph in the Roman Republic: Frequency, Fluctuation and Policy." In Lange and Vervaet 2014, 197–258.
Richardson, J. S. 1986. *Hispaniae: Spain and the Development of Roman Imperialism, 218–81 B.C.* Cambridge.
———. 2008. *The Language of Empire: Rome and the Idea of Empire from the Third Century B.C. to the Second Century A.D.* Cambridge.
Richardson, L., Jr. 1978. "*Honos et Virtus* and the *Sacra Via*." *AJA* 82:240–46.
Rieger, M. 2007. *Tribus und Stadt: Die Entstehung der römischen Wahlbezirke im urbanen und mediterranen Kontext (ca. 750–450 v. Chr.)*. Göttingen.
Rilinger, R. 1976. *Der Einfluss des Wahlleiters bei den römischen Konsulwahlen von 366 bis 50 v. Chr.*, Munich.
Rives, J. 2012. "Control of the Sacred in Roman Law." In Tellegen-Couperus 2012, 165- 80.
Rodrigquez-Almeida, E. 1981. *Forma Urbis Marmorea: Aggiornamento generale 1980*. Rome.
Roselaar, S. T. 2009. "Evidence for Gracchan Activity in the *Liber Coloniarum*." *Historia* 58:198–214.
———. 2010. *Public Land in the Roman Republic: A Social and Economic History of "Ager Publicus" in Italy, 396–89 BC*. Oxford.
———, ed. 2012. *Processes of Integration and Identity Formation in the Roman Republic*. Leiden.
Rosenberger, V. 1998. *Gezähmte Götter: Das Prodigienwesen der römischen Republik*. Stuttgart.

---. 2005. "Prodigien aus Italien: Geographische Verteilung und religiöse Kommunikation." *CCG* 16:235–57.

---. 2007. "Republican *Nobiles*: Controlling the *Res Publica*." In *A Companion to Roman Religion*, edited by J. Rüpke, 292–303. Oxford.

Rosenstein, N. 1995. "Sorting Out the Lot in Republican Rome." *AJP* 115:43–75.

---. 2006. "Aristocratic Values." In Rosenstein and Morstein-Marx 2006, 365–82.

Rosenstein, N., and R. Morstein-Marx, eds., 2006. *A Companion to the Roman Republic*. Oxford.

Ruoff-Väänänen, E. 1972. "The Roman Public *Prodigia* and the *Ager Romanus*." *Arctos* 7:139–62.

Rüpke, J. 1990. *Domi militiae: Die religiöse Konstruktion des Krieges in Rom*. Stuttgart.

---. 2007. *Religion of the Romans*. Translated by R. Gordon. London.

---. 2008. "Livy, Priests' Names, and the *annales maximi*." In *Fasti sacerdotum: A Prosopography of Pagan, Jewish, and Christian Religious Officials in the City of Rome, 300 BC to AD 499*, by J. Rüpke, translated by D. Richardson, 24–38. Oxford.

---. 2012. *Religion and Ritual Change: Rationalization and Ritual Change*. Philadelphia.

Russo, F. 2008. "Su alcuni aspetti dei *Ludi Saeculares* del 249 a.C." *SCO* 54:115–36.

---. 2012. "The Beginning of the First Punic War and the Concept of Italia." In Roselaar 2012, 35–50.

Ryan, F. X. 1998. *Rank and Participation in the Republican Senate*. Stuttgart.

Sabbatucci, D. 1954. *L'edilità romana, magistratura e sacerdozio*. Rome.

Salmon, E. T. 1969. *Roman Colonization under the Republic*. London.

---. 1982. *The Making of Roman Italy*. Ithaca.

Salvatore, J. P. 1996. *Roman Republican Castrametation: A Reappraisal of the Historical and Archaeological Sources*. BAR International Series 630. Oxford.

Salway, B. 2012. "Putting the World in Order: Mapping in Roman Texts." In Talbert 2012, 193–234.

Sandberg, K. 2009. "Isis Capitolina and the 'Pomerium.'" *Arctos* 43:141–60.

Santoro, R. 1991. "Il tempo ed il luogo dell'*actio* prima della sua riduzione a strumento processuale." *Ann.Sem.Giur.Palermo* 41:281–308.

Santangelo, F. 2013. *Divination, Prediction and the End of the Roman Republic*. Cambridge.

Satterfield, S. 2012. "Livy and the Timing of Expiation in the Roman Year." *Histos* 6:67–90.

Schaberg, D. 2001. *A Patterned Past: Form and Thought in Early Chinese Historiography*. Cambridge, MA.

Scheid, J. 1984. "Le prêtre e le magistrat: Réflexions sur les sacerdoces et la droit publique à la fin de la République." In *Des ordres à Rome*, edited by C. Nicolet, 243–81. Paris.

---. 1987. "Les sanctuaries de confines dans la Rome antique: Réalité et permanence d'une représentation idéale de l'espace romaine." In *L'urbs: Espace urbain et histoire (Ier siècle av. J.-C.–IIIe siècle ap. J.-C.)*, 583–95. Collection de l'École française de Rome 98. Rome.

---. 1990a. *Romulus et ses frères: Le collège des frères arvales, modèle du culte public dans la Rome des empereurs*. Rome.

---. 1990b. "Rituel et écriture à Rome." In *Essais sur le rituel*, edited by A.-M. Blondeau and K. Schipper, 2:1–15. Louvain.

---. 1994. "Les archives de la piété: Réflexions sur les livres sacerdotaux." In Nicolet 1994, 173–85.

———. 1998. "Les Livres Sibyllins et les archives des quindécemvirs." In Moatti 1998, 11–26.

———. 1999. "Hiérarchie et structure dans le polythéisme romain: Façons romaines de penser l'actions." *ARG* 1 (1999), 184–203. Reprinted in *Roman Religion*, edited by C. Ando, translated by P. Purchase, 164–89. Edinburgh.

———. 2003. *An Introduction to Roman Religion*. Translated by J. Lloyd. Edinburgh.

———. 2006. "Oral Tradition and Written Tradition in the Formation of Sacred Law in Rome." In *Religion and Law in Classical and Christian Rome*, edited by C. Ando and J. Rüpke, 14–33. Stuttgart.

Scheidel, W. 2006. "The Demography of State Formation in Italy." In *Herrschaft ohne Integration? Rom und Italien in republikanischer Zeit*, edited by M. Jehne and R. Pfeilschifter, 205–26. Frankfurt am Main.

Schiavone, A. 2012. *The Invention of Law in the West*. Translated by J. Carden and A. Shugaar. Cambridge, MA.

Schofield, M. 1986. "Cicero for and against Divination." *JRS* 76:47–65.

———. 1991. *Stoic Idea of the City*. Cambridge.

Schubert, C. 1996. *Land und Raum der römischen Republik: Die Kunst des Teilens*. Darmstadt.

Scuderi, R. 1991. "Decreti del senato per controversie di confine en età repubblicana." *Athenaeum* 79:371–415.

Scullard, H. H. 1981. *Festivals and Ceremonies of the Roman Republic*. Ithaca.

Sehlmeyer, M. 1999. *Stadtrömische Ehrenstatuen der republikanischen Zeit: Historizität und Kontext von Symbolen nobilitären Standesbewusstseins*. Stuttgart.

———. 2003. "Die Anfänge der antiquarischen Literatur in Rom: Motivation und Bezug zur Historiographie bis in die Zeit von Tuditanus and Gracchanus." In Eigler, Gotter, Luraghi, and Walter 2003, 157–71.

Serrati, J. 2006. "Neptune's Altars: The Treaties between Rome and Carthage (509–226 B.C.)." *CQ* 56:113–34.

Shatzman, I. 1975. *Senatorial Wealth and Roman Politics*. Collection Latomus 142. Brussels.

Sherk, R. 1969. *Roman Documents from the Greek East: Senatus Consulta and Epistulae to the Age of Augustus*. Baltimore.

Sherwin-White, A. N. 1973. *The Roman Citizenship*. 2nd ed. Oxford.

Skutsch, O. 1986. *The Annals of Q. Ennius*. 2nd ed. Oxford.

Smith, C. J. 2008. *The Roman Clan: The Gens from Ancient Ideology to Modern Anthropology*. Cambridge.

———. 2012. "The *Feriae Latinae*." In *Greek and Roman Festivals*, edited by J. R. Brandt and J. W. Iddeng, 267–88. Oxford.

Spaeth, B. 1996. *The Roman Goddess Ceres*. Austin.

Stek, T. D., and J. Pelgrom, eds. 2014. *Roman Republican Colonization: New Perspectives from Archaeology and Ancient History*. Rome.

Stevenson, A. J. 2004. "The Roman Antiquarian Tradition." In *The Worlds of Aulus Gellius*, edited by L. Holford-Strevens and A. Vardi, 118–55. Oxford.

Stewart, R. 1998. *Public Office in Early Rome: Ritual Procedure and Political Practice*. Ann Arbor.

Sumner, G. 1970. "The Legion and the Centuriate Organization." *JRS* 60:67–78.
Suolahti, J. 1963. *The Roman Censors: A Study on Social Structure.* Helsinki.
Takács, L. 2013. *The Social Status of Roman Land Surveyors.* Budapest.
Talbert, R. J. A. 2004. "Rome's Provinces as Framework for World-View." In *Roman Rule and Civic Life: Local and Regional Perspectives,* edited by L. de Ligt, E. A. Hemelrijk, and H. W. Singen, 21–37. Amsterdam.
———. 2010. *Rome's World: The Peutinger Map Reconsidered.* Cambridge.
———, ed. 2012. *Ancient Perspectives: Maps and Their Place in Mesopotamia, Egypt, Greece, and Rome.* Chicago.
———. 2013. "The Roman Worldview: Beyond Recovery?" In Raaflaub and Talbert 2013, 252–72.
Tatum, W. J. 1993. "The *Lex Papiria de dedicationibus.*" *CPh* 88:319–28.
Taylor, L. R. 1934. "New Light on the History of the Saecular Games." *AJPh* 55:1–20.
———. 1960. *The Voting Districts of the Roman Republic: The Thirty-Five Urban and Rural Tribes.* Rome. Reprinted with a postscript by J. Linderski. Ann Arbor, 2013.
Taylor, R. 2000. "Watching the Sky: Janus, Auspication, and the Shrine in the Roman Forum." *MAAR* 45:1–40.
Tellegen-Couperus, O., ed., 2012. *Law and Religion in the Roman Republic.* Leiden.
Thommen, L. 1989. *Das Volkstribunat der späten römischen Republik.* Stuttgart.
Thomsen, R. 1947. *The Italic Regions from Augustus to the Lombard Invasion.* Copenhagen.
———. 1980. *King Servius Tullius: A Historical Synthesis.* Copenhagen.
Tiersch, C. 2009. "Politische Öffentlichkeit statt Mitbestimmung? Zur Bedeutung der *contiones* in der mittleren und späten römischen Republik." *Klio* 91:40–68.
Timpe, D. 1988. "Mündlichkeit und Schriftlichkeit als Basis der frührömischen Überlieferung." In, *Vergangenheit in mündlicher Überlieferung,* edited by J. Ungern-Sternberg and H. Reinau, 266–88. Stuttgart.
Torelli, M. 1966. "Un templum augurale d'età repubblicana a Bantia." *RAL* 21:293–315.
———. 1969. "Contributi al supplement del *CIL X.*" *RAL* 24:9–48.
———. 1999a. *Tota Italia: Essays in the Cultural Formation of Roman Italy.* Oxford.
———. 1999b. "Religious Aspects of Early Roman Colonization." In Torelli 1999a, 14–42.
Troiani, L. 1984. "La religione e Cicerone." *RSI* 96:920–52.
Turfa, J. M. 2006. "Etruscan Religion at the Watershed: Before and After the Fourth Century B.C.E." In *Religion in Republican Italy,* edited by C. E. Schultz and P. B. Harvey Jr., 62–89. Cambridge.
———. 2012. *Divining the Etruscan World: The Brontoscopic Calendar and Religious Practice.* Cambridge.
Vaahtera, J. 1993. "On the Religious Nature of the Place of Assembly." In *Senatus Populusque Romanus. Studies in Roman Republican Legislation,* by U. Paananen, K. Heikkilä, K. Sandberg, L. Savunen, and J. Vaahtera, 97–116. Helsinki.
———. 2000. "Roman Religion and the Polybian *Politeia.*" In Brunn 2000, 251–64.
———. 2001. *Roman Augural Law in Greek Historiography: A Study of the Theory and Terminology.* Stuttgart.
———. 2002. "Livy and the Priestly Records: À propos *ILS* 9338." *Hermes* 130:100–108.
Valeton, I. M. J. 1889–90. "De modis auspicandis Romanorum." *Mnemosyne* 17:275–325, 418–52; 18:208–63, 406–56.

———. 1892–98. "De templis Romanis." *Mnemosyne* 20:339–90; 21:62–91, 397–440; 23:15–79; 25:93–144, 361–85; 26:1–93.

Valvo, A. 1997. "Terra Italia, Terra Etruria, Terra Istria." *AN* 68:10–20.

———. 2001. "Formula amicorum, commercium amicitiae, filias koinonia." In, *Linguaggio e terminologia diplomatica dall'antico oriente all' impero bizantino. Atti del Convegno nazionale, Genova 19 Novembre 1998*, edited by M. Gabriella, A. Bertinelli, and L. Piccirilli, 133–45. Rome.

van der Meer, L. B. 1979. "*Iecur Placentium* and the Orientation of the Etruscan *Haruspex*." *BABesch* 54:49–64.

———. 1987. *The Bronze Liver of Piacenza: Analysis of a Polytheistic Structure*. Amsterdam.

van Haeperen, F. 2012. "Auspices d'investiture, loi curiate et légitimité des magistrates romaines." *CCG* 23:71–112.

Venturini, C. 1979. *Studi sul crimen repetundarum nell'età repubblicana*. Milan.

Versluys, M. J. 2004. "*Isis Capitolina* and the Egyptian Cults in Late Republican Rome." In *Isis en occident. Actes du IIème Colloque international sur les etudes isiaques, Lyon III 16–17 mai 2002*, edited by L. Bricault, 421–48. Leiden.

Versnel, H. 1970. *Triumphus: An Inquiry into the Origin, Development, and Meaning of the Roman Triumph*. Leiden.

Vervaet, F. 2014. *High Command in the Roman Republic: The Principle of the summum imperium auspiciumque from 509 to 19 BCE*. Stuttgart.

von Hesberg, H. 1985. "Zur Plangestaltung der Coloniae Maritimae." *RM* 92:127–50.

Walbank, F. W. 1957–67. *A Commentary on Polybius*. Oxford.

Wallace-Hadrill, A. 2008. *Rome's Cultural Revolution*. Cambridge.

Weinstock, S. 1946. "Martianus Capella and the Cosmic System of the Etruscans." *JRS* 36:101–29.

———. 1950. "C. Fonteius Capito and the *Libri Tagetici*." *PBSR* 18:44–49.

———. 1951. "*Libri Fulgurales*." *PBSR* 19:122–53.

Wilcox, D. J. 1987. *The Measure of Times Past: Pre-Newtonian Chronologies and the Rhetoric of Relative Time*. Chicago.

Williams, J. H. C. 2001. *Beyond the Rubicon: Romans and Gauls in Republican Italy*. Oxford.

Wiseman, T. P. 1969. "The Census in the First Century." *JRS* 59:59–73.

———. 1988. *Roman Drama and Roman History*. Exeter.

———. 1994a. *Historiography and Imagination: Eight Essays on Roman Culture*. Exeter.

———. 1994b. "Monuments and the Roman Annalists." In Wiseman 1994a, 37–48.

———. 1994c. "The Origins of Roman Historiography." In Wiseman 1994a, 1–22.

———. 1995. *Remus: A Roman Myth*. Cambridge.

Woodard, R. D. 2006. *Indo-European Sacred Space: Vedic and Roman Cult*. Urbana.

Zack, A. 2012. "Forschungen über die rechtlichen Grundlagen der römischen Außenbeziehungen während der Republik bis zum Beginn der Prinzipats. II. Teil: Fragen an Varro *de lingua Latina* 5,33: Die augurale Ordnung des Raumes." *Göttinger Forum für Altertumswissenschaft* 15:61–128.

Zanker, P. 2000. "The City as Symbol: Rome and the Creation of an Urban Image." In Fentress 2000a, 25–41.

Zevi, F. 2002. "Appunti per una storia di Ostia repubblicana." *MEFRA* 114:13–58.

Ziółkowski, A. 1992. *The Temples of Mid-Republican Rome and Their Historical and Topographical Context*. Rome.
———. 1999. "Ritual Cleaning-Up of the City: From the *Lupercalia* to the *Argei*." AncSoc 29:191–218.
———. 2009. "Frontier Sanctuaries of the *Ager Romanus Antiquus*: Did They Exist?" *Palamedes* 4:91–130.
———. 2011. "The Capitol and the 'Auspices of Departure.'" In *Studia Lesco Mrozewicz ab amicis et discipulis dedicata*, edited by S. Ruciński, C. Balbuza, and Ch. Królczyk, 465–71. Poznań.
Zorzetti, N. 1980. *La pretesta e il teatro latino arcaico*. Naples.

Index

Ager: definition of, 141; Gabinus, 140–42, 144, 149; peregrinus, 140–42, 143, 144; Romanus, 140–41, 143, 144, 145–46, 149, 151–52, 199, 228, 253n100; Romanus antiquus, 146–49
Agrarian Law of 111, 217–18. See also Laws, legislation
Antiquarians, antiquarianism, 33–38, 113–14, 125, 141, 247–48n119
Arx, 124, 131, 155, 182, 183, 222–23, 227, 249n17, 250n46
Augurs, 5, 25, 27, 28–29, 31, 122–25, 140, 142–43, 145, 222, 225
Auspices (auspicium), 26, 28–29, 46–47, 56, 111, 123–24, 179, 249n19; at crossing rivers, 137, 143; at crossing fines Romani, 143; of departure, 46; of investiture, 45; urban, 132, 136–37, 138, 251n64

Bacchanalian conspiracy, 51, 73, 74, 97, 194, 197, 200, 206–10, 215. See also Senatus consultum de Bacchanalibus
Beginning and end of commands. See Rome, urbs Roma: departure and reentry
Boundaries, 49, 56–57, 58–59, 185, 188–89. See also Fines

Camps, 145–46, 178–81; prodigies in, 100, 105, 180
Capitoline Temple of Jupiter Best and Greatest, 20, 45, 46, 121
Cardinal directions. See Orientation
Census, 4–5, 105–10. See also Tribes
Citizen, Latin and ally, as formula, 88, 202, 204–5, 207–8
Civitas sine suffragio, 10, 88, 89
Colony, colonies, 9, 22, 50, 167–78; citizen colonies, 66, 168–69, 182; Latin colonies, 168–69, 182; and roads, 52–53; and urban cores, 171–75. See also Sulcus primigenius; Surveying; Triumviri coloniae deducendae
Comitium, 20, 121–22, 123, 126–27, 128, 135, 150, 161–62, 165–67, 171, 172, 173, 182, 185, 248n1, 251n59, 257n43, 257n44
L. Cornelius Sulla, 67–68, 80, 151–52
Counterclockwise over clockwise. See Orientation

Decemviri agris dandis, 3, 49
Decemviri (or quindecemviri) sacris faciundis, 5, 25, 27, 28, 31, 46, 100, 102, 204, 222, 225
Departures from Rome. See Rome, urbs Roma: departure and reentry
Dilectus, 45, 110–18; and roads, 116

Domi et militiae, 1, 24–25, 28, 70, 87, 133, 136, 202, 251n51
Duumviri aedi locandae/dedicandae, 3, 50

Enumeration of elements from the center. See Zones
Exilium, 199
Extortion Law of 123, 80, 204, 211–12. See also Laws, legislation

Fines, 56–57; of *provinciae*, 74–75; *Romani*, 143–44, 146, 149, 199, 209, 238n55; of Roman people (*fines populi Romani*), 58–59, 225, 238n55, 238n57; of urban auspices, 56
Formae, 8, 177
Formula provinciae, 69
Formula sociorum et amicorum, 86, 151
Formula togatorum, 45, 85–86, 151, 168, 202, 204
Fundus fieri, 203

Haruspex, haruspices, 27, 28, 30, 46, 59, 100, 102, 134, 138, 157, 163–64, 175–76, 225, 238n57
Hostages and prisoners, places of detention of, 200–201

Imperium, 21, 45, 46–47, 55–56, 57, 63, 64, 68–69, 132–34. See also *Domi et militiae*
Italy, limits of, 83–84, 199, 209

Jurists, jurisprudence, 35–38, 141

Law of Praetorian Provinces of 100, 72, 75–76, 77–78, 139, 204–5, 236n107. See also Laws, legislation
Laws, legislation: form of, 5–6, 38–42, 187–89, 236n106, 254n4; sumptuary laws, 194–95. See also Agrarian Law of 111; Extortion Law of 123; Law of Praetorian Provinces of 100
Left over right. See Orientation
Legate, legates, 49, 56–57, 68–69

Lex, leges: Baebia, 63; *coloniae Iuliae Genetivae* (Urso), 41–42, 150; *curiata de imperio*, 130, 135–37; *Oppia*, 194–95; *Ovinia*, 4, 106; *Porcia*, 80; *Porciae*, 192–93; *Sempronia*, 215–16 (see also *Triumviri lege Sempronia*)
Livy (T. Livius), 15, 16–17, 21–23, 44–45, 155

T. Maccius Plautus, 29, 162–63
Milestones, 52, 91–92, 146–47, 222; fiftieth milestone from Rome, 177, 196, 227; first milestone from Rome, 132, 190–92, 194, 195, 212, 213, 214, 227; as limits of official activity, 75, 132; at other settlements, 150, 194–95; tenth milestone from Rome, 75, 195–96, 197, 227
Movement to and from Rome, structural significance of, 49, 54, 79–80, 206
Q. Mucius Scaevola, 32, 36
Municipium, 10, 88–90, 243n27

Oikoumene. See *Orbis terrarum* or *terrae*
Orbis terrarum or *terrae*, 1, 55, 57, 69, 150, 159, 221, 225
Orientation: to cardinal directions, 154–57, 175–77; counterclockwise versus clockwise, 94–95, 183–84; left over right, 159, 176, 179, 182

Peregrinus, 87–88, 142
Polybius, 12, 14–15, 23–24, 32, 48, 55, 83–84, 110–14, 178–79, 201
Pomerium, 17, 56, 107, 126, 130–32, 134–35, 136, 140, 147, 149–50, 172, 173, 181, 190, 209, 250n45; at Latin colonies (see *Sulcus primigenius*); limit of urban auspices, 56; at Urso, 150
Pontiffs, 5, 25, 27, 28, 46, 100, 222, 225
M. Porcius Cato, 14–15, 24, 56, 78, 79–80, 84, 114
Praefectus iure dicundo, 91, 97–99, 104, 244n59
Prodigies, 44, 99–105, 180; in camps, 100, 105, 180; locations of reports, 102–5;

nature of, 100, 180; rites of expiation, 100–102
Profectio. See Rome, *urbs Roma*: departure and reentry
Promagistrates, promagistracy, 45, 63, 64–65, 68, 138; and auspices, 138–39; origins of, 64–65
Provincia, 45, 48, 49, 59–69, 76–77; annual distribution of, 45, 49; as army, 65, 71–72; Farther Spain (*Hispania Ulterior*), 60, 61, 62–63, 67, 198; and judicial coercion, 61–62; meaning of, 69; military nature of, 70–71; as moveable object, 50; and movement, 77–78, 227; Nearer Spain (*Hispania Citerior*), 60, 61, 62–63, 67, 198; as opponent, 72–73; permanent versus ephemeral, 62–63; *provincia Africa*, 240n82; *provincia Asia*, 67, 71, 75; *provincia Macedonia*, 67, 71, 72, 75–75; *provincia Sardinia*; 59–60, 61–62, 62–63, 66, 70; *provincia Sicilia*, 59–60, 61, 62–63, 66, 70; as region or ethnic group, 72–73; spatial implications of, 69–78, 81–82; and triumphs, 65, 80; urban and peregrine, 60, 61, 66, 96–97
Provocatio, 134, 192–94

Quindecemviri sacris faciundis. See Decemviri sacris faciundis
Quinqueviri uls cis Tiberim, 194, 208

Reentry into Rome. *See* Rome, *urbs Roma*: departure and reentry; Triumph
Roads, 51–55, 58, 77, 213–14, 226–27; and *dilectus*, 116; and tribes, 94–95; used to organize activity, 197. *See also Via, viae*
Rome, *urbs Roma*: departure and reentry, 46, 48, 77, 78, 133–34, 226; first milestone as urban boundary, 132, 192–95, 212, 213–14; as origin of roads, 51–55; *pomerium* and walls as urban boundaries, 130–32; tenth milestone as urban boundary, 196–97. *See also* Zones

Secular games (*ludi saeculares*), 87
Senatus consultum de Bacchanalibus, 204, 207–8
Sententia Minuciorum, 184–85
Sulcus primigenius, 172–73
Surveying, 173–74, 175–79, 182–83

Tabula Heracleensis, 108, 213–14
Templum, templa, 125–29, 154–67, 179–80, 181–82, 192, 228, 250n42; and laws, 160–63, 189, 225
M. Terentius Varro, 32, 125, 127, 128–29, 155, 156–57
Terra: meaning of, 85; *Italia*, 84–86, 140, 142, 149, 151
Tribes, 92–93, 94–95, 95–99, 103–5; nature of, 92; order of, 94, 243n44; and roads, 94–95
Triumph, 46–47, 78–80
Triumviri capitales, 194, 208, 209
Triumviri coloniae deducendae, 3, 49, 169–70, 189, 217
Triumviri lege Sempronia, 54, 178, 197, 215–16, 219
M. Tullius Cicero, 139, 219–20; *On Divination*, 27–30, 123, 138; *On the Laws*, 38–42, 124–25, 157, 159; *On the Nature of the Gods*, 25–27, 138; *On the Republic*, 12–14, 15, 23–25
Twelve Tables, 13, 14, 15, 40, 161–62, 167, 190

Via, viae: *Aemilia*, 52, 53; *Appia*, 50, 52, 53, 54, 57, 94–95; *Aurelia*, 52, 57; *Cassia*, 52, 57; *Egnatia*, 52, 77; *Flaminia*, 52, 57, 77, 94; *Latina*, 50, 52, 53, 94, 183, 222; *Valeria*, 52, 53, 94–95

Year, consular, 21–22, 59

Zones: around other settlements, 179, 184–86; contrast between inner and outer, 136, 152–53, 181–83; enumeration of elements from center, 94, 140, 143, 183–85, 204–5, 206; formal, 139, 140–52, 196, 200–201, 227–28; informal, 90–91, 92–94, 95–99, 103–5

www.ingramcontent.com/pod-product-compliance
Lightning Source LLC
Chambersburg PA
CBHW032032300426
44117CB00009B/1034